Capitalism: An Ethnographic Approach

EXPLORATIONS IN ANTHROPOLOGY
A University College London Series

Series Editors: Barbara Bender, John Gledhill and Bruce Kapferer

Capitalism

An Ethnographic Approach

Daniel Miller

BERG

Oxford • New York

First published in 1997 by
Berg
Editorial offices:
150 Cowley Road, Oxford, OX4 1JJ, UK
70 Washington Square South, New York, NY 10012, USA

*HF5415.33
.T7
M55
1997*

Berg is an imprint of Oxford International Publishers Ltd.

Library of Congress Cataloging-in-Publication Data

A catalogue record for this book is available from the Library of
Congress.

British Library Cataloguing-in-Publication Data

A catalogue record for this book is available from the British
Library.

ISBN 1 85973 123 6 (Cloth)
        1 85973 128 7 (Paper)

Typeset by JS Typesetting, Wellingborough, Northants.
Printed in the United Kingdom by WBC Book Manufacturers,
Bridgend, Mid Glamorgan.

For Rickie

Contents

Acknowledgements

I have an enormous debt of gratitude to the companies with which I worked. I think I was very fortunate in the degree to which companies in Trinidad are mainly run by Trinidadians. I can't imagine many places that would have been quite so 'laid back' about my presence or taken me at my word as an explanation of my presence and purpose. There are far too many firms that helped my work for me to name them individually. I probably owe most to the various soft drink companies and to David Martin, who was then President of the Advertising Association and facilitated my work with the various advertising agencies.

I have kept my side of the bargain with commerce, which is that this would be a generalized academic text rather than a more journalistic exposé. I am prepared to be considered an academic 'wimp' for this, but would justify the precedent it creates. I believe that academics require access to many institutions, and if need be should agree to the anonymity of their objects of study, just as they do with individuals. As it happens Trinidadian commerce is faced with a barrage of critical commentary in the local weekly newspapers, of a far more acerbic variety than anything I could produce. My own critique of capitalist practice is constructed in much more general terms, and relates to the wider issues that I feel are most important in the long term.

In commenting upon my work I have again had considerable assistance. In particular I would like to thank, within Trinidad: Bridget Brereton, Paul Charles, Ralph Henry and Kim Johnson. Outside Trinidad I have received constant critical advice from: James Carrier, Richard Wilk and Kevin Yelvington. In all my trips to Trinidad I am very grateful for the continued friendship and assistance from the family of Moonilal Seemungal-Dass, Renita Griffith, Angela and Pulchas Jonas, Jackie Lewis, Linda and Claude Kahn, Ann-Marie Mohammed and her family, Dennis

Singh, and my research assistant Shanaz Mohammed. Above all I owe a considerable debt to my wife, Rickie Burman, who sacrificed a year from her own work in order to become the companion of mine.

As I noted in my earlier volume, my experience of Trinidad was overwhelmingly positive; I have never been treated with such hospitality and friendship. I have probably also never had so much fun or felt so relaxed. I have found that this sometimes makes people sceptical of my academic commitment; but I do not feel that my research suffered unduly from the fact that I enjoyed it.

Grants towards the fieldwork in Trinidad between 1987 and 1989 and return trips in 1990, 1993 and 1995 were funded by: The British Academy, The Central Research Fund of London University, The Nuffield Foundation, and The Wenner-Gren foundation for Anthropological Research, to all of whom I am very grateful.

1

Capitalism, Ethnography and Trinidad

Shiny Peanuts

Just after returning to London from the main period of fieldwork in Trinidad in 1989, I decided to interview the director of the firm that supplies the majority of the peanuts to Trinidad. I was interested to know why his particular firm seemed so well established as the dominant supplier, especially when, in the context of a deep recession, packets of salted peanuts seemed a relatively expensive product. He explained to me something of the global trade in peanuts and the main sources of competition. What stuck in my memory was the suggestion that the key advantage he had over his rivals was that he was mainly exporting Chinese peanuts rather than American peanuts. Chinese peanuts are a little shinier than American peanuts, and Trinidadians, he explained, preferred shiny peanuts.

In countries such as Britain or the United States the relationship between our supermarkets and the global economy is not only transparent but widely accepted. That a few products are actually locally grown is almost something of a novelty, to be promoted in specialist gift shops to holiday-makers. In other respects the supermarkets in London or New York take credit for providing goods from throughout the world. The shoppers may well include some whose ancestry lies in exotic regions, and for whom specialist sections are developed; but the majority also now take for granted access to the products of most areas at most times. The major characteristic of this supply is that it is constant, predictable and of uniformly high quality. These goods are expected to compete in terms of attributes such as their glossiness and hue, and to appear, in effect, perfect.

When people in Berlin or Chicago think of Trinidad, by contrast, they assume that none of these things will be true. They imagine foodstuffs that are largely locally grown, and are a much closer reflection of the variety of quality that actually comes up from the ground or down from the tree. In fact, during the time of my first fieldwork (1988–9) agriculture provided only 2.5 per cent of Trinidad's gross national product. The proportion of imported foodstuffs was therefore even greater than in most metropolitan countries, and most foodstuffs are also purchased in supermarkets. Goods are also expected to come to the shopper in branded products of uniformly high quality and without blemish. Attributes such as being shiny or of a particular hue will help determine what sells. In Western Europe this presumption of quality is taken for granted more or less as a right. The same applies in Trinidad.

In Britain the major supermarket chains are increasingly subject to a system of backwards vertical integration in which the retailer controls distribution and, increasingly, production, in the sense of at least the packaging of these goods. These are displayed alongside the well-established brands of the major global transnationals, such as Nestlé and Procter and Gamble. The situation in Trinidad is very similar. The dominant supermarket chain is part of the largest conglomerate in the region, with considerable power of distribution and packaging. The branded products are mainly the ones familiar from most other countries in the world.

Throughout the contemporary world there is a general recognition that we live within a world dominated by capitalism. The degree to which this was diluted by alternative ideas such as socialism has diminished significantly in the last decade. In Trinidad capitalism is if anything rather more taken for granted than in Europe. As in the United States, there has never been a period in which it has been under serious challenge, nor has there ever been a government much interested in experimenting with alternative forms of economic control. The only rival to the free market was the growth of state control during the oil boom of the late 1970s; but this was far more influenced by a strident nationalism than by any antagonism to capitalism itself.

To use the shiny peanut as a symbol to justify Trinidad as an exemplar of contemporary capitalism is to acknowledge one of the most significant changes within capitalism itself. This is the increasing centrality of consumption rather than production. We are moving from a time when manufacturers made goods and then sought markets, to a time when retailers tell manufacturers what to produce (see Miller 1995). What has become critical is the development of a huge range of imperatives behind demand and the desire by people throughout the world to possess a wide range of modern commodities. It is this that makes the shiny peanut crucial to modern analysis: that even a country as peripheral to the major metropolitan states as Trinidad has its economy determined by consumers' focus upon the highly specific attributes of the commodities found on supermarket shelves.

The present volume is a continuation of work by myself and others to redirect attention to the importance of consumption. But more specifically it is a description of the results of fieldwork that was undertaken in response to a criticism of this study of consumption. The criticism (for a recent example of which see Fine and Leopold 1993) was that current studies of consumption had neglected the wider context of consumption in production and distribution, and in the same way that earlier studies of production had ignored consumption. We were swinging the pendulum of academic study so far that we might produce an equally disarticulated study of consumption that ignored its relationship to business. As Fine and Leopold have argued, a proper study of capitalism requires consideration of the articulation between all these processes, and my intention was to see to what extent an ethnography might be able to address these issues.

The Aims of this Volume

The aims of this volume follow from the intentions behind the fieldwork it describes. I will outline these, and then consider how they differ from some of the expectations that may have been raised by choosing the title *Capitalism: An Ethnographic Approach*. This implies, of course, an attempt to justify this discrepancy, as one of my intentions is to expose the narrowness of these expectations.

The first aim of this volume is to give a sense of how commodities come to the consumer with particular attributes. The commodities selected to exemplify this process are those that appear on the shelves of supermarkets in Trinidad, with a particular emphasis upon non-alcoholic beverages. These commodities do not appear to the consumer merely as utilitarian products matched with utilitarian demand functions such as hunger or thirst. Rather, as with the shiny peanut, the key to their relationship to the consumer is a complex amalgam of attributes that they obtain through processes such as branding, marketing, advertising and retailing. These attributes are intended both to create consumer demand and to appeal to existing consumer demand for highly nuanced and complex symbolic attributes of commodities.

This book examines several of these contexts for the production of commodities as complex symbolic formations, and seeks to show how ethnography as a method can reveal something of the context within which each process occurs within one particular region. Thus Chapter 3 focuses on the firm, Chapter 4 on branding, Chapters 5 and 6 on advertising and Chapter 7 on retail. In moving through these various institutional contexts the commodity comes to exist as a potential object of consumption.

The second aim of this volume derives from my own particular interest in consumption. I do not believe consumers are merely the end-point of these processes, who then 'choose' to accept or reject what commerce has produced. I certainly do not recognize in them the optimizers of economic theory. Consumers turn out to be among the most active players in the construction of the commodity from its inception. They are constantly involved through their reaction to branding, to advertising and to strategies of selling. For this reason consideration of consumers is not relegated to a final chapter, which as it were ends the sequence of commodity trajectory, but is a clear presence within the process of commodity formation. This varies from market-testing in the early stages of creating new brands to the dual personalities executives acquire through their being themselves consumers. Fieldwork also revealed, however, times when consumers were in a sense absent at key moments when one might have expected them to occupy centre stage. For example, in advertising and marketing the atmosphere of intense competition sometimes creates a fixation on rival firms that pushes out any interest in or concern with consumers.

To say, therefore, that my aim is to integrate consumers does not mean that I give them unwarranted agency. Any attempt to determine the relative power of consumption and production must also face up to what turns out to be a core issue of relative autonomy. In both cases each may be legitimated with respect to the other. Business constantly justifies what it does in the name of the consumer, and in a belief that it understands the behaviour of consumers. Similarly, consumers constantly credit business with the power of determining what they do as consumers. In general, however, each of the central chapters reveals considerable autonomy. The viewers of television reconstruct the meaning of adverts in a manner that has only a limited effect upon the adverts themselves. In the drinks industry, consumers and producers blithely ignore major trends and changes in the other. There are, of course, many instances where this is not the case. Campaigns are described that appear to have of themselves transformed consumer demand, alongside others that vanish without trace. This book therefore aims to integrate the perspective of the consumer as part of the process of commodity production, but only where appropriate.

If the second aim is to turn the consumer from passive endpoint to active agent within the process of the production of commodities, the third aim is to effect a parallel transformation in the concept of regional context. Trinidad is therefore presented throughout this volume as much more than merely the place where these processes happen. The emphasis is rather on Trinidad as itself constructed out of the very activities that are studied here. The book to which the present volume is a sequel (Miller 1994) demonstrated that Trinidad is a product of tensions in modernity, that it is a highly dynamic context that is constantly changing. It would be quite naive, therefore, to tackle Trinidad in the way that anthropologists approach Hawaii or Benin, that is to look for the way some long-standing structural relations that make up 'cultural' predispositions continue to constrain or influence some new institutional activity (e.g. Sahlins 1988). Trinidad, by contrast to these regions, was born out of the particular concerns of capitalism to create a periphery – in this case sugar production, followed by oil production (Brereton 1981; Mintz 1985a). As the material in this volume will indicate, Trinidad continues to evolve in tandem with capitalism, and is not separable as a 'context' to capitalism.

The fourth aim of this volume is to attempt to exploit the

advantages of ethnography both as a methodology and a
perspective on capitalism. As a methodology, ethnography represented a commitment to the long-term study of these processes
in their contexts. As far as possible they were observed as they
occurred in their typical setting. The emphasis was on qualitative
observation of events as they unfolded. My contention is not that
ethnography is a better or worse method for studying these
phenomena; it is clear to me that it should be complementary to
other methods. Rather, my concern is that in writing up the
results I should emphasize that which ethnography – as against
other methods – contributes, without falling into the positivistic
trap of assuming that the entirety of what constitutes these
activities is merely what such a method is able to capture as
observation.

My fifth and final aim arose subsequent to the fieldwork,
and was fortuitous in that it emerged out of events that
happened to coincide with my study. This was a growing
realization that there was another form of capitalism that was
certainly not contained in the kind of business practices that were
studied, but was grounded instead in the application of certain
abstract economic models. This was embodied in what has been
termed structural adjustment – a phenomenon that was just
about to impinge upon Trinidad when the fieldwork was being
completed.

From these five aims emerges the structure of the volume as
a whole. This introductory chapter contains an attempt to
contextualize this rather particular perspective on capitalism
within the wider comparative literature. It also briefly addresses
Trinidad as a context. It is followed by an exploration of the fifth
aim, which is the current exposure of Trinidad to structural
adjustment, and, in that guise, to a particular model of 'pure'
capitalism.

The following five chapters form the substantive core of the
study, and trace four major contexts through which the
commodity comes into being as a consumer object. The first
explores business through the selection of one particular form –
the transnational companies concerned with the production and
distribution of supermarket goods. The next chapter is concerned
with the single most important symbolic frame through which
the commodity is constituted, both for commerce and for the
consumer, which is the brand. It also provides one of the clearest

examples of a direct encounter between consumer and producer, through exploring the meaning of brands within the soft drink industry.

The next two chapters take different perspectives on advertising. The first situates advertising entirely within the institutional framework of the advertising industry as a highly competitive set of firms whose primary orientation turns out to be – not the consumer, but – their rivals. The following chapter shifts to the analysis of the actual advertising produced and includes an element of the consumer reading of these adverts. The final chapter of this section then follows through to the next stage, retail. Once again it divides between taking retail from the perspective of retailers, and the analysis of retail from the perspective of the consumer as shopper.

The final chapter starts by examining the ways the consumer is objectified as such through consumer organizations, but then moves to more general questions about the contextualization of capitalism in Trinidad. The conclusion to the volume then attempts to integrate the implications of Chapters 3 to 8 with the larger macro-perspective provided in Chapter 2. From this it derives a model of capitalism as the practice of commerce that then gives rise to a more general model of the contradictions of the consumer economy in the contemporary world.

It is important that the order in which the book unfolds should not be seen as of itself an argument for directionality. As was noted in describing the second aim, the idea is not to see the consumer merely as the end-point in the process, which is why the consumer has an equally clear presence in Chapters 4, 6 and 7 as they do in Chapter 8. Furthermore, one of the conclusions of Chapter 8 is that the whole process can also be seen in reverse, so that the consumer appears as the starting-point for macro-economic shifts such as structural adjustment.

A final aim of this volume is more modest and descriptive than those already discussed. For whatever institutions and aspects of capitalism the ethnographer sets out to describe, the information must be scholarly enough and full enough that the material can be used in the future as part of a larger project of comparative studies. I do not then apologize for what might be seen as the 'boring' substantive sections of this work. There are certainly parts of my description of the soft drinks industry, advertising agencies and retail that are not intended to make any immediate point, but simply to provide sufficient detail and coverage that any individual points are properly contextualized and that any comparative work has a foundation for assessing similarities and difference.

This volume is committed to a description of capitalism as I encountered it. It differs from most parallel books on the Caribbean economy, which describe and deplore current conditions and then concentrate on the alternatives. Books such as McAfee's admirable (1991) critique include detailed descriptions of community groups and the variety of NGOs (non-governmental organisations) and others working for the benefit of Caribbean peoples. While such bodies should certainly be supported, they remain of limited importance within a country such as Trinidad. The larger problem posed in this book is that Trinidad is vulnerable to a movement towards forms of capitalist control that make its present situation relatively benign by comparison. The key struggle at the moment is between a not particularly good form of capitalism and the threat of a far worse version. I call this the move from organic to pure capitalism. There seems, then, good reason for being closely tied to the grim realities of the historical moment.

These, then, are the basic aims that account for what follows in the rest of this volume. I fully recognize that someone coming from a different academic trajectory and working mainly from the book's title would have other expectations. In the following section I would wish to persuade you, through reference to the comparative literature, that the aims outlined here are just as valid an exploration of capitalism as those aims that you might have expected to have taken their place.

A Particular Perspective on Capitalism

I will not attempt to define capitalism. I assume that, as a kind of Wittgensteinian language game, the word 'capitalism' has many definitions, depending upon its context. Capitalism may achieve its most precise definition within neo-classical economics. Neo-classical economists attempt to construct algorithms that model particular relationships within capitalism, which is thereby rendered a general and ideal system. But this activity bears very little relation to the arena where the term has traditionally been most fully employed, which is in Marxist discourse. Here capitalism has moved from the analysis of a particular system by Marx to become, after a century and more, largely a figure within rhetorical politics. Each of these academic and non-academic fields generates its own language-game, within each of which the term capitalism finds another particular scope and meaning.

In practice, an ethnography reduces capitalism to those aspects manifested within the ethnographic encounter. This will be mainly the workings of commerce involved in creating commodities for supermarkets. In addition, however, the first and last chapters deal with capitalism as derived from a particular economic model manifested through structural adjustment. Indeed, one of the main points made by the volume as a whole will be that there is a marked difference between what I shall call 'pure capitalism', which comes directly from economists' models, and the kind of organic capitalism that describes the day-to-day practice of commerce. The possibility of incorporating plural definitions of capitalism is one of the main advantages of starting from the field encounter rather than from an abstract model. I shall be examining the effects of economists' models, but this book will not attempt to address the validity of economists' approaches to these topics, such as theories of transaction costs.

The significance of the term as selected for the title of this book is perhaps best clarified in relation to the alternative term which is not used, that is 'the market'. The obvious temptation would be to follow current semantic fashions, and replace the term 'capitalism' with the term 'market'. In today's debates it is usually 'the market' that seeks ever increasing degrees of commodification. It is also the market (as it was once capitalism) that seeks to ensure that all transactions are dependent upon competition for profit, with minimal interference from other bodies such as the State. On library shelves it is clear that many books published in the 1990s that would previously have used the word 'capitalism' in their titles now use the term 'market' (e.g. Crouch and Marquand 1993; Lane 1993). By comparison, the term 'capitalism' appears to have an almost antiquated ring to it, evoking a generation of academic analysis now doomed to extinction in the face of more fashionable concerns. It is worth fighting a rearguard action on behalf of the term 'capitalism' rather than 'market', since although the two are increasingly being used synonymously in political and popular debate they differ significantly in their evocations.

Once accepted, the term 'market' appears to achieve another stage in the naturalization of capitalism and the replacement of politics by economics. The term 'market' evokes a sense of an innate propensity to exchange, and is less open to challenge, which probably accounts for its current prevalence. A 'market' sounds much more like a given, natural phenomenon that simply exists in the world and that must be allowed to manifest its own inherent logic. At least the term 'capitalism' implied a system of relations that was historically circumscribed and could be challenged. It also evoked a sense of the larger system of relations and ideologies that are characteristic of the contemporary global system. The term 'market', in its colloquial use at least, seems less demanding of such wider considerations. For these reasons I prefer to use the term 'capitalism', to imply both the actual system of economic relations prevalent in the modern world and also an idealized system of economic relations revolving around the concept of a pure market.

In practice, the problem posed by my title and the expectations it may have raised derives less from any definition of capitalism than from the fact that academic studies of capitalism to date have formed mainly around two dominant genres that purport to cover the implications of this term. In browsing the social science (as opposed to economics) section of a library two core concerns stand out within books using the term 'capitalism' – the study of the industrial proletariat and the study of the 'world' or 'global' system. Both arose for particular and entirely valid reasons. Both might have been expected to be considered in a volume with this title, yet neither is in fact well covered – for rather different reasons.

The inherent conflict between capital and labour lies at the heart of the Marxist analysis of capitalism, but left-wing social science has tended to undertake far more concrete studies of the industrial proletariat than of the capitalist (though see Janelli 1993 for a recent wider ethnography in Korea). Indeed, the concept of 'worker' has become almost synonymous with that of the industrial proletariat. I have no wish to decry the importance of such work; but there are two reasons why it does not feature in the current study. The first is that in Trinidad as in other areas it is one of the topics that has already received considerable attention. Indeed two of the best recent publications on Trinidadian society are directed to this topic. The first is Rhodda Rheddock's thorough historical analysis of the position of women in the labour force (Rheddock 1994), and the second is an equally exemplary ethnography of a factory by Yelvington (1995). There was already a concerted focus of work on the development of industrial relations (and especially industrial strife) within Trinidad history centred on leaders such as Butler and Rienzi (Brereton 1981: 177–90) that these new works build upon. These studies are particularly important as a complement to the current volume, and should be consulted by any reader interested in this topic.

The other reason why the topic is not covered within this volume is that there is quite a considerable description of workers and work contained herein, but it is of a corps of workers who have been relatively neglected in the literature on capitalism. The workers in this volume are mainly middle management and those among the self-employed that dominate advertising agencies, marketing and retail. There is indeed equally impressive recent literature on the Trinidadian entrepreneur, which has been created mainly under the auspices of Selwyn Ryan (e.g. Ryan and Barclay 1992; Ryan and Stewart 1994). These writings are discussed in Chapter 3; but most of the workers discussed here are employed by large corporations, and would no more fit within the category of entrepreneur than in that of proletariat. They have been relatively ignored because they don't fit within the larger categories projected from models of capitalism as a system. Furthermore (as explained below with respect to organizational studies), the perspective of material culture used within this volume leads to both workers and work being addressed from a rather different perspective here than in the comparative literature.

The other major topic that has developed within the social science study of capitalism is that of 'world' or 'global' systems. I suspect that the emphasis on global capitalism emerged because it represents the vanguard, the latest development, in capitalism, and therefore excites particular interest. This tradition has arisen from two main trajectories. The first was historical work on the world-system, influenced in particular by Braudel (1972) and Wallerstein (1974); the other is studies of the emergence of global institutions, such as finance (Corbridge *et al*. 1994; Harvey 1989), and of local–global relations more generally (e.g. Featherstone *et al*. 1995; King 1991). Sklair (1990, 1994) more than most within this tradition has noted the importance of consumption; but within all this work consumption remains a rather shadowy untheorized and unstudied process, to which this and its sister volume on modernity are intended to provide a complementary perspective.

The fact that this book is based on an ethnography should not of itself preclude the study of global systems. Marcus (1995) has recently argued for multi-sited ethnographies, which is quite proper after decades of ethnography based on small sites. His argument is entirely reasonable when set against topics that have been studied for decades through focusing upon extremely small units of analysis such as the street, the factory or the tribe. In a world where capitalism increasingly uses highly extensive global chains for agrarian products (Goodman and Redclift 1991) or clothing (Gereffi 1994) there is clearly scope for this kind of multi-sited study of capitalism. But from the point of view of the topic just described, that is, of the articulation between pro-duction, distribution and purchase of commodities, the argument is perhaps premature. Multi-sited ethnography is intended to complement decades of single-sited ethnography; but on the topic of this volume there does not yet exist any single-sited ethnography to be so complemented. There is a tremendous amount of work still to be done on the articulations that exist within one site, where studies of production are completely separated out from studies of marketing and retail. For this reason the present volume does not yet attempt to travel beyond the shores of Trinidad, but rather analyses the various inter-national links through an examination of their consequences within this particular site.

The context for the study of business for this volume is the nation (more correctly the island, since it is Trinidad, not Trinidad and Tobago, that is its context). As Carnoy (1993) has recently pointed out, this focus remains a great deal more justified than is commonly realized (see also Kogut 1993). Although academics have been fascinated by the trend from multinational to transnational companies, they may thereby be projecting beyond the realities of the present. Carnoy notes that 'despite all the talk about the "globalization" of world business, most multinationals' performance is still closely tied to the competitiveness of their "home" economies' (1993: 53). He shows that multinationals tend to keep most of their sales and assets in their home base, tend to operate according to the economic culture of their home base, often take orders from their home government and are often helped in gaining a better position by their government's interventions (p. 84). Therefore the fact that Chapter 3 takes a national rather than a transnational perspective on transnationals does not seem overly parochial, especially when it is found in that chapter that the key transnationals are surprisingly enough Trinidadian.

The inverse of the approach to capitalism as a global system is the study of comparative capitalism, which assumes that it remains a system that is still subject to regional and localized difference. There are, of course, important traditions devoted to precisely this question, within which Weber's work (e.g. 1978) stands supreme. Economic historians also compare the development of the capitalist firm in different regional contexts (e.g. Chandler 1990). To a degree sociologists have reinvented this concern more recently through examining what Granovetter has called the 'embeddedness' of economic action (Clegg and Redding 1990; Granovetter and Swedberg 1992). This is exactly where one would expect the anthropological contribution to be sited, especially that based on ethnography. The concern is to discern the retention of local difference expressed within business practice, as in an 'African' style of commerce (Bayart 1994; Rowlands 1995; Warnier 1995). Similarly there are many articles on 'Eastern capitalism'. A typical example (*Cultural Anthropology* 8 (1993): 388) notes the problems for capitalists working in China, where 'the consolidation of social relationships built on gift exchange provides a substitute form of trust that can improve the profitability of investment and reduce the risk of arbitrary bureaucratic interference that is not in the interests of investors' (p: 398). Such comparative capitalism is an obvious concern for anthropology, and in this volume my intention is to look beyond the legacy of ancient historical difference, to consider also whether new forms of diversity arise out of the regional contextualization of capitalism as practice.

Where this volume differs from most studies of comparative capitalism is that, as already noted, the relationship between capitalism and its context is seen as dialectical. In every chapter, prominently posed behind the material discussed, is the question 'How is Trinidad as context created by these processes?' (though this may also be found in some business studies, e.g. Smith and Meiksin 1995: 261). By contrast, most texts in comparative capitalism tend to presume a given abstract entity that is then differentially contextualized within what is taken to be *a priori* cultural difference.

There is also a long tradition of anthropological work on markets (e.g. Dannhaeuser 1985; Geertz 1979; Plattner 1985), often highly contextualized in local cosmologies (e.g. Belasco 1980). This has been complemented recently by a powerful and sustained critique of the economists' concept of the market (Dilley 1992). Alexander (1992), for example, questions whether the concept of price almost ever works in practice according to the principles assumed by economists and others. Mature anthropology, such as that exemplified in Dilley's volume, does not take up the position of more extreme relativism. It is open to making generalizations about economic activities that follow theories of the market, and also open to the influence of such theories and models in homogenizing actual market practice. Nevertheless, it insists that these have to be demonstrated in ethnographic description. Just because economic models are long held does not mean that they therefore describe any social reality.

Ethnographers and anthropologists should not be over-generalized as relativists. Having carried out an ethnography of Japanese advertising Moeran (1993) argues that what this has in common with the practices of advertising elsewhere is much more important than any local differences that might otherwise be considered 'Japanese'. Similarly an impressively detailed ethnography of Norwegian marketing in a recent Ph.D. thesis also suggests a trend away from a stress on diversity (Lien 1995). But this flies in the face of a tradition, particularly within British anthropology, for regional and micro-expertise (e.g. Fardon 1990). Moeran is subject to the rather 'cheap' criticism from the traditional anthropologists that the differences were there if only he had looked 'deep' enough. They might argue that global institutions tend to look superficially similar wherever one finds them, but that if anthropologists are able to examine the evidence carefully they will find that underneath this façade of similarity may be discerned authentic difference.

I for one would not accuse Moeran of any such thing. Indeed, his is the product of a full ethnography, while many of the articles that stress difference seem to be written on the basis of rather more anecdotal evidence, often seizing on a choice 'exotic' example of difference on which to build their argument. My own presumption is that capitalism, or more generally modernity, will bring new homogeneity, but equally spawn new heterogeneity. What I would oppose is that anthropology that is prepared to study comparative 'capitalism', but only inasmuch as deep historical traditions have left a legacy of difference that continues to create distinctions within contemporary institutions. Instead, I would rather anthropology was open to the idea that institutions that generate new differences are just as important to us as new forms of homogeneity or old forms of separation. This does not mean we are committed to difference. Moeran and others are correct to assert homogeneity where it is the product of their encounter. It is simply that neither can be assumed.

From within business studies there has also arisen an extensive literature that focuses on the anthropological term 'culture' (Alvesson 1993; Hofstede 1980), though sometimes using this concept rather loosely to examine regional differences in the practice of business. As well as a great variety of accounts from within business studies (contrast Hampden-Turner and Trompenaars 1993 with Smith and Meiksin 1995), approaches include contributions from sociologists (e.g. Clegg and Reading 1990; Prus 1989) and anthropologists (Hofstede 1980, 1994). As well as anthropologists who have moved into organizational studies, such as Hofstede, noted above, or Czarniaswka-Joerges (1992), increasingly anthropologists are working on organizations from within anthropology (see Ouroussoff 1993; Wright 1994). Although much of this volume is about the world of work, I hardly make any reference to this literature. To explain this is to turn from an emphasis on what this volume has not tried to do and start to return to the topic of what it seeks to achieve.

Apart from a concern with consumption, the other trajectory that led to the present work is that of material culture studies (Miller 1987, Miller forthcoming). As noted in the aims outlined above, the primary intention of this book is to trace through the processes by which commodities are formed. The dramatis personae of this book are commodities, not people. Organizational studies, by contrast, are based not around objects, but persons. Most such studies are written either from the perspective of industrial workers, their rights and conditions, or more usually today from the perspective of how a company can ensure the efficient running of its labour force. The emphasis in this book, however, is not on these topics, but on the commodity within its social context. Its concerns are with how advertising agencies come to attribute certain characteristics to the goods they sell, on how they attempt to sell them and people to purchase them, although the context for such topics is often the social organization of these institutions. This orientation to commodities allows for some quite surprising conclusions. Often neither workers nor profitability nor efficiency seem to be nearly as important as is claimed by those involved. This is often because their primary orientation is also to the commodity being created – its prestige, its competition, the way it objectifies the institution that creates or sells it. This focus is on culture, where society is constructed through its material context, rather than on a reified concept of society, which tends, as Latour (1993) has argued, most often to be the other pole to a reified science or, in economics, a reified commodity.

Given this perspective from material culture there are two other literatures that might seem relevant, those of economics and cultural studies. Material culture differs considerably from both. Economics tends to focus on aggregate behaviours and models of abstract relations, producing a fetishized sense of the commodity. Cultural studies (e.g. Grossberg *et al.* 1992) tends to be devoted to the analysis and decoding of texts, many of them highly relevant texts, such as advertising and media forms. Material culture, as exemplified in this volume, is contrasted by its ethnographic focus. My focus upon the commodity is an acknowledgment of its importance within modern life. By showing how it emerges from social contexts and its subsequent consequences for those contexts this account is intended to contribute directly to the general project of de-fetishizing the commodity.

For ethnography to be the prime agent in this de-fetishization it needs to be understood as more than mere methodology. It is also a series of commitments that together constitute a particular perspective. The first commitment is to be in the presence of the people one is studying, and not merely of the texts or objects they produce. The second is a commitment to evaluate people in terms of what they actually do, i.e. as material agents working with a material world, and not merely of what they say they do. The third is a long-term commitment to an investigation that allows people to return to a daily life that one hopes goes beyond what is performed for the ethnographer. This reflects a commitment to the refinement of the act of observation itself that is essential to the plausibility of anthropological scholarship outside a context of naturalistic science. All of these are tempered by a fourth commitment, which is to holistic analysis, which insists that such behaviours be considered within the larger framework of people's lives and cosmologies, and thereby is to include the speculative construction of much that is not observed, but conjectured on the basis of what can be observed. This last commitment explains why a study that relies so much on observation lies quite outside the normal form of positivistic enquiry. This ethnographic tradition is equally distinct from that which cultural studies appears to have inherited (above all from Walter Benjamin), where capitalism became a kind of spirit of the age read off through textual forms such as reconstructed arcades (Miller 1997 for critique).

I do not claim that my approach is the only, or even a better, approach to capitalism than those that have been discussed in this section. I do claim, however, that there is remarkably little work to date that defines a research project remotely similar to the one attempted in this book. I further claim that these areas are just as important to the overall understanding of capitalism as the foci of concern that dominate current studies of capitalism and capitalist societies. This is particularly important with respect to the context to which I now turn, which is the specific situation of Trinidad. There is a considerable legacy of studies in the Caribbean on capitalism, including a contribution by anthropologists such as Mintz (1985a). The context for my study is, however, worlds apart from that of most previous ethnographic accounts. If I were studying a plantation system and a tradition arising out of the peasantry I would have hundreds of comparative studies by anthropologists to refer to. Even if this were a factory system, such as that recently studied by Yelvington (1995), there would be comparable work, both historical and contemporary, to use. But ethnographic work amongst white-collar professionals in areas such as media and shopping malls as yet has little in the way of comparative ethnography within this region, or indeed in any region.

The Encounter

This then is the setting for my work. I started this research with a very specific agenda and some relevant experience. I have had some indirect encounters with business concerns from childhood. My family worked in the clothing trade, and meal-time conversation at my home was almost always directed to business concerns. This certainly left its legacy, in the sense that I possessed certain kinds of tacit knowledge that others did not have. Partly this took the form of cynicism about business. I was scornful of the degree to which I felt people around me ignored business imperatives. When friends asked the waiter to recommend something from the menu that day, I assumed they would be sold whatever dish the management had agreed to give the waiter commission on, since it needed to be used up. I saw the language and culture of selling as part of the norm of humanity around me, while in most English society it seems regarded as a kind of dirty secret that should not usually be alluded to.

I suspect this made me more ready than most to accept my second major influence, which began with the reading of the *Communist Manifesto,* which was the set text for my school politics exam. Marxism continued to be the dominant influence on academic life during my time as a student and when I first began teaching. I still believe it was one of most valuable and indeed accurate accounts I have received of the world, and this remains just as much the case when 'Communist regimes' have fallen and the topic is no longer in academic fashion. At the least I hope to retain the Hegelian dialectic, which I regard as one of the most profound and sophisticated means for understanding the nature of human culture and history, together with the sense of morality and conviction that was wedded to this tradition by the early Marx. The main deficit was that it made me think I knew what capitalism was from a series of theoretical models, and that leads to the agenda of this current work, which strives to achieve a better descriptive grounding prior to the reformulation of any critical perspective.

My own academic agenda, which arose originally from training in archaeology, was focused first upon material culture and then the study of consumption, as the main context through which people today enter into their association with objects. These remain my central academic concerns. It is clear, then, that for me the study of business is subsidiary to these other topics. The writing of this book came rather from an acknowledgment of a critique of works I and others had written on the topic of objects and consumption, and in particular a lack of articulation between work on consumption and on production. But because my family background was in retail, I could not simply refer the term production to proletarian labour, which often seemed the only image of production within academic Marxism.

Having written a largely theoretical work on consumption (Miller 1987), I also set out to undertake an ethnography in Trinidad with the aim both of observing consumption in a comparative context, and of re-contextualizing consumption within the larger framework of business. I chose Trinidad because the recent experience of an oil boom and recession seemed likely to give the topic a particular salience, as against a region in which mass consumption was gradually absorbed over decades and could now be taken for granted. Furthermore the size of the island suggested that I would be able to achieve the kind of coverage I had in mind between various levels within the economy, which would have been far more difficult if I had returned to India, where I had carried out a previous ethnography. I believe these were generally correct assumptions.

I had thought that this would result in a single-volume ethnography in which the cultural context would be an opening chapter to the rest. The fieldwork lasted for one year, from 1988 to 1989. Return visits were made in 1990 and 1993. A final visit in 1995 was made specifically to revise the manuscript of this book. As this writing up developed it soon became obvious that the task of contextualizing the imperatives of consumers within a more general ethnography would amount to a book-length monograph in its own right. Since it also became concerned with the encounter between ethnography and rather over-generalized models about the nature of 'modern' life, it was published under the title *Modernity: An Ethnographic Approach* (1994). It is strongly recommended that the present book is read in conjunction with that volume, since the first volume contains a much longer exposition about consumers and their imperatives than is included in the present volume.

The emphasis upon consumption within the cultural ethnography, rather than within this volume, arose as fieldwork
confirmed my expectations that consumption imperatives are
generally derived from the social and cultural contexts of
consumers rather than from anything constructed by business. In
this volume I will be concerned with the articulation between
consumption and business concerns, but I feel that I have
understood much more about why consumers have particular
desires for clothing, cars, food and other such forms through
studying topics such as kinship and ethnicity than I gain by
studying what Fine and Leopold (1993: 20–35) have called the
'systems of provision' through which they obtain these goods.

Description and History of Trinidad

The island of Trinidad is the larger part of the state of Trinidad
and Tobago. Tobago will not be considered in this book, since it
has a very different history, population structure and self-
characterization, and in terms of its economy it is being developed largely through tourism, which is a resource of very little
importance within the larger island. Trinidad itself is 4,828 sq.
km., and lies in the south-eastern Caribbean 16 km. north-east of
Venezuela. There is one major range of hills in the north, and
today 50–60 per cent of the land is forest.

Trinidad's emergence into modern history[1] is best situated at
the end of the eighteenth century. Prior to that date the main
feature is the decline of the original population of Arawak and
Carib, following the arrival of Columbus in 1498. Although the
Spanish first colonized and ruled Trinidad, the numbers involved
were always very small. By contrast, the last two centuries have
witnessed the arrival of an abundance of peoples to produce the
highly heterogeneous contemporary population. Slavery developed later in Trinidad than on other Caribbean islands, and it
was also less dependent upon massive sugar plantations, with
crops such as cocoa having a major influence. By the time a
significant slave population of around 10,000 was established the

---

1. The standard reference for the history of Trinidad is Brereton (1981), but see also
Williams (1964) and Wood (1968), which are complemented for the most recent period by
Ryan (1972, 1988).

slave trade was being abolished, and within forty years there was the slave emancipation of 1834. Already at that time there was a significant urban population. The colonial population was also divided into a number of competing groups, essentially British by political control, but French-dominated numerically and culturally.

Trinidad continued to see the arrival of diverse populations during the nineteenth century: the largest immigration was of around 144,000 South Asian indentured labourers brought in between 1845 and 1917. Perhaps next most significant in population was the migration of *peons*, a Spanish-speaking peasantry from nearby South America. A full list of immigrant sources would include Chinese indentured labourers, Portuguese shopkeepers, French royalists and republicans, economic migrants from the Middle East today known as 'Syrians', settlers from other West Indian islands (e.g. Barbados, St Vincent, Grenada) and others. Today the two main ethnic components of the population describe themselves as Indian and African/Negro, each in census terms comprising around 40 per cent of the population. The remaining 20 per cent is mainly composed of those who describe themselves as 'mixed', but there are a host of small populations such as Chinese, Syrian, and White. The 1990 census gives the total population as 1,234,388.

The sense of creolization and heterogeneity has been as much assisted by emigration in the twentieth century as by immigration in the nineteenth. Trinidadians have migrated in waves to London, Toronto, New York and Miami. The élite colonial population has seen its scions depart at various moments of political emancipation. This has included the establishment of the government by Eric Williams, leader of the People's National Movement (PNM) in 1956, Independence, granted in 1962, or the black power struggles of 1970, when a combination of popular protests and demonstrations together with a mutiny in the army came close to overthrowing the government. As a result of these movements an extraordinary number of Trinidadian families are in effect transnational. In a survey of 160 households I found that 101 could name a member of their immediate family (parents, children or siblings) living abroad, 38 mentioned more distant relatives, and only 21 stated that they had no relatives living abroad (see Olwig 1993 for an even more extreme case).

The two most important factors in the history of the Trinidadian economy are both largely irrelevant to this particular study. Prior to the twentieth century the bulk of the population has been principally concerned with plantations of sugar, cocoa, coffee and coconuts. For much of the twentieth century oil has increased its importance as the primary source of income, but agriculture, and in particular sugar, remained more important as a source of employment. Today, however, agriculture is a minor component of the Trinidadian economy, and does not feature within this volume except as the supplier of a few of the raw materials. The Trinidadian economy continues to be dominated above all by the price of oil. There have been a number of important studies of this aspect of the Trinidadian economy (e.g. Alleyne 1988; Hintzen 1989; Singh 1989). My study, however, does not deal at all with either oil or its associated industries, so again the history of these developments will not be considered.

The true ancestry of the aspects of capitalism that are the subject of this study probably lies in a third element within the development of the Trinidadian capitalist economy, which is its role as an entrepôt. In the nineteenth century the capital, Port of Spain, was considered one of the most sophisticated and cosmopolitan sites in the Caribbean. In order to supply the local élite with high-quality goods there were a considerable number of import agencies, which were founded and run by members of this same élite. Below this was a level of marketing and 'hucksters' dominated by the African segment of the population that redistributed some items such as cloth to the larger population. The early impact of such business is made clear in the Red Book of 1922, which describes Port of Spain as 'the largest and handsomest town in the British West Indies' (Macmillan 1922: 164). The 73,000 inhabitants are described as fully supplied with clean water, electricity, telephones, and an electric tram system. Details of over 150 companies are given.

A large number of the businesses I dealt with had their roots in the kind of 'merchant capital' represented by such firms, mainly headed by local whites whose families had been in Trinidad for several generations. The origins of this community in linkages between early capitalism and slavery have been documented by Eric Williams (1942) and incorporated within more general accounts (e.g. Brereton 1981; Wood 1968). Most historical materials on Trinidad are on its political history, and dwell on the events leading to the gradual distancing of the

white population from government before and after Trinidad
gained its independence from Britain. But it is also clear that the
same post-independence period saw if anything a consolidation
of this group's control over local business.

This community, whose core group became known as the
'French Creoles', remains of considerable importance. At the
level of the interlocking directorship of the major companies they
still control much of Trinidadian business (Parris 1985).
Unfortunately there are no contemporary studies equivalent to
that recently carried out by Douglass (1992) for the Jamaican
white élite that can provide a portrait of the relationship between
their business involvement and their social milieux. In the area
of grocery and retail trades with which I am principally
concerned there were, however, from early on a number of other
groups that became rivals to the original élite. Indeed the term
'white' becomes quite problematic in this context. While the
Chinese, Portuguese and Syrians have been considered 'white' as
against the majority population from Africa and India, they
nevertheless appear historically as a kind of marginalized in-
between set of groups that mediates between the 'French Creole'
and the rest of the population.

A number of recent studies have provided us with much
better information as to the commercial development of these
groups. This is in part because these historical studies have taken
place under the auspices of a larger programme designed to
investigate the link between ethnicity and entrepreneurship.
Ferreira (1994) provides a concise history of the two thousand
'Portuguese' migrants who came from the island of Madeira.
Many of these developed small retail outlets or ran rum-shops.
Some of these developed into large companies that still exist. In
the oral histories I collected about the Chaguanas district where I
worked, the Portuguese wine-maker and retailers occupy a
similar niche to that of the Chinese, also the subject of a recent
study (Millett 1993; also Bentley and Henry 1969). The Chinese
influence in small businesses has perhaps remained of
importance for longer, in that in the 1960s they are recorded as
still running some 500 grocery shops and 15 supermarkets
(Millett 1993: 51).

Just as the influence of the Chinese and Portuguese declined
in the second half of this century, partly through emigration
and absorption, the influence of the small 'Syrian' community

(actually mainly Lebanese Christians) has increased. Although Ryan (1991c: 179) notes that they were unable to open their first shop in the main commercial street of Port of Spain until 1954, today their influence in retail is a greater rival to white dominance than any of their predecessors (see Barclay 1994). Given their small numbers they are extremely important to the history of commercial development, particularly in the clothing industry, but more recently to commerce as a whole.

The gradual emergence into commerce of the largest groups in the population, the East-Indian and African, is discussed further in Chapter 3. On the whole it was a population that graded from African to 'off-white' and mixed that was favoured both by foreign companies and the independent state in recruiting management for the transnational and government-controlled firms. Outside of the small ethnic élites, it is probably they that have the major role in 'running' business in Trinidad on a day-to-day basis. This would, however, be quickly denied by most Trinidadians, who would point instead to the much more visible East-Indian population, who have a rapidly growing influence in the development of small and medium-sized private firms, as well as some notable major entrepreneurs recently described by Ramsaran (1993).

Although one thinks of the contemporary period as one in which local economies are buffeted and unprotected against sudden and often disastrous shifts in the global economy, this situation has always been true for Trinidad. Whether it was acts of nature, as in the witches' broom disease that devastated the cocoa plantations, or acts of the market, with sudden falls in the price of sugar, Trinidad was always quite precariously situated. If in the nineteenth century fate seemed largely to intervene in terms of disasters, in the twentieth century it has been equally sudden and unpredictable booms.

The Second World War had an enormous impact on the consciousness of the people of Trinidad, not least because the wages paid by the Americans were of an altogether different level to anything paid to workers before. This followed a period in the 1930s in which Trinidadian labour organizations achieved a strength and militancy which, however, did not outlast the events of the war. The Second World War also seems to have marked a gear change in the speed to with which Trinidad entered into the modern economy. In oral traditions it is remembered as a kind of earlier mini oil boom. The war had brought Trinidad to the attention of various transnational firms, and the period from 1950 to 1970 may well have seen a greater level of direct foreign involvement in Trinidadian business than either before or since. A typical example is given in the history of the advertising industry described in Chapter 5, where indigenous development was succeeded by the incursion of large foreign-based transnationals. Indeed, the newly independent government of Eric Williams was much influenced by economic theorists such as Arthur Lewis, who advocated the attraction of foreign capital as a means of ensuring progressive development in the economy as a whole.

Eric Williams's economic policies, embodied in three five-year plans between 1958 and 1973, were not a particularly successful strategy for Trinidad, whose economy largely stagnated, and where very little employment was created by foreign investment. Carrington provides a critique of these policies as applied to Trinidad, especially with respect to employment (Carrington 1971). Over the decades, however, Trinidad continued to develop the same niche that it had occupied now for a century. This saw the dominant oil industry supplemented by some primary manufactures. More important were firms that specialized in the redistribution of imported goods, the local completion of industrial manufacturing using parts made elsewhere, as in car assemblage, or the repackaging of basic groceries for supply to the islands of the Southern Caribbean. This produced the typical 'screwdriver' industries that today make up much of the manufacturing activity described in this book. A detailed example of such an industry is also given in Yelvington (1995: 99–120).

The hopes raised by political independence were clearly not being fulfilled, and the continued stagnation led to increasing unrest. This culminated in the Black Power disturbances of 1970, which posed a serious threat to the government and led to a clear shift towards more populist measures and a more strident nationalism. But there was little benefit to most of the population, and the situation looked increasingly bleak, until . . .

The Oil Boom

The effects of the oil boom were dramatic by any standard. The government saw its revenue grow from TT$494 million in 1973 to TT$7117.8 in 1982. Over the same period GDP grew from TT$ 2,560 to TT$18,121. By 1986 most people had seen their wage packet grow by something between a factor of 5 and 8 over the previous decade. There was massive investment in the development of new industries, especially around the Point Lisas area, including fertilizers and steel. This period also saw the nationalization of many of the main industrial sectors. There were also the development of welfare programmes, enormous subsidies, and a huge expansion of the public sector.

The effect of the oil boom is discussed by Auty and Gelb (1986; also Gelb 1988), and the latter has investigated the effect of the oil boom on a comparative basis. These authors were concerned with the degree of dependence upon oil that was fostered and the decline in other sectors, though they note that for Trinidad, unlike most other countries, these effects were well in evidence even before the oil boom (p. 1163). When the oil boom did come the windfall was proportionally large, even in comparison with other oil-boom countries. They note that after initial caution the money was increasingly used for across-the-board subsidies, for maintaining and creating employment, and for risky large-scale industrial development.

Meanwhile other sectors, noticeably agriculture, declined. The priorities of the government have been seen as closely related to political and ethnic considerations, favouring the development of an African public sector while ignoring an Indian-dominated rural sector (Hintzen 1989). The symbol of misspent revenue was seen as the DEWD programme, which became notorious for lax supervision of the casual labour employed and was seen as creating a tradition of taking money for little work. On the other hand, many such criticisms are class-specific, and, compared to other oil-boom countries, Trinidad was probably unusual in the degree to which ordinary working people were given access to the benefits, so that the gap between the richest and poorest segments narrowed during this period.

By the time I conducted fieldwork the oil boom had become a thing of myths and legends. The experience depended on the level one was starting from. One individual recalled the oil boom as follows: 'In '73 I felt it first, I got a raise in salary from $250 a month to nearly $475 a month and that was a big raise and I was able to go to the grocery and have money until next pay. Before that used to get credit.' By contrast, a member of the middle class saw it in the following terms: 'People had money coming out of their ears. You would see people go into a store and buying 100tt whisky and whatever because the top brands of everything. Everybody had on Gucci jeans, Calvin Klein, Reebok shoes. They knew from *Vogue* magazine, you had them all here.' As a businessman put it with respect to commodities coming into Trinidad: 'We were even close to importing winter coats and so on because everything was being brought into Trinidad. You know things had gotten so out of hand I was ashamed.' Food and drink imports shot up in this period. It was the period that saw the establishment of basic electrical goods such as fridges and television as standard. Indeed, it is the odd statistics, like Trinidad's becoming the third largest international market for Harvey's sherries, that give the vividest sense of what had occurred.

The most dramatic accounts of the oil boom are available from ethnographers who were able to observe its effects amongst what had been the least developed population of Trinidad – the rural East-Indian hamlets and villages. Klass (1991: Chapter 3) returned in 1985 to study the village near Chaguanas where he had originally conducted fieldwork in 1957. He not only reports immense differences in wealth and possessions, but notes that most of the distinctive cultural traits that originally he had been able to link to their South Asian roots had virtually disappeared by 1985. One had to look rather to structural continuities. For example, he notes that the pattern of international visiting by families in 1985 had many similarities with inter-settlement visiting in 1957.

Vertovec (1992: Chapter 3) provides a more detailed account of these changes from the perspective of an equally remote Indian village. The sense is of a move from a sleepy agricultural village to a well-educated, modern settlement, well connected to urban employment and developing its own extensive commercial facilities, including shops and cars. In contrast to Klass, however, he has noted that wealth should not be viewed as necessarily a sign of the neglect of traditions. For example, some of the new wealth was used to fund the revival of certain costly religious ceremonies amongst the Hindu population he studied.

From 1982, however, an inexplicable growth was replaced by an equally inexplicable decline. Neither had much to do with anything for which Trinidadians were responsible. Unemployment grew, and subsidies were increasingly withdrawn, so that expectations, which had been so dramatically raised, were now being crushed. As a friend remarked to me: 'People feeling a lot of pressure from recession. If they have money they drinking. Some drink because they have no money.' Vertovec, who conducted fieldwork as recession was beginning to bite, notes the climate amongst youths hanging around the rum-shops and facing suddenly much poorer prospects (1992: 157). A useful contrast to these studies is given by Yelvington (1995), who undertook fieldwork during the same post-oil-boom period as Vertovec, but amongst the urban proletariat on the outskirts of the capital. Here the ethnography gives a keen sense of a struggle against declining prospects. Between them Vertovec and Yelvington provide important portraits of what it was like to live through the times that form the background to my own study.

Trinidad in 1988–9

A useful summary of the general condition of Trinidad and Tobago at the time of fieldwork is provided in Yelvington (1991). Politically the National Alliance for Reconstruction led by Robinson had come to power in 1986. The NAR had replaced the PNM, which had been in power ever since Independence in 1962. The PNM had been seen as being in decline during the increasingly autocratic government of Eric Williams, and even more after his death in 1981. Its fall was no surprise, although it left a civil service which was largely constructed under its patronage and protection and was clearly not well disposed to any successor. As the first multi-ethnic government the NAR carried the hopes of the East-Indian community in particular. It also tried to appeal both to the business sector and the mass population. But my fieldwork coincided with the year the government fell apart, in what is locally termed 'bacchanal', with the core of the traditional Indian opposition party leaving the coalition. The low popularity of the government was to continue to its complete demise in the election of 1991.

My sense of the difference between the beginning and end of fieldwork was that when I arrived many people still hoped that the oil boom represented the new norm, while the recession was a temporary problem. By the end, most people accepted that the recession was to be the norm, and it was the oil boom that was a one-off exception. That year per capita GDP was TT$14,267. It declined by 3.9 per cent, the fifth contraction in succession. The oil boom, which had seemed likely to place Trinidad as one of the richest countries in the Americas, was definitely history. Unemployment was at 22 per cent and inflation was 7.8 per cent. In fact, although the recession was bottoming out, with small rises in GDP in 1990 and 1991, the general sense in the six years since fieldwork is that the economy is continuing at more or less the same level reached during the recession. This meant that some things were getting better, as well as some getting worse. In particular, a number of the heavy industrial complexes con-structed under Eric Williams, which had been thought to be 'white elephants', were to prove reasonably profitable in the medium term.

During fieldwork several events highlighted the sense of recession, and indeed depression. The TT dollar was devalued from TT$3.84 to the US$ to TT$4.25 to the US$. There was a crisis over reserves of foreign currency, leading to periods when companies simply could not find the funds to pay for imports. There was a sudden surge of mainly East-Indian economic emigrants leaving for Canada, which was only stopped when Canada made it clear that the claims being made for refugee status would not be confirmed. There was a host of 'belt-tightening' measures in that year's budget, among which most publicity went to a 10 per cent cut in the salaries of all civil servants. The events with respect to the IMF will be discussed in the next chapter.

According to the household budgetary survey of 1988 the average household income was $TT1,872 per month, and average household size was 4.1 persons; 21.5 per cent of households had an income of less than TT$999 a month, while 3.3 per cent had incomes of more than TT$6,000. The oil boom had created a relatively high standard in many fields: 70.5 per cent owned their own accommodation, and there was a 97.2 per cent literacy rate, while 35.5 per cent of children were reaching secondary school education or above. Life expectancy was 68.7. A taste for consumer goods is more easily gained than lost, and shopping trips abroad were still on most people's theoretical agenda, though in practice it was more likely that they would buy one or two items from a semi-professional 'suitcase trader' who was going abroad on behalf of many. This was a time when most people had videos, and most of these videos had ceased to work.

The degree to which people could continue to have a sense of themselves as a middle class within a developed country varied considerably between the different communities which I studied. By my return visit in 1991, there were a number of households in the poorest community whose children were visibly not going to school, as the parents were embarrassed at not being able to afford proper clothing and books for them. By 1995, although I did not come across it directly, friends in the medical profession were telling me of malnutrition cases being dealt with in the hospitals. Nevertheless, even in 1995 the manufacturing and distribution sector that I studied was in approximately similar shape to its condition when my fieldwork began, and there was a considerable amount of construction activity. The wealthiest community studied appeared thriving, with a number of very large houses being constructed. The schoolchildren in the squatters' settlement seemed to have largely returned to school. But with structural adjustment about to take hold, the most likely prospect was for a renewed decline.

In general, then, the feeling was that the oil boom had disappeared, leaving Trinidad still a relatively wealthy island compared to many of those around it, but one with an increasing disparity between rich and poor, and with expectations that each year became harder to fulfil. Behind this lies the reality of dependence upon oil and gas. In effect, the actions of government often matter little compared to a combination of commodity prices and the World Bank. In 1985 there was still the prospect of substantial gains from gas reserves in the area, and it is unlikely that Trinidad will sink below a certain level, simply because it has a natural resource that is going to be worth a substantial amount for some time to come.

The Ethnographic Context

A detailed description of the fieldwork context is given in Miller 1994: 24–57. This includes a discussion of my use of 'ethnic' labels. I spent a year (1988–9) and three subsequent return visits living in the small town of Chaguanas in central Trinidad. Chaguanas was one of the fastest growing commercial centres, with a well-established market and three more recently built shopping malls. It is often seen as a centre for the East Indian population, though the four communities I studied in the area reflected the overall ethnic make-up of the population, at 40 per cent African, 40 per cent Indian, and 20 per cent other or mixed. For the study of consumption I worked with four communities: (1) St Pauls, a largely East Indian 'village' that had become incorporated within the town; (2) The Meadows, one of the wealthiest residential areas in the town; (3) Newtown, a National Housing Authority scheme mainly occupied by Africans working for government in sectors such as the police; and (4) Ford, a squatters' community, one of the poorest areas in central Trinidad. I will on occasion make reference to a survey I conducted, which was based on 160 households, 40 from each of these areas.

The aspect of fieldwork that is not described in the earlier volume but forms the core to the present book is my work within companies. Not surprisingly, most of the major companies reacted with some suspicion to my initial enquiries for permission to observe their work. In many cases it took several months to obtain the degree of access I required. Nevertheless, with only a single exception all the companies I was most concerned to work with did in fact grant me permission. In some cases, this was merely an interview or two with executives. For others, however, this meant a long-term commitment to following their activities and being present when discussions were taking place. In all cases I explained that I was writing an academic book whose main concern was to use Trinidad instead of the usual metropolitan countries to exemplify business practice. I assured executives that I would not release commercially sensitive information to rivals, and that my publication would be concerned with general practices rather than some kind of journalistic exposé, and that any commercially sensitive information would be years out of date by the time it appeared.

Probably the most sustained fieldwork was based on the relationship between advertising agencies and their clients. Here I attempted to ensure that I would receive a call about any meetings taking place with respect to the particular campaigns that I was following. I would then turn up and in most cases tape-record the entire proceedings as unobtrusively as possible. Much of my time was also spent in hanging around in offices waiting to see people, and I think I learnt as much from the conversations and events that were taking place around me at these times, as when I was explicitly focusing upon some or other meeting or event. Obviously in some cases the conversations and what was presented were affected by my presence. In general, however, these were large commercial companies operating to deadlines, and much more keen on impressing each other and thereby securing their accounts than with addressing themselves to me. I believe I was generally regarded with some accuracy as inconsequential. I felt, therefore, that in many cases where I attended several meetings I was able to achieve the 'fly on the wall' status of being simply a taken-for-granted presence.

Most of the businesses I studied were in Port of Spain or what is called the East–West corridor – a commercial and residential spread eastwards from the capital. By contrast, the study of retail described in Chapter 7 was entirely based in Chaguanas, as was my fieldwork with consumers. There was something of an overlap, however, since during the course of the year I made a large number of friends and acquaintances in Chaguanas who spoke to me about the companies for whom they worked. These ranged from people in senior management positions to workers at much more modest levels, but also included accountants, government workers, and others with particular kinds of knowledge. It is probable that more of the information about transnationals given in Chapter 3 derives from these informal contacts with various friends who also happened to be employees of the companies than from the more formal approaches made to the companies during the course of the year.

I would finally wish to defend my constant use of the term 'Trinidadian' during the course of this volume. The question of whether Trinidadian business differs from any general model of business practice becomes one aspect of more general questions about the nature of Trinidadian norms and expectations, since it is shown that business is far more socially contextualized than is often thought. As was argued in Miller (1994), the very idea of being able to talk about 'Trinidadian' practices is itself in some ways an astonishing discovery. In an older anthropological tradition the use of such a general term was not seen as problematic. But Trinidad is in no respect similar to those 'tribes' and 'villages' traditionally studied by anthropologists. Indeed, many of these have now been discovered to be far less homogeneous and with a more chequered history than was often admitted to in anthropological accounts, which tended to generalize out of convenience.

Trinidad, by contrast, is much more characteristic of a modernity that evokes a picture of heterogeneity, as is evident from its history of immigration and its current transnational links. Nevertheless, my account does generalize and describe normative behaviour as much as when anthropologists talk of 'tribal' groups. The reasons behind this are one of the main conclusions to Miller (1994: 314–22). That book concluded that, despite the recent expectations of anthropology, I had found people quite capable of creative normativity around recently developed or adopted rituals that blithely ignore all those transnational factors that should have counted against this. At Christmas, for example, virtually the entire population may be found eating the same things, highlighting certain values that centre very clearly on a common notion of being Trinidadian. Of course, differences are always masked by generality, but normativity remains just as important an area of social behaviour as difference, and just as subject to empathetic understanding. Although I argue that being Trinidadian means working between two highly opposed and contradictory possibilities, these operate for most of the population and are constantly reinforced in popular culture, such as the weekly newspapers, or national events such as Carnival.

The point made in Miller (1994) was that the homogenized normativity of behaving like a 'Trinidadian' was quite different from that assumed by anthropologists of 'traditional' societies. Much of it is based on the 'virtual' community that comes from a standardized education system, including the models inculcated in business schools, and constant exposure to the same television shows and newspapers. It is a normativity that is characteristic of the condition of modernity, but it is still normative. Furthermore, it often did not represent a conformity to international homogenization, but rather the specific construction of a level of difference through the local appropriation of consumption forms. I believe that whether anthropologists approve or disapprove of a nationalist category, they cannot ignore the degree to which groups with extraordinarily heterogeneous origins and with every modern facility for transnational contact still manifest forms of sameness with which they have a powerful sense of identity and that can be evoked in a volume such as this by reference to the 'Trinidadian' tendency to act in this or that way. As such the term recognizes rather than naturalizes sameness within the framework of academic analytical generality.

2

Pure Capitalism

The Legacy of Bretton Woods

It might be thought that theoretical ideals of a model of pure capitalism would be of little significance to a small marginal country such as Trinidad and Tobago. This is not the case, because Trinidad's historical legacy of actual commerce is increasingly likely to have to give way to what is proving a more powerful trajectory – the history of theories of ideal capitalism and their manifestation in a powerful series of institutions. Business in Trinidad can no longer be considered outside the context of this encounter with pure capitalism.

In 1989 the government of Trinidad and Tobago decided to request from the International Monetary Fund (henceforth the IMF) financial guarantees. This was followed in 1990 by a request for further stand-by credit, and then the development of a restructuring programme under the auspices of the World Bank. This was a reluctant move, inasmuch as in 1987 the government had declared this to be the worst option available to them. But by 1989 they had come to the conclusion that the worst option was actually the only option open to them.

Fortunately, there have been a number of recent publications that examine in some detail the effects of the IMF and the World Bank upon the countries of the Caribbean, and in one case on Trinidad in particular. Pantin's (1989) work is a polemical and pre-emptive strike against the IMF written at the time of the decision by Trinidad to go down this path (for a later Trinidadian perspective see LaGuerre 1994). McAfee (1991) is a more general but equally critical assessment, based on the Caribbean as a whole and written from the perspective of a development officer with Oxfam. Ramsaran (1992) might be expected to provide a more sympathetic appraisal, given his background as an economist who has also been a consultant for the World Bank. The tone is certainly less polemical, and more a drawing-up of a systematic balance sheet; but the conclusion in many respects differs little from those of the other two authors.

The reason for this consensus seems to lie with the evidence as to both the local and the global effect of IMF/World Bank involvement. In almost every respect this seems to have been a disastrous encounter, which in and of itself seems to be a significant factor in the increase in poverty, social conflict and general suffering in the Caribbean, as also in other regions. The tone of the writings reflects the fact that despite this evidence there is as yet little suggestion that the future policy of these institutions is going to change. Apart from academic work the message was clear from other events. For example, the Trinidadian economist D. Budhoo resigned from the IMF after 12 years as a senior official, and made public his dissatisfaction with their effects on the Caribbean (Yelvington 1991: 467). It is not surprising, therefore, that the government itself regarded a move to the IMF as its last resort.

This very refusal to reflect upon considerable evidence for deleterious consequences may provide a good place to begin a more general account of these institutions, which today provide the key 'global' context for the development of Trinidadian business. There are some striking parallels with the period of Communist government in many areas of the world. Marxist governments often debated ideology at the level of an abstract model derived from an often formalistic reading of Marx. The fixity of ideology was a major problem in its application. It depended upon adherence to an ideal of communism, which did not yet exist anywhere, but would inevitably develop as a result of historical transformations. In practice, for those wishing to speed things up when history seemed to be 'forgetting' its proper role, the task was to transform the societies in question, irrespective of their actual diversity, into something approximating to the model prescribed. Thus, in so far as Russia did not accord with predictions as to its historical development through capitalism to communism, the Soviet Union would be transformed to meet its destiny.

In recent years neo-classical economics seems to have developed a similar role. As is often remarked, the premises behind academic economics are at least as far removed from the actual practices of any given social group as were any of the idealized formulations of academic Marxism. The ideals of a totally free market, of a pure optimizing rationality choosing freely between utilities, etc., would seem quite bizarre to lay individuals reflecting on their own society, but have been maintained in the esoteric textbooks of this increasingly influential academic discipline. In this case there are also powerful institutions, such as the banking establishment, which in their ordinary practice have achieved sufficient abstraction as to actually approximate some of these economic assumptions, and to have a vested interest in the further development of such abstraction.

To provide one Caribbean example (James 1983): a respected economist, with I imagine sincere motives, published an important analysis entitled *Consumer Choice in the Third World* based almost entirely on a study of washing powders in Barbados. Through a number of carefully constructed experiments the author was able to demonstrate a discrepancy between the actual qualities of different forms of laundry soap and powders and the choices made by consumers based on their claimed properties. He therefore concluded that there were distorting factors, such as advertising, that invalidated key assumptions about rational utility choice in economic theories of consumption. I do not wish to disparage this book, whose 'heart' was clearly in the right place, but merely point out that, for probably the entire global population outside those trained in formal economics, the assumptions about consumer utility functions that this book sought to challenge would have appeared to be absolutely daft.

In the case of Communism it was largely explicit political revolutions that led to the formation of governments committed to transforming societies into a closer approximation to its ideals. There was often a clear moral intent, and sometimes (but only sometimes) popular acquiescence in this project. In the case of economics the actual reasoning and premises remain esoteric, far too bizarre to be comprehended without several years' specific inculcation through academic institutions. Nevertheless, these ideas have been promulgated with sometimes missionary-like zeal by persons who have access to the kind of power that can once again change societies to fit their models.

This portrayal of these institutions is hardly novel, and there is a recent similar (but much fuller) portrayal of the World Bank by George and Sabelli (1994). Their primary argument is that the institution most closely approximates to a traditional religion in its hermetically sealed structure of legitimation, which seems quite impervious to the enormous weight of evidence that it has consistently acted in diametric opposition to its own claimed purpose of assisting the poor of the world. Perhaps because I am rather more influenced by Bourdieu (the author of books such as *Homo Academicus* 1988), I would ascribe much more power to the academic discipline of economics. I see the content of their book as supporting the claim that rather than emerging from any particular national or class interest, the World Bank is a relatively simple expression of an academic drive to construct a pure theoretical model. As George and Sabelli show (pp. 112–34) the bank is recruited almost entirely through creaming off the most talented and academically successful members of economics departments around the world. It should hardly surprise us that the result, to use their words, is that 'The Bank's declared new, or at least renewed, "poverty focus" shows that it is groping for a mission, but in practice it has no grand design beyond the casting of all economies in the neo-classical mould and the refashioning of all men and women as *Homo economicus*' (p. 8).

There are of course many versions of economists' models as to an ideal world, and economists may complain that my homogenization of what internally is seen as a highly divided and quarrelsome profession is therefore merely the building of a straw man. Certainly there were quarrels in the formation of that version of economics that I am principally concerned with here. This is evident in the almost entire absence from current influence of the ideas of Keynes, the most important economist to have contributed to the final programme developed at Bretton Woods in 1944 (Acheson *et al.* 1972), from which was developed the IMF and later on the World Bank.

My prime concern is with the post-1980 period, when the World Bank became increasingly involved in policy-based lending (see Mosley *et al.* 1991). From this point, although the two institutions (the IMF and the World Bank) may not always work in harmony, there is considerable continuity in the kinds of demands being made by them in relation to any particular local economy. At this period the World Bank shifted from an emphasis on trying to find specific 'projects' to invest in, towards a desire to effect a more fundamental structural transformation of particular national economies – a set of programmes that became known as 'structural adjustment'.

In effect, many of the classic premisses of the academic discipline of economics (almost since Adam Smith) became the intended attributes of actual economic systems. Above all there was a commitment to a free world market, with all local barriers to this ideal being understood as 'distortions' that had to be eliminated. Thus there would be the elimination of all barriers to free exchangeability of currencies and goods. All products would be produced at the site where they would be cheapest in terms of costs. All attempts to subsidize alternative loci of production would eventually be prevented. The logic behind these intentions – that the world as a whole would have access to the widest range of the cheapest goods – makes theoretical sense, but clearly exists at a vast distance from the actually existing world we inhabit. It assumes quite immense disruptions and transformations from a world that historically grew up in a situation of relative regional self-sufficiency, with trade largely an appendage to, rather than the foundation of, economic life. Such zeal made sense when Bretton Woods was responding to the great depression and the war, but as a 'solution' its costs are only now becoming evident.

At the time of Bretton Woods the concerns of the Third World were largely covered by their incorporation within colonial regimes, and therefore of little immediate concern. The new institutions were expected largely to concern themselves with the largest economies, the central objective being global agreements such as GATT, while aiding states that were having problems accommodating to these changes through either short-term assistance through the IMF or longer-term aid from the World Bank.

In practice many of the larger economies are of sufficient power that they have been able to be highly strategic in their acceptance of Bretton Woods goals. Not surprisingly, they are trying to eliminate protectionism only where doing so would be in their interests, while retaining considerable autonomy and control over local economic decisions such as interest rates and subsidies. Given the extreme economic orthodoxy of institutions such as the IMF and the World Bank, which were understood by all to provide help only with potentially devastating strings attached, most states have hardly leapt into the arms of these 'aid' agencies. For this reason their greatest impact has been on those countries that have least power to resist them. It is above all in what George and Sabelli note are 'euphemistically called less developed' (1994: 1) countries that everybody has heard of the IMF and the World Bank. Even in these countries, Mosley *et al.* (1991: 128–9) argue that one of the main factors governing the conditionality of World Bank loans has been the negotiation between the political pressure that the bank can exert against the political weight (or sometimes economic ability) of the debtor country.

There were many shifts between the original Bretton Woods conference and contemporary policies. The World Bank, in particular, has shifted according to the priorities of particular presidents such as Robert McNamara (George and Sabelli 1994: 37–57). Mosley *et al.* (1991: 13) argue that it was the development of a particular economic model that lay behind the development of more recent policy-based lending. 'This New Political Economy of development uses the assumptions of neo-classical microeconomics – methodological individualism, rational utility maximisation and the comparative statics method of equilibrium analysis – to explain the failure of governments to adopt the "right", i.e. the neo-liberal, economic policies for growth and development.' They imply that there remained considerable flexibility between this ideological foundation based in the research departments of the World Bank and the actual implications drawn for any particular issue, which remained more pragmatic and dynamic. Nevertheless it provided a basis for a consistent anti-State stance, which to a degree also built on neo-Marxist criticisms of the State (pp. 13–26).

Pantin (1989) provides some useful imagery to account for the power of the IMF/World Bank in the developing world. He suggests that these institutions are best understood as equivalent to the receiver to which a bankrupt business may be forced to resort. The only states that are served by these bodies are those that declare themselves bankrupt in the sense of being unable to secure any further monies to maintain their current commitments, which most usually take the form of servicing already incurred debts. It is at this stage that states have no choice but to ask for IMF aid. The theoretical option of reneging on debts is only credible if the state is itself a powerful economic player. The IMF and the World Bank do lend money on favourable terms; but their main role is not as lenders but as guarantors. In effect what they provide is a credit rating that allows a state that was unable to procure further monies now to secure them. It follows that, in the first instance at least, this involves an increase in debt. Apart from this the IMF, and in the longer term the World Bank, are suddenly in a position to attach conditions to this 'receivership' that force the states in question to acquiesce in the pure model of a capitalist state. Thus the only countries that are actually eliminating all protectionism and restrictions on currency exchange are those developing countries that are now dependent states of the IMF and World Bank.

If Communism was castigated by the West as the power of extreme left-wing ideologies to reconstitute societies in their image of the future ideal society, it seems just as reasonable to suggest that the IMF and the World Bank are agencies that have allowed extreme right-wing ideologies to activate their transformation of the world into their pure market ideal by starting with the weakest countries of the world. Just as with Communism, the ultimate justification is constantly reiterated as being the elimination of world poverty. In this case we have the further poignancy that what we have here are institutions constructed by former colonial powers foisting themselves in extreme fashion upon those countries that had once been their colonies. The term 'neo-colonial' is then no mere rhetorical device of liberationist philosophers, but an accurate depiction of the relationships of the First and Third Worlds that are currently being created. That this is to some extent a coherent 'plot' to transform as much of the world as possible in a particular direction is quite evident in the statements made by these organizations. For example, a World Bank official complained about loans being made by donor countries that might help the Caribbean states of Antigua and Barbados because they allowed them to put off accepting the need for structural adjustment: 'It allows them to postpone the inevitable' (quoted in McAfee 1991: 77). Indeed, on leaving the IMF the Trinidadian economist Budhoo accused the IMF of altering its financial statistics on Trinidad and Tobago in order to enhance the case for that state to adopt the fund's recommendations (Yelvington 1991: 467).

Most of the academics I have discussed these issues with take the view that these institutions are effectively the tool of the major powers, and use the principle of liberal economics as a cover for discretionary intervention. I disagree, although I would acknowledge that the effect is just as it would be if these academics were correct. Instead, I would argue that these institutions embody a particular academic model based on a particular academic training. But since, in practice, major powers are better able to resist the imposition of this model, the effect is to favour powerful states over impotent ones. Given a free hand, however, the economists would probably enact the same transformations universally, without respect to any particular regions or states.

For this reason I would argue that these institutions may be said to embody a 'pure capitalism', to contrast with what might be called the 'organic capitalisms' of actual commerce. Pure capitalism is that which is envisaged in economic theory, and is dependent upon the construction of certain ideal conditions that would facilitate capitalist enterprises' working 'efficiently'. With respect to its Caribbean impact, therefore, it has been suggested that 'the IMF's strategy . . . is derived from its role in the Capitalist world economy . . . (its role) is to maintain an environment that facilitates the accumulation of capital on a world scale. This requires the complete international mobility of capital and commodities' (quoted in Thomas 1988: 225). For these reasons the World Bank is notoriously insensitive to the particularities of any given region. Since the solution is always going to be the same, they need almost no knowledge about the particular local problem (George and Sabelli 1994: 58–72).

Economists might argue that they are the wrong target here. The World Bank is, after all, a bank. It is bankers who have dictated the interests that these institutions represent, and made the repayment of loans the overriding priority. This is partially the case; but the one conclusion does not negate the other. The term 'bank' today should not evoke high street banks that deal with personal financial orders, but rather the radical transformations that have occurred in global financial practices, especially in the decade that culminated in 'The Big Bang' in London in 1986. The implication of these changes has been the growth of stateless and 'fictional' monies until they rival any of the more familiar currencies. In recent years money has become increasingly indifferent to space, time and place, and is emerging as an increasingly abstract form that comes ever closer to pure exchangeability. That is, fictional money is essential for realizing the imagination of pure money (Corbridge *et al.* 1994: Harvey 1989: 159–72).

As such, money is the one form that is coming to correspond to what up to now has been the fantasy of the discipline of economics, a virtual asocial economic fact, and thereby a building-block of pure capitalism. Actual markets are always constrained by their facticity, the commodities exchanged and the institutions exchanging them, with all those extraneous factors with which economic theory has always had a highly ambivalent relation (see Fine 1982: 12–18). As Harvey suggests 'If we are to look for anything truly distinctive (as opposed to "capitalism as usual") in the present situation, then it is upon the financial aspects of capitalist organisations and on the role of credit that we should concentrate our gaze' (1989: 196).

It was the oil crisis of 1972 that was responsible both for Trinidad's temporary wealth and also for the establishment of the typical sequence of events that led Trinidad to the IMF. International debt for Third World countries has often had severe consequences. Even in the nineteenth century, debt sometimes provided the excuse for an expansion of colonial domination. Post-war debts remained at manageable proportions for most states until the oil crisis. This began a spiral of indebtedness, with increasing use of expensive private loans to pay off previous debts. The commercial banks were keen to lend money, since they had considerable surplus monies coming from the oil-rich countries. In addition interest rates, which rose in the 1970s, exacerbated the problem, as did the rise in the 1980s of protectionism in industrialized countries against Third World countries (Korner *et al.* 1986: 6–41). The Caribbean in general has been caught up in this sequence. 'In 1987, the Caribbean as a whole paid out US$207 million more to the foreign governments, banks and multilateral agencies that are "aiding" the region than it received from all of them combined in the same year' (McAfee 1991: 13). This was the pattern to which Trinidad in 1989 found itself having to conform.

The Effects of Pure Capitalism

Turning to the implications of these developments, the demands made by the Bretton Woods institutions to Third World countries are easily understood given the basic premises from which these institutions operate, and the Trinidadian case is a fairly typical example. The underlying principle is that a free market will be the most efficient mechanism for producing the maximum quantity of goods at the cheapest possible price, and therefore increasing world wealth. Thus a given region should concentrate on producing that which, in a pure competitive market, it can produce at the lowest price. These commodities should then be free to circulate in trade without distortion, backed by financial institutions in which the value of local monies gives a true reflection of the position of that economy. The language is therefore constantly one of removing distortions, which is why the term 'pure' capitalism is a particularly apt one.

In order to ensure these aims, the first demand is the removal or at least relaxation of these 'distorting' elements. This means deregulation: removing price controls, import licensing and subsidies for local producers. Trinidad had an extensive 'negative list', which was intended to protect nascent local industries. This either prevented the import of, or imposed higher duties on imports of, certain goods, in order to allow a local company to develop to a level at which it might eventually be competitive with foreign producers – sometimes it simply allowed the existence of a local producer. In order to apply to the IMF Trinidad had first to reduce and then to promise to eliminate this 'distortion' to free trade. This was of course of enormous importance to local business, because if a new import could come in at a lower price than could be matched by the local manu-facturer, then it was likely that the local manufacturer would go out of business. The IMF's logic was that this would force the country to specialize only in that in which it was competitive, and there was a suggestion that such local manufacturers were anyway inefficient. This rests on the belief that institutions such as the negative list protected companies from the pressure of true competition. Trinidad has not only been relatively swift in adopting these measures, but has taken the lead in reducing the overall Common External Tariff (CET) that applies to the local Caribbean trading block (CARICOM) (Tewarie 1994).

The same logic applies to privatization. A state monopoly is understood as protected from the logic of the market, and able therefore to run at a loss. It is therefore assumed that state companies are, by definition, relatively inefficient and should be abolished. Trinidad was therefore expected to divest itself of much of its involvement in business. This was not inconsiderable. By 1985 the Trinidadian government held participatory interest in 66 enterprises, owning 37 outright, mainly in petroleum-related industries. These had net assets of around 3 billion US dollars, and accounted for 16 per cent of direct employment. The government had embarked on some divestment prior to IMF involvement. For example, the National Commercial Bank was sold to 25,000 local investors. This later turned into a flood of disinvestment, ranging from telephone companies to airlines, sold to a mixture of foreign and local business and employee concerns (Ragoonath 1994: 182–3). Unfortunately, this has occurred at a time when so many companies are being subjected to similar processes in Trinidad and elsewhere that the market for divested companies is not particularly good.

For the IMF privatization is merely one part of an attempt to reduce government debt. Equally important is a reduction in public services and other government expenditures such as welfare provision. This implies a reversal of a long-term commitment in Trinidad to the expansion of the public service. 'In 1992, ten years after the first decline in oil prices the Government's public service payroll numbered in excess of 45,000. It is interesting to note that the increases continued even after the oil bubble burst in the early 1980s' (Henry 1994: 101–2). The NAR government attempted to lower wages rather than reduce numbers, and by 1990 there was a loss in real income of around 28 per cent (p. 122). Not surprisingly the effects on government popularity were dire. The problem is that if employment through state companies is also considered the government is responsible for about a quarter of all employees (p. 107), a significant proportion of the electorate. The other negative feature of these changes, pointed out by Samaroo (1994), is that a complex transformation such as structural adjustment requires a highly competent government service to oversee the changes and make them work. This is rather unlikely when the government service is being drastically reduced in numbers, income and morale. From the point of view of the World Bank, however, Trinidad has certainly made a considerable effort, reducing gross government expenditure from a high of TT$9.5 billion in 1982 down to TT$5.6 billion in 1988 (Ragoonath 1994: 180).

Equally important to IMF programmes is the idea of a pure

trading of currencies without 'distortion', since in most cases developing countries have tried to protect their currencies. It is almost always the case that the IMF logic looks towards a downwards shift of the local currency value in either a managed or, preferably, a free-floating devaluation such that the currency can reach its 'natural' level. A further advantage of this logic is that devaluation should produce a rise in the cost of imports, favouring import-substitution industries and a decrease in the cost of exports, allowing local companies to respond by finding exporting niches that will then improve the balance of payments. Of course, in practice this may mean other countries in the area also reduce prices in order not to lose their own competitive advantage, and in the Caribbean this has threatened a destructive downward spiral of incomes from some exports (McAfee 1991: 177). It is generally assumed that foreign capitalists are more 'efficient' than local ones, and that anyway, given the initial state of debt, there is not the local money available for investment in these new export-oriented projects. It follows that the country should take measures that are designed to attract foreign capital, through, for example, setting up export-processing zones and the removal of most of the taxes and other limitations placed on foreign investment in (exploitation of) local resources. Trinidad finally floated its currency in 1993: it fell 26 per cent against the US dollar in the first day (*Financial Times* 14/5/93). It has also set up export-processing zones, at first with little effect; but in 1995 it changed the terms of reference to make these more attractive to foreign capital.

It is of course the balance of payments that is the crux of the problem that leads to the involvement of the IMF. Most important is the legacy of national debt and debt repayment. One might think that a sensible strategy would be to view such enormous debts as the most important 'distortion' for developing countries. A proper evaluation of the countries' economic health might be an assessment of whether they could balance their books in the absence of such heavy debt repayments. Unfortunately, institutions in which banking plays a predominant role are hardly likely to approve such a perspective. It is therefore this 'distortion' that is allowed in many cases to determine all other concerns, so that the country has to sacrifice any strategies that might make sense in terms of local balancing of budgets to the short-term need to pay back debts and thus secure the 'credit rating' that is the IMF's main 'gift' to the country concerned. The Bretton Woods institutions that pose as aid agencies are therefore largely the instruments by which ever greater amounts of money are exported to lender countries. In the Caribbean it is these agencies rather than private banks that are the prime holders of debt. For the region as a whole over two-thirds of external debt is owed to non-commercial bilateral and multilateral aid donors and lending institutions (Thomas 1988: 220), which is far higher than the figure for most underdeveloped regions.

To restore the balance of payments means in effect reducing the borrowing requirement of government, which, given that in a period of recession revenues are hard to come by, is translated into reducing government expenditure. Thus government welfare and job-creation schemes are likely to be cut in order to pay foreign debt. This is one of the most troublesome of all the IMF concerns. The logic by which government and commerce reduce costs is by increasingly regarding the population as in essence a 'cost', whether as wage-earners or as recipients of benefits. Here at least the economists approach an older form of political economy, inasmuch as the outcome of such an ideology is likely to lead to a re-emergence of the most naked form of opposition between the interests of capital and of labour. This is recognized in the clear anti-union and anti-welfare bias of these institutions (Moonilal 1994). Not surprisingly, this is the major focus of resistance from the population at large. Here the Trinidadian government need not look very far for an example of the likely consequences. In Venezuela, literally in sight of the coast of Trinidad, there has been a sequence of social and political unrest that is generally regarded as a direct consequence of the implementation of IMF policies. Despite this, and its parallel in the form of the attempted coup by Abu Bakr in 1990 in Trinidad, apart from a couple of mentions of welfare costs being preserved, there is not much sign in the letters of intent given by the Trinidadian government to the IMF that the lessons of this particular short-termism had been learnt. The lesson that is not lost on the Trinidadian population is that by 1995 there has been a return to real destitution for a significant part of the population, and that this is not unrelated to what many people regard as a terrifying increase in violent crime.

The background to this is a country now almost entirely sacrificed to its external debt. The context and content of the 1994 budget clearly spell this out. Trinidad at this time had a per capita debt of TT$2,416. The year's debt servicing of TT$608m amounted to a third of export receipts. The budget therefore included taxes on almost everything the government could lay its hand on. It also saw the continued divestment of companies that the state had actually probably run just as well as private firms in areas such as urea and ammonia, which had proved lucrative. It included plans to sack thousands of workers from public sector areas such as transport and energy. As seems to be frequently the case, even such drastic measures are usually taken in budgets based on a given forecast for the price of oil, which then proceeds to fall well below this price, rendering all such 'good' works of little value to the government (*Financial Times* 25/1/94).

The IMF is officially only concerned with the ultimate ability of the country to perform according to certain criteria. It is the country's government that takes the decision to request that it be allowed to conform to IMF policies! Thus for Trinidad we do not have a series of explicit dictates by the IMF, only a series of letters of intention that summarize what the government of Trinidad is intending to do in order to secure the backing of the IMF (the details are provided in Ramsaran 1992: 177–94). Trinidad is by no means the first Caribbean state to have had to concur with IMF and World Bank dictates, and it might have been hoped that by now this latest relationship would be the beneficiary of the voluminous literature on structural adjustment. One of the best established examples is that of nearby Jamaica. As Ramsaran has recently noted 'The Jamaican experiment stands out as a monument of the Bretton Woods institutions' fallibility' (1992: 4–5; for details of the disastrous effects see also Iqbal 1993). In this Jamaica, however, merely echoes the experience of many countries in Latin America, Africa and Eastern Europe, who have had faithfully to follow structural adjustment programmes, only to find that, far from achieving improved, stable economies with benefits to their peoples, the results seem to be worse than the often dire conditions that led to that eventuality. Ramsaran, quoting from a United Nations Survey, notes the increase in almost all measures of poverty and suffering in Jamaica, such as a rise in malnutrition and a decline in education, that has accompanied structural adjustment (1992: 20). Furthermore, in Jamaica as in most other countries, a decade and a half of structural adjustment has led to no significant changes in the underlying structure of the economy. Countries dependent upon the international exchange rate for a few natural resources, such as bauxite for Jamaica and Guyana or oil for Trinidad, are simply not going to be much affected by any shifts towards purity in the course of their economic deregulation.

Furthermore, this experience has provided the basis for a challenge to a number of the key premisses of pure capitalism. To give a few examples: the Bretton Woods assumption was that trade liberalization will lead to fewer imports and higher exports, with a saving of foreign exchange. But in countries such as Trinidad imports are not simply added luxuries, but represent the bulk of basic goods, such as foodstuffs and schoolbooks, so that structural adjustment is more likely to lead to greater sums' being spent on imports and a loss of foreign exchange and higher inflation (Ramsaran 1992: 127). Similarly, there is evidence that higher profitability for companies does not lead to greater investment in production, but rather to greater disposable income, which may lead to a still higher level of imports again, with a damaging effect on the balance of payments (Ramsaran 1992: 11–12). IMF ideology precludes what are likely to be much more effective instruments of increasing investment in local productivity that would have come from the state's raising money in taxes and ensuring that it is spent in investment. The IMF has also been accused of short-termism. That is to say the austerity measures needed to reduce local demand and change the balance of payments in the short term are precisely the opposite of those that might be necessary to invest in dev-elopment for the long term (Korner *et al.* 1986: 59). There are similar questions surrounding most of the other key policies, which assume that, for example, private-sector near-monopolies are more efficient than state monopolies.

The usual model for the 1980s has been short-term IMF assistance followed by a structural adjustment programme, which was developed when the World Bank agreed in 1980 to, in effect, continue the role of the IMF over the longer term. The World Bank is a little different from the IMF in that the con-straints imposed are often looser and more open to negotiation, at least in their implementation, and that their negative impact is in some cases less clear. Furthermore, there is clear confusion between the conditionalities imposed by these two bodies (see Mosley *et al.* 1991 for cases). Nevertheless, those writings that are concerned with welfare effects seem to concur that IMF lending followed by World Bank structural adjustment has been an almost unmitigated disaster. In general, early insistences that this was because the policies did not go far enough are thankfully in retreat as against the opposite conclusion, that the medicine was applied in such strong measure as to leave the nation too weak to respond positively to any new opportunities for export, for example, that might have been created by these measures.

Overall the problem is that the IMF assumes that economic decline is a result of local mismanagement. While there might have been some local mismanagement, in general the causes of economic decline and indeed economic success have always been in the larger economic environment, over which local politicians have no control whatsoever. Against such a one-sided critical appraisal of the IMF could be put the argument that these institutions did not of themselves cause the problems that resulted in their being called upon. As Ramsaran (1992) notes, it is not fair to consider this a choice of structural adjustment as against no adjustment. The sharp decline in the balance of payments had already occurred, and could not be left unattended.

There is at least one cynical but possibly genuine reason for seeing the recourse to the IMF as a beneficial move from the point of view of local politicians. Some adjustment at this stage is inevitable, and the term 'adjustment' almost invariably means extremely unpopular and unpleasant changes to the economy, such as cuts in expenditure and increases in taxation. Without the IMF it may appear that it is the government itself that is 'choosing' to take such measures, and an opposition can posit alternative possibilities whether these are in fact realistic or not. In such a situation a government under IMF tutelage can at least make the largely true claim that the measures being taken are forced upon it by an outside body, and the only thing an opposition can really complain about is that the government went to the IMF in the first place (Ramsaran 1994: 32). The IMF may therefore be looked to as a syphon for negative criticism of the local government. There are also sections of the local élite, for example major capitalists, who support such measures because they believe both they and the economy will benefit. It is likely that they will be wrong on both counts. I expect that the business élite will not benefit from trade liberalization, but if anything are more likely to be severely hurt by it.

Irrespective of political interest, the idea that the necessity for difficult action of itself provides a defence for what the IMF does would only hold inasmuch as the IMF is correct in its own premiss as to why these recessions occur. Although in countries such as Trinidad some internal mismanagement may have been present, the unimportance of this factor as against the effects of the world economy were made crystal clear by the oil boom that preceded these events. Trinidad did not experience an economic boom because it was suddenly behaving with increased economic sagacity, but because a Middle Eastern conflict produced a huge increase in the value of its main export. Similarly, its recession is almost entirely a product of fluctuations in the price of the same commodity, as previous recessions were associated with sugar, cocoa and other commodities. Indeed, it was as much the desire of First World countries to lend in previous periods as their desire to refuse further credit in the latest period that created the problem of debt that now results in effective bankruptcy for the government.

If it is the macro-environment that is the real problem, it is perhaps no surprise that the IMF policies represent an exacerbation rather than a solution. A country that is suffering because it is unable to curb forces acting beyond its control needs above all some defence against those forces. It needs the stabilization of world commodity prices, and some amelioration in the ruptures caused by global events. Theoretically Bretton Woods is supposed to supply this through its other arm of GATT; but, as might have been anticipated, powerful countries are much more reluctant than weak ones to acquiesce in outside prescriptions. What in fact the IMF represents is an increase in interference in internal economic management by global forces, and thus an increase in the very forces that are responsible for the problems in the first place.

As an aside, it may be noted that this creates a particular local perspective on efforts to renew the GATT agreement. At one level Trinidadians might be expected to favour these moves. At present they face powerful countries such as the United States, France and Japan refusing to accept the economic disciplines that they themselves have been compelled to adopt because they are not equally empowered. It must be galling to hear the cries and complaints of highly subsidized French farmers on the world media. One should, however, hesitate before assuming therefore that GATT and its ilk are necessarily good news for developing countries such as Trinidad. If it turns out that 'pure capitalism' produces anything like the effects on the First World that it has had on the Third World, then the mere desire to see French farmers 'beaten' is hardly good enough grounds for desiring the continued encroachment of Bretton Woods ideologies on the world at large.

What would be much more satisfactory from the point of view of countries such as Trinidad would be to see the muscle of these large institutions at least able to secure true bilateral terms of trade for less powerful countries. At present we have a situation where the United States can claim to be providing aid with favourable duties on Caribbean goods (through the Caribbean Basin Initiative), but can then refuse to include any product such as sugar, where the Caribbean desperately requires a market, because the United States wishes to continue highly protectionist policies. Trinidad is still in 1995 hard hit by United States protectionism against any of its own industrial goods such as steel and urea.

The same period that has seen developing countries' markets opened up by IMF decree has seen an increase in the general level of protectionism by bodies such as the EU against exports from the developing world. This problem is exacerbated by the degree to which the share of world trade held by primary products such as food has been falling as against that held by commodities such as chemicals and telecommunications. The most impressive exporters are those with advanced manufactured goods, not raw materials (Ramsaran 1992: 29).

The other agencies and institutions that complement those established through Bretton Woods are if anything more clearly partisan. The United States has established several bodies, such as that for 'Caribbean–Central American Action' and the 'Caribbean Association of Industry and Commerce', and most importantly the 'Caribbean Basin Initiative'. These bodies were officially established to assist the economic development of the region; but the evidence of their work to date suggests that this was only inasmuch as it served the security and economic interests of the United States. Often they served to establish bilateral connections that allowed the smaller states to be played off against each other. The most damning criticism has come from one of the founders of the CAIC, an American congressman who suggested that these bodies were merely an arm of a larger strategic plan and of security interests that would involve military intervention as readily as economic relations (Thomas 1988: 334–6). Slightly less partisan has been the Canadian involvement, which Caribbean countries have tried to promote as an alternative to the United States in terms of providing a market for their exports. Historically rather more important had been the Lomé Agreement (now Lomé IV), which established that there remained some responsibility of European governments for former dependencies and colonies. But while the original terms were helpful, the period since the foundation of this agreement in 1975 has seen a gradual lessening in favourable terms and an increase in European protectionism (Thomas 1988; but see also Sutton 1986).

There are even worse prospects for the future. The European block is likely to become increasingly concerned with internal trade and its eastern neighbours. Trinidad, like most of the Caribbean, is still largely dependent upon trade with the United States. Indeed, the Caribbean is one of the few places in the world where the USA has a trade surplus. It is estimated that for every dollar earned in Caribbean Basin Initiative countries 60c. is spent on USA products (Rosenberg and Hiskey 1993). But with NAFTA the United States has made a decision that is likely to shift trade towards Mexico, which has lower labour costs and would be hard competition for countries such as Trinidad. Trinidad is desperately looking for alternatives, such as an expansion into Venezuela and through that into Colombia and thence Mexico, and thereby NAFTA through the back door. This is imaginative, but rather far-fetched. Indeed, the same article has suggested that the Caribbean's best bet is to force the issue in Florida, which has 30 per cent of its trade with the Caribbean, and thereby to create an internal lobby in the South-East against the development of the South-West United States.

Finally, it is hard to see how liberalization could ever work for this region. What by this logic would constitute an 'efficient' Trinidadian economy? To produce goods cheaply Trinidad might reduce wages to compete with the starvation levels that allow certain countries to produce goods at very cheap rates. But even if such an appalling thing happened, several economists have noted that even such low labour costs are increasingly being undercut. This is because metropolitan regions that have high labour costs also have highly developed technologies that allow them increasingly to produce goods within minimal labour and through enormously efficient uses of modern science and technology. These writers (various papers in Watson 1994) have recommended that Caribbean states should also emphasize high technology; but it seems difficult to believe that this would ever allow them to compete with Japan and Germany.

There is no sphere that is free from this conclusion. For decades Trinidad has attempted to develop its industrial base. If this seems doomed to be uncompetitive it might have to move back on an agricultural sector that at present contributes only 2.5 per cent of GNP. But even here it is likely that within a decade or two new biotechnologies will make science once again supreme over labour costs as the key factor in producing cheap foodstuffs. Thus even with the best (in the sense of the most liberal) will in the world, there seems nothing that Trinidad could even envisage doing that would allow it to prosper under pure capitalism. As Ryan has recently noted (*Trinidad Express* 5/3/95) GATT is explicit about trying to push the South out of agricultural development, to such a degree that it is hardly surprising that the only option available to most of the peoples of the South is to become illegal immigrants in the North.

Organic Capitalism

The institutions that rose from Bretton Woods have been with us for quite some time, and have developed their own institutional culture. There is an accumulating sediment of their own traditions and myths of tradition. Many of the writings on the role and impact of these institutions personify these traditions as particular personalities who have had a commanding role, such as Robert McNamara. In the above section, however, the emphasis in my argument is that this is in some ways a mistaken focus, since the role and impact of these institutions derives not from their own internal institutional development but through their acting as the instruments that make manifest more abstract economic theory as concrete action in the world.

I now want to suggest that the opposite point is true of the kind of business corporations with which this book is largely concerned. Here again we are faced with a similar choice of emphasis. There are plenty of theoretical texts available about the capitalist firm. There are many models of the major factors that produce or inhibit profitability for individual firms and competition between them. Indeed, there might have been just as much a case for arguing that it is the capitalist firm as much as the Bretton Woods institutions that manifests the basic principles of economic theory.

The alternative I will follow is to suggest that at least by comparison the role and effect of the capitalist firm owes rather more to institutional trajectory, internal norms and historical precedents. It owes therefore rather less to the firm's manifesting some more abstract logic of capitalism or profitability. The evidence behind this claim is given in the following chapters, based on the specific case study of Trinidad. These provide the foundation for my description of the kind of businesses studied in this book as 'organic' rather than 'pure' capitalism. The implication of a pure capitalism is that it is comparatively ahistorical. That is to say, while firms that embody it obviously have a history and have gone through important stages of development, they are better understood in relation to abstract models that drive them forward in a teleological sequence. History here is more an encumbrance than a root or route. The 'grocery brand' capitalism that I studied is, by contrast, deeply historical, which is to say that its present norms and procedures are more a result of the way the culture of the institutions has developed, than of any abstract model or ideal.

Certainly the historical evidence suggests that, so far from being a highly dynamic set of institutions that rise quickly and fall decisively according to how at any given moment of time they have read and exploited the market, Trinidadian business is a sluggish resilient beast, remarkably unaffected by the slings and arrows of outrageous fortune. Profitability is not only the avowed aim, but is conceptualized as a rather dramatic instrument of fate. A company that fails to honour it should quickly fall victim to this hubris, while efficient and conscious pursuit of profit should quickly and literally pay dividends. The past few decades in Trinidad have been as turbulent in terms of business conditions as anywhere in the world. There are few states that have seen such violent lurchings of the business climate as Trinidad's sudden and explosive oil boom and its deep and trenchant recession. One would think that unless firms had a remarkable ability to keep their eye on this twisting and tortuous road they would soon be off the track.

Despite this, the picture of business in Trinidad today is one in which history is written deep. In the main area of business studied, that of soft drinks, the dominant business today was written up in the *Red Book* of 1922 (Macmillan 1922) as having been dominant in the soft drink industry since 1913. In the field of groceries more generally the main multinational company, Nestlé, that dominates the field in Trinidad in 1994 was again the dominant transnational purveyor of branded groceries in the same *Red Book*. Most of the other main players were on the scene soon after the Second World War. A historical perspective on the grocery trade suggests that the turbulent times of the oil boom and recession have had to all intents and purposes a negligible effect on the main industry studied! Far more important has been the gradual decline of the élite white class, at least with respect to middle management. Even here there have always been alternative groups, such as the Chinese, Syrians and Portuguese, that have played an important historical role.

This sense of stability is even more evident amongst consumers than the grocery firms that consumers have in mind when they think of the capitalist firm. Capitalism is most readily associated with the major branded goods that consumers buy. As such these goods are constantly claimed to represent a radical modern presence without historical roots. The present is seen as a 'fall' into an overly materialistic world, saturated by branded commodities. The past was stable, based on social rather than material relations.

So says the rhetoric. The evidence could, however, support the opposite contention. My previous book on Trinidad was largely concerned with what might be seen as 'traditional' elements, such as social structure and ethnic difference. The evidence presented there (1994: Chapters 4 and 6) was for remarkably rapid change. I argued that, for example, the stereotypes of ethnic groups, which are rhetorically argued to be ancient and intrinsic, have in fact been highly dynamic. Those current today bear little relation to those of a generation or two previous to the fieldwork. There have also been remarkably rapid changes in social structure. By contrast, brands and commodities may often be relatively stable markers that are remembered from childhood and from the tales of one's grandparents. Could it be that one of the major appeals of brands is that they represent a kind of bedrock stability in a world of rapidly changing social structures and social relationships? The likes of Heinz tomato soup, Nestlé milk and Unilever soaps and oils may be experienced as historically rooted points of refuge at a time when no one knows where the family or individualism is going. As in so many areas, I suspect that it is consumption that plays the major role here. That is to say, the reason business can be fairly lax and amateur in its approach to the market is that its place is often secured by this consumer desire for stability in certain types of capitalist firms. Obviously this may not be true of fashion-based industries that serve quite different consumer imperatives, and it may mask the dynamics of global take-overs. Nevertheless, as will be shown in the next chapter, even such take-overs can often have remarkably little effect upon businesses operating within Trinidad.

Despite all that has been argued in this chapter it is possible to write the following chapters on organic capitalism with very little reference to pure capitalism. This is because even in 1995, the time of my most recent visit to Trinidad, the effects of the IMF and World Bank were only just becoming manifest. The major changes, such as currency flotation, the removal of the negative list and continued divestment of assets by the State were only now coming into place. The world that is described in the following chapters is therefore almost an elegy for a relatively benign period in which the post-Second World War settlement permitted the local emergence of capitalist institutions behind a kind of protective reef. This may have been in some ways a more unusual period, if one recalls the nineteenth-century periodic destructions of local plantation economies by the typhoons of global commodity price crises. The future may well then mark a return to a pattern that was well established in the past.

Having, then, introduced pure capitalism, I will now leave the topic and present a series of chapters on the workings of the organic capitalism that contrasts with it. The implications of pure capitalism will, however, be returned to in the concluding chapter, where the relationship between these two forms of capitalism will be considered in more detail. It will be shown there that this is part of a much wider relationship, which equally involves a surprisingly close articulation between the consumer and these Bretton Woods institutions.

3

The Local-'Global' and the Global-'Local' Companies

Introduction

The last chapter provided a larger context to capitalism in Trinidad with respect to what I have termed 'pure' capitalism. For most people, however, the World Bank is not the first institution that is called to mind when they consider capitalism. The key image in the nineteenth century was probably the factory owner with top hat and cigar; at the end of the twentieth century it is the rather less conspicuous figures of the managing directors of transnational companies and their relationship to commercial bankers that comes to mind. This chapter will take as its theme those transnational companies that deal in supermarket goods. It will also start to introduce some further themes within the volume. Its main focus will be on the relationship between identity and locality in the construction of Trinidad as the context of commerce. It will also start to address the relationship between production, distribution and consumption. Both these themes continue through several further chapters.

There has been a clear shift in the general and academic perception of large companies. The gradual replacement of the term 'multinational' by 'transnational' signified awareness of a development from companies having a clear national base with branches in other countries to the modern corporate group, where there is no spatial focus and the significance of national boundaries is diminishing. The evidence from Trinidad suggests there remains much more regional diversity than is often assumed, and that companies do not always accord with any simple model. As was noted in Chapter 1 Carnoy (1993) has argued strongly against exaggerating the transnational nature of most modern business corporations.

It is with the development of the European-based conglomerates that this model probably works best (Franko 1993: 46–68;
Hedlund and Kogut 1993: 343–58). It was here that companies
that had a secure and often long-standing national base first
regarded their other branches as an 'international division' and
developed what has come to be called a 'mother–daughter'
relationship. This led, however, to a failure to utilize the potential
benefits of a true transnational character. It could also lead to
internal conflict between the two segments, since there was often
no sense of the overall profitability of the corporation. Reduc-
tions in trade barriers tended to lead to more genuinely global
operations. This allowed companies to take advantage of worldwide differences in production costs, to such an extent that,
for example, 'profits in the chemical industry are to a large
extent influenced by the ability to shift production according to
exchange rate movements' (Hedlund and Kogut 1993: 350). The
same authors quote a Phillips executive wishing that production
could be aboard a ship, so that facilities could sail to wherever
conditions were most favourable at any given time. This sometimes led to parallel structural changes in company organization,
creating a heterarchy instead of traditional hierarchies (p. 344),
though some of the more adventurous repudiations of older
structures seem to have proved cumbersome and were later
abandoned (p. 351). These changes did not occur uniformly,
and Japanese companies, for example, have been much slower to
transcend their regional identity, carrying out almost all research
and development in their home country first.

At the same time there have been other changes working in
the reverse direction. Capitalism has undergone some radical
restructuring over the last two decades, which to a degree has
reversed what were assumed to be long-term tendencies in its
evolution. Apart from the term 'local-global', concepts such as
'postfordism', 'postmodernity' and 'disorganised capitalism' (cf.
e.g. Harvey 1989; Lash and Urry 1987) have been developed to
describe and account for these changes. Many of the key theorists
have retained certain key Marxist concepts in accounting for
these developments. Harvey, for example, sees the new flexibility
and divergences as based on internal contradictions within the
previous system of production. Postfordism is thus a temporary
respite to problems of rigidity and overaccumulation in Fordism,
leading to greater internationalism, the growth of fictitious

monies, and flexible accumulation. Some, such as Harvey, would see this as a reflection of productive transformation, such that companies require differences in the market where once they required long production runs to secure profitability. The alternative explanation, which I prefer, looks to changes in popular culture in the 1970s that led to a new concern with roots and difference, in opposition to several decades of modernism. The new diversity was therefore consumer-led, and production forces had rather quickly to develop new technologies, such as computer-aided design systems, that could respond to the new forms of demand without losing profitability.

Irrespective of whether this new concern with the local comes from changes in production or consumption, it seems to offer a golden opportunity for anthropologists to become involved. If the 'local' is said to be increasing in significance, how is this new significance manifested locally; indeed, is there local evidence for any such trend? What are the perspectives of those involved at the level of local managers or workers in such companies? To what extent do they identify companies as local or global, and how does this affect their sense of relationship with the company for whom they work or from whom they buy?

In Trinidad there are 'local' globals – that is, actual transnational companies represented within Trinidad by their local office, which may be granted relative autonomy or may be circumscribed by its affiliation with a global enterprise. There are also 'global' locals, in so far as (to my surprise) the local offices of global transnationals are increasingly dwarfed by home-grown Trinidadian companies such as Neal and Massy or ANSA McAl, originating in Trinidad, but today starting to emerge as transnationals in their own right.

In addition to describing these companies in terms of their activities and scale, this chapter begins to develop ethnographic evidence. This extends from interviews with local management to observations made when given the opportunity to be present inside the companies while work was taking place and decisions were being made. In the second half of the chapter the focus shifts to still more local issues that provide the immediate context for business development, such as the State and the ethnic identity and composition of companies. By the end of the chapter it will be evident that, notwithstanding the considerable evidence already presented for the global impact on local companies, there is still a pressing need to consider local factors that turn out to have an important bearing even on the Trinidadian branches of true transnational companies.

The Local 'Global' Companies

The companies that produce goods for supermarkets include a number of well-known transnationals. Some of these have been in the area for a considerable time. For example 'Nestlé and Anglo-Swiss condensed milk' is described in the *Red Book* (Macmillan 1922: 201) as selling 11 brands, including Milkmaid brand evaporated milk, Peter's breakfast cereal and Fussell's confectionary. The company had been present in Trinidad since 1914, and has been prominent ever since. In its publicity it claims that in 1972 it opened up in Trinidad the first Tetra Pak aseptic filling facility in the Americas. Another of the largest and best-established grocery companies today is the local manifestation of Unilever (Fieldhouse 1978). Based in Trinidad, Lever Brothers West Indies Ltd was responsible for exports from that island to other Caribbean countries in a manner comparable to the local conglomerates. Turnover in 1990 was TT$167 million, of which TT$38 million were exports. It managed on its profit of TT$12 million to give a dividend of 22c. In that year it paid TT$5 million in tax. Since the parent company has close to 50 per cent local share ownership, it would have exported half the TT$5 million it distributed in dividends back to Unilever Overseas Holdings.[2]

At the time of fieldwork these were amongst the largest transnationals, with Nestlé ranked 18th and Lever Brothers 12th in the world (Dicken 1992). Local shareholdings in such companies most often belong to major financial institutions. The local Republic Bank holds 2 million shares in Lever Brothers. Companies may also hold shareholdings in their rivals. Normally this is seen as providing the potential for aggressive bids, although it seems unlikely that Neal and Massy had this in mind when they took nearly half a million shares in Nestlé. Most transnationals in Trinidad are recognized through their leading brands, such as

---

2. Not surprisingly, companies that are mainly foreign-owned tend to give much larger dividends than local companies as a means of exporting their profits back to the parent company.

Pepsico, Johnson and Johnson, Colgate Palmolive, Cadbury-Schweppes, Bristol-Myers and many others. Such companies are often represented in 100 countries or more, and have worldwide sales of several billion UK pounds (Stafford and Purkis 1989).

The transnational may not be instantly recognizable in its local form. For example, Nestlé is represented by a wholly owned subsidiary called Trinidad Food Products, representing a corporate decision to work under a claimed local identity rather than the transnational image. In practice this was not often successful, and Nestlé today have gone back to giving their own name prominence on the packages of their goods, although officially they are produced by TFP. The status of companies is not always easy to ascertain. For example, the dominant blue of the Republic Bank was instantly recognizable from other countries in which I have worked as a clone of Barclay's International. I immediately assumed that Barclays was retaining its control, but had localized the name in deference to post-colonial sensibilities. In fact, after the two wholly local banks, it had the highest degree of locally owned equity, at 68 per cent (Yawching 1991). Given the rather complex history of this localization, often under nationalist pressure, it is hard to extrapolate from such figures alone the actual degree of local control (Besson 1987). I also assumed that the biggest companies, such as Neal and Massy, would reveal a lurking foreign interest behind the apparent claims to local identity, which was not the case. It also did not occur to me that a company called 'Colonial Life Insurance' could be a focus point of almost strident nationalistic identity, since it was perceived as the largest 'Black' company!

The first place to try and define what is a local as opposed to a foreign-owned company would seem to be the investigation of who holds equity in that company. Some companies with 99 per cent or 100 per cent local equity seem unambiguously local, such as the Co-operative Bank[3] or the two major conglomerates or state-owned companies such as British West Indian Airlines.[4] Others are clearly foreign-owned, such as Bata shoes[5] (since sold) or McCann Erikson advertising. Many more are around 50 per cent locally owned, with either the balance just going to foreign

---

3. By 1995 this had merged with others to form the First Citizen's Bank.
4. BWIA was privatized as part of the government divestment of assets in 1995.
5. In the case of Bata the private international company later sold its Trinidad branch to a local entrepreneur.

control or, as in the case of Angostura bitters, to local control. Levels of equity may signify degree of interest, control and co-operation. Alternatively they can represent a financial investment and little else. Several firms that were wholly or largely foreign-owned still acted as though they were little more than franchises, being mainly concerned with company image and quality control, while leaving the running of the firm to local executives.

Sometimes this relationship is not clear to the companies themselves. For example, a local advertising agency that was wholly locally owned successfully sought out a transnational agency to purchase some equity in the local firm. As far as the local firm was concerned this was to be the start of an active relationship, such that the local firm would be able to rely on sophisticated facilities and advice which was not available locally. There was also the hope that international products that were tied up with this advertising agency in global agreements would thereby also accrue to the local agency. In fact, after quite some time the local firm had to admit that they had not received a single piece of business or help with a campaign, despite the purchase of equity.

The establishment of Lever Brothers West Indies Limited in 1987, although it left the majority shareholding with the international firm, seemed to represent more than a tokenistic sop to localization when it came to decision-making. Indeed, in many respects the actual loci of decision-making might be considered as important a criterion in determining whether a company should be deemed local as is the pattern of equity. The Trinidad media clearly regarded Lever Brothers as a local company. Certainly by 1988 it was manufacturing some 50 brands locally, ranging from detergents through oils to cold cream. Most of this was for local consumption, with 13 per cent going in exports. This point was demonstrated forcibly when it came to trade liberalization. Most commentators assume that such transnationals favour trade liberalization, but Lever's became quite vociferous in the 1990s in trying to lobby the Trinidadian government to retain elements of protectionism against, for example, cheap imported soya oil products.

Transnationals not only differed in terms of equity but also in relation to their overall commitment to the local site. Those companies that manufacture within Trinidad are obviously engaged in much longer-term commitments, and will tend to engage in expenditures that involve enhancing their corporate image as an 'at least in some ways' local company. Although it would not broadcast the fact, Colgate-Palmolive tends to operate a different strategy. It avoids manufacturing costs in the area, so that it can be very competitive when foreign exchange is in its favour, but simply pull out when protectionism or devaluation threaten its profitability. By, contrast, Nestlé is recognized to be highly decentralized, with considerable autonomy granted, so that in some respects it is really a confederation of operating units (Stafford and Purkis 1989: 877).

Even in these transnational corporations the personnel is almost entirely local. Today Trinidad represents a much smaller market than during the oil boom; but that event left a legacy with regard to corporate responsibilities. For example the Trinidadian managing director of one local office of an immense transnational also sits on the international executive board of the global corporation. More commonly, the Trinidadian who controls the local operations of a transnational may be responsible for either the whole of the Caribbean or more often the southern section, which may include Guyana. This will be complemented by an office in Jamaica or Puerto Rico for the North Caribbean. In such cases the 'globe' is most often an American office, for example, Miami, but may also be European, for example in England or Switzerland.

The relationships of control and decision-making vary considerably. If we move to smaller companies than Nestlé and Lever Brothers, the most common scenario could be considered versions of the typical franchise operation. Although Felstead (1993) has recently argued that in general franchise operators have less autonomy than at first appears, in the Trinidad context effective autonomy was often considerable, at least with regard to the general conduct of the business. In several cases it was stated that there was no financial liability on either side: 'If anything happens to either side the other has no financial obligations towards them . . . no bailing out.'

There were two points of contact that were commonly emphasized in discussions: the public image and quality control. With respect to the first the local business uses the logo, colours and other stylistic attributes. Usually it is keen to do so, since the main interest of the local owners and management is precisely to capitalize on the established identity in the public mind, although I also found executives frustrated by what they saw as a slow global administration that insisted on vetting any stylistic distortion of the conventional logo created for advertising purposes. In one telephone call the local representative was venting his frustration: 'How it looking . . . you enh feel you could get into trouble for that, separating them? Are we allowed to split the logo like that? – the manual doesn't say. The manager say they have to be together and all that shit.'

Equally if not more important was the issue of quality control. The global corporation would permit the use of its logo, name, etc., providing the local company was seen as living up to global standards and not in any way detracting from the international reputation of the firm. Most commonly quality control consisted of annual inspections of the Trinidadian premises and operations. This could range from a car manufacturer's checking the local car assemblage plant, to a firm of accountants inspecting the books of the local 'franchise'. The visit of the owner or head of a transnational would usually become a feature in the local press. For example a local newspaper (*Mirror* 10/1/93) has a photograph and profile of the chairman of the Courts furniture group, which has 95 shops in Britain and had recently expanded in Trinidad following a long association with St Lucia and Jamaica. Perhaps third in importance to quality control and use of logo were the possibilities of training for local executives in international training schemes. In the larger companies, in particular, it was part of the overall agreement that such training would be carried out on a regular basis. Behind this arrangement lies the assumption that the local consumer identifies the global company with particularly high standards and dependability, which makes it worthwhile for the local company to act within the umbrella of the global label. This may not always work, and there are certainly cases where the local company gains a reputation for poor quality that in turn affects the reputation of the international firm, and makes it quite difficult for the transnational either to take on, or even to be a desirable label for, some alternative local firm. On the whole such reputations seem more easily lost than gained.

In such franchise-like operations the equity of the local office is entirely locally owned, so that there is no direct transference of profits out of Trinidad. I had assumed that in most cases there would instead be a 'fee' for holding the franchise that would be a proportion of the local profits or sales. While this occurred, it seemed to be less common than an alternative relationship that gave even more autonomy to the local operation. In effect, the value of the local firm was held to be the level of purchases it made of the constitutive materials. Most Trinidadian firms are in effect packaging and assemblage plants that rely to a considerable extent on imported materials. Thus a food may be 'cooked' and packaged locally, but both the concentrated raw material in its established proportions and the packaging materials may be imported. Obviously car parts and machinery are imported; but so may be the half-worked leathers and smaller machine parts for assembling shoes locally. In all such cases the main concern of the global company is that the local franchise is selling as many products as possible, and so becomes the key purchaser of the global goods. In effect this is the subcontracting of the final stages of a global manufacturing process, so that the relationship of global to local distributors has become quite similar to that between global and local producers. This places Trinidad in the vanguard of what may be a larger shift from producer-dominated to buyer-dominated global commodity chains (Gereffi 1994).

This 'franchise' model represents the greatest level of autonomy for the local firm. There are other transnationals that continue to maintain a much clearer control over the local branch. The financial relationship may be directly exploitative, with both a royalty charged for the sale of the product and various forms of management fee imposed to cover contributions to product research and development as well as personnel training. There is little by way of restriction on the export of profits in Trinidad once a dividend has been declared and a withholding tax has been paid to ensure that proper local taxes will be received. There may in effect be very little difference between the way profits are distributed within the local conglomerate and a global transnational, although the former obviously does not have to sort out complications such as double taxation treaties.

In cases of tighter control the local executives may advise as to which brands should be pushed and which have their image localized, or where new capital should be injected. But in all these areas final decisions have at least to be approved, if not made, in regional or global offices. Commonly the global company launches a new product at a global level, and the local office may simply be informed as to how the product is being constructed in marketing terms. At the most extreme there may be an insistence that only 'canned' global advertising is used, and even events such as promotional competitions will be organized at a global level, with the Trinidad office merely being informed of the dates. For example, the transnational may have an agreement with a firm organizing promotional events who have developed a particular strategy around the sale of a certain children's toy (e.g. a transformer) or a token-collecting scheme. The promotional firm goes to each of the national or regional offices and explains how the promotion works, what resources are needed, what media time has to be booked, etc. The local office may be obliged to carry out the promotion because of the international agreement made by the transnational with that promotional firm. In practice, however, I came across very few cases of such an obligation. It was much more common for a global office to suggest a promotional venture and to send executives to explain the working of the scheme to the local office, but for the local office to retain the power to opt for or opt out of this particular promotion, depending upon whether they saw it as appropriate for local conditions. The local offices often stressed that the degree of compliance was not a result of coercive pressures but simply because the international offices could provide high-quality materials that they could not otherwise afford and competitive prices based on the sheer scale of the international group.

Despite this degree of autonomy, tensions between local and international control often came out in conversations. For example a local manager noted

> you do feel the hand of Head Office as it were, but in frustrating areas, because any small change in our logo in Trinidad they want to go all the way to Head Office and the lawyers, which pisses me off, but the main thing which affects us is the creative material. The international division is bringing out material which is mainly developed for European markets which I feel is not suitable, and our region is too small. We are not like a Japan to say we want our own advertising. They say, well, you don't have the budget for it, you can't afford it. Each advert has to be 250,000 US dollars to get the kind of . . . image that they want, but we are working on that.

For the biggest transnationals there may be global strategies that are so firm that they seem almost oblivious to local conditions. For example there are goods where two global brands compete in virtually every country in the world. In one case at the time of fieldwork one of these brands had a virtual monopoly, while the other was almost unobtainable in the shops. Nevertheless, more money was being spent on advertising and sponsorship by the absent brand than the present brand. The argument given for this was that such global brands can afford to take a long-term view. For the last decade the absent brand had failed to find an efficient local producer and distributor, but was concerned that at some stage such a link would be obtained, and it was important that the popular conception of the brand should be maintained until that time. I confess that, although this was clearly an important point of legitimation, I was not convinced as to the efficacy of such policies. Rather it seemed to be that the local franchiser was simply far better at persuading the global company to part with money to pay for advertising than it was at creating an effective distribution system that would actually sell the product.

Two Global 'Local' Companies

There is one major obstacle in attempting to follow the usual analysis of business in a small developing state based on the dominance of global transnationals. This is the rather (to me) surprising fact that by far the largest transnationals operating in Trinidad groceries are entirely Trinidadian-owned and of Trinidad origin. The activities of the big two local 'global' conglomerates often dwarf the activities of 'local' offices of global companies. The companies concerned are the Neal and Massy group and ANSA McAl. Indeed this is a proper reflection of the Trinidadian economy more generally, where apart from the oil sector local control is dominant. A 1994 survey by the accountants Deloitte and Touche gives the top 50 companies in terms of assets, employees and revenue. In terms of assets the top six companies are all either government-owned or public companies. The same is true for the top fourteen companies in terms of employees. Amoco oil actually tops the list of revenue, but the next six are all local.

When it comes to the grocery trade Levers and Nestlé are indeed the largest foreign firms, but they are dwarfed by the two local conglomerates, as shown below:

Firm	Employees	Assets (TT$mill.)	Revenue (TT$mill.)
Neal and Massy	6,794	1,907	2,364
ANSA McAl	3,143	1,703	996
Lever Bros	593	Not in top 50	223
Nestlé	503	152	240

In some ways the comparison in unfair, in that the local conglomerates are involved in far more than just trading in grocery goods; but there are no foreign firms with an equivalent range of interests present in Trinidad.

Neal and Massy

The origins of the Neal and Massy group of companies lie in 1932, when English-born Harry Neal combined with Trinidadian Charles Massy to create the Neal and Massy Engineering Company. The company became public in 1958 and then started to establish subsidiaries, for example in Auto Rentals. The two key developments since then have been the establishment of the first Automotive Assembly Plant in the West Indies in 1966, and then in 1991 the take-over of the Geddes Grant/Huggins Group of Companies, which has allowed the company to consider itself a Caribbean rather than just a Trinidadian conglomerate, and thus a true transnational.

Some idea of the scale of the company during the period of initial fieldwork may be gleaned from the 1989 *Annual Report*. In that year group sales were TT$943 million, down from TT$1,151 million in 1986. Profit before tax was TT$29 million, which allowed a dividend of 8c. Export sales were of TT$32 million.[6]

The Annual Report provides a complete list of companies as follows (Rev = Revenue in TT$ million, Shareholding given where

---

6. Growth in the company since fieldwork has been prodigious, as can be seen from the figures given in the Deloitte and Touche report. Profits for 1994 were TT$43.8 million before tax.

this is not 100 per cent, Staff and Revenue noted where this information is given in the report):

NEAL AND MASSY GROUP:
Auto Rentals Ltd, staff 68, rev 22m.; Automotive Components Ltd, staff 187, rev 44; Climate Control (refrigeration and air conditioning), staff 23, rev 9; Massy Enterprises Ltd, staff 214, rev 105 (Nissan, General Motors, Mazda and Suzuki sales); Tobago Services Division, staff 21, rev 2; Tracmac Engineering Division, staff 159, rev 50; Neal and Massy Industries Ltd, staff?, rev 17 (Nissan and Mazda car assembly plant).

CANNINGS GROUP:
Canning and Company Ltd, Dairy staff 115, rev 27; Cannings and Company Ltd, Soft Drinks, staff 253, rev 42; Hi-Lo Food Stores, staff 580, rev 205; Melville Shipping and Trading Division, staff 55, rev 9.

SYSTEMS ENGINEERING GROUP:
Nealco Enterprises Ltd (Borde communications, printed circuits, etc.), staff 53, rev 10; Grell-Taurell Division (Dry goods trading), staff 186, rev 101; Complete Computer Systems, staff 199, rev 63; Nealco Travel Services Ltd, staff 5, rev?; Polymer (Caribbean) Ltd, staff 129, rev 26.

OTHER COMPANIES:
Industrial Gases Ltd, staff 97, rev 22; Electrical Industries Ltd (50% shareholding), staff 105, rev 14; General Finance Corporation Ltd (60% shareholding), staff 45, rev 27; Management Information Systems, staff 42, rev 8; Nealco Air Services, staff 25, rev 4; Neal and Massy Caribbean Ltd (Exports), staff?, rev 21; Nealco Properties Ltd, staff 31, rev 20; Universal Metal Co. Ltd (78% shareholding), staff 80, rev 9; Caribbean Home Insurance Co. Ltd (40% shareholding), staff 175, rev 114; Securicor (Trinidad) Ltd, staff 327, rev 12; *In Addition*: R&M Brokerage Services Group, staff 36, rev 5, including: Risk Management Services Ltd; R&M Insurance Intermediaries Ltd (80% shareholding); Industrial Risk Consultants Ltd (50% shareholding); Employee Benefit Services Ltd (33% shareholding).

OVERSEAS COMPANIES:
ANTIGUA: Copy Services Ltd, staff 13; General Finance Corporation Ltd, staff 6; BARBADOS: Caribbean Computer Systems (Barbados) Ltd, staff 55, rev 29; Liquid Carbolic (Barbados) Ltd, staff 10, rev 2; Plantrac Industries Ltd (60% shareholding), staff 58, rev 27; GRENADA: Office Services Ltd, staff 10, rev 2; GUYANA: Associated Industries Ltd, staff 92, rev 6; Demerara Oxygen Co. Ltd (87% shareholding), staff 80, rev 11.1; Transportation Services Ltd, staff 15, rev 1; JAMAICA: Jamaica Oxygen and Acetylene Ltd, staff 73, rev 23; Neal and Massy Investments Ltd, staff 5; Neal and Massy (Jamaica) Ltd, staff 72, rev 25; MARTINIQUE: Trimarg SARL, staff 25, rev 14; ST LUCIA: CCS (St Lucia) Ltd, staff 9; General Finance Corporation Ltd, staff 3; PUERTO RICO: Ambrosiani Hermanos Inc. (tyre retreading, etc.), staff 19, rev 4; SURINAM: (name not given), staff 23, rev 2; USA: Neal and Massy Inc. (Miami) (purchasing and export), staff 12, rev 59.

This already seems like an impressive conglomerate, though largely of Trinidadian concerns. In the years after fieldwork, mainly thanks to the take-over of Geddes Grant, Neal and Massy expanded rapidly into becoming the major conglomerate of its type in the Caribbean. By 1995 it had over 20 companies in Jamaica, and had expanded into Costa Rica, Cuba, St Kitts, Guadeloupe and Venezuela. Trade liberalization was starting to have an impact. On the one hand exports from Trinidad had become a major part of its business; on the other hand the car assembly plants upon which the company had originally been founded had now been closed down.

Neal and Massy is one of the most personalized of all businesses in Trinidad, in the sense that both the public and businessmen tend to associate it with a single person, W. S. Knox (normally known as Sidney Knox), who is both Chairman and Chief Executive Officer. In local parlance the term French Creole has been used since the nineteenth century for all who are seen as unambiguously local whites (even with names like Knox!), so that the company is seen as a 'French Creole' company. The 1992 Board of Directors was described by a company executive as consisting of 4 French Creole, 3 Black, 1 Indian, 1 Spanish, 1 Mixed. The executives were seen as 7 French Creole, 4 Mixed and 1 Indian. All were men, and several of the Board of Directors were seen as token appointments based on their ethnicity.

ANSA McAL

This company traces its origins to 1881, when George R. Alston started a small cocoa export/import firm with one room in Port of Spain. In 1969 this company was taken over by Charles McEnearney and Co. Ltd, which was also started as a one-room firm in Port of Spain, though in this case in 1919. The final take-over was in 1989 by Anthony Norman Sabga, who bought TT$30 million of new shares in 1986 and became majority shareholder through the acquisition of another TT$10 million of shares in 1989. Sabga is identified by all Trinidadians with the Syrian community, which in turn was originally identified largely with the cloth trade. But in 1945 Anthony Sabga at the age of 22 started Standard Distributors Limited with tremendous success in electrical goods, to establish by 1964 the ANSA group. He became the major shareholder of McEnearney Alstons in 1986 and changed the name to ANSA McAL in 1992.

The biggest component of the company is its manufacturing sector, which includes chemical plants. Perhaps best known locally is the Caribbean Development Company Limited, which manufactures the main Trinidadian beer 'Carib'. This is closely tied to a major glass production company. There are also large manufacturing operations in paint, building and matches. In the trading sectors there are car assembly and trading (e.g. of Mitsubishi cars), business machines, electrical goods, a company called Hardware and Oilfield Equipment, tyres and general marketing, and products such as pharmaceuticals and foodstuffs, as well as a specialist trading enterprise for Tobago. In the service sector there is a publishing company responsible for the daily newspaper the *Trinidad Guardian*, a broadcasting company with several radio stations, and also life assurance, business insurance, finance, travel and shipping companies.

The history of this company since fieldwork has parallelled that of Neal and Massy, inasmuch as it has also attempted to develop as a Caribbean company, and by 1995 was also trying to establish key links with Latin America through Guyana and Venezuela. The sheer scale of its ambition may be illustrated with a report on just one subsidiary, the Carib brewery (*Trinidad Guardian* 12/3/95). Following fieldwork Carib had taken over its main rival, and followed this with large investments. It claims that when complete it will be producing 15 million cases per annum which would make it equivalent to the tenth biggest brewery in the United States. By 1994 it was also exporting 1.9 million cases of brewery product worth TT$75 million to 24 countries.

In many respects these conglomerates were exhibiting the typical behaviour of a major transnational. In general there is some logic to the make-up of the subsidiary services, so that, for example, the manufacturing sectors are assisted by the trading facilities, and many of the service operations, such as shipping, insurance, finance and business expertise, exist largely to service intra-company needs. This means that a separate internal economy may develop between the various subsidiaries, which decreases any reliance on external businesses. The move to intra-company trade has become a feature of a number of advanced economies, as indeed has a kind of return to 'barter' that characterizes relations between the largest of these companies. So, for example, it is reported that Neal and Massy exchanged shipments of urea to Japan instead of cash to pay for its Nissan franchise holding (*Express*, 23 August 1988).

Certain products have been of particular significance in the development of local companies. In the case of both the local conglomerates it was probably the highly profitable car trade that (especially during the oil boom) provided the kind of profits that enabled them to aspire to true transnational levels. It was also probably the post-oil-boom decline in car sales that weakened Charles McEnearney to the extent that it could be taken over. In 1990 it looked as if AMAR (a company particularly identified with the East-Indian community) was attempting to become the third major local conglomerate, once again developing through car sales, in this case a franchise arrangement with Toyota. A different route, through insurance and finance holdings, but spreading into commodities, is represented by the rise to potential transnational status of Colonial Life Insurance (a company particularly identified with the African community).

Once a company is taken over by a conglomerate there is a rapid loss of autonomy, with most major decisions now having to be at least approved by the corporate head office. One complication here is the presence of any minority interest. In general Neal and Massy have avoided this, with a preference for full take-overs. In contrast ANSA McAl developed an earlier tendency to work with minority interest status, although there was increasing pressure from their accountancy advisers either to divest or fully incorporate such companies.

In general conglomerates seem to look to establish dominant brands or monopoly conditions. An example occurred when ANSA McAl purchased its main brewing rival at a time when it posed a growing threat to its dominant brand. This created a virtual monopoly operation, with one company selling all the major beer brands and 'malted' drinks brands. Advertising expenditure obviously dropped up to a point. The advantages of the monopoly conditions are most evident in the ability to fix prices, and the take-over may well have been prompted by what had been several years of aggressive price wars between the rival beer brands. Competition still exists in relation to other products, in this case as part of a longer-term rivalry between beer and rum as the national drinks.

On the other hand, there may be some permitted brand competition within the company. This may take the form of products split between subsidiaries, resulting in a situation in which for instance the Alston Marketing Company Ltd trades in vitamins such as Seven Seas, while another ANSA McAl company, Trinidad Distributors Ltd, trades in Sanatogen. As another example, within AMCO there are several rival wine products, such as Papillon, Deinhard and Piat d'Or. And with respect to beer, most members of the public would have seen the three major brands of stout, Guinness, Mackeson and Royal Extra, as highly competitive brands, whereas in fact all three were produced by ANSA McAl, with only the Jamaican Dragon Stout in a state of true external competition.

The local 'global' companies are by no means always the direct rivals of the global 'local' companies. They often act in direct collaboration. For example, a recent success story in Trinidad has been the entry of Court's, Britain's third biggest furniture firm. Although not strictly a transnational, Courts has branches in a large number of countries, including eight within the Caribbean. Indeed, its foreign stores earn on average some 2.5 times their British equivalent in turnover per unit area. Its success comes from radical localization. Most of its goods come from local manufacturers, the management is mainly local, and it only retains a few elements such as the logo and competitions, in common. In the case of Trinidad (and also Grenada and Guyana) the firm works as a joint venture with Neal and Massy (*The*

Economist 8/1/94). This would be only one example of many where the two local conglomerates act together with foreign or transnational ventures.

The Local Versus the Global

Given the limited number of the larger transnationals present in Trinidad, in many cases it is the local conglomerates that have the dominant share of the market. It is often they who represent the brand of some other leading transnational through their reassemblage and trading operations. In those cases, however, in which the transnational is itself present in the form of key global brands, the local conglomerate has to decide whether to attempt to compete with its own local brand or in alliance with a rival transnational. In an interview with a Neal and Massy subsidiary a senior executive provides many reasons why in general the local conglomerates do compete, and only some of these come down to questions of profitability.

Certainly, the fact that they are part of such a large group gives the conglomerate's subsidiaries some support in feeling that there is a point to competition; but the sense of being a local company also impinges: 'We cannot withdraw our egos, so we have to try and beat them or meet them.' Whereas in larger markets there may be an attempt to find a specialized niche as against the global brand, this is relatively rare for the local conglomerates, who tend to see the market as insufficiently segmented for such strategies. 'In terms of income and demographics I don't think we operate or go for a lower end niche. I think we are both going after the same piece of the pie.'

At first it seems that there are good commercial grounds for local production. 'No company can maintain 100 per cent, the cost of trying to maintain 100 per cent would make [it] . . . operate at a loss. Our experience shows that on entry of another producer in a situation of virtual monopoly they lose between 15 and 30 per cent of their market.' There is, then, a market which one is likely to obtain; but at least in the case this manager was discussing that did not imply profitability: '[It] is an ego thing, it is in operation because of ego, it has not been profitable, the losses are starting to diminish, we expect that under this new regime we can bring our loss down to a break even'. In other words, the local conglomerate feels almost under an obligation to have a presence in markets where the global brand has tremendous power and back-up. There is a self-consciousness that it represents the 'local'; and it is likely that at least some of the consumption of its local brand is predicated upon the same principle.

Complications may also arise because of international takeovers. Commonly, the two local conglomerates who at a level of brands had represented the local marketing of a global competition between dominant brands would suddenly find that they were both now marketing brands owned by a single company. On occasion the local situation was able to retain its stability. So, for example, in its 1991 *Annual Report* ANSA McAl was able to announce 'TDC was the only distributor in the world not to lose the Carnation brand name when Nestlé took them over in 1989.' In this case there would be particular pride, since Nestlé exists in its own right as a major company within Trinidad and would normally assume control of any brands the global company had taken over. Similarly, a local company may take on the franchise of brands that in other areas are in competition: 'We opted at that time for A, but they are competitors for B, so A and B fight for market share throughout the world, but here there are no problems as far as our franchise agreement is concerned, no conflict.'

Behind this rivalry is the question as to which companies do indeed represent the 'local' and the 'global'. On the one hand, the local conglomerate is associated with many global brands, which diminish the sense of it as Trinidadian. Cannings (a subsidiary of Neal and Massy) certainly produces Cannings label products; but it is also the local bottler for Coca-Cola. Neal and Massy's car brands, like those of ANSA McAl, are all Japanese. By contrast, as already noted, Nestlé attempt to pose as essentially a local company.

With Lever Brothers, British West Indian Tobacco and the like there is considerable use made of the fact that the transnationals have often existed in Trinidad for a good deal longer than their 'local' rivals. There is after all no *a priori* reason why it is ownership alone that would secure the concept of location. Furthermore, there is no absolute correlation between the localized nature of the company and the furtherance of local materials. A prominent newspaper advert read: 'In 1914 two greats came together into existence. One was the City of Port of Spain and the other was Nestlé.' The major transnationals may have greater capacity to produce their global brands from local ingredients, while local companies have to import their materials. This would be particularly true of Lever Brothers. This company dominates local sales of oil-based products, but given that it was originally established more to secure raw materials than to sell goods it is not surprising that it probably has the best capacity for the processing of local oils. So, for example, the *Express* (28/5/88) quotes the company Chairman as noting, 'The increasing displacement of local indigenous and regional coconut oil by soyabean oil, produced from imported beans, continues to threaten the future of the coconut industry.' Lever is said to have submitted proposals to Government for regulation of the present uncontrolled situation. In other words, it is often the transnational that is applying for local protectionist policies, as against the local company, which wants free access to imported goods.

Equally, a local company may be producing products under licence: for example, ANSA McAl's subsidiary Penta Paints manufactures under licence from ICI of the UK, just as all car assemblage also takes place under licence. There are clear advantages for a local company in working with a foreign brand: 'In many cases they share the advertising and the marketing budget on a 50:50 basis, yet on the other hand whenever we introduce a local flavour we have to spend 100% of the advertising budget.' In many such cases the product is a mixture of imported and local elements, and it would be very difficult to disentangle the local from the foreign component. Even the proportion of 'value added' based on local work would be difficult to calculate. The absurdity of trying to locate a true 'local' and 'global' in sourcing products was very evident when the question was put to a dairy and juice products manufacturer. He was clear that his bottles were local and that the concentrate was imported; the water is of course local, but the milk purification treatment is based on a franchised machine from a French company; the tin cans are imported as plate from Metal Box England, but then made up locally. Artificial flavours are bought locally from a company that imports them. Juice content had been local, then became entirely imported, and was now (under pressure from restrictions on access to foreign currency) again increasingly local. This in turn was threatened by future trade liberalization, which meant it might well become imported again. But the executive became really tongue-tied when it came to sugar. This is because of the special agreements held by the local company CARONI, which runs all the Trinidadian sugar cane plantations. CARONI has an arrangement with the European Common Market (the Lomé Agreement). Under these terms Trinidad has quotas for sugar exports, which it will lose if it does not fulfil them in any given year. For this reason it is quite common for CARONI to export all the sugar it can produce, and then become the main importer of sugar. Is sugar then local because it is being bought from CARONI, or foreign because CARONI imports it!?

In my surveys most consumers, including schoolchildren, seemed reasonably clear as to which companies should be regarded as foreign-owned, picking out AMAR, CLICO and the big two conglomerates as local firms. It is, however, at the level of consumption that the expectation of local versus global reasserts itself, since in the main there is the desire to advertise the quality of transnational goods on the basis of their global presence, pandering to the assumption that global branding means higher quality. So Colgate would flaunt the fact that it is marketed in 160 countries and has 40 per cent of the world toothpaste market in order to make claims about product quality.

The ambivalence about the location of one's company in image construction reflected a genuine concern amongst executives in almost all companies as to what the meaning of locality represented for the general public. In short, companies simply didn't know whether it was better for them to be local or global. The construction of images had little to do with actual locality. A company might hide the fact that Trinidadian cocoa, which is regarded by the industry as of exceptionally high quality, was in fact Trinidadian if it thought that Trinidadians would simply assume that a local product was inferior to an imported raw material. But whether in advertising, product name or materials used, there was also a sense that a nationalistic localism might be appropriate or of benefit. The ambivalence of executives was a reasonable reflection of actual consumer values. That is, most consumers simultaneously held contradictory beliefs about the value of local and global goods, constantly denigrating the failure of local brands and firms to match the quality of global goods, but in a manner that suggested that this concealed a fierce potential loyalty to and defence of the local in the face of similar criticisms from any quarter that was not itself local.

The Revolt of the Local

The problem of assigning the label 'local' and 'global' to particular companies is mainly discussed in terms of inter-company rivalry and competition. Less well-documented is a tension in local–global relations that may occur within the contemporary transnational company. Once again the case study that I will present of this tension also indicates how limited the drive to profitability may be as a factor in determining what a company actually does. The clear point of potential rupture arises when companies staffed almost entirely by Trinidadian personnel are nevertheless supposed to be organized according to the imperatives of the profitability of the global enterprise.

Most of my information was derived from the study of advertising agencies in relation to their clients, and I cannot tell how far this may be generalized; but at least within this industry the potential for rupture and contradiction quickly became apparent. On one morning I arrived for what had become a fairly routine 'checking in' at an advertising agency to see what was taking place that day, and was permitted to observe a briefing session. The briefing was concerned with the relationship to a client who was known to favour global brands and images, in opposition to certain recent trends towards greater localization. This was manifested in the advertising for a particular product, which traditionally showed it in use by actresses. This had become a standard feature, and the adverts were entirely familiar to me from television and cinema viewing in London. The briefing I witnessed represented what to the agency appeared as a kind of revolutionary cell operating in secret, but about to be launched against the global company.

It appeared that the separate national agencies throughout Latin America had been meeting in secret because of their collective sense that a localized version of this advert using actresses known to South American audiences would be prefer-able to the use of the established European or North American actresses. Given the scale of these operations, they had been able to go ahead without permission and create the local adverts which they preferred. What I viewed was thus a succession of around a dozen adverts, each created by a different South American agency and employing local personnel. None of these had at this stage been revealed to the global corporation, and the question that the Trinidadian agency was being asked to consider was whether they wanted to join this rebellion from the regions or to stick with the global advertising programme.

Mattelart (1991: Chapter 3) has carefully documented the relationship between the failure of Saatchi and Saatchi as a global agency and the decision by that firm to embrace a particular image of the future as leading towards greater use of global advertising images that would 'work' in a wide variety of contexts. The implication of his study is that advertising executives assumed that the well-established global bands were in some sense a vanguard of an increasing global homogeneity. What this large-scale failure seems to suggest, by contrast, is that global brands such as McDonald's and Coca-Cola are not the tip of some globalizing iceberg, but rather the markers of a particular superordinate level of identity on a par with world music and saving the rainforest. These are significant precisely because they are contrasted with highly localized images. In other words, a few global brands exist that stand conspicuously for the idea of being global, mainly because most brands have no such image.

It might follow from this argument that the lesson to be learnt from this regional revolt was that the local advertising offices, knew their markets better than the global offices, and could see that adverts sensitive to the local context would sell better than global adverts. Although representing a rebellion at one level, the overall effect was merely to enhance the overall profitability of the global company. On further investigation, however, I became increasingly unsure as to whether this was really what such revolts from the local represented.

If local personnel were entirely concerned with the overall profitability of the transnational company they represent, then their concern would be to limit costs to that company while expanding sales. As most of my evidence comes from the relationship between advertising agencies and these companies, this becomes a question of the relative costs and impact of advertising campaigns. All transnationals produce adverts intended for transnational use. There are clear economies of scale here. By producing a single advert in a country that is in the vanguard in advertising skills, a transnational can produce the quality of advert that attracts attention by virtue of its sheer professionalism. Its 'expensive' feel is intended to evoke the guarantee of a high-quality product. Once produced, this can be shown in a multitude of settings, also helping to establish the product as a global brand that can be met with equally in a wide variety of national contexts. The head of the agency team that produced Coca-Cola advertising for a considerable period makes it clear in an interview that this strategy is quite explicit (O'Barr 1989).

From the point of view of the local agency these are 'canned adverts', the term coming from the days when it was simply a question of importing a can of film and showing it in the local cinema. In such cases the sole task of the local office and the local advertising agency today is to determine the best placing in the media, usually television, and negotiate the best terms. The advertising agency itself receives some commission on this activity, but this is likely to be modest. By contrast, if the local agency persuades the transnational company that the product requires a locally made advert, then a number of the local advertising agencies have sufficient professional abilities to produce high-quality television adverts. These may not be quite up to the standard of American or British adverts, but compensate by containing local elements that the canned advert cannot contain.

When an advert is made locally, the overall advertising budget is far larger. The advertising agencies' own staff must be employed in writing the ad, they must employ models and film crews, secure locations, etc. Quite commonly, if there are sophisticated animations involved, these may be subcontracted to advertising studios in Venezuela or Florida; but the bulk of production costs are within Trinidad. As a result the advertising agency may employ many more people and is altogether a much larger concern than would be the case if it were merely placing canned adverts. The local office of the transnational also sees far more money passing through its hands, since the global offices will normally be supplementing the budget if not paying a substantial proportion of the costs, and their own staff are needed for common briefing sessions and overseeing production, which again justifies their own expansion.

While many adverts for products such as perfumes around Christmas time are purely canned, it is more common for imported adverts to have some localizing treatment such as the use of local voice-overs, or the interpolation of some local scene. What is surprisingly common, given the expense, is the number of entirely locally made adverts shown on Trinidadian television. Indeed, given the relatively small size of the local market, it would have been hard to predict that the greater part of television advertising is in fact locally produced. There need be no contradiction between the interest of global profitability and that of the local office if it is clearly the case that such local adverts increase sales as against imported adverts.

Perhaps fortunately for the local executives, the study of the effects of individual advertising campaigns is a very inexact science. There are too many other factors (e.g. product quality, the competition, retailing strategy, etc.) that might have affected results. Overall, in my conversations with senior executives of transnational companies I gained the distinct impression that they strongly suspected that the glossy imported adverts were often more effective at selling the product than local advertising campaigns, but were willing to be constantly persuaded to the contrary, since this in general resulted in the augmented importance of their local office. It was not necessary for them to make the case, since the advertising agencies, who had no reason to be so coy about the advantages of local production to themselves, volubly argued for the necessity of a locally produced campaign.

The revolt of the local may therefore be interpreted in two distinct ways. The first would be a perception of an actual movement towards localized imagery and its effectiveness as against the global advert, the point made by Mattelart (1991). Alternatively, we find a structural contradiction in the logic of profitability such that the 'profitability' of the local arm of the company may be at the expense of that of the global company. It is, of course, very likely that the degree of localization of personnel in Trinidad lends itself to this second factor, with in essence the Trinidadians of the advertising agency and the local office colluding against the influence of the global firm.

That there could be conflict in profitability between the central and subsidiary offices of a company has been recognized in the general literature on the firm. It is seen as particularly characteristic of the early stage of 'mother–daughter' relations, where there is a clear hierarchy between the original and subsidiary offices. The Trinidad evidence suggests something different, however. Partly this is an aspect of the new decentralization discussed in more general debates on post-Fordism or disorganized capitalism. But these approaches would suggest that the looser relations between regional offices of transnationals return them back to a variant of 'mother–daughter' relations, inasmuch as it is harder for the global firm's management to see an overall picture of profitability and more likely for internal contradictions to arise (Franko 1993). In Trinidad the continued importance of national identity is itself a major cause of contradiction. Although my evidence is largely restricted to advertising, I strongly suspect that there are many other areas from production through to distribution where the relationship between local and global becomes a point of structural contradiction in the logic of profitability, rather than merely an instrument for simple profit extraction.

Big Business in a Small State: Two Factors

There are many peculiarities that result from large firms working in a small state. The small size of élites, the impact of personal gossip, the degree to which an individual is likely to be recognized in the street and the details of company personnel known to the public at large are all different from the case in a larger country. Other topics to which an ethnography could contribute by its localized focus might include gender, class, religion and any number of other social parameters that clearly impinge upon business organization. There is not the space here, however, to engage with more than a couple of examples of these issues, which will then have to stand for the others. I have selected two topics here that I think illustrate the more general issues particularly well – ethnic identity and the role of the state. By selecting them as examples of contextual issues, I am not making any claim that they are in any sense more fundamental than other topics that could equally well have been addressed.

Company Identity and Ethnic Identity

Perhaps the main difference between the perception of business in Trinidad provided by historical records and that of the present day is the far more complex ethnic composition of contemporary business. The historical legacy, as pointed out above, is that of largely White-run business. This was strengthened rather than diminished with independence, as the White population moved from political power into less conspicuous but entrenched economic power. In contemporary business it is important to distinguish between foreign control and local White control. Until recently it was still the case that a network of White families dominated Trinidadian big business. Of course, not every senior executive is White, but a group making up less than 1 per cent of the population until recently dominated most of the board of directors of the major companies (Parris 1985). This suggests that, despite all the pressure from Eric Williams that followed the 1970 attempted Black Power coup, a tiny minority still dominated the country's private sphere, perpetuating a colour hierarchy that stretches back in unbroken line to the barbarism and oppression of slavery. But the period of fieldwork was probably that which marked the end of this historical truism. The take-over of McEnearney Alston by Syrians was probably its symbolic end. Although Syrians could easily be defined as White, they are not part of the historical élite of 'French Creoles' in Trinidad. There is very little academic study available on the Syrian group (though see Barclay 1992, 1994). The White élite are, however, likely to have many similarities with those in Jamaica, who were recently studied by Douglass (1992: 223–6).

Most Trinidadian companies remain unambiguously ethnically labelled by the mass population. By 1990 there was no ethnic group that did not have major business corporations associated with them. Perhaps the most 'watched' developments were in specifically Indian-associated companies. There were some older examples, such as Seereram brothers, a construction firm, or Solo for soft drinks. Several more recent entrepreneurs have been important in the development of shopping malls and hotels, amongst other industries. Ramsaran (1993) provides a brief history of a number of these business developments. As already noted, the Amar group of companies seemed to be quite systematically trying to join the major two conglomerates, although in this case with a firm ethnic affiliation. Partly as a result, Amar has a clearer identity as a conglomerate than its two larger rivals, since there is less tendency to identify its subsidiary companies as separate entities.

This sense of ethnic designation can also apply to the subsections within a given company. For example, one salesman described his firm classified management in ethnic terms, with hardware as White, non-food as Indian, drugs as White/Chinese, etc. In many cases there is also an expectation that ethnic management will lead to ethnic recruitment lower down. On the other hand it was perhaps equally common for workers as much as managers to claim that employment was no longer as dependent as before upon ethnicity, and largely followed educational qualifications. For example a new recruit at Neal and Massy noted that the group of high-flying graduates who had been recruited that year from the Universities included no Whites.

The ethnic community that is least associated with big business in relation to its overall numbers is the African community. The role of Africans in business is presently part of a large-scale study by a leading social scientist, Dr Selwyn Ryan, who has previously written extensively about the relationship between ethnicity, commerce and the State (e.g. Ryan 1972, 1991a, 1991b, 1991c). In books about Ray Edwin Dieffenthaller (1990) and Cyril Duprey, Ryan is clearly making claims for some larger companies (such as the Hardware and Oilfield equipment business and the Colonial Life Insurance Company) with respect to their 'African' leadership. Ryan's recent work also (Ryan and Barclay 1992; Ryan and Stewart 1994) provides the clearest arguments for continued deliberate networking amongst the White business community to frustrate attempts by others to break into the control of the largest businesses. For example, he has argued that the network of overlapping boards of directors could collude against attempts by CLICO to succeed in key takeover battles (Ryan and Barclay 1992: 67–71). Ryan and Barclay, working largely on a survey of smaller businesses, provide considerable evidence for African perceptions of discrimination. This is shown to have had an important historical dimension in the fleecing of nascent African planters in the nineteenth century (pp. 1–11). In his more general account Ryan seems to give more or less equal weight to anti-African discrimination and attributes of Afro-Trinidadian culture, including family structure, as causes for relative lack of success in business. The work seeks to juxtapose the quotations of African businessmen who claim that it is discrimination by the banks that has led to their problem with the evidence of the bankers themselves, who imply a consistently favourable policy towards black nascent entrepreneurs, particularly under the political regime of Eric Williams, and contest the suggestion that post-Independence failures resulted from the same kinds of discrimination as pre-Independence failures (p. 80).

There may, however, be one problem with assessing this research. Within this project the section on Indians has focused on highly successful individual entrepreneurs (Ramsaran 1993), while that on the Africans has focused on the problems for much smaller firms (Ryan and Barclay 1992). In addition there has been a study of the Syrians as a commercial community (Barclay 1992). Ryan's starting-point is the observation that there are few major companies owned by Afro-Trinidadians compared, for example, to Indians. In ordinary conversation one constantly hears remarks about the apparent competence of Indians in business as opposed to the supposed incompetence of Africans. But there may be grounds for suggesting that it is in fact the African population that provides most of the 'competence' behind what must generally be regarded as a relatively successful national business community.

If one asked within the Indian community for an explanation of the relative placement of ethnic groups there would be at least as strong a tendency to invoke discrimination as amongst the African community (Ramsaran 1993). Most Indians see the British colonial authorities as having shown clear preference in their historical recruitment strategies for Africans and coloureds, who had passed through the élite educational system that would in large measure take over the running of both the private and public administration of the country. The Indians were by and large seen as more naturally suited to their rural occupations when compared with urban Africans. Indians were also tarred by an earlier association with criminality and by a later association with militant trade unionism (Trotman 1986; compare Williams 1991: 127–200 for the case of ethnic recruitment in Guyana). The PNM government marked a shift to Africans from coloureds, but not towards the Indian population. Inasmuch as under Eric Williams a considerable proportion of economic power lay with the state sector, this gave Africans considerable experience in running larger economic institutions. The term African has now come to subsume, through reincorporation, the 'coloured' population, and is today mainly defined as against the Indian population (see also Yelvington 1993: 11–14).

Furthermore, the situation with regard to the private sector may not be as different as might be at first thought. The key economic agents are not the smaller local companies, with their clear ethnic associations, but the transnationals. On the whole these have sprung from a historical recruitment policy that favoured Whites, and after them the mixed and African. By 1990 recruitment policy had become much less ethnically biased, and there were probably as many Indians as Africans being recruited into these businesses; but the historical legacy means that the middle management ranks may remain largely those recruited during the earlier period. Although ownership and boards of directors may remain controlled by Whites, the general management is probably dominated by this 'African' (defined in its larger sense) component. The recent report by Ryan and La Guerre (1993) on employment and ethnicity notes the higher proportion of Indians than Africans in management within the private sector; but I suspect this relates more to the higher ownership of small firms by Indians. My own observation in the number of large transnationals where I was conducting fieldwork was that a Mixed–African group of various gradations still dominated numerically in management, other than senior management which was dominated by Whites and Off-whites. If we include here the public sector, where Africans clearly dominate, it could be argued that the lack of success of Africans in independent entrepreneurship is matched by their considerable success in state and private sector management, where they have been highly effective.

In turn it is likely that many Indians would consider that their high-profile involvement in independently owned, entrepreneur-led business enterprises arose out of their exclusion from those routes to power that led through established state and business enterprises. Indians are often thought to have considerable economic power in the private sector because of their dominance in some highly visible retail sectors. Sudema argued (*Express* 11/

12/1990) against general assumptions about an Indian take-over of the economy. He notes that none of the eight main banks are Indian-owned, and that Indians represent between 10–13 per cent of the boards of directors of banks, in most cases token appointments, so that at the level of directorships their influence on the economy would be very small (see also Ramsaran 1993: 18–20). There are exceptions, for example the construction industry, where the Indian presence is probably a great deal stronger than that of Whites; and Ryan has noted other exceptions, such as the water authority.

None of this need detract from the important questions being asked by Ryan and his associates as to the effect of discrimination against attempts to establish African businesses and the question as to whether social structure and historically derived cultural tendencies lead particular communities to be more or less pre-adapted to those skills required for profitable entrepreneurship. For example, the research by Ryan and Barclay does seem to suggest a relative individualism and lack of family support and intra-ethnic patronage (Ryan and Barclay 1992: 21–6, 60–5, 116–28) compared to my own fieldnotes on Indian retailing in Chaguanas (though see Ramsaran 1993: 33).

All such discussions about ethnicity and business are also held against a background of equal concern about the levels of ethnic representation in the public sector. The idea of Indian entrepreneurial success is always held against an image of entrenched preference for Africans by the PNM government. The survey by Ryan and La Guerre (1993) included the public as well as the private sector, the emphasis in its public reception being on the latter. Although there are clear exceptions, this largely confirmed the public sense of the low representation of the Indian population in the public sector. In particular, it confirmed the virtual absence of Indians in sensitive areas such as the Police and Armed Forces. The authors are, however, unwilling to see this as simply a product of racial discrimination, noting a wide range of factors that have contributed to this result.

What is clear is that larger stereotypes are pervasive in Trinidad that imply quite distinct differences in commercial ability. These stereotypes are quite dynamic. Williams (1991) has put forward a powerful argument with respect to nearby Guyana for the abiding influence of colonial prejudice upon contemporary debates. She suggests that throughout the colonial period

it was the élite Europeans who 'reserved for themselves the right
to allocate economic roles and social privileges and to manipulate patterns of interaction among subordinate ethnic groups'
(p. 151). So, for example, Africans could be seen as industrious
and trustworthy or lazy and indolent, depending upon the
economic niche for which they were being designated at any
particular time. Williams's evidence for the colonial period is
persuasive, though I am not sure that these have remained quite
as frozen during the post-colonial period as she implies, at least
in the case of Trinidad.

The malleability and dynamics of such stereotyping of
economic aptitudes are ethnographically observable. One of the
most recent shifts is the self- and public designation of the White
community. Until very recently the overwhelming dominance of
White business went with an assumption of experience and
competence as natural entrepreneurs. With the recent success of
Syrian and Indian businesses, one finds a clear realignment
amongst the White population. For example, in a dinner-time
conversation with one of the most powerful White business
families I was given a long account of the role taken by Whites.
On this account the Whites represent 'old' business ethics, which
have a strong sense of honour and paternalistic concern for the
welfare of their employees. By contrast, Indian and Syrian
business is characterized, as so often is the case with *nouveau*
wealth, as vicious, aggressive and unfair. They are seen as purely
interested in profit, with no compunction about firing or
displacing employees or using various dishonourable and illegal
business practices that have given them an unfair advantage over
White businesses. Although there was a sense that this positioning is still not fully worked out, I was certainly left with the
impression that the more the balance tips against White control
and in favour of other ethnic communities, the more Whites are
likely to try to concretize this image of Whites as almost business
'victims' to provide potential political alliances with African-
dominated state control. The ironies of this tactic, which
represents almost total amnesia with respect to the historical
evidence of White rapaciousness and cruelty, are evident enough,
and demonstrate that one should not underestimate the dynamics of such ascriptions of business aptitude to ethnic groups.

These are all normative generalizations. The distribution of
traits amongst ethnic groups in my ethnographic observation

was far less clear-cut than colloquial discourse suggested. But such stereotypes have a major impact. As I have noted elsewhere (1994: 273–88), these arguments over ethnicity within Trinidad have often little to do with any actual appraisal of ethnic values or aptitudes. Rather they have become part of a much larger symbolic and material struggle, in which ethnicity is itself being defined and manipulated through a wide variety of positive and negative attributions of supposed traits or supposed contributions to 'Trinidad' itself. In short, it is generally much more reasonable to regard ethnicity as the end-product rather than the initial premiss of cultural conflict.

The State

The public perception of the relationship between big business and the State is grounded in the rather convenient existence of two major local conglomerates and the long-term dominance of a party of government and a slightly less stable but generally identifiable main party of opposition. In the main gossip centres on the idea that each party has one of the two conglomerates behind it. Alternatively, the two conglomerates themselves are often remarked upon as wielding such power that irrespective of the political affiliation of government the decisions taken reflect their will, so that they thereby make up an alternative 'government' of their own.

Such is the dominance of this model that there is surprisingly little discussion of any other form of potential relationship between government and business. Although academics and some workers, for example in the sugar and oil industries, may talk of the impact of 'capitalism' as a generic form and of the State's involvement, this was almost never encountered in my ethnography of the four housing areas, nor was there much mention of the other large companies that dominate the Trinidadian scene. The expected questions on the role of transnationals or of class conflict occasionally came up, but tended to be subsumed within these more dominant concerns. By contrast, the two conglomerates seemed almost to stand for business in general, and all 'conspiracy theories' revolved around their activities.

The politics of the conglomerates were of particular interest because of the sense in the late 1980s that government could in fact change. During the initial fieldwork period the most popular conspiracy theory was that Neal and Massy had been closely involved with the National Alliance for Reconstruction (NAR) and had worked hard for its final success at overcoming the PNM (People's National Movement). Its opponents saw the NAR as a more middle-class party, with greater sympathy for business and free enterprise and less concern with welfare. The PNM had been forged by Eric Williams amidst a strong anti-colonial rhetoric, and people had assumed it would follow a radical politics. In practice, the party once in power had seemed keen to repudiate these origins and demonstrate its concern for business development, although this embracing of capitalism had received a jolt with the 1970 Black Power revolt, after which a certain recommitment to welfare concerns had resurfaced.

This legacy set the scene for what would otherwise appear as rather bizarre relationships between the conglomerates and the political parties. In the context of fieldwork within the company I found less evidence than I had expected of any actual favouring of Neal and Massy by the NAR. For example, during late 1988 the State started to wield a particularly strong measure of control over business because of the weakness of the Trinidadian dollar. This meant that companies were under tight control over their export of foreign currency, and many smaller companies genuinely feared that they would go out of business because they simply could not get the US dollars they needed to buy the imports they sold. This foreign exchange squeeze dominated the news and almost all business conversation, and became a critical issue for a while. At that time I was conducting fieldwork in a number of the subsidiaries within the Neal and Massy group, which was the company that local rumour suggested was most closely in cahoots with central government, and therefore able to obtain the dollars that others found unavailable.

I was able to overhear a number of conversations within the Neal and Massy company which suggested that they were far from immune to this constriction, and had failed to obtain a number of special requests for currency from the central bank. These were long detailed debates among very senior management, such that I feel quite sure they were not 'staged' for my benefit. Indeed, there were a number of subsidiaries that were predicting short-term layoffs and other desperate measures because of their failure to obtain foreign exchange.

What this and other similar evidence suggested was that the government was not nearly as corrupt in paying back its supporters as many people on the street believed was the case at that time. In general, I found less evidence of corruption than was suggested by the local media and conversation. This is not to say that government was handling the crisis particularly well. Many of the companies were complaining that it was the raw materials needed for making export goods that should have been allowed in, but that the government was just imposing blanket refusals without any consideration of priorities. This seemed both a reasonable and a sustained complaint.

Although the relationship may not have been of quite the corrupt form often assumed, this is not to deny that a clear link between the conglomerates and party politics existed. Indeed the clearest evidence for this came after the fall of the NAR. The election of the PNM allowed a kind of test of the two popular hypotheses with regard to the nature of alignment between business and the state. On the whole ANSA McAl was regarded as the more rapacious capitalist organization, with a stronger commitment to untrammelled business enterprise without interference from the State. While both political parties were regarded as very far from any overt socialist principles, the PNM was clearly regarded as more interested in state involvement and welfare commitments as opposed to pure *laissez-faire* capitalism. Thus if ANSA McAl was to follow ideological principles it should have immediately set itself up in opposition to the new government.

In fact, the opposite occurred. The political affiliation of ANSA McAl was easy to determine, since it ran the *Guardian* newspaper. The *Guardian* was in many ways its natural ally, since of the two dailies it was clearly more orientated to business interests than its rival the *Express*. The *Guardian* generally was seen as more right-wing, more sympathetic to élite groups and more informed with regard to business matters. The *Express* went through a period when the Neal and Massy group had direct influence in terms of share equity over the paper, but was less clearly aligned than the *Guardian* to one of the two conglomerates. By 1992 the *Guardian* had quite clearly taken a sympathetic line to the PNM government, and this was seen by one and all as indicating a clear affiliation between ANSA McAl and the PNM. In practice what this demonstrated was that ANSA McAl was much more concerned with its business rivalry with Neal and Massy than with political ideology, and it therefore chose to establish its links with the alternative political base. On the whole this outcome not only conformed to most people's views about the dualist conspiracy of 'one party, one conglomerate', but also conformed to most people's expectation that pragmatic rivalry was far more important than business or political ideology to the running of both business and politics. On this my evidence and public opinion coincide.

The two examples that have been presented in this section could certainly be added to by many others. What they indicate is that in such a small state there are many issues of contextualization that take on a highly specific and often contingent character that would not easily be assimilated into general models of the localization or contextualization of business.

The Employees' Perspective

From the perspective of many Trinidadians the concern is mainly with whether in considering a company as local it may therefore become a point of local identity, as Trinidadian or at least Caribbean. I use the term 'many Trinidadians' deliberately, since there are also a great many who clearly have very little interest in knowing anything about companies, where they are based, or who they are thought to represent, dismissing them all under a generic notion of 'business'. In a way these two public attitudes reflect a key academic debate about contemporary capitalism. There are many academics (Sklair 1990 provides a recent clear example) who might see the latter attitude as appropriate, in that it really does not matter where the capital base or personnel of a company come from, since (Sklair argues) simply working in business management puts one in a class apart, a class whose international connections and common interests have become far more important than the connections between that class and the locality. Buying the same goods, watching the same media, founded on similar educational resources and having to be prepared to be 'posted' to any regional office, they become an international class constituting the management of global capitalism. It is thus reasonable for those Trinidadians (and they tend to be those of lower income and educational levels) to show little concern over differences that would merely mask the larger unity of that class that continues to oppress them irrespective of their localized identity.

By contrast, the opposite pole is held by a view of capitalism that is extremely nationalistic. This assumes that while there is considerable rivalry between Trinidadian companies they unite at a higher level in opposition to outside forces that would be bad for them all, and they not only claim but actively pursue a collective national interest. This view is generally proposed at the political level, since politics is largely defined in national terms and the government is responsible for running state companies that do indeed occupy such a niche. The media is almost entirely national as opposed to regional or international, and thus the profitability of capitalism is assessed less by companies or by global shifts than by a concern with the 'political' accountancy of the nation-state.

In the ethnographic encounter one finds both these expectations realized in terms of the identity of employees, but their opposition is diluted by an extraordinarily complex set of diverse alignments between what might be called local and global interests and identities. During the course of the year I was saddened when one informant for whom I had enormous respect and who was working for a transnational company was offered the opportunity of a senior position in the company's Mexican office in recognition of his considerable abilities. He took this job, and it seemed clear that his future lay in a transnational managerial class within which Trinidad would soon become little more than a point of origin. In general it seemed that Trinidad was much more a recruitment ground than a repository for such figures.

While the occasional high flyer might be picked up in this way and redeposited abroad, virtually the entire personnel of both Trinidadian-owned and foreign-owned Trinidadian offices were actually Trinidadian. Only a few of the largest continued to have foreign personnel, and then usually only the most senior executive. According to most accounts this degree of localization was largely a result of the political clout of Eric Williams' combining the post-1970 popular impulse towards localization expressed in the Black Power uprisings of that year together with the national authority derived from the post-1973 oil-boom wealth. Another factor must have been the high educational levels in Trinidad and, increasingly, the proven ability of local personnel in running successful businesses. Finally, there is the diminishing importance of Trinidad in the recession. There is less incentive for transnationals to post international figures to what has become a declining market.

The question of a national élite is therefore rather more pertinent than that of an international élite. There is a considerable degree of informal contact between the senior management of companies, be they local conglomerates or transnationals. The status and respectability of such senior figures rests as much in their ability to turn profits into esteem as in success in obtaining profits *per se*. For this reason most are well represented at various forms of clubs and charitable endeavours, such as Lions, Rotary and Kiwanis. These clubs were not mere token social gatherings, but had become serious institutions of status and self-valorization for many members of the Trinidadian élite. Rotary commands the highest status, as representing the more established élites. It secures its prestige by its membership being granted from above, and not open to application. Thus it was said of a senior member of the White business establishment, 'Since he got into Rotary the sky's the limit.'

There is no attempt to separate off such social intercourse and the conduct of business. It was widely recognized that this could have the effects both of promoting and equally of undermining business success. An example of the former is evident in Ryan's (Ryan and Barclay 1992: 67–71) critique of the handling of the take-over of T. Geddes Grant, where he implied the strategy was to keep assets within a network of companies run by the White élite and out of the hands of the African-dominated CLICO corporation. Here there was the reasonable assumption that the White chief executives who commonly sit on the same boards of directors have every opportunity to collude on take-over measures or indeed any other aspect of business strategy that appears advantageous to those participating.

Such 'collusion' could however work the other way. Middle-ranking executives commonly complained to me about the behaviour of senior management in this regard. For example, they would suggest that they could have more cheaply produced a promotional competition in-house, or would have been better off signing up with this as opposed to that advertising agency. The factor that constantly undermined their profitability was the personal relationships between their senior executives and those of other companies, so that the tender for the competition was said to have been promised to a particular firm over drinks, or that the relationship with the wrong retail group was sustained because the directors of the two companies were close friends and would never consider breaking off this particular business contract. There is considerable overlap between boards of directors, so that, for example, the Directors of the Neal and Massy group include the chairman of the powerful drinks group Angostura, the Chief Executive of *Express* newspapers, and the chairman of the National Commercial Bank (Parris 1985). Given that the élite is often divided along ethnic lines, this leads to some very 'small worlds', where personal relations constantly interfere with simpler logics of profitability.

Another problematic area is evidence of nepotism within companies. One of the assumptions made about the failure of McEnearney Alston was that it promoted on the basis of ethnicity rather than ability. As one person put it, the company came to represent jobs for the 'White dunce-ee boys' who could not gain employment elsewhere, but then could not effectively run a company. On the other hand, the inclusion of family members in some Indian businesses was seen in a quite different light, as ensuring tight control and co-ordination between different aspects of the same business.

Although all countries have a few more flamboyant or notorious business executives who become well known, I doubt that most British or American citizens would recognize many corporate chief executives in the unlikely event that they should encounter one in a social setting. In Trinidad, by contrast, senior business figures are relatively identifiable, and associated with the acts of their companies. The knowledge held of business people by the general public is often inaccurate and out of date. It is often based on gossip, or that form of media gossip represented by the weekly newspapers, which implies that there are other reasons behind personal success than that which individuals might claim. These may be seen as an ethnic advantage, such as being White or Syrian; as having gone to a certain school; or as embodying ideas of unfair practice that might range from supposed use of Obeah (magic) to the maltreatment of employees. All of these may, of course, be the case; but in a sense the accuracy of the knowledge may be less important than is the sense that ordinary citizens might expect themselves to have such knowledge, and might thus personalize businesses with respect to the individuals who run them.

At this point many Trinidadians would be willing to tackle business executives on the policies followed by their companies. When listening to the discussion of policies within business offices I sensed that key business decisions could be often affected by a sense of potentially having to answer for them. This may be partly responsible for the degree of nationalistic emphasis in the symbolism of products that is described in subsequent chapters. The main grounds on which a member of the public might tackle an executive were their common identification with the interests of 'Trinidad'. This may also account for the unusual degree of direct sponsorship in which larger companies are involved. Members of the public faced with senior businessmen are often at least as concerned to secure favours for particular interests as they are interested in general castigation of corporate policy.

The discussion so far mainly pertains to the more senior executives of the company, in whom the company was embodied for others. Lower down the scale the relationship to the company was more complex. For many people the nature of the company is not especially relevant. Their work is merely a job, and whether it is in public service or a private corporation is irrelevant. Yelvington (1995) provides a good case of the lack of attachment to work amongst factory workers. Indeed, my supposition, based only on qualitative experience, is that compared to many countries Trinidadians tend to have less identification with their workplace, because they resent being identified with work itself. One of the most inappropriate questions one could ask at a Trinidadian party is, 'And what do you do?' The examples I will now give are therefore not typical, but relate rather to middle management and, within that category, mainly to those whose values accord with 'transcendence' (for which see Miller 1994), and who are more likely to identity with institutions. I will first consider employment in the local 'global' companies and then the global 'local' companies.

An example of close corporate identification is an employee who worked for a transnational company (I will call it 'Blue') for 23 years, and is now involved in restructuring the local company that bought over Blue, having given it a new name and reduced the retail outlets from 18 to 13. Her identification with the owner's perspective almost amounts to a form of fictive kinship: 'Even Mr Blue himself used to come to visit. They show so much appreciation for the staff and everything. In working for international you felt better, you felt proud', 'and Mr Blue's status in "Sweden". They are real experts in that they are so scientific in everything they do, all the systems.' She therefore enters into dilemmas from the company's point of view as to whether paternalism is preferable to quick profit-seeking. As she notes 'I think the grandson, right now if he does not reduce the size of the operation in every part of the world. There are problems and he is looking at the bottom line – are you making money or not? If you are not making money, start again. He is not sentimental, he is not like the father you know.'

The role of the transnational is supervisory: 'every three months you would get a visit by regional co-ordinator, and above him another guy and then Mr Blue, they check on administration, and problems and what you have identified as weak points and advise on what you should do and what you shouldn't.' In turn the Trinidadian section are viewed as child to the father. When asked why the company was not saved by its international group she replied, 'but sometimes when you have a child you can't keep on supporting them. So obviously Blue Trinidad supposed to be able to make something to happen for itself. But there are union problems – we had difficultly with benefits, heavily debt-ridden with severance.'

The attraction is also pride in the sheer scale of the company:

Even the employee feels a different sense of belonging and pride when you are working with a foreign company, you know like Blue was in 97 countries in the world and they are really massive. In Trinidad they were nothing but in places like India where they have 25,000 employees Blue is a household name . . . Now when you are working for a local company it is different. I have no doubt that given time the present management will rise to that level, but Blue International . . .

The position taken was always that of the foreign as against the local:

> Many things caused problem of Blue in Trinidad. The factories paid the highest wage in the country compared to any other manu-facturing. Started with having one of the most militant unions in the country and the pressure we came under because we were international, so you can do this and give the workers that, etc., and the additional benefits which we give are really a package so the costs were really high . . . but while they were getting all the benefits and so on, there are several other companies that have been springing up overnight.

It took prompting from me to suggest that there could be any disadvantage to working for a transnational. For example, she reluctantly admitted that the rules for ordering replacements could limit the flexibility of local responses: 'So sometimes you may have a situation where you know you need some . . . in this category since there are a couple of items that are sitting there, they are not moving. So now this category is blocked so you cannot even buy to replenish, but you know you need it, but you full up, you don't have any money, you can't buy anything, you need to do something. Sometimes they have some hard and fast rules . . . but you know.'

This employee demonstrates a clear ideology of the sup-eriority of the global over the local. She reflects the corporation's concern to transcend regional identity through a commitment to corporate identity. Edstrom and Galbraith quote the Chairman of Unilever as stating: 'The intent is to de-emphasize national cultures and to replace them with an integrating company culture' (1993: 253). The main strategy to achieve this has been through the kind of transference of managerial staff that Sklair sees as a major component of the socialization of an international capitalist class. In fact, as already noted, very few Trinidadians are co-opted into these élite cadres, and the employee extensively quoted above is more typical, in that she identified with the com-pany in terms of its transnational status *per se*.

The global 'local' companies are, of course, at least as much concerned to foster positive identification on the part of their employees. They had an equally successful means of obtaining this, through fostering internal competition using employee identification with individual subsidiaries. This arises in part through the long history and cohesive identity of some of the companies that were taken over by Neal and Massy in its expansion: for example, Cannings, which still retains its own credit union, or Grell-Taurell. This is in turn aided by competitive sports events that are held by the company, such as a cricket final between the Hi Lo head office and Cannings Dairy Products divisions. Sports are a major enterprise, with the 1991 Neal and Massy annual sports day attracting around 5,000 family members.

A similar situation exists within ANSA McAl. For example, a worker at the glass works contrasts her experience with that of workers in another subsidiary. She claims that her subsidiary is relatively egalitarian, and is not burdened by the conservative hierarchy of other divisions. She is equally concerned that, as a separate company, her firm has its international reputation for the quality of its glass and that it should win awards based around competition within the conglomerate. In both conglomerates a key issue for fostering pride in one's own subsidiary is how far the Chief Executive of that subsidiary is seen as able to stand up and fights for its corner against Naim Sabga or Sidney Knox. In general, then, credit for developments goes to the subsidiary, while blame for retrenchment is passed on to 'head office', that is, the conglomerate as a whole.

It could, of course, be argued that this is entirely in the interests of the conglomerate; and certainly it is true that internal competition between subsidiaries has probably contributed markedly to overall profits for the conglomerates. Nevertheless, my evidence (which included discussions with personnel officers in both conglomerates) suggested that this strategy has often developed as much despite, as because of, company policy. In the main, the companies saw this internal rivalry as a throw-back to earlier stages of development, and vigorously sought, without success, to replace this by positive identification with the conglomerate itself. Certainly, the mass of public sponsorship comes under the name of the conglomerate rather than the subsidiaries, so that one is increasingly seeing the 'Neal and Massy' steelband rather than the 'Grell-Taurel' parang group. This suggests that the employees are active agents in using these possibilities of identification, rather than merely following company strategy.

Neal and Massy followed many strategies used by companies

to create positive internal identification. For example, there are discounts at conglomerate companies, a fact of some significance for a group that owns the main supermarket chain. There is also medical insurance, an investment plan, a counselling pro-gramme, a credit union, and funds available to help employees establish their own businesses. Indeed, by international standards, and certainly with respect to the usual role of big business in recently industrializing countries, this company does stand out as relatively (but only relatively) benign with respect to its policy for the workforce. This is not, however, the perception of the workforce, who do not on the whole consider the company in a positive light, preferring to dwell on more negative aspects such as increasing retrenchment (firing). This is true even when it is compared with Trinidadian companies that have much harsher employee conditions.

These tensions between identification at a conglomerate as against at a subsidiary level are evident in the development of intra-company publicity and activities. Neal and Massy produces an internal magazine, *Nealco News*, six times a year, which highlights the degree of activity aimed at internal identification. Typically this might include reports on training programmes for executives, or seminars for learning to use new equipment; new export developments; reviews of new products; prize-giving for long service or high sales; new appointments; community events, such as a fashion show; sponsorship, such as for local craft; a philanthropic endeavour or arts groups, such as steel bands; and an advice column, such as 'Managing Mid-Life Crisis'. ANSA McAl also produces a journal for employees, called *Focus*, with a similar range of concerns. The local 'global' companies may also have company magazines, but these are on a smaller scale than those of the conglomerates.

The activities of these company journals are complemented by the two daily newspapers. According to journalists in 1992, the *Guardian*, in particular, had, under its ANSA McAl control, embarked upon a period of clear opposition, and even aggres-sion, against the Neal and Massy Group of companies. Business gossip suggested both that there was a formal policy not to accept advertising associated with that company. My own analy-sis of adverts appearing in the *Guardian* during the end of 1992 suggested that this might well have been the case. Also, in the sample of the 74 adverts over five days that took a quarter page or more, 25 were for companies within ANSA McAl. The *Guardian* also provides an obvious source for the dissemination of company news. Thus the *Sunday Guardian* of 13 December 1992 reproduced in full Anthony Sabga's speech at a company awards function. The public (and the weekly newspapers) generally saw the daily newspapers as pawns of the conglomerates.

Turning from the employees to the general public, the latter's knowledge of the companies themselves and their relationship to their products is often weak. Perhaps not surprisingly, few consumers store information about companies as such; rather they follow the kind of news items that personalize or entertain. Thus where there has been a scandal or a scam, the public shows relatively high knowledge about a company. Where there has been little of newsworthy interest, the company may be almost entirely unknown except through its brands. Despite the high commercial profile of Chaguanas few people in my surveys had an accurate image of the main conglomerates, unless they had worked in a related company (which many had). When asked which companies were owned by Neal and Massy, some noted Hi Lo and their various car subsidiaries. Rather more noted their near-monopoly over chickens, but surprisingly few recognized their ownership of Cannings as a whole. A typical response would be to assert that they own many, if not most, of the companies in Trinidad, but that while 'I think I know a good few, right now I can't name any of them.' Even less is known of the precise details of ANSA McAl. In a sense the relevant information for the public is merely the scale and power of these enterprises, while the precise details of who owns what are of less importance, especially given that take-overs can change these relationships every few years, with few perceptible consequences for the consumer.

Neal and Massy has made considerable efforts to secure a positive image amongst the general public. Discussions suggest that some of its policies in this regard have failed, but others have succeeded. On the whole its overall image is negative. 'Mean and Nasty' is just one of a wide range of alternative names given to the company. Although Sidney Knox is in no sense the owner of the company, unlike Sabga, people could less imagine Neal and Massy without him than ANSA McAl without Sabga. As a key member of the 'French Creole' élite, he is considered to be in cahoots with the chairmen of other big Trinidadian companies.

The White dominance that he represents is still a major cause for complaint amongst the majority populations of Trinidad, and may account in some measure for the unpopularity of the firm as a whole.

Conclusion

Although this volume is concerned with capitalism, I have particularly focused upon the terms 'local' and 'global' in my analysis of the major firms that supply grocery products. This is because these terms seem to be in danger of becoming just as glib generalities as the term capitalism itself. In this chapter it has been shown that the concepts of the local and the global cannot easily be applied to the ethnography of the major companies in Trinidad. The transnationals that would most easily be identified as global may have existed in Trinidad for longer, with local personnel, answerable to local judgement, than some Trinidadian companies. On the one hand, they may lead to an identification with an outside world that extracts the most able executives and leads to a sense of loyalty that denigrates mere localism as inferior quality. On the other hand, tensions within the company may lead the local branch to become amongst the most important agents in the fostering of nationalistic pride. Equally, local Trinidadian companies have themselves developed as transnationals, with increasingly ambiguous attitudes to what might be called the local.

In considering the general articulation between consumers and business much of this information, while essential as a background to understanding capitalism in Trinidad, does not relate directly to issues of concern to the consumer. As noted above, consumers in general do not reflect much upon the internal dynamics of companies, and are much more interested in them when they encounter them as employees. There is, however, another level at which the identity of corporations and those of the consumers do become closely interwoven, and this is at the level at which the products of the corporation become manifested for the consumer – the level of brands. For this reason the next chapter will begin the task of examining the relationship between the consumer and the producer through an ethnography of brands.

4

An Ethnography of Brands: The Trinidadian Sweet Drink Industry

The intention of this chapter is to provide a case study of one particular industry. The emphasis will be on carbonated beverages as an example of the kind of branded commodity for which one can study the links between the interests of the producers and their conceptualization of the consumers (for comparative work see Clairmonte and Cavanagh 1988; Tollison *et al.* 1986). It thereby provides a specific case study of what Fine and Leopold (1993) call 'systems of provision'. Obviously, this will touch upon issues of advertising and consumption, which will be addressed in this chapter as they relate to this particular product area. More general treatment of these topics is to be found in subsequent chapters.

The main aim of the present chapter is to provide a 'feel' for an industry at work inasmuch as this could be encountered through ethnographic fieldwork. Fieldwork in this context meant rather more formal interviews with executives than might have been wished for, but also a good deal of time simply accompanying executives in their activities: driving with them around the island as they check up on their distributors; listening in to their conversations with advertising companies and others; hanging around enough to be forgotten about as the office continues to deal with the relentless demand for responses to events as they crop up within a fast-moving, highly competitive commercial context. Ethnography also means the reportage of such events within an analytical framework that betrays my specific reasons for embarking upon such an inquiry: for example, a concern to know how far profitability can be isolated as a causative factor for action as against the various competing concerns that are brought to bear on decision-making. In particular, I was concerned with the relationship between consumers, actual and imagined, and the various forces that produce products and images.

The term 'sweet drink' is used by most Trinidadians for carbonated beverages, though it is increasingly being replaced by the international term soft drink (the two terms are used synonymously in this chapter). As will be shown below, this is not considered (as might have been expected) a luxury or expendable item of consumption. Instead, it is understood by most Trinidadians as a core necessity, constituting the ordinary drink of the mass population. It exists within a wider field of beverages, including milk drinks and fruit juices, though its most important competitor might well be the home-made drinks made from liquidized fruits or artificial drink crystals. For some sweet drinks there is also an important relationship to alcoholic drinks, for which they are considered mixers. The concept of 'rum and coke' is the single most important linkage of this kind, though there are other carbonated beverages, such as soda water, which, unlike Coke, are primarily purchased as 'mixers'.

In order to understand the industry the core 'players' must first be introduced. It had been my intention to use code names for the companies, since I promised during interviews that I would preserve anonymity. I find it impossible to keep this promise, inasmuch as there are so few companies that any description would immediately tell most Trinidadians which company I am referring to. I would therefore wish to make very clear the fact that much of my evidence is based on interview material, most often with one company talking about its rivals. It is important that many of the negative comments made should be understood in terms of this source of information, and I *cannot attest* to the truth of the statements made. The material should therefore be taken as a flow of claims and counter-claims, not as a description of actual events. It is typical of the kind of gossip and denigration that occurs between companies in direct competition. I would, however, claim that, since I conducted at least some interviews with all the companies concerned, I do not see my material as biased in favour of any particular company. I also preserve anonymity for some of the criticisms made where I feel that the information would not in anyway have revealed who is being discussed. I have, however, kept throughout this chapter to what I took to be the most important component of my assurance of anonymity, which is never to reveal who has been the source of my information, or to provide information that would allow this to be detected.

The Sweet Drink Companies

Solo

Solo Beverages is in many respects the core provider of sweet drinks. Many people suggested that it is the brand against which other brands would be judged. This is because it is the only brand that evokes a strong element of nostalgic identification in the minds of a great many Trinidadians, who constantly refer to the length of time it has been operating in Trinidad. This is perhaps because it stood relatively early on for the principle of local Trinidadian production success against imported or colonial goods. Ramsaran (1993) provides a short biography of the founder, Joseph Charles, who started the business in the 1930s, and who, after working his shift in a bakery, produced 1 or 2 cases a day, using old beer bottles and syrup boiled up by his wife (p. 94).

The Solo firm was founded in 1941, replaced this hand production with semi-automation in 1944, and achieved full automation in 1950, which the owner claimed was a first in the Caribbean. The factory moved to its current site on the East–West highway in 1959, and now employs 120 workers. It is owned by an East Indian family, who have other production interests such as in chocolate and sweets, but are best known for this particular brand. Its origins at the lower end of the market are evident, in that it is not recorded in the *Trinidad Year Book* until 1952, and does not seem to have had much advertising until the 1970s.

A typical description of the firm is given by one of its main rivals:

> Solo has a niche, the Solo drinker has drunk Solo from childhood, he is not about to change. He will not buy any other product unless Solo is not available. His quality is poor, he has troubles with his production side, distribution side, capacity side. What Solo does have going for him is he buys quality concentrate, but his process . . . he has not spent money on it for years, when he does, it is to patch it up rather than fix the problem. In terms of tests we do in the lab, his

yeast content is astronomical . . . maybe that's why he tastes so good. His product is a good product. His Apple J is the finest drink in the market.

These sentiments are common. Solo is also usually credited with being constantly one of the most innovative producers in Trinidad. The Apple J referred to in the quotation is generally seen as a fine example of a sweet drink, with real fruit juice included and added vitamin C, and without artificial flavours or preservatives. It had won several international prizes. Other examples are innovation in canning, where the company imported the first machines to produce 600 cans per minute, and in the introduction of diet range drinks. The firm has a good reputation within the business community for paying on time and general business probity. It has only one franchise, for a cola marketed as R.C. Cola.

I will use this company to give an example of the kind of range of products that are found in the island:

The full Sola range in 1993

Product	Return	16oz	1 litre	Can	10oz glass	10oz plastic
Own Brand						
Banana	+	+	+	+	+	+
Grape	+	+	+	+	+	+
Kola Champagne	+	+	+	+	+	+
Orange	+	+	+	+	+	+
Pear	–	–	–	+	+	–
Pineapple	+	+	+	–	–	–
Sorrel	–	–	–	–	+	+
Diet Orange	–	–	–	–	+	+
Diet Kola Champagne	–	–	–	–	+	+
Diet Cola	–	–	–	–	+	+
Diet Bentley	–	–	–	–	+	+

Product	Return	16oz	1 litre	Can	10oz glass	10oz plastic
Cream Soda	+	+	+	+	+	+
Club Soda	–	–	–	+	+	+
Bentley Lime	–	+	+	+	+	+
Apple J	–	–	–	+	+	–
Ginger Ale	–	–	+	+	+	+
Ginger Beer	+	+	+	+	+	+
Upper 10 (Lemon–Lime)	–	–	–	–	+	+
Made under Licence						
R C Cola	+	+	+	–	+	+

+ = Made in that size
– = Not made in that size

They also produce a tonic especially for flights by the national airline BWIA. According to Ramsaran (1993) Kola Champagne and Banana were the original flavours from the 1930s, while grape, cream soda and orange were added in the 1950s.

Cannings and Coke

The firm of Cannings is one of the oldest-established grocery firms in Trinidad. Associated with a white family, it was established in 1912 with a grocery and a bottling works. According to the *Red Book of the West Indies* (Macmillan 1922: 188) 'His establishment became the leading place in Port of Spain for groceries, provisions, wines and spirits. It gives employment to about one hundred and ten persons. . . . An example of the firm's progressive policy in all they undertake is also found in the electrical machinery equipment of their contiguous aerated water factory, where all kinds of delicious non-alcoholic beverages are made from carefully purified waters . . . the turnover of the business is about one million dollars per annum.' Aerated beverages were quite common, with the *Year Book* for 1930 listing 15 factories. The franchise for Coca-Cola was obtained in 1939, and this led to a consolidation of the firm's own soft drink division in the following year. The connection with groceries is maintained today, in that Cannings also owns Hi-Lo, the largest and most prestigious supermarket chain in the country. The firm attracted two investors from the United States, though this investment was withdrawn when the firm was taken over by the Neal and Massy group in 1975, at which point it lost its autonomy. But in the public mind its products are still as much associated with the name Cannings as with Neal and Massy. It may be noted that the firm is thus as old as if not older than Solo. Despite this, it is rarely discussed by consumers with the same sense of nostalgia and longevity as is Solo, and this is therefore not a salient connotation of its products.

Instead, Cannings and Coke between them represent a particular form of authority and respectability in the market. Coke has much the same connotations here as in the international market, as a brand leader for American culture. It is also assumed to represent international standards and quality, to which Trinidadians will often compare their own products unfavourably. But the attitude is clearly ambivalent, since there is also pride and nationalism associated with the local product. Cannings is itself an entirely local firm, as is Neal and Massy; but Cannings, in particular, is associated with the legacy of white élites and white colonial rule. This is notwithstanding that this is a white family that has been in Trinidad for a considerable period, and that (as with many of these commercial families) would see itself as much an integral part of West Indian cultural life as any other group.

As such, Cannings, with its association with Coke, is able to stand for high-quality product and purity, but is rarely viewed with particular affection, and is not often singled out for its flavours or positive qualities. Since, however, there are no negative associations either, it is treated as simply one of the main contenders, as a high-quality key player in the general sweet drink market, and one that is destined always to have a significant part of the market. Coke on the other hand is easily the dominant cola product. While in some countries the phrase 'rum and Coke' may signify any cola drink's being used as a mixer, in Trinidad at present it is indeed Coke that easily dominates the rum-mixer market. Given the centrality of rum to drinking in Trinidad, this ensures an immense role for this drink, quite apart from its use in its own right. It is clearly the best-selling single sweet drink in Trinidad.

The sweet drink section is reported in the 1991 Neal and Massy *Annual Report* to employ 317 staff and have a revenue of TT$77 million. It is usually twinned with the dairy division, which produces ice-cream and milk drinks, and there are associated food products, such as Arawak chickens. The Canning range would be similar to that of Solo. They have a mango and a green drink in addition. They have a 2-litre range, but not a 1-litre range, and probably slightly more emphasis on returnable bottles. Associated with Coke are also Diet Coke and Sprite (a lemon–lime drink) and Diet Sprite. Coke expanded largely in order to supply the American forces stationed in Trinidad during the Second World War. It was the associated boom time that probably also stimulated the development of Solo and Cannings as modern industries. Cannings also has associations with other international products. It is the local producer of Lucozade, which is a very minor brand. At times they have been the distributor for Schweppes. There is also a tie-up with Canada Dry, which during the period of fieldwork had an enormously successful launch.

S. M. Jaleel

This firm claims in its publicity to have been founded in 1924. In the early days it was mainly associated with a 'red' sweet drink (Red Spot) in the area of San Fernando, the second biggest town in Trinidad. The family went through a difficult patch, as much concerned with its political involvements as with its commercial concerns. The problem in part rested on the fact that, being an Indian family and based in the South of the country, which is dominated by the Indian population, there was a clear ethnic connotation to the drink itself. This particular family belonged to the Muslim population, which as a minority within the Indian population sometimes, as in this case, tended to side on occasion with the 'Black'-dominated PNM government against the local DLP 'Indian'-dominated opposition (see Clarke 1986 for the local politics of San Fernando).

The redevelopment of the company by the founder's grandson Dr Aleem Mohammed from 1980 was seen by some as an attempt to rescue the family reputation through commercial success. Certainly, this is regarded by all as the most aggressive company in the sweet drink market today. This includes a negative and a positive component. On the negative side, the company is often accused of exploiting its workforce beyond the hours they are recruited to work, and it is also said to delay payment and to go back on promises made in informal agreements with other companies as to price-fixing and other such measures. Typical would be a story about how it collected up non-returnable bottles and refilled them, which led to a large number of bottles breaking. The matter had to be investigated and put right by the bottle supplier, Carib Glass, which had guaranteed to pay back money on any of its bottles which broke (on the assumption that these were returnable bottles). I should note that these are only examples of many stories collected, and I cannot vouch for their veracity. It is likely that as an aggressive competitor Jaleel attracts negative stories.

On the positive side, the firm is seen as highly dynamic in its technical division. One quote suggested an investment of TT$18 million. It was a pioneer in establishing high-tech factories for plastic bottle production, and is the company most committed to plastic containers. It is also a pioneer of the larger plastic bottles since 1984, to the extent that the litre-size bottle is generally known by consumers as the 'Jaliter' and asked for by this name even when it is another company's product that is meant. Less well-known to the public is that it was a pioneer in mass distribution of its product. By focusing on small vans (approximately 3 tons) it was able to reach areas that the larger trucks (approximately 5 tons) had difficulty with. It also established warehouses in places such as Tobago that helped provide quick distribution far from its source. It has attempted to draw public attention to its particular availability through a campaign termed 'Zero in on a Cole Cold.' Overall there is probably a wide gulf between the public perception of this as a low-tech Southern 'Indian' company and the reality of its being a very high-tech national and international brand.

Its own flavour range has been marketed under the title Cole Cold since 1981 (and to a lesser extent an export-orientated label of Caribbean Cool, made with 10 per cent fruit juice). In addition it has various franchise arrangements with companies such as Schweppes, Seven-Up and a cola called Dixi Cola. Such arrangements are flexible, and Trinidadian companies would have a hard time keeping up with the rapid changes in the ownership of such brands in the international merger market (Clairmonte and Cavanagh 1988). Although the concentrate for its own products is not viewed by its rivals as of particularly good quality or taste, the company is seen as a modern efficient producer, and in business circles its aggression is viewed with ambivalence, since profitability is as much a virtue as trustworthiness. It is also one of the firms with a strong commitment to export. The range would echo those of the previous two, though with some differences in their flavours and a stronger emphasis on plastics. They produce both 1- and 2-litre containers, but did not have a returnable range in 1993.

Pepsi

The situation of Pepsi Cola is rather a strange one. On the one hand, it had historically been a rival for Coke in the Trinidadian market after it was first launched by a firm made up of people who had previously been part of the Cannings/Coke production team. In the late 1980s and early 1990s it still would have seemed a major player in the market if one judged by the amount of advertising, in that it often outspent Coca-Cola on television and on other media. Despite this, it was actually quite hard to find it in the shops, and, apart from areas where it was tied into vending machines through fast-food outlets, it was in no sense a match for Coca-Cola. Partly this was because it had failed to team up with an established Trinidadian firm that could match the scale and expertise of Cannings.

The local producers of Pepsi, a firm called Bottlers, have been through several strategies to revive their place in the market. They also associated themselves with other franchise arrangements, as for a drink called 'U.S.A. Pop', which was in effect a flavour range, including typical local items such as Sorrel and Kola Champagne. The situation seemed about to change in 1990. First Bottlers was acquired by Amar, which was trying to follow Neal and Massy and ANSA McAl in moving away from its foundation in the car industry into diversification as the third major Trinidadian transnational. This seemed more likely to come to fruition with a tie-up arrangement with S. M. Jaleel through which the product would be distributed by that company. Jaleel had an enviable distribution system and good facilities for blowing plastic containers. But rumours suggest that the two companies soon accused each other of taking advantage, and the partnership broke up. Another rumour suggested that Amar had persuaded Pepsi to spend a considerable quantity of money (around TT$8 million) on advertising in Trinidad, which seemed to relate to a situation found in Latin America where Pepsi was attempting in effect to buy markets dominated by Coke. In this case, however, the local firms were unable to match any new demand that would result. Indeed, rumours suggested that Amar was trying to use Pepsi to bail it out of its own financial difficulties.

L. J. Williams

This firm is seen by outsiders as an old established Chinese trading company (though local managers defined themselves as White), which would normally have been involved largely in importing goods, but had moved to some degree into local production partly under the prompting of the negative list, which prevented the import of finished drinks but allowed concentrate to be imported. This was a problem for a firm that was associated with one of the best-established imported sweet drinks – Peardrax from Britain. Just as this once well-established drink was dying out in Britain, the Trinidadian firm found a highly profitable niche through the local production of Peardrax, making it, for a while, the world's largest market for this drink. The profitability arose from the fact that it was able to retain the relatively high price of what had been seen as a 'premium' sweet drink by the consumer, even though its costs were much lower once it was producing the drink within Trinidad.

In addition, the firm launched in 1984 an American range called 'White Rock', using taller but narrower cans than had previously been available, and this has become established as one of the flavour ranges of drinks now available, though not in as large a quantity as the previously established flavour ranges. The White Rock brand also has some mixers, such as club soda, that were being promoted at the time. The company also fills Ribena for another import–export company, Hands Arnold.

Minor Players

Some sweet drink products come and go in a relatively short time, and this includes both local and foreign products. A small bottling plant was established in Chaguanas in 1979, but was in receivership during the fieldwork period of 1988. It had produced very low-cost and low-quality drinks with names like 'Bubble up'. These were still an important part of the market in, for example, the squatting area at the fringes of the town that was one of my fieldwork sites. There were also various foreign products such as Dr. Pepper that did not last long in the local market.

A 1987 drinks survey by a marketing company produced the following figures for who had drunk each product over the last month: Coca-Cola 62%; Solo 40%; Cole Cold 31%; Cannings 31%; Diet Coke 23%; Pepsi 23%; Diet Rite 14%; Dixi Cola 11%; Pear D 10%; Cannings diet 10%; Sprite 9%; Apple J 9%; R C Cola 7%; Diet Cole Cold 6%; Seven-Up 7%; White Rock 5%. Brand share of the market is probably around half these figures, at around 35% Coke, 20% Solo and around 10% each for Cole Cold and Cannings.

The Financial Base

Fieldwork took place when recession was well under way, and this has only deepened during the subsequent five years. The investments in new machinery made by some companies during the latter part of the oil boom were no longer viable, and production lines that could work at two shifts a day had been reduced to a single shift, if that. In 1988 everyone was hoping for sales to peak during the long hot season, but this did not happen. Sales had already gone down an average of 10 per cent the year before. Through the 1980s at least recession could be set against oil-boom levels, which meant that the decline remained relative. As one executive noted, 'they all complain that they can't make profits, but all wear Rolex watches and drive Mercedes Benz'. This would be true even of the top managerial staff of the conglomerates. The wealth of private capitalists is hard to gauge, since most Trinidadians assume that a large proportion of private profits is banked abroad. Even in recession losses can be fed down to the work force in the form of redundancies and poorer conditions without necessarily having much effect on the personal fortunes of the capitalist class.

Overall the industry was probably worth around TT$200 million in annual revenue, with the Cannings/Coke combination as the largest group, accounting for around a third of the total. The cost to the consumer is around a dollar per bottle. An exception would be a drink such as Peardrax, which would cost at least 2 dollars. Trinidadians were therefore drinking an average of around 170 bottles a year. The mark-up to retailers would be from 25 per cent up to 45 per cent. Company costs, apart form raw materials, machinery and labour, also include the costs of promotion, increasing bank charges on loans taken for investment in new technologies, and a government 20 per cent purchase tax.

All the industry executives tended to claim in discussion that this was one of the most competitive areas of local capitalism. The reasons for this may not be straightforward, however. Even a highly prestigious international company of accountants gave me what I would regard as a quite spurious explanation for what was going on. They suggested that this competition was due to the relatively low inputs required: 'In soft drinks all you need is a bottling plant, a bag of sugar and water and in you go.' In fact this is much too simple, as can be seen from the fact that many of the West Indian islands have few or no local producers (for an economist's view on problems of entry into this sector see Tollison, *et al.* 1986: 68–95). As will be shown, there are many other inputs, such as distribution and advertising, which make for a much more difficult market. Many small scale producers have attempted to break into the market, as in the Chaguanas example, but seem to have completely failed. The key players are large-scale and long-term, with in most cases high technological investments.

The degree of competition is reduced only by the degree to which the major players can come together and agree mutually supportive policies such as price-fixing. This practice has certainly existed, and is defended by the producers in terms of their relationship to retailers:

> The industry meets from time to time, generally the purpose of the meeting is to minimize price cutting. Now it is a highly competitive industry and a dealer might switch his business for a dollar a case,

which is 4c on a bottle, and the dealer will carry a very strong influence, and very often play one against the other. Very often they say
they get a 10 per cent discount when they don't, but they break the
competitor down. When they get it they go to the next one and that
is the way they effectively bring the prices down. The industry
needs to try and eliminate being taken for a ride by the trade.

There are occasional prosecutions for price-fixing in the United
States, but this tends to be at the level of bottlers rather than
product manufacturers (Tollison *et al.* 1986: 103).

When this fails then prices decline across the trade, which has
tended to be the case in recent years. 'In the sweet drink market
we are getting half the price that Barbados is getting. They sell
soft drinks for about 36 dollars; we are getting 26 dollars a case.
There are only three over there so they can get together. Ten,
fifteen years ago we had a cartel. We sat down and made a
decision and stuck to it.' Today competition tends to come back
in the form of promotions offered to retailers, such as a free case
for every ten. This is then followed by the other players. The
highly competitive environment had the positive consequence
for local firms that they were probably a good deal less worried
by the forthcoming trade liberalization than many other producers: 'Even without the duties, freight rates would be too
exorbitant and I am sure no one could compete with our pricing.'

Overall the situation in Trinidad seems to reflect that of the
United States. In the US, despite the enormous power of the two
main colas, the industry has been intensely competitive, leading
to a general reduction in real prices between 1965 and 1986. This
has occurred together with an enormous increase in consumption,
from 2.1 billion gallons in 1960 to 12.4 billion gallons in 1988. Soft
drinks were also the most heavily promoted item in the supermarkets (Tollison *et al.* 1986). I do not have as exact figures for
Trinidad, but I suspect all of these three trends would also apply
there.

Local and Global Factors

When I started working on this industry I had expected that it
would typify the problem of a country largely reliant upon
imported goods and expectations as against local production and

needs. I had anticipated that sweet drinks would stand as a symbol for international domination and actually contribute to the country's indebtedness. It was soon evident, however, that this industry sees itself from the opposite perspective, as an important contributor to the country's balance of payments and as batting as it were for the home side. Furthermore, this perception is often shared by the general public.

This may not be an unreasonable claim. Although concentrate is imported, this may be the only part of the product that is not in some sense local. Flavourings may be obtained from abroad: for example, according to a newspaper article one Canadian company wholly owned by La Roche Switzerland makes the flavour for Cannings's Big Red, Bentley and King Orange, the ginger in Shandy Carib and the vanilla in Supligen (*Express* 23/12/90). Flavours may also be obtained locally, though this is admittedly only because a Trinidadian company is importing them for local distribution. On the other hand the CO_2 is locally produced as a by-product of one of the country's heavy industrial plants. The glass bottles are almost entirely produced by Carib Glass, which is part of the ANSA McAl group of companies. Carib Glass uses local silica sand, though limestone is imported from Guyana and potash and some specialist chemicals from the United States. It also produces the labels for its own glass products. It is a major producer of glass bottles, with more than 30 bottle lines at any one time. The ANSA McAl *Annual Report* for 1991 describes it as having 494 employees and 5 lines producing containers. Around 40 per cent of its production goes to the soft-drink market. Figures from employees suggest that the company earns between a quarter of a million dollars from a small producer to one and a half million dollars each month from one of the largest producers of sweet drinks. The company was also aiming for exports to the USA worth $US four million in 1988. Cans are mainly produced locally under franchise from Metal Box UK, using imported plate. Plastic is imported, but blown into bottles locally. Machinery may be imported or locally produced: for example, a newspaper report commented on the success of 'Metal Industries Company Ltd in producing a fast response to Solo's decision to produce a 16oz size. The mould was delivered within a month and after months of 24 hour use was still working well' (*Express* 21/12/92). The complexity involved in trying to decide whether sugar is local or imported was described in the last chapter.

As well as mainly using local materials, the Trinidadian sweet drink companies almost all have an export section of 5 per cent or more, which they attempt to expand. Most wanted ideally to take this up to 20 per cent or more. Most cola products are also produced in other West Indian Islands, but products such as Solo and Cole Cold are found in those islands, such as Grenada, that seem to be increasingly dominated by Trinidadian products. Most sales are within Caricom, but Solo, for example, has small niche markets with expatriate Trinidadian communities in Toronto, New York, Miami and London. These may be small-scale: for example, they claim a 40-foot container a month to the UK. Even where the finished product is not exported, components may be, as in the case of Carib Glass, which has a contract to manufacture bottles for Pepsi in Florida compared to which the local Pepsi market is relatively small. As a result, it is probably fair to say that the sweet drink industry is a net asset for the Trinidadian balance of payments.

From the point of view of the companies the recession and the restrictions on foreign currency in 1989 were making them consider the possibility of further local substitution for imported elements. It was hoped that the supply of local fruit juice, which had been devastated by the oil boom, would recover to levels where it could replace Florida as the main supplier of orange juice. This was also the incentive to consider local flavours such as soursop, passion fruit and mauby. The same logic would apply to a brand. For example, given Cannings's relationship to Coke, it came under pressure (on occasion perhaps considerable pressure) to take on Fanta. The fact that it has not done so suggests that it feels its own orange drink is sufficiently strong, and that the increase in sales generated by the international label would not equal the loss of foreign exchange and margins that would result from the shift from its own product. Obviously this acts against the interests of Coca-Cola, and it is an example of the way in which the link between local and global firm can provide some conflicts of interest in terms of the profitability of each. In general, companies made much better profits from the flavours than from colas, since they were selling both at the same price, but the premium cola brands obviously charged far more for their concentrate.

In general, there is surprisingly little sense of local versus international competition in the sweet drink trade. This is partly due to soft drinks' being included on the negative list. This is a government restriction on the importation of any product that is already manufactured in Trinidad and that the government seeks to protect. These regulations were largely destroyed by the trade liberalization enforced through IMF agreements in the 1990s. The difference between a local company that imports its concentrate and a foreign company whose product is bottled in Trinidad may be not very significant, particularly when franchises and other arrangements complicate this distinction.

A tie-up in one country may have little bearing on what is happening next door, even when it is largely Trinidadian companies that are involved. Grenada, for example, one of the nearest neighbours, presents a quite different scenario, although it has in common a primary rivalry between the two Trinidadian conglomerates. In Grenada Pepsi and Seven-Up are both linked to a brewery owned by ANSA McAl. Rival firms prefer to be attached to different local companies, but there is a general feeling that the island is too small for more than one bottling company at present, so they have little choice but to share facilities. The main groceries, by contrast, are now owned by Neal and Massy, since they belonged to the Geddes Grant group, which had been brought up by the Trinidadian firm. Although they certainly stocked a considerable quantity of Cannings drinks, in practice their rivals Solo and Cole Cold were also easily available. This is partly because actual trade between the two islands is heavily influenced by 'traffickers', that is, independent boats who quickly respond to any sense of shortages, and are less subject to import controls than formal trade. The need for traffickers was occasioned by the degree of import control practised by most Caribbean islands in the 1980s. At that time only Jamaica had a free market in sweet drinks, while Barbados only let in about 4 containers a month.

In most cases the local drinks company does not pay royalties or even a percentage to the foreign firm. The most common relationship is one where a local firm is given exclusive rights to purchase the concentrate and to market the product. The interest of the foreign company is then in the local firm's being as successful as possible, since they can then sell greater quantities of concentrate. In effect, the foreign firm may put the 'royalties' into the price of the concentrate, which can also in effect then represent a percentage on the sale price of the drink locally.

Retaining a notion of merely selling concentrate often has the beneficial result as far as both companies are concerned of simplifying the tax implications of this transaction *vis-à-vis* the local country's excises and tax laws.

Even with the major cola companies there can be a considerable degree of autonomy. Theoretically, the local company may be able largely to ignore the international marketing and advertising schemes used by the cola company and develop its own. In practice, this does not happen, largely because no local company can afford to produce the kind of material and expertise that a major cola firm can develop. Although several of the companies discussed their desire for still greater local autonomy, in general this industry reflects the point made in Chapter 3 that there is already a surprising amount of relative autonomy for local franchise holders. For one major transnational drink, the representative of the parent firm was not expected to visit more than once a quarter from Miami. Marketing, pricing and other plans were largely left to the Trinidadian firm. Promotional costs would be shared. Typically, the parent company would match whatever spending the local company chose to commit to the product. In some cases this lack of involvement caused a problem. A cola company that has only one division for all the non-USA regions tended to be dominated by its European section. As a result, Trinidad was largely being supplied with European-orientated promotional materials that were seen locally as unsuitable.

Competition between companies may focus upon the relative advantages of exploiting one's local or foreign connotation. On the one hand, brands such as Coke and Seven-Up can deliver advertising campaigns made on global budgets of a vastly sophisticated variety. Yet, as will be shown in Chapters 5 and 6, these may fail both against low-budget adverts with particular local appeal and, as in the Canada Dry case (see below), a local campaign that can rival international production values. There is some advantage in promoting international brands, since half the costs will often be borne by the parent company. On the other hand, a local firm may have greater flexibility. This point was made by Solo with respect to Canada Dry. They noted that Canada Dry have to retain their international brand image, while a local producer can make a Ginger Ale that is promoted as relatively 'hot and spicy', which they argue is closer to Trinidadian tastes.

The lack of flexibility of the foreign product may have a bearing when it acts as a brake on local autonomy. One particular franchise was argued to have failed on these grounds. In this case the range was sold as mixers, in particular for gin. This market collapsed during the oil boom, when Trinidadians went *en masse* for premium label scotch whisky, and gin sales fell to a fifth of their pre-oil-boom sales. The local firm could see the possibility of a rapid shift in image; but this demanded a larger range. The parent firm failed to deliver what the local firm required, and as a result sales kept declining, leading to the end of this partnership. At this point another local firm took over the link, but also failed in its bid for local promotion, and now mainly exports this brand to other islands.

Local executives not surprisingly try to emphasize in conversation the superiority of their local knowledge. A typical story (though relating to alcohol) was how they advised against the importation of half-bottles of whisky, but were overruled by the parent company. Sensitivity to local conditions meant that a Trinidadian 'would have known' that since whisky is always given as a luxury item, to give a half-bottle would be to suggest that one could not afford to give a whole bottle. The story concludes with the moral that the stuff that was brought in could not be sold.

Finally, the local firm may be frustrated over those domains where control is retained by the parent company. 'You do feel the hand of [the named corporation] as it were, and the lawyers, which pisses me off. But I am most concerned about the creative material.' I attended one meeting in which much time was spent poring over manuals to find ways of shifting the logo in a manner that would not be rejected by the parent company.

Companies and the Trinidadian State

The 1989 crisis over foreign exchange was a good opportunity to investigate the actual as against the often supposed nature of the relationship between companies and the State. The company executives constantly noted that the effect of this crisis was extremely unfair. The government, which was worried about the leaching of its foreign currency as the recession appeared ever deeper, placed a blanket restriction on the use of foreign exchange. What the companies objected to was that this policy in some cases appeared misdirected, since it stopped companies earning more foreign exchange than they would have spent. Thus Jaleel suffered, since it had a large investment in plastic bottle production and could not bring in the resins. Indeed, rumour had it that they planned to move to Antigua and use the freedom of Caricom to import their product back to Trinidad.

In the national press and in general conversation it was usually assumed that the state was intimately involved with particular companies whose interests it favoured, for example, the relationship noted in the previous chapter between the NAR and Neal and Massy. In fact I was present at quite a number of meetings with subsidiaries of that conglomerate during this period and it was quite clear that far from being favoured the subsidiaries were in as much despair as any other company with regard to their lack of foreign currency. Overall the impression was that the government had produced a very simple guillotine on supplies with often negative consequences. Companies that used their purchases of imported materials for largely export-led manufactures and thus were net earners of foreign exchange, were hit just as hard as companies which were mainly importers. Indeed at one point Coca-Cola threatened that it was 'considering reducing its Trinidad and Tobago operations by 30 per cent because of foreign exchange problems' (*Express* 13/10/88).

Companies certainly employ the State as a kind of 'judge' in their competitive rivalries. Thus each one has an interest in pointing out to the authorities any illegal promotion attempted by its rivals. Most common is recourse to the State to protect an image from being copied. For example, Solo, having secured the considerable reputation of its Apple J brand, was concerned that its competitors would copy it. Similarly L. J. Williams sought government backing to ban a rival company that launched a Pear D brand in a purple container with a fruit image that was in clear emulation of its premium Peardrax brand.

The State is not necessarily an independent arbiter. Its potential for bias was particularly evident in the development of diet sweet drinks. According to one company, the government granted permission for them to import the machinery to manufacture diet drinks, but then a few days before the launch passed new legislation to ban it, arguing that this was necessary to protect the local sugar industry. The company suggested that this move was connected with the alignment of the firm with the political opposition, together with lobbying by the franchise holders for a cola company. A journalist working on the case at that time suggested that the reasons were racist rather than political, since the owner of the company was East Indian. Some rival companies supported this version of events; others referred to older legislation directed against all companies equally. A similar accusation was made to me about the government's allowing of the importation of cans for a company that was associated with the government, while forbidding it for a company associated with the opposition.

One of the key episodes in the developing relation between the State and the industry was the decision to put sweet drinks under price control. This meant that retailers would be fined if they charged anything above the nationally published price for these goods. To be included the product had to be perceived as a 'basic' item of consumption rather than a luxury. Various arguments were said to have been used in the discussions. For example, it was said that sweet drinks were based on clean purified water, while tap water would have to be boiled. It was also argued that sweet drinks provided an important supply of sugar for active schoolchildren, and thus that schools were promoting their availability on grounds of health. Both arguments are almost entirely spurious.

The industry as a whole was opposed to price control, and provided quite a different explanation. They saw it as a political gambit by Eric Williams to gain popularity at a time of political weakness prior to the oil boom. The assumption was that politicians were trying to get the industry to subsidize what was seen as 'the poor man's drink'. As it was told by the industry:

> We were making a small margin but then your inputs keep going up with increased duties, etc. Then you would meet with the price commission and ask for an increase, which we could justify based on increased costs and so on, and they keep stalling you. You have a long drawn-out meeting which will take 6 months or a year and they will give you another cent on a bottle or something, by which time your costs going up again and it now requires 3 cents instead of the cent.

If the State exaggerated the positive effects of this move, the companies had their own exaggerated claims as to the negative effects, arguing that they were virtually forced out of business. In practice, the impact of the government's intervention may well have been detrimental, even if there was some cutting of company profits to the benefit of the consumer. One negative effect was on investment: 'At the time it created a terrible shortage of drinks on the market, because everyone had old machinery, machinery that was breaking down all the time. So while the government made us lose money we were not able to invest in updating our machinery and that kind of thing.' Secondly, the move did not help the balance of payments. It was locally made bottled drinks that were controlled, and the accusation made against one company was that it used the opportunity to bring in large quantities of its franchised canned cola product from Florida. These were not price-controlled, and could be sold at much higher prices. This was seen as the precedent for companies going in for canning. Indeed, with respect to governmental intervention the industry was keen to see this as a kind of 'revenge' against the State, in that the effect was to reduce trade in the almost totally indigenous returnable bottle market, and favour the development of a can market, where cans cost over 30c. each and were just thrown away.

Production

The first concern of any of the companies has to be with consistency in the quality of the product. As already noted, Trinidad is what I have termed a 'shiny peanut' market, where expectations are on a par with those of a developed industrial country. This means that as far as consumers are concerned industrial commodities should come to them perfect every time. An imperfect product, or even a rumour of imperfection, can prove disastrous for food and drink companies in First World contexts. In Trinidad there is the added poignancy that such a product in a sense lets down the overall pretensions of Trinidadians for the kind of country to which they belong. It threatens to expose the realities of a developing country under the façade of an industrialized commodity realm. As noted in

Miller 1994, this idea of exposure or revelation would become an example of 'bacchanal', which is what the public is half hoping will erupt and what professional companies are at pains to avoid. This would be particularly true for a company such as Cannings, which has more pretensions to Western 'perfection' than say S. M. Jaleel, which might be more expected to 'try it on' and therefore in a sense suffer less when it is found out. The latter behaviour also follows a specific form of 'typicality' in what might be expected from Trinidadians, conforming to the notion of 'Boldface' (see Miller 1993).

This means that each company is exposed by the fragility of any of its component commodity parts. The drink and the bottle may be fine, but the whole product may be let down by a defective screw cap. As the *Annual Report* from ANSA McAl noted in 1989, this need not be company-specific. The whole soft drink industry was massively hit (nearly 50 per cent down on sales) after a particular batch of defective tops, which then became the problem of Carib Glass as supplier to all the drink producers. In this case the reports suggest that an aggressive consumer information campaign managed to get sales back to normal within two months. Similar problems arose on occasion with blowing plastic and with cans. At one point L. J. Williams used a three-piece can that leaked and tasted of metal. Again, drastic recuperative measures were called for, and in this case a reduction of sale price to cost price for a period was necessary to win back the market share that had been lost. These problems may arise equally with imported stock, especially where firms have gone to a 'bargain' supplier. If the problem is found prior to sale then it is only production targets that suffer. The real disasters come from loss of consumer goodwill. In the Carib Glass case recovery was fast, since there was no alternative supplier; but for the individual sweet drink company there are plenty of competitors waiting to take advantage of any consumer loss of confidence.

Before consumer goodwill becomes an issue there are three potential points of quality control. The first is the government, which will monitor potential contamination and other health hazards on the one hand, and also look out for claims that are either fraudulent or defined in local legislation as illegal. The most common application of the latter is the ban on the use of pictorial representations of fruits on products where the flavouring is entirely artificial. In such cases the representation must not be made to look like a real fruit. For example, some Solo drinks were challenged under this ruling (the 1960 Food and Dairy Act section 6.1), and there are several other cases of drinks companies being forced to change their labels. A typical investigation by the food and drugs division took place as to the use of the terms 'natural' and 'new improved' on a drink label. The terms 'new improved' turned out to refer to new technology used to extract essential oils and nutrients from pulp and rind. The term 'natural' was, however, challenged and referred to the Director of Public Prosecutions. Meanwhile, the company was told to make the term 'reconstituted' more prominent.

These restrictions become more tightly controlled in cases where the company wants to export to large markets such as the United States and Britain. Indeed, the companies suspect that both those markets create artificial criteria, which are not fully applied to locally made produce, as a form of protectionism. They feel that every time one test is passed the local customs find some other restrictive regulation in order to prevent importation.

The third quality control comes from the companies with franchise or other arrangements with Trinidadian firms. The concern of the parent company is that any incident that affects its product in one market might by association affect its reputation in all its markets. Features such as water purity, bacterial content, bottle quality, representation of logo, etc., are carefully scrutinized through regular sampling, with the potential sanction that the local company will lose its contract with the parent group. A report by the research section of the consumer affairs division on one such company shows weekly samples tested for purity in England and Switzerland, and checks for leakages every 7 days for juice drinks and every 5 days for milk drinks.

The relative importance of production quality will depend in part on the self-conception of the company in terms of its reputation. A firm such as Cannings may feel that it is essential to be more conservative and spend more on various forms of quality and other controls simply because it sells itself partly on the larger reputation of the firm. A loss in reputation in the drinks division might also affect the reputation of other Cannings products, or indeed the Neal and Massy group as a whole. Furthermore, it is long-term reputation that guarantees retaining the arrangements with Coca-Cola that are the linchpin of the drinks division's continued prosperity.

The situation is different for smaller family-run firms that specialize only in this product area. Here there is likely to be more risk-taking. On the other hand, in such cases the company's reputation in commercial terms is closely linked by both the press and the public with the reputation of the family that owns and runs the firm. Motivations are constantly projected by the public as being based as much on the family's general social prestige, for example their role in politics, as on the desire for profitability *per se*.

Another factor is the sheer expense of quality control. A company may decide that the money saved by staying with relatively low-tech production is worth the risk of possible contamination. This is, however, only an option for local companies that don't have international quality controls breathing down their necks. Indeed, one company noted with some degree of envy: 'You have this Solo product that has got a niche market. He's got no overheads and if you got into a price war with him you would be hardpressed.' The implication being that Solo is able to spend much less on its production than rival companies.

The final major factor is the relationship between the company and its labour force. I have rather less information on this than in other areas, since my interviews did not include line workers.[7] Certainly there are many stories about the uneasy relationship between the workforce at S. M. Jaleel and the company. Solo also had to close their plant in 1979 as a result of a labour dispute. My lack of material on this issue is, however, balanced by the excellent recent ethnographic work by Yelvington (1995), which provides a thorough portrait of a typical Trinidadian capitalist firm from the point of view of its labour force (see also Rheddock 1994).

There is, however, another form of associated labour. The present recession makes it clear that the final point in the soft drink cycle lies within the harshest poverty found in Trinidad.

---

7. This was based on a deliberate decision on my part. Although it clearly represents a gap in such a study, as was already noted in Chapter 1,labour is the only area of business that has already received substantial research attention from academics both within and outside Trinidad, and, since I could not hope to be comprehensive in my coverage, it was not included.

The most notorious estate in the country is probably the Beetham, which borders one of the main highways. The *Sunday Punch* (21/8/88) reported of an individual that 'like scores of youths from the Beetham Estate, he earns an income from scavenging'; this is done from the national dump, which lies next to the estate. The scavenger reports: 'Bottles need a lot of patience and hard work. At the end of each fortnight they collect about ten bags containing some 2,000 bottles, which Carib buys from them for $200 per 1,000 kg.'

Distribution and Retail

Distribution is generally seen as one of the key factors in company competition. This seems to be a factor that has been remarkably neglected in the comparative literature on capitalism, but the emphasis placed upon it by executives certainly echoed that suggested by some recent accounts (Wrigley and Lowe 1996). A larger firm will have 45 trucks serving around 8,000 outlets, and employ around 100 persons as salesmen, supervisors and area managers who do the trade research. As one firm put it: 'Remember a major part of the sales is the effectiveness of the distribution, who has the best fleet, who has the most motor vehicles, who has the best supervision.' This last point is taken very seriously. Whether the company runs its own distribution or uses a separate subcontracted firm that takes responsibility for this, the managerial staff of the company make regular checks on the reliability of the distribution. They will visit various retail outlets on a regular basis and find out whether the driver of the truck visited at the right time, took the order and supplied the outlet properly. For example, while I was researching one firm it was running a check-up because the managers of another product that they were distributing alongside their own complained of its unavailability. The drivers who had skipped deliveries were found, and two were fired.

The managers also find surveys enable them to have direct feedback by chatting to retailers, ensuring that they do not lose touch with the market. For example, on one such visit the retailers commented on a wide range of aspects of their relationship. One suggested a particular television show that should be targeted for adverts, since his customers particularly watched that. They will also comment on how helpful the supplier has been in responding to their various requests. Larger retail outlets may be concerned with merchandising and special promotions. Most of all they try to obtain bargains, both with respect to price and period of credit. These visits may also be used for systematic marketing research and for dealing with aspects of merchandising such as the shelf space given to a product.

In general the industry sees retailing, alongside the government and labour, as the main negative force to be blamed for its problems. This is not surprising, given that retail is their main competitor for the extraction of profits from price. As was noted above, retailers create competition between firms by claiming that rival companies have given them discounts that should be matched. Similar arguments can occur with regard to credit, in that retailers can choose to buy products from the companies that give them most credit. An exception is Cannings, where the most important retailer, Hi-Lo, is part of the same group of companies and may be expected to favour its products. One of the ways retailers are said to cheat producers is through promotions. One firm tried to team up with a nappy company (Johnson and Johnson), providing free sample of an orange drink with each pack of nappies, but: 'The shops, they took the orange as something to sell. So they tend to take off the free gifts as a gift to them. So now we do coupons, that is: "Buy the nappies and get 40c. off." '

The question of the relative power of retail and the consumer emerged in the difference between the views of two senior executives of the same firm with regard to returnable bottles. This was one of several firms that were trying to promote returnables, as an obvious response to recession. The market for returnables, which had once been the backbone of the industry, was largely destroyed by the affluence of the oil boom. Given constantly diminishing incomes, it seemed likely that consumers would want to return to the lower prices that are secured through returnables. According to one executive the problem lies with the retailer: 'He is also the man who helped kill returnable bottles by not stocking it at all. Saying he has limited space, and saying that it encourages cockroaches in the empty bottles, although the consumer might save. If he hears he is not stocking, says "That's OK, give me a can." ' He assumed therefore that the consumer might not want a returnable (i.e. the consumer would not care much that the retailer did not have returnables). Another executive in the same company did not see this as the issue, and was more concerned with the degree of consumer resistance to a new stress on returnables, assuming that if the consumer could be persuaded the retailer could not or would not block this move.

All firms agree that promotional activities are as much directed to retailers as to consumers. 'The dealer has a big role to play. They are influenced by promotions, so feel that quite a few customers will ask for that product and thus give a lift to their business and it will bring them in so they can sell the things.' In accompanying executives on their visits to retailers I was surprised how often the retailers brought up this question of advertising and promotion, giving advice to the firm as to how it should promote its products. In part this relates to the point discussed in more detail in Chapters 5 and 6 about advertising as a national popular art.

The relationship of production to retail also brings up the issue of ethnicity, since retail is assumed to be dominated by one particular group. As one executive noted of sales outlets: '90 per cent are Indian, so 90 per cent of the sales people are Indian. We have to face facts. In Central we had a Negro sales manager, not doing especially well, so we moved him to Barataria (a predominantly African area). We found that Central sales with a new Indian rep doubled, while Barataria also went up.'

If we move from the comments of the executives to the perspective of retailers on producers, then the dominant representation is obviously quite different. Retailers complain constantly that credit is granted to major chains that could make profits without it, while the small single shops and parlours that are often forced to supply credit to customers cannot get it from their suppliers. Such shops may find the scale of these large companies intimidating. For example, the supervisors of the distribution systems have a problem in that shops will claim they want to purchase stock but that the van did not call. In fact, it may be that they did not want to, or could not afford to, purchase further stock, but were unwilling to say this to the supervisors, who then falsely accuse distributors of not doing their job. One supervisor would carry stock with him to challenge the claims made by the shopkeeper. In general, the small shop feels both persecuted and intimidated by the firms.

The final voice here is that of the consumers. Consumers may also see retailers as the barrier between production and its true reflection of the nature of demand. Thus any consumer who dislikes a particular product may account for its prevalence by concluding that retailers have chosen to stock this against better-tasting products because they have a higher margin. Behind the accusations of both producers and consumers is the assumption that sweet drink preferences are simply not important enough to most people to make them forgo the most easily available brand and search out the brand they prefer. This gives the retailer particular power. Clearly, with products where consumers do comparative shopping the power of the retailer would be considerably diminished.

Building Market Share: Creating the Niche

The sweet drink industry is highly dynamic, and every year sees innovations in flavour, container type, size, franchise arrangement and so forth. This is partly due to the degree of competition, with each company looking for some niche to open up an advantage over their rivals. However, the same competition tends to close down such advantages quite quickly, as other companies move to copy any evidently successful innovation. A new flavour is easy to copy once it has proved itself on the market. Even a link-up such as the promotion of Canada Dry through Cannings can become diffused in the general promotion of various ginger drinks by the rival companies.

Nevertheless, there may be a premium on being the first with a particular innovation. As one executive put it:

> Now in the beverage market we are to a great extent very copycat. Solo was the first to launch in cans, and it was a great success and everybody had to follow. Solo was the first to go into the disposable glass bottle. He ran away with the market. The consumer favoured that product, all had to follow. Jaleel goes into the 2 litre pep [plastic], all got to jump in. Cannings came first, they had a 16oz massive. Solo brought out a 16 oz called tall boy, Jaleel has a 16oz, so does Pepsi.

Innovations can succeed well beyond expectations, as Solo found when it first brought in cans. 'Within two months we could not supply all the demand. People were getting up at 4 in the morning to buy the product. At that time we were paid 15 dollars for a case of 24, but sidewalk vendors were snaffling cases and selling them at two dollars a can.' The company's rivals tend to try to damage this tale of success by various negative stories. For example, they claim cans were priced very high to overcome price control, and that in its success Solo failed to honour its obligations to returnables, which created longer-term consumer loss of goodwill. They can also try to vary their imitations, as Solo did by stretching the mould of their 10oz plastic bottle to produce their 16oz rival to the Cannings massive. The other side to these gains is the cost of innovation. An executive noted: 'There was a plan, it was three years before it was launched. Then [rival company] came in within two months.'

The point here is that there is a sales potential for newness in and of itself. Most of the flavours start out with considerable sales, before diminishing to much more modest levels as consumers show a pronounced interest in trying new possibilities. The question is often merely whether the innovation will subsequently diminish to viable levels or to complete extinction. An example is Sorrel, based on a traditional Christmas drink made from a local flower. Brought out as a sweet drink flavour it was able to break out of its traditional associations, but only while it was an innovation: 'Early on it used to be consumed all the year round, we find now during the year it is very slow and the peak time is Christmas.' New angles may prolong this strategy, as for example the very apt advert for 'Diet Sorrel Fizz' that suggested, 'Enjoy the Christmas cheer . . . without some of the calories.' Even the beer market tried to cash in on this, with the production of a 'Shandy Carib Sorrel' drink.

Not all companies have equal access to particular kinds of innovation. Some Cannings executives implied that the reason that innovations are most readily associated with companies such as Solo and Jaleel is that as private companies they are less cautious and freer to take risks. These points were made more forcefully when I was working with transnationals in other product areas, where it was often assumed that they were at a disadvantage because of their more cumbersome decision-making processes. The notion of always having to refer back to some 'head office' before innovations could be launched and risks taken was used to explain any success of local companies over transnationals.

While there are clear forces behind the drive for innovation, things may not be so evident when it comes to determining which innovation to follow. The decision to produce a new flavour or form rarely follows any systematic research or clear marketing strategy. There are two main forces at work from the production side. The similarity between what is produced by the various companies is in part a reflection of the global nature of this industry. 'Most of the players go to the beverage show in the States every year, and whatever is new in the soft drink industry is there. So each can see, and then it is who decides to go first into one area.' At this point the companies have to decide whether it is worth the investment in terms of its likely performance in the Trinidadian market, and whether they should go first with it or only invest if another company has shown it may work. The risk is that the innovator will retain the specific connotation and market advantage even after the others have followed, as happened with the concept of the 'Jaliter'.

There is a considerable difference between a flavour innovation and an innovation that involves new production equipment. A new flavour is not necessarily a large investment for a major company. Although the example given was of a milk drink, one executive put the cost of importing the new concentrate in addition to the plate charges for printing a new label at around 20,000 US dollars. Then, reverting to TT dollars, he suggested that costs depended considerably on whether advertising is used. Flavours can be and are launched with virtually no advertising; but more often there is press coverage, costing around TT$20,000, and point of sale coverage of TT$10,000. The big difference comes with a television campaign, at TT$90,000–100,000. These costs may be set against overall revenues of TT$20–50 million for a large company.

This culture of innovation and copying is what produces the range that was described for Solo at the beginning of this chapter. Jaleel claimed it was producing 114 products when all the permutations of flavours and packages were taken into account. With some exceptions the main players are represented in most of the varieties and in most of the packages. This relentless force expanding the variety of forms available has its negative consequences, and would certainly not have been an aim of any of the companies if they had been left to work out their production strategies outside this competitive environment.

From the point of view of the logistics of distribution, the result is a nightmare. The companies have to create cases made up of a selection of their drinks, which are then made into pallets to be loaded on to trucks. This is a relatively simple operation when there are few products in few sizes. The logistics of representing all these varieties in loading the trucks and then matching them to the specific quantities required by a wide variety of outlets is a far more tedious and time-consuming operation than the companies would wish, and allows room for all sorts of mistakes and confusion. At the end of the line shoppers can often be seen walking around the cases of sweet drinks making up their own 'pik 'n' mix' selection, which creates the problem of left over less popular flavours.

This is not the only disadvantage. The addition of new flavours and sizes does not necessarily increase sales. The retailer who previously was buying ten of each flavour, faced with a larger range will buy only eight of each. Once the flavours are launched there is then a commitment to the consumer who becomes attached to it. 'This is why we keep market share, because someone would like an orange, and another a grape, so we try to satisfy everyone.' The implication appears to be that much of this innovation has little to do with planned policy, marketing research or choices made by the firms. It is in some sense inherent in the competitive environment itself, and the marginal position of this small market to global developments of new possibilities.

Decisions that might have been left to 'planned policy' are often merely the whim of senior executives who feel that they are close enough to what is a relatively small market to have a sense of what will work. As one such executive said: 'A lot of our product decisions are based on gut feeling. Now I hope this never gets back to my boss, but the large majority of decisions are gut decisions. We think that it will work so we try it.' Indeed, where companies have tie-ups that lead to foreign experts coming in and writing long reports on the state of the industry and suggesting innovations, the local executives take pride in dismissing such materials. They complain about the money spent and how these 'experts' don't really understand the local situation. Indeed, this often produces a desire to innovate in the opposite direction, and thereby 'prove a point' (proving a point is a commonplace of intrusion between the social prestige of the individual executive and any overall search for profitability). There are exceptions, and the beer market, for example, underwent its most radical change (with considerable success for one company) as a result of such an outsider report's being taken seriously. But on the whole local executives attempt to protect their notion of an aura of expertise that only a 'local' could ever have.

In the discourses of the executives there is a constant fluctuation between their concept of the rational market and their sense of the actual market. Normally they will attempt to assert that a given event has happened because of some logic of consumption that they can understand or have predicted. Despite this, they will often in the same conversation allude to some event in the market that contradicts their supposed knowledge. In a typical example one executive noted: 'I tried to stay out of it [2 litres] because unless you have a party or something like that and you could consume a 2 litres, it's all right, but if you put it in a room overnight, no matter you tighten it the soda comes out and it goes flat.' In general business executives (conforming here at least to their Marxist critics) wish to assert their ability not only to understand but to control markets. They do so largely through these claims for knowledge as to why consumers do what they do.

The reality is somewhat different. The logic of production is based largely upon a relationship between the use of international trends in the beverage market and the decision by one of a series of highly competitive firms as to which will take the risk of being the local innovator with this possibility. The innovation may be a flavour, a package or a franchise/link-up with an international brand. The logic of competition then tends to dictate the pattern of emulation. Actual knowledge of markets and consumers seems to play relatively little role in product innovation and development. This is complemented by decisions based partly on the internal prestige rivalries within companies, but even more on a highly aggressive idiom of 'warfare' in which company executives take on the role of 'warriors' against rival brands.

Advertising

The conclusion of the previous section with respect to the source of innovation is less true of the specific niching of products through advertising and the construction of images. This topic is dealt with in more detail in the next chapter, but a brief examination of advertising within this particular market shows two very different possibilities. Often advertising may be no more than the shoehorn that eases a product into a niche that is already constituted by the existing field. On occasion, however, imaginative ploys on the part of advertising agencies in collaboration with production company executives can be clearly seen to have acted as substantial agents in changing the market.

The first aim of advertising was to promote those specific attributes of the product chosen by the executives. During the period of fieldwork Jaleel used advertising to advance on two fronts. The first goal was to render Cole Cold stylish, with some fast-moving modern images. This tended to centre upon the idea of the coldness and freshness of the drink connoted by the brand name. The other aim was to focus upon those strengths that could be claimed against other companies. Thus the slogan 'Zero in on a Cole Cold' highlighted their superior distribution system, which was also alluded to in a television commercial featuring a glamorous female DJ who could 'deliver' on request (which in turn referred back to a radio request programme sponsored by the company).

This forefronting of positive attributes is obviously carried out in the context of competition. As in the above case, advertisers often seek simply to promote the drink without direct acknowledgement of competition; but where there are important differences in company strategy this rule may not hold. A key campaign during the fieldwork period was the drive to returnable bottles, seen by many executives as bound to themselves 'return' to prominence given the recession. After a series of adverts that promoted the advantages of returnables, particularly with respect to good value, it is not surprising that there was a counterattack. An advert from S. M. Jaleel for its 2-litre 'Jaliter' starts with the caption, 'Don't be fooled, Cole Cold 2-litre is still the most economical package you can buy.' It notes that at 4.75 dollars the package saves 3.48, as against the 7 returnables that would be needed to make up the same amount. (This was based on the idea of returnables being at the rather unlikely price of 1.25!) Given this sales pitch, the next stage in explicit comparison was the promotion of a third package by a company that did not produce 2-litres. This was found in a concurrent Solo advert, whose caption was, 'Mr Solo exposes the facts. The big one from Solo gives you the unbeatable edge over ANY 2-litre soft drink.' The advert goes on to suggest that the consumer should buy two separate 1-litre bottles, and thereby be able to choose two flavours instead of just one, and further that these would be less likely to go flat than a 2-litre bottle.

Each company has also to decide whether it should promote flavours as a whole range or as individual 'characters'. This seemed to be the subject of general trends across the range of companies. There had clearly been a period in which companies had concentrated on the generic brand label for their advertising, – the relative merits of Cole Cold *v.* Solo *v.* Cannings *v.* White Rock as a group. This strategy could only be considered a success where it resulted in particular attachment by consumers to a brand name. But, as an executive noted, 'If [we] had developed a loyalty factor there might have been some point to it, but since this doesn't really happen in the market, one might as well allow individual flavours to develop.' The label was said to be 'stifling the individuality of the flavours'.

Cannings found that once it had decided to move from generic brands to a policy of picking out particular products, it needed to exploit the remnant individualism that had been retained by particular drinks. It found that there was already considerable potential for the concept of its red drink, which was therefore promoted as 'Big Red'. Other flavours were more difficult. It decided at one point to try to individualize its orange. It first tried to add a small amount of juice, which in combination with added vitamins might make the drink a 'healthier' version of the sweet drink. This strategy was completely rejected by the public. Rather more successful was the idea of focusing on a particular kind of orange, the 'King Orange', which was a traditional Trinidadian variety. They were surprised by this success, given the negative feature that many younger Trinidadians had never heard of this rather antiquated category. They were about to embark upon the next project of individualization, directed at banana. This had already been attempted by another company, which noted, 'Banana also did better than expected and is now one of the leaders in our range. We did some TV and radio to single it out from the range of our products and that really took off.'

It is rare to advertise to particular niched target consumers in Trinidad. Most advertising is of a general variety, focused upon a sense of youth and excitement. The one brand that saw itself as based around a particular segment of the market was L. J. Williams, which knew from marketing reports that its White Rock range was mainly drunk by children. Since these children made more of their particular preferences for individual fruit flavours, these were highlighted in its advertising. Although this company was less involved in promotional activity than most, it would be more inclined to child-based promotions, such as a cool box for a school. Its narrow can was also seen by some as suited to a child's grip.

I had the impression that these last two observations, the trend to individualizing flavours and the targeting to children, had not been put together by the company executives. The problem for the executives is that they tend to see such questions in terms of supposed general trends and fashions in advertising across the whole industry. For them, either individualizing was the way to go for the industry or it wasn't. They thereby failed to appreciate that there may be reasons why a flavour range as a concept might fail for one company and yet succeed for a rival, where the appeal was to a slightly different market.

Instead of targeting a particular type of consumer, a company can attempt to capitalize on a particular consumption occasion. The clearest evidence for this kind of niche marketing is the case of Peardrax – the premium brand sweet drink. Here both the producers and consumers are quite clear why it should hold this position. The drink has long been regarded as a substitute champagne. At one time it is possible that this was a substitution necessitated by expense. But during the oil boom the need for a substitute was more directed to the teetotal market, and to some extent to children-centred celebrations. Champagne itself has expanded its semantic field, given the expense of the authentic product, and most fizzy white wines with the right kind of bottle shape and cork will serve as champagne. Peardrax has in turn attracted its own substitute, in the form of Jaleel's Pear-D. As one person commented on the advert for Peardrax: 'If you don't have champagne you could do the Peardrax, and if you can't do the Peardrax you could do the Pear-D.'

The strongest association I found with Peardrax was not surprisingly amongst East Indian teetotal families, where the drink would be called for within many kinds of family celebrations, such as for the success of one of the children in education. To that extent the consumers required that the brand retain its price differential from other sweet drink products. Of course the company was only too happy to oblige the consumer. As a rival executive noted:

> L. J. Williams also do Peardrax and Cydrax. Well what happened, over the years they were bringing it in as a high cost item. So now they have a plant and producing it. But still selling it at the same high-cost, so they can afford to have a very high margin on it. . . . It does not cost them any more than our apple and our pear because, we bring in our apple juice and after manufacturing we have to pasteurise and sell it at same price as a soft drink. Once you have natural juice and we do not use preservatives, we have to pasteurise.

This account is backed up by the history of the parent company in Britain. Whiteway notes that Trinidad became a huge importer during the oil-boom period. In the decade after 1973 they exported no less than 5 million gallons to the region. 'This remarkably successful sales position overshadowed other countries and dominated the Whiteway's sales department at the time' (Whiteway 1990: 127). Obviously from their point of view, sales declined once L. K. Williams moved to importing concentrate only from 1983 on.

Companies could also use spatiality as a key attribute, whether by localizing an international brand, internationalizing a local brand, or, as it were playing the hand they have been dealt by stressing their actual origins. But such strategies were not always successful. An executive discussed the problem with a failed campaign for a non-fizzy range of tropical juices. The executive noted that:

> The central theme was 'It tastes so great it's like being there', meaning you are in paradise. Now, as far as it goes, we are in paradise in the tropics. They had a lovely girl on the beach, 35mm film, excellent production. One of the best to have come out of our advertising agencies. We got a Venezuelan guy to direct the ad. Great stuff BUT 'It tastes so great it's like being there.' We're here! What are we going to do? It would have worked in the States, but then again you try and buy media in the States we can't do that on our losses!

The specificity of the Trinidadian market is made most evident to local firms by the differential success of products even in neighbouring Caribbean islands. As one executive reported: 'You can't generalize. The recent launch of Hawaiian Punch was a huge success in Barbados but a complete flop in Trinidad. Canada Dry is great here, but failed on the smaller islands. A favourite in Grenada is a green drink which is not popular here.'

A final example of advertising within this industry comes from the most successful campaign during the period of fieldwork, which was for Canada Dry. There seemed no doubt at all that the enormous sales were a direct result of the advertising campaign. Cannings already had a ginger ale, which had been quite unsuccessful up to that point. The agency achieved this goal by never referring to Canada Dry as a ginger ale drink while marketing the product, and thus never relating it to the extant field of ginger drinks. The reason for this was that the field was already constituted by a distinction between colas and flavours. This is already quite different from the market in other countries, where there are different segments for, say, lemonade, ginger ale and colas. The common practice was therefore to launch a new drink as an addition to a flavour range, in the hope of some rapid sales before the novelty wears off. In the Trinidadian context ginger ale had become largely absorbed as the flavour drink 'ginger', though not entirely, since it was also a known mixer as a 'ginger and rum', but this was not a particularly common rum variety.

The approach of the advertising agency was not to promote ginger as a flavour but, more on analogy with Coke, to try to form an independent category. As they put it: 'The point was to ignore the ginger ale category and go for something unique without rivals.' The agency looked at the international material available, and found the concept of a 'tough' soft drink within previously created international advertising. This image had not been particularly followed up internationally, but was very successful in Trinidad, so they decided to develop it locally. In turning this into a local campaign they had to confront local issues. As so often in advertising, this was above all a question of how best to appeal to the two main communities.

The advertisement that they produced was in two versions, based on a Cowboy and an American Indian. In each case the figure faces a line-up of bottles on a wall and shoots a gun at them/throws a tomahawk. All are smashed except the Canada Dry bottle, which the impressed fighters then take up, replacing the weapons in their belts with this new, tougher instrument. The slogan suggests that the drink is 'tougher than your thirst'. As the advertisers noted: 'The cowboy is not a white or black but a glamorised gunfighter, superficially white by tradition, but a gunfighter image beyond this. So both a Negro gunfighter and also an American Indian were acceptable images. As a result any group in Trinidad could identify with them.' The firm checked first that the Indian community would not be offended by the American Indian image. Indeed it is likely that most Indians may not even have appreciated that the Indian image stood for them in the advert. The point, however, that would have emerged was that there was a plurality of positive identifications with the drink.

The advertisement is generally regarded as having some of the finest production values produced in Trinidad. The 'Wild West' setting was established through filming in an arid zone within Venezuela. The advertisement went on to win an international prize within the global advertising industry, and did a great deal to establish the reputation of this new advertising firm. The firm claimed sales of half a million cases of Canada Dry in the first year. What comes over clearly from this example is the possibility of relatively autonomous creative work by an agency. The advertisers simply chose to ignore the apparent attributes of the drink and thereby to transcend its competitive context, and could then ignore most of the factors that have been discussed in this chapter.

It might seem that to end the section on advertising by showing the creative ability of advertising agencies to manipulate images with considerable material effects would demonstrate the passivity of the consumer in this domain. This is far from the case, since even in the case of Canada Dry, which was much more the exception than the rule, there is evidence that its success does not necessarily imply that the consumer had followed through with the agency's own logic. One of the by-products of its launch seems to have been the increase in sales of other ginger drinks, suggesting that the public did not necessarily agree to define Canada Dry outside this flavour range as the advertisers had intended. Solo claimed that its own Ginger was becoming just as successful (though other companies were highly sceptical of this claim).

Solo's response was to localize Ginger as a 'hot and spicy' Trinidadian drink, implying that Canada Dry was bland by comparison. Even if it did not rise to Canada Dry's sales levels, it seems that this campaign was a success. As part of the general rise of ginger this must have been in some measure emulatory of Canada Dry's launch. The active consumer is still more evident in the many more examples of innovations and campaigns that failed, either altogether, or only succeeding after several failed campaigns.

Consumption

In order to consider the whole field of sweet drink consumption in Trinidad, one must recognize that it is constituted first by the other drinks against which it must be chosen by the consumer. The most important 'other' to sweet drinks is probably fruit juices. These had once been a major local product, particularly the canned version that was produced by the Citrus Fruit Growers Co-Operative. This was founded in 1930 and had been canning juices since 1935. It reached its peak in the mid-1960s but was a victim of the success of the oil boom and the move away from agriculture. Production, which was once over a million crates a year, collapsed to 63,000 crates of orange juice and 49,000 of grapefruit juice in 1986–7. More robust was the market for packeted imported juices, dominated by Nestlé's Orchard brand. This was the main competitor with sweet drinks. Although grape, grapefruit, sorrel and lemonade were amongst the flavours usually available, the brand was dominated by sales of orange juice, which alone was not that much smaller than the sweet drink market. The other competitor was milk drinks. A marketing company that asked about drinks consumed within the last 24 hours found orange juice the most popular at 15.1 per cent, hot drinks at 14.1 per cent and soft drinks at 10.7 per cent.

The context for the consumption of these drinks is also important. Most families continue to produce their own drinks within the home. Probably most common is the use of fruits grown in the yard or purchased in the market to make fruit drinks such as soursop mixed with water and sugar. In between home-made and commodified drinks was the practice of using canned citrus juice as the basis for home-made drinks, again through adding sugar and water. In general consumers showed a good knowledge of the contents of sweet drinks. A day spent with schoolchildren at a secondary school in rural Tabaquite in central Trinidad showed this very clearly. They were well aware of what contained caffeine, and of the relationship between artificial flavouring and actual fruit juice in different products. They assumed the sugar was local and the rest imported. They also assumed that plain water was more thirst-quenching than a sweet drink. In turn, as predicted by the industry executives, they showed far more concern with particular flavours, such as pear and banana, than might an adult group.

Consumers' opinions did not always concur with producers' knowledge, however. A good example of this could be found in the consumption of fruit juice. Surveys constantly showed that consumers viewed tinned orange juice as of higher concentration and without the addition of sugar as compared to packet orange juice. In most cases the two were either identical or it was the tinned product that contained additional sugar. No amount of publicity by the packet juice companies seemed to be to shake off this belief, which simply fitted with the traditional practice of using canned, but not packaged, citrus fruit juice as a substitute for fruit in making home juices. Thus while adverts for the tins could claim 'most everybody mixes our juices 1 : 1' (1 can juice to 1 can water), the rival packet juice could only match this with the rather more lame 'and it can stretch just as far', the problem for them being that what would be a cheaper product is made into a more expensive one by a consumption practice they are unable to change.

If the sweet drink exists within a field of competing drinks, it occupies a particular niche, as a 'basic' drink, a point confirmed by the debate over price control. As was noted above, most outsiders would be astonished by the kinds of claims made by the government with respect to sweet drinks. Even locally, the idea that this was done for the benefit of the nation's health was seen as spurious. Today, this basic status of the sweet drink remains evident. It is very rare to find a Trinidadian asking for water as a drink when purchasing food to eat. The sweet drink was commonplace in all public drinking contexts, from the squatting community of Ford to the middle-class area of The Meadows. If anything, the main rival would be the food or snack vendors' own vending machines, which may provide their own made-up flavoured drink rather than a franchised product.

These connotations of the drink again raise the question of the 'active' or 'passive' consumer. This idea that a sweet drink is a basic necessity cannot be assumed to be just successful company promotion that results in people 'wasting' their money on what 'ought' to be a superfluous luxury. Nor was it an invention by government that became accepted. This may be shown by reference to an equivalent contemporary example, which showed how consumers do not necessarily obey the whims of the industry. A primary target of the drinks industry during 1988–9 was the return of the returnable bottle. This represented a case of the industry's attempting to second-guess the consumer's concern with thrift and price. The industry, so far from trying to 'waste' the consumers' money, was guessing that its profitability would be best served by trying to save them money. It was the executives who felt that the public 'ought' to respond to the depths of recession by favouring the returnable bottle. The problem was that, despite heavy advertising by more than one company, the consumers seemed unwilling to respond to what all the agencies were loudly announcing to be the next stage in the development of the industry. The campaigns were generally not particularly successful, especially given that they were intended to collude with a trend rather than to 'distort' public demand.

Instead of looking to producer or state interests our under-standing of the situation is perhaps better advanced by considering the nature of drink consumption. A prime factor seems to be encapsulated in the local term 'sweet drink'. The food category of 'sweet' and its associated category of chocolates is a much smaller domain of food than is found in many other areas such as Europe or the United States. There is no equivalent to the 'sweet shop' in Trinidad. Although sweets are sold in super-markets and parlours they do not seem to be quite as ubiquitous as elsewhere. There is therefore good reason to see this domain of consumption as not simply equivalent to the category of soft drinks in other countries. This is one of the reasons I have often retained the term 'sweet drink' as opposed to 'soft drink'. I do not want to read too much into semantic connotations, but it does seem that the sweet drink in Trinidad occupies at least some of the niche which would be taken by the category 'sweet' in other countries.

There is further evidence for this from the neighbouring market of milk drinks. The market leader in this field is usually chocolate-flavoured milk drinks. Although I do not have any comparative figures, my observations suggested that chocolate milk drink achieved unusually high sales in Trinidad. Chocolate itself, though certainly present, and of exceptionally good local quality, does not command the same sales as in many other developed regions. One could conclude that the combined field of sweet drinks and milk drinks occupy a related niche to the sweet and chocolate market in other areas. Although it is hardly surprising that we find a market for solid forms in temperate climates and for liquid equivalents in this tropical environment, I do not want to suggest that this need necessarily have been the case. I am sure it would be possible to find counter-examples in other countries. Nevertheless, this attribute of drinks that both quench thirst and also fulfil the demand for sweets and choco-lates works well to the advantage of those companies involved in their production.

Such localisms with respect to the drinks are not necessarily fostered by the local companies. Indeed, the opposite may be the case. If my analysis of the importance of the 'sweet' element in sweet drinks is correct one might expect this to be exploited by the industry. But, as is so often the case, the social milieu of the executives is more important than some abstract drive to profit-ability. The producers are part of an international cosmopolitan culture within which high sugar content is increasingly looked upon as unhealthy. In this milieu sweetness increasingly stands for vulgarity, and is taken to represent an old and outdated tradition. The executives would wish to see themselves, by contrast, as trying to be in the vanguard of current trends. There were, therefore, several cases of companies trying to reduce the sugar content of their drinks, and finding that this resulted in complaints and loss of market share. As a result the sugar content remains in some cases extremely high. A good proportion of the cases of failure in the market that I recorded seemed to be of drinks with relatively high juice content and low sugar content. As one executive noted: 'We can do 10 per cent fruit as Caribbean Cool. We are following the international trend here to higher juice, but this is not a particularly popular move within Trinidad. Maybe because it not sweet enough.' This suggests that, while producers and advertisers are sometimes keen to find explicit images of locality in their image construction, the more foundational distinctions in their market are not always evident to them, since they live in worlds that are closer to international élites than local mass populations. To generalize, the company executives would wish to see themselves as in the vanguard of changing taste both as a strategy of profitability and in terms of their own status prestige. Where these two come into conflict profitability seems to be placed in a secondary position, only to revenge itself in the form of product failures.

The Red and the Black Sweet Drink

The importance of understanding the local context of consumption as opposed to production is also evident when we turn to other qualities of the drinks. From the point of view of producers, as I have noted, the key categories are those of 'flavours' and 'colas', so that all the major companies have evolved by producing a local flavour range tied to a franchised cola production. These are not, however, the categories used by the general population. In ordinary discourse the key categories which emerge are those of the 'black' sweet drink and the 'red' sweet drink.

The 'red' sweet drink is a traditional category, and in most historical accounts or novels that make mention of sweet drinks it is the red drink that is referred to. The attraction of this drink to novelists is probably not only nostalgia but the sense that the red drink stands in some sense for a transformation of the East Indian population. While originally the 'ethnicity' of that community would have been registered in its traditional material culture, the red sweet drink may have been an early example of the community's being also objectified in a commodity. There is a sense that the red drink is the quintessential sweet drink, inasmuch as it is considered by consumers to be in fact the highest sugar content drink. The Indian population is also generally supposed to be particularly fond of sugar and sweet products, and this in turn is supposed to relate to their entry into Trinidad largely as indentured labourers in the sugar-cane fields. They are also supposed to have a high rate of diabetes, which folk wisdom claims to be a result of their over-indulgence of this preference for sweet food and drink.

The present connotation of the red drink contains this element of nostalgia. Partly there is the reference to older red drinks, such as Jaleel's original 'Red Spot', which was primarily drunk by Indians. There is the presence of the common flavour 'Kola Champagne', which is itself merely a red sweet drink. Today adverts that provide consumption shots will most often refer to a 'red and a *rôti*' as the proper combination. The implication is that non-Indians also would most appropriately take a red drink with their *rôti* when eating out, since the *rôti* has become a general 'fast food' item that appeals to all communities within Trinidad.

The centrality of the black sweet drink to Trinidadian drinking is above all summed up in the notion of a 'rum and Coke' as the core alcoholic drink for most people of the island, and just as rum is the most common alcoholic drink, Coke is by far the most common mixer. This is important, as rum is never drunk neat or 'on the rocks', but always with some mixer; and even a small segment of the rum-mixture market would constitute high sales. Coke does not stand on this relationship alone, however. The concept of the 'black' sweet drink as something to be drunk in itself is nearly as common as the 'red' sweet drink. As such, Coke is probably the most common drink to be conceptualized as the embodiment of the 'black' sweet drink. It is not alone, however, and for some people any black drink will do. At the cheapest end of the market a brand such as 'Bubble-up' that sells exclusively to the poorest rural community (they were the dominant brand in Ford) has no real pretence to being a cola. It simply produces cheap versions of the 'red' and 'black' sweet drink for a community that would tend to order them by these labels.

This distinction between drinks may be related to the much more general discourse of ethnicity that pervades Trinidadian conversation and social interaction. Thus an Indian talked of seeing Coke as a more White and 'White-oriented people' drink. The term White-oriented is here a synonym for African Trinidadians. Many Indians assume that Africans have a much greater aptitude for simply emulating White taste and customs, to become what is locally termed 'Afro-Saxons'. Africans in turn would contest this, and claim that, while they lay claim to White culture, Indians are much more deferential to White persons.

Similarly, an African informant suggested that '[a certain] Cola is poor-quality stuff. It would only sell in the South, but would not sell in the North.' The implication here is that sophisticated Africans would not drink this substitute for 'the real thing', while Indians generally accept lower-quality goods. In many respects there is a sense that Black culture has replaced colonial culture as mainstream, while it is Indians who represent cultural difference. Thus a White executive noted that, in terms of advertising spots on the radio, 'We want an Indian programme, since marketing soft drinks has become very ethnic.'

This issue of ethnicity and advertising is more fully explored in a later chapter, but I do not want to give the impression that there is some simple semiotic relationship between ethnicity and drinks. What I have described here is simply the dominant association of these drinks – red with Indian, black with African. This does not, however, reflect consumption. Indeed market research shows that, if anything, a higher proportion of Indians drink colas, while Kola champagne as a red drink is more commonly drunk by Africans. Many Indians explicitly identify with Coke and its modern image. This must be taken into account when comprehending the associated advertising. In many respects the 'Indian' connoted by the red drink is in some ways the African's more nostalgic image of how Indians either used to be or perhaps still should be. It may well be, therefore, that the appeal of the phrase 'a red and a *rôti*' is actually more to African Trinidadians. Meanwhile, segments of the Indian population have sometimes used foreign education and local commercial success to overtrump the African population in their search for images of modernity, and thus readily claim an affinity with Coke.

In examining the connotations of such drinks we are not therefore exploring some coded version of actual populations. Rather, as I argued in more detail in Miller 1994, both ethnic groups and commodities are better regarded as objectifications that are used to create and explore projects of value. As such, they relate more to aspects or potential images of the person than actual persons. What must be rejected is the argument of those debating about 'postmodernism' that somehow there is an authentic discourse of persons, and this is reduced through the inauthentic field of commodities. Indeed, such academics tend to pick on Coca-Cola as their favourite image of the superficial globality that has replaced these local arguments.

Nothing could be further from the Trinidadian case. Here

Coca-Cola both as brand and in its generic form as 'black' sweet drink becomes an image that develops through the local contradictions of popular culture as part of an implicit debate about how people should be (what I call 'projects of value'). They refer to aspects of persons, temporalities or groups, frames within which particular ideals can be worked out. As such they are closer to the place of myth as analysed by Lévi-Strauss (e.g. 1969) than the more fetishised mythologies analysed by Roland Barthes (1973). If one grants that the red sweet drink stands for an image of Indianness, then its mythic potential emerges. This is an image with which some Indians will identify, and some will not; and more commonly, some will identify with it only on certain occasions. Furthermore, it is an image with which many non-Indians will identify, either as an aspect of their 'Trinidadianness' or as an 'otherness' that they define themselves against. In the former case the object stands for a sense of being Trinidadian which incorporates plurality. An individual's identity may be experienced simultaneously as African but also Trinidadian, where the latter transcends any specific group and acknowledges the plural contribution that makes up contemporary Trinidad. Individual non-Indians cannot literally apply a piece of Indianness to themselves to resolve this contradiction of alterity. Instead, they can consume mythic forms that in their ingestion in a sense provide for an identification with an otherness that therefore 'completes' this aspect of the drinker's identity. It thereby allows them to be both African and Trinidadian.

A final example of this importance of a 'deeper' logic by which the drink's relation to the consumer may be understood returns to an observation made at the start of this chapter: the considerable nostalgia felt towards Solo, as against other companies that have been in Trinidad for just as long. Solo continues to use for its returnables a fat bottle with a narrow neck that would seem to be more in place in a museum of the beverage market than as a presence within a highly competitive contemporary market. The explanation of its longevity may lie in the observation volunteered by several informants that this is the very bottle with which a generation of Trinidadians were given milk as babies!

Conclusion

The history of a particular product is based upon the whole range of factors which have been described here. These include the international trade and the relationship of local companies to the State, to foreign suppliers, and to distribution and retail. It also depends upon the social setting of the executives as this influences their decision-making, as well the separate concerns of advertising agencies, and last but not least of consumers. It is not just that within this a simple notion of profitability can become swamped by competing pressures. Given this complexity of factors, neither the executives nor I as anthropologist can claim with much confidence what did or did not contribute to the success or failure of a particular product. Even though both they and also this chapter work within the framework of what Fine and Leopold (1993) might call a 'system of provision', it is very hard to disaggregate any particular factor. Any specific response, such as the reaction of consumers to a particular new flavour, may be determined in large measure by a longer-term relationship between consumer and company. Consumer attitudes to a company develop over a considerable time, and it is this that may make the consumer feel that it is, or is not, the 'appropriate' firm with which to associate this flavour. It may be this that makes a consumer feel that one company's version 'tastes' better than its rivals. Indeed, as I have argued, the equivalent to this product in another country may even include a different domain, such as sweets and chocolates.

Most companies have some background information, such as blind tests on the popularity of particular brands and information from point of sale on the relative success of both their own and their rivals' brands. At times of dramatic change they can therefore sometimes isolate particular factors such as an advertising campaign. But even then it is unlikely that much of this information is actually used. Most key decisions are taken by individuals either as owners of the company or as senior executives. On the whole these seem to be based on personal opinions and a generalized 'gut' sense of what might or might not succeed, sometimes tempered by other senior executives in the advertising agencies.

In general then the firm as an independent decision-maker

may often be squeezed between a logic of trends that emerges out of the international beverages industry and its own competitive context on the one hand and a consumer response that has more to do with the resolution of contradictions in the dynamics of a popular culture that uses goods to objectify its discourses on the other. One would expect to be able to argue that capitalism works by attempting to capitalize on consumer desires or trends. I feel after surveying the evidence that it supports a slightly different relationship between commerce and consumer. It is rather that when, as is often the case, commerce *refuses* to capitalize on these developments in popular culture and instead follows the logic of its own system of categorization that it mainly fails in the market-place, although this may also be where it achieves its most spectacular and original successes. To conclude, it is precisely the complexity of the contributory factors and the difficulty in assigning specific blame for failures that allots a considerable role to 'cultures of production' and 'cultures of consumption', allowing them to operate without appearing to conflict with the rhetoric of hard-nosed instrumentality and the drive to profitability. This may well be true also for the more diverse cultures of consumption that await anthropological investigation.

Epilogue

By way of an epilogue to this chapter it is worth noting the results of questions asked about sweet and other drinks in the questionnaire. The title of this chapter is 'an ethnography of brands', and this might imply that the topic of drinks and the study of brands as commodified forms are synonymous. This would tend in turn to reinforce an assumption that consumers are living within a material culture whose dominant represent-ation is that of commerce. There is, however, a wider context to this. Branded goods such as Coca-Cola and the like are certainly significant drinks; but their importance should not be exagger-ated. The questionnaire showed that it is not at all unusual for branded goods to be reduced in consumption to more generic categories such as black and red drinks that are out of the control of commerce *per se*.

In the survey I asked householders to name their favourite drinks. A total of 191 opinions were received. The main contenders were:

Fruit juices: 72
Sweet drinks: 30
Local drinks: 20
Malta: 15
Milk drinks: 14
Shandy: 12

Of those who chose sweet drinks, 10 simply said sweet or soft drinks, and 6 noted specifically Peardrax and 6 Coke. Pepsi received one vote, although it was the third most popular television advert. In total, of the 191 responses only 24 were brand names. I was even more surprised when brand names only accounted for 25 out of 97 alcoholic drinks, and out of that 25, 12 were for VAT, which is often used as generic term for rum. With a total of 7 out of 191 voting for Coke or Pepsi this hardly suggests that Trinidad has become merely an adjunct to global Cola corporations. The articulation between business and consumption that is the subject of this chapter matters, but it is certainly not the whole story as far as drinks in Trinidad are concerned. Even in a country that seems as devoted to capitalism as Trinidad, it cannot be assumed that material culture has become merely the logic of commodity culture.

5

The Production of Advertising

Introduction

Various approaches to the study of advertising have been developed in the last two decades, mainly depending upon other interests than those of this book. Cultural studies, for example, has been principally concerned with how advertising reflects the essence of capitalist society. Others have been interested in how advertising language works as compared to other linguistic forms, or in applying semiotic textual analysis. With respect to the title of this book there exists a tension in the study of advertising. Here if anywhere people have seen the quintessence of capitalism. Advertising is often treated as 'the business end', the bit where we see the effects of business on society most clearly. This may well be to the detriment of the study of advertising. Firstly, it is not clear that this is the case. Rather in the same way that people have tended to blame shopkeepers rather than 'high capitalists' for their misfortunes, since they were the more visible business community, so also academics may have over-estimated the importance of advertising simply because of its visibility and because it is the most immediate source of information on business. There is also a tension in some critical studies between the desire to come to grips with the specificity of advertising as an institution and this desire to employ it to represent some more general essence of capitalism. I hope that taking a relativist perspective on capitalism will make this less likely to occur in the present case.

This degree of 'projection' on to advertising in critical analysis may sometimes lead to obfuscation rather than elucidation of the effects of the industry. Nevertheless, there can be little doubt that there has been an enormous increase in the sophistication with which adverts have been subject to analysis. This is concurrent with an increasing sophistication in advertising itself, which is well able to learn from such critiques. The literature on advertising is certainly extensive today, and I note only a few books that appear to me to have provided particularly important contributions. The tradition of textual analysis through the decoding of the structures of the genre has been one of the most common sources of analysis. Williamson's (1978) work is particularly useful, both because of her success in prising open the underlying technologies of ideological construction, and through her application of post-structuralist theory to a substantial body of material.

One trajectory of this work has developed into largely linguistic analysis (e.g. Vestergaard and Schroder 1985; Tanaka 1994). Another major strand of analysis looked away from the texts themselves to investigate both the context of their production in terms of the advertising industry and its executives and also the context of their consumption in terms of their effects. The most original and to my mind significant contribution here was made by Schudson (1993), who strives for a balance between critical analysis and evidence for this wider context of consideration. Less original, but useful as syntheses introducing the wide range of literature on aspects of the profession was first Dyer (1982) and later Leiss *et al.* (1990). Various books have tried to deal with the larger social message of advertising, often through Marxist critique (e.g. Jhally 1987); but to my mind the most effective in showing how the overall impact of advertising was articulated with key ideological questions of a particular period is the scholarly account of American advertising earlier this century by Marchand (1985).

The work on the international context of advertising is less effective, and I am not aware of any particularly helpful examples of ethnographic relativism applied to a particular local advertising industry, though this may be in the offing with Moeran's ethnographic work in Japan (1993; see also Wells 1994). These certainly are showing the similarities in the institution of advertising across the world, but also the importance of regional trajectories. For example Wells (1994) notes how transnationals entering the former Soviet Union failed to appreciate that advertising had previously been mainly used to persuade Soviet citizens to buy up produce that was in surplus and might go to waste, and was therefore associated as a practice with poor-quality unwanted goods. Matterlart (1991) provides what should be a starting-point for anyone interested in the larger question of the impact of the internationalization of advertising itself. Matterlart's book is particularly instructive in showing the failures of the industry in cases where they have made the same grandiloquent claims for themselves as a global influence as have often come from their critics.

My own analysis has a number of specific aims. Firstly, to demonstrate an ethnographic approach. Not that this would be the first such example, since various ethnographies have been conducted in advertising agencies. But here 'ethnographic' means more than just being inside an agency, since this experience was part of a wider ethnographic encounter with commodity construction and consumption. Furthermore, tensions within agencies may be referred to observations of the same tensions in society at large. The other obvious intended contribution of this study derives from its situation in Trinidad as opposed to metropolitan studies. This should introduce relativist and comparative components, and a consideration of the implications of the relatively small scale. The material I collected on advertising has been divided between four sections of this volume. This chapter considers the industry itself and its relationship to the media and to marketing, ending with a detailed case study of a campaign. The next chapter looks at the content of advertising on the basis of the viewing of adverts on television, as well as of fieldwork within the agencies and society more generally. Some discussion of advertising also formed part of the chapter on sweet drinks. Finally, material on the consumption of advertising will be used within the concluding chapter, concerned with the consumption of business forms and products generally.

History and Size of the Advertising Industry

There has been some excellent general work on the history of advertising, which may provide a backdrop to the developments in Trinidad. Books on the development of consumption (e.g. McKendrick *et al.* 1983), on general trends (e.g. Leiss *et al.* 1990: 225–348) or on advertising as a cultural form (e.g. Williams 1980) are amongst the many that mark the increasing sophistication and importance of this industry over the last century and a half. Marchand's work on American advertising is outstanding as an example of how the relationship between advertising and society may be tackled. He demonstrates the problems in assuming that advertising can be used as some kind of mirror of society, but shows that, once this limitation is accepted, careful analysis can throw considerable light upon key conflicts in ideology at a given time. He also shows that, as against the rather simplistic conspiracy theories of some of the critiques of advertising, it is often more insightful to examine the degree of collusion between producers and consumers in constructing the dominant concerns represented.

In Trinidad early representations (e.g. etchings), particularly those set in Port of Spain, suggest a thriving use of billboards and shop fronts in the nineteenth and early twentieth centuries, and in many respects there is no reason to assume that the early history of advertising here was particularly distinct from that in many other areas. This tradition of sign painting as it took place in provincial Chaguanas in the 1930s is also illustrated by the character of Biswas in V. S. Naipaul's classic *A House for Mr Biswas* (1961: 74–82). Oral histories taken from current advertisers suggest a rather surprising sequence to the development of the modern agency. In effect, the industry appears to have emerged out of local initiatives, and only when well established to have been taken over by larger foreign concerns. This process then went into reverse, to produce the high degree of local control that may be found today.

Trinidad was probably in the vanguard of Caribbean advertising, inasmuch as Port of Spain was one of the most cosmopolitan centres in the nineteenth century, and the oil revenue that started to flow from the 1920s on ensured a higher standard of living than that in most of the other islands. Advertising (as with so much of the local economy) will have been boosted by the American presence in the war and by the rise of multinationals. The early agencies were developed by Whites, both recent immigrants and established local élites. Companies such as Colonial Advertising or Davies and Chislett developed in Trinidad and in one case from Barbados, building up over the 1950s. As has been the case ever since, their best hope of profitability was to be tied in with one of the larger multinational firms. Local firms were here at a disadvantage against multinational advertising agencies that had agreements to represent particular clients in whichever countries both should be represented (for which see Leiss *et al.* 1990: 170).

Early sources of revenue included poster campaigns and press such as the *Gazette* and the *Guardian*. The use of cinema became much more systematic through the increasing involvement of Pearl and Dean, while the growth of radio through Cable Rediffusion provided another major outlet. This was not always without opposition; for example, hoarding advertisements never developed to the extent found in the United States owing to action by Town and Planning authorities. As well as representing international concerns, advertising became involved in local business development. For example, there was an early case of an advertising battle between two major local shirt manufacturers called 'New Yorker' and 'Elite'. Other early mass campaigns developed around the beer market, such as Carib and Guinness. At least one early campaign slogan, 'The Spirit of Trinidad', survives today as the mark of a popular rum brand. As with advertising elsewhere the historical development must be set alongside more general shifts in marketing that necessitated increased advertising, of which the most important factor is the development of brands (Jones and Morgan 1994).

In general, advertising was more orientated towards British concerns and models until the 1960s when the growth of American international agencies was reflected in the relative loss of independence of several of the local firms. At one point only two of the nine agencies could claim majority local ownership. Given the importance of international tie-ups between major companies and agencies, this situation would probably have continued but for the impact of the Black Power revolt of 1970, followed by the power given to the localizing rhetoric of Eric Williams (then prime minister) by the oil boom after 1973. After Black Power the advertising industry was singled out by Williams for attack as an example of a force representing outside interests and destructive of local autonomy and concerns. Since at that time the economy was in poor shape and expatriate interest was anyway in decline, this call for localization was swiftly complied with. This was fortunate, since soon afterwards the boom period was obviously an enormous boost to the industry, and permitted the growth of quite substantial local firms mainly controlled by Trinidadians, several of whom had been involved since the 1950s.

The local agencies gradually built up their talent and creative sections with reference first to graphics, then to voice-orientated material for radio, and finally to the visual material required for television advertising. Localization was much assisted by the development of videotape technology, since previously film had had to be developed abroad. At the same time more recent recruitment has been from Trinidadian graduates trained in foreign universities in the business and marketing fields. For much of its history the local advertising industry supplied small-scale materials, while brands such as Esso, Coca-Cola, Colgate and Shell provided the international imagery. In many cases the transformation of promotional material to fit local contexts could be accomplished gradually. For example, imported material could be given a new local 'voice-over', or a scene with local models and views incorporated within and harmonized to the international material.

Thanks largely to the oil boom Trinidad for a time became a significant market in its own right, and this led its advertising workers into larger international exposure than might have otherwise been the case. An example is McCann Erickson, which has stood out against the political pressure for localization and remained the main example of a transnational firm with no local equity. Trinidad rose to become ranked nineteenth in importance out of 64 offices worldwide. The head of Trinidad's McCann Erickson office became responsible for all four Caribbean offices, and a member of the worldwide board of the transnational. Many local personnel are sent for training for within agency courses in the United States. McCann Erickson also had advantages because of its international connections, which could be offered to clients. For example, an executive claimed they had found a wholesaler in Brazil for a local product through their own networks.

The situation when fieldwork began was of a formally established Advertising Agencies Association to which the eleven largest firms belonged. Of these, only McCann was foreign-owned, though it claimed to work with considerable autonomy in all areas except finance, where it had to justify capital expenditure and keep within budget. It was also the biggest agency in Trinidad, though only by a small margin over local firms such as Lonsdale. At the start of fieldwork there were three other agencies with some foreign equity involved. At that time and since, other local agencies were considering reinvolving global firms, and companies such as Saatchi and Saatchi were being drawn in. Although some foreign equity was involved, these agreements did not always have the major impact the local companies were hoping for. The idea was that foreign equity would provide for better access to sophisticated foreign production facilities and information and also would bring in international clients associated with the equity-owning foreign agency. Some contracts were thereby acquired; but in one case two years of such a relationship had not contributed a single client. The main effect was access to research material, and sometimes more sophisticated technical assistance. For example, where an agency had to advertise an automated banking system it used its international links to go to New York to examine what had been done in this area and what computer-generated graphics might be available.

Advertising expenditure in 1987 was estimated as around $TT100 million, representing 0.7 per cent of GDP or about half the international average. According to an industry report 750 persons were directly employed, and ancillary service organizations accounted for another 1,550 persons. The personnel involved in advertising were entirely Trinidadian citizens or permanent residents, even in the case of McCann. If anything the influence was in the other direction, as McCann recruited the best Trinidadian executives for work in other countries. This was not just true of personnel. The *Sunday Guardian* 20/12/92 noted that their current advert for Milo was now being shown in Kenya, as an example of the international quality of Trinidad-made adverts. In several cases the Trinidadian firms had considerable influence on other Caribbean islands' advertising. Throughout the 1980s advertising continued to be an important export industry for Trinidad.

It is possible that this relatively high degree of local involvement in advertising is connected with the unusually wide range of responsibilities taken by agencies in Trinidad. Oral histories talk of advertisers not only constructing campaigns, but helping to offload products from trucks as part of their participation in expanding the presence of certain products. Today, when a Trinidadian advertising agency is given responsibility for a product it expects to do far more than simply create or place an advert in the media. In many respects it seems to appropriate the position of the marketing section of the client company. It will often try to devise a complete campaign, including television, radio and press and point of sale advertising. It may itself carry out or commission market research. It also acts instead of the company's design team to create corporate logos and images and to obtain all promotional materials and objects. It suggests competitions, sponsorships and a wide range of promotional strategies, and often sees itself as the force that pushes the client into more aggressive marketing on all fronts. This degree of control is more likely to occur when a large agency is dealing with a relatively small producer or importer. The major transnationals have their own marketing sections, and resist 'bullying' by the agency. As the recession developed some tried to save money by developing more in-house activities. But in general the advertising agencies have preserved a situation where for a company to go directly to the media rather than through them is seen as somehow 'suspect'.

This position of power is maintained alongside considerable competition, and often outright animosity, between agencies. They are constantly looking for ways to poach clients from each other. The major transnationals and conglomerates exploit this degree of competition by distributing their brands amongst the agencies, so that they maintain close relations with several at once (see Moeran 1993: 75 for a similar situation in Japan). Nestlé, for example, might have its fruit juices with one agency, its coffee with another and its milk products with a third. For large-scale campaigns, such as the construction of a new corporate image and logo for a state enterprise or large firm, the agencies are expected to tender for the work. In a sense it is the structure of capitalist competition itself that ensures the survival of at least a minimum number of agencies, since no company is happy to put its brand in the hands of an agency that is also representing a major rival. One rival argued that McCann, in particular, had already reached its maximum potential for that reason. The situation is complicated, in that rival brands do not necessarily represent rival companies. West Indian Tobacco was only the most evident example of a company that had gone for a policy of highly segmented brands in order to occupy all available niches, and thus keep out any effective opposition. Thus while there might be several brands advertised as though in competition, they were in effect more concerned with targeting particular groups of smokers for the same company.

The volatility should not be exaggerated. In its publicity for 1988 Corbin Compton was able to claim that it had 6 clients that had been with it for 20 years or more, and 14 more for more than 5 years. Its list of main clients gives an impression of the range a typical advertising agency is dealing with. These included S. M. Jaleel and its associated franchised drinks, the Republic Bank (Barclay's), British Airways, Berger Paints, and Fuji Film.

Ethnography of Agencies

My 'ethnography' of advertising consisted in the main of obtaining permission to follow through particular campaigns. Ideally I wanted to be present when the original brief was given to the advertising agency, at the meetings within the agency when the strategy was developed, and at subsequent meetings between the agency and the clients. This would permit the whole story of the campaign to be recorded, preferably by my sitting quietly in a corner with my tape recorder on. It took me several months to obtain permission for this work, since this had to be from both the agency and the client. In practice I tended to see snippets, for example the beginnings and ends of campaigns, rather than seeing many all the way through. But I was also able to overhear many more informal conversations while hanging around. I also conducted some interviews with key personnel. Since I do no want to break my promises of confidentiality, many of the observations I shall provide have been generalized. Sometimes the name or product has been disguised, sometimes more than one campaign conflated into a single example. On the other hand, where information was in the public domain, since the source was outside the company or in newspapers' reportage, I have used the actual name and product. In addition, I collected samples of adverts and conducted studies of viewers watching advertising, which will be presented in the next chapter.

The Structure of Advertising Agencies

In many respects the Trinidadian advertising agency and its main practices follow what has become a common structure to advertising around the world. The key figures in most companies are the company directors/owners. They may not be involved in the day-to-day details of creating and conducting campaigns, but they are responsible for the recruitment and promotion of key personnel, and are often involved in obtaining key clients. Partly this is because of the degree of personal contact that influences what are supposedly commercial decisions. The directors are members of the same élite as company directors, and go to the same clubs and social events. An executive for a large firm complained of the results: 'I am not satisfied with the way G. did our calendar. It cost TT$400,000 when they did it. In house it was TT$60,000 less. They did a crappy job, but got it since they are friends at directorship level.' Another, talking about why a particular agency obtained a contract: 'His office next door, as simple as that. I always see D. scrunting around to see C.' ('scrunting' is a kind of begging/borrowing role). In the 'small world' of the Trinidadian élite individuals may either engage in such activities pragmatically from the point of view of their self-interest in their own companies' profitability, or this may dovetail with their social ambitions. As a more junior individual commented: 'Since he got into Rotary the sky's the limit. I think he is a Mason too now, but they live in their own little worlds.' Obviously this leaves those concerned subject to the same kind of criticism that Ryan made of company take-overs (see Chapter 3 above).

No agency seemed to have such a distinctive style or consistent image that a client could look to this in order to determine which agency to employ. It was quite difficult even for those in the trade to be sure who had made which advert simply from the style of the advert alone. Oral history suggested that this had not always been true, and that there had been, for example, more English-style or American-style agencies in the past. So it could not be said that directors have stamped their personality on their agencies, though they might often believe this to be the case.

Below the level of the company director the agency breaks down into its several component parts, here as elsewhere (see Leiss *et al.* 1990: 176–93). These are the account managers, who represent the main interface between the agency and its clients, and the creatives, who are responsible for developing the advertising materials. Creatives may be divided in turn between those who work more with print materials and those who specialize in television work. In addition there are technical staff who range from secretarial services, through production personnel, who print and transport materials, to specialists in electronic media. One agency has its creatives divided into three copywriters, six artists, the art director and media producer, and 'the lady who runs the computer'.

The key structural tension here, as in advertising agencies internationally, is between the account managers and the creatives. A creative noted that 'where you have one [an account manager] with creative ability he is much more amenable and acceptable to the creative group'. Creatives will only tend to meet the clients in the case of major campaigns. Often the agency, in effect, sets up a tension between these groups, since many directors feel that creatives will tend to indulge their own artistic ambitions at the expense of commercial interests unless the account managers keep a firm grip of the overall goal of the campaign. To that extent the account manager in a sense represents the client within the advertising agency.

The traditional view is of agencies that closely reflected the overall power structure of Colonial and post-Colonial Trinidad as represented by Braithwaite's (1975) [1953] sociological analysis of the 1950s. 'They would be upper middle class, where you pretend to be all this high falutin' sort of stuff. Where they put on all sorts of accent and thing and pretend. The ad agencies are dominated by the upper class. Most of them, like the accounts executives, the creative director, are Whites, and the Black people would be the paint artist, the messenger, that sort of thing.' The pattern that I observed largely conformed to this. Most directors of agencies are White, although there are also Chinese and African agency directors who are actual rather than token heads of their firms. At senior management level the 1980s had seen a considerable rise in the presence of Indians, from what may have been a relatively small presence in earlier periods. Nevertheless, many Trinidadians would share the view of one informant: 'Advertising is a monopoly led by a French Creole group who act together as a pressure group. There are constant complaints about their influence from (television) production companies and others.' From the points of view of such critics, celebrations of the degree of 'local' control only obfuscated the degree to which power was indeed local, but wielded by the inheritors of a local plantocracy whose wealth and influence were taken to be at least as inimical to the mass population's interests as that of foreign firms. Such accusations raise larger questions. I cannot claim that I engage in the detailed examination of the distribution of power in contemporary Trinidad that would be required for a fuller assessment of such criticisms (though see Yelvington 1995 and for Jamaica Douglass 1992).

Agencies vary in personnel policy. One at least seems to run a deliberate policy of remaining understaffed, and then recruiting temporary staff on the strength of particular campaigns they had acquired. A rival company was hoping that by taking the costs of more permanent staff it would build up a reputation for superior quality and consistency. There is some seasonality to employment, since agencies that are slack during much of the year may still find that there is considerable demand around Christmas.

The agencies like to think of themselves as the 'brains' behind campaigns, having all the initiatives and working against conservative clients. They are sometimes piqued by having ideas pushed from other sources. For example, one agency complained 'Basically this is not our campaign, this was a theme which was very successful in Jamaica, which they have decided to use here. The theme of the campaign is not one this agency particularly agrees with, but we don't always have our way.' In general, they are disdainful of the client's ability to comprehend the processes involved. In one briefing the client suggested using the calypsonian 'Tambu'. Later on, the advertising creative noted scornfully 'With them, before they have even decided what the piece of music sounds like, they have decided who is going to sing it. Now Tambu has a particular style, which is not suited to everything. They tend to get a little excited like that.' Clients are particularly resented by creatives for their power to alter the material. A typical complaint was 'Slowly but surely the scripts were watered down to the extent that there was no real message in the ad . . . they know what they want but they are afraid to take a stand so they end up diluting it.'

In many ways the creatives in practice may be as conservative as their clients, because the influences upon them are just as narrow. One creative noted that when she was stuck for an idea she would spend the weekend going through as many ads as possible. In her case this was a combination of American magazines such as *Esquire, Vanity Fair* and *Harpers,* and the adverts of American satellite TV, which is broadcast at night in Trinidad. She noted the problem that 'MTV is what everybody is imitating, so there aren't many new visual ideas.' She noted that she preferred the English ads 'because they tend to say we are going to say this and they use the most unusual vehicles to do it. The Americans tend to go for a hotch-potch of visuals and a nice catchy jingle. Not particularly saying anything except hitting it home to you: "Use jello, use jello, use jello," whereas the British, it's more intellectual.' In practice the influences do indeed come from both sides of the Atlantic, as is reflected both in the use of imported 'canned' adverts and in the television programmes that surround the adverts, though the bias is increasingly towards North America.

Commercial Concerns and Competition

The first concern of agencies is to ensure that a company will actually decide to advertise. Many companies noted with interest examples of their own successes achieved without advertising. For example, a new flavour was widely taken up simply through being made available. The advertisers will take pains to explain these as exceptional circumstances: for example, that the situation is complex, because one success is riding on the back of another success that did involve advertising. Advertising obviously represents a considerable additional cost to a firm's activities. For example, a firm considering the costs involved in producing a new flavour estimated this at around TT$80,000 investment. It would be unlikely to have no advertising to launch the product, but might well decide to opt for just press coverage, at around TT$20,000, and point of sale material at TT$10,000. But a major television campaign could cost as much as all of these other costs put together. Agencies depend on having a few major accounts, rather than a host of small ones. One agency, for example, concentrated on its five largest accounts, which were worth between 0.5 and 1.2 million TT$ in expenditure per year. In 1988 the advertising agency of Kenyon and Eckhardt had to close down, with 18 employees and debts of TT$500,000 to TTT (Trinidad and Tobago Television), when it lost its last transnational client.

As one listens to these debates it emerges that the key decision to invest in advertising emerges less often from the power of the agencies to sell themselves as essential to their clients than from the intensity of competition between the clients. As is the case in so much of commerce, decisions are often simply reactive. The dialogue between agencies and clients tends to reflect the 'militarization' of company rhetoric. Decisions are constantly cast in relation to doing battle, winning wars, and laying waste the competition. Thus, the decision as to whether to spend money on advertising seemed to be as much the result of an anxiety that one would not keep up with some move by a competitor as of any long-term strategy with regard to one's own product. Indeed, as one executive admitted: 'You really have to justify every cent you are spending, if your competitor is not spending.' By implication, if the competitor has a current campaign it is far easier for product managers to justify such expenses within their own company.

An example comes from a telephone conversation by a transnational A. concerned with the promotional activity of its rival company B. 'You see how whenever a film comes in B. get their logo on that. So why not liaise with the cinema-owners. Tell them give us stuff for promoting their film in our 15-minute thing, and also give away ten free tickets for every major film which is launched. The youth study we just did shows that cinema is one of the top four types of entertainment. This is a means of blocking B. which is coming in with them. They should give us a concession in selling the stuff in the cinema, we should get exclusivity there.' Later on he notes, 'I ent having my backdrop next to that company. That's bull.'

The advertising agencies do what they can to foster client's paranoia by keeping them informed as to any new strategies being attempted by their rivals. Agencies often compete head-on through competitive tendering or through knowledge that a given transnational employs several agencies across its brand range. Here the paranoia of competition is returned by the client to the agency. As in all advertising, it is hard to gauge which factor is responsible for a given failure. Failure is therefore not in itself necessarily the reason why an account may move. Rather more important is the 'smell of success': as one executive noted: 'The fact that we won in a short space of time H., and L. people said, "There is something going on in that agency, boy. We had better get a piece of the action," and we are getting people coming to us to present whereas before we had to go out there and work for it.'

Once the decision is made to advertise, the spirit of competition becomes still more crucial in considering how the brand is positioned. There is often a dynamic history resulting from such competition. For example, in the domain of flavoured milks there are two main rivals: Nestlé and Cannings. Nestlé dominated flavoured milks in 1982, but Cannings's new range in 1983 made substantial inroads, including new flavours such as banana and strawberry. In 1985 Nestlé counter-attacked with its own new range, which (thanks more to difficulties on the Cannings side than any advances made by Nestlé) resulted in the collapse of part of the Cannings market. But Nestlé did not do much better, as the public rejected its own concept of low-fat drinks targeted at children. By the end of the decade Cannings had again moved forward with its Peanut Punch, Eggnog and Chocolate Milk, while Nestlé responded by relaunching its own series with a new name. Each would ideally wish to drive out the competitor, since the profits that can be squeezed from a situation of competitive price cutting clearly bear no relation to a 'what the market can bear' pricing policy where competition is not an issue.

In a big company there is also the problem of the internal relation to other brands of the same company, where competition must be avoided in order to (as one executive put it) 'minimize the cannibalism'. For example, when Nestlé wants to fight back against Cannings by developing new advertising for its flavoured milks such as eggnog and peanut punch, it acts within certain constraints. It cannot advertise on the basis of energy and athletics, because that would conflict with its own brand 'Milo'. It cannot emphasize sexuality, energy enhancement and meal substitution, since that would conflict with its 'Supligen'. It cannot be too child-centred, since that would take away sales from its own brand 'Quick'. This internal rivalry is particularly important because of the practice of merchandising, where companies fight for shelf space as a unit within the retail outlets. This means that the products of the same company are grouped together in the shop, and appear as immediate competitors to the shopper.

Having avoided internal rivalry the company then has to turn its attention to its rival Cannings. Here, by contrast, it must try to accentuate any innovations in flavour, such as a choc-nut or coffee that Cannings does not have, or any innovations in packaging, targeting, etc. that it can devise. The same, of course, follows for Cannings. Such factors are typical of the context within which an advertising campaign must be conceived and constructed.

Internal Controls

As noted above, the agencies formed themselves into a general association mainly to act as a lobbying group to the government and in response to general criticisms of their influence. Probably the most important factor was the sense that unless they took some voluntary measures to control their activities the likelihood of government intervention would be far higher. When inspecting the files of the Association it became clear that once again it was competition between the agencies rather than outside authority *per se* that seemed to be the foundation for the Association's authority. Rival companies were far more ready to make a complaint than a government agency. Controls over advertising were not the only role for the Association; they could also agree to mutually beneficial procedures, such as exchanging information on delinquent (that is non-paying) clients.

There are a variety of voluntary agreements and statutory rules that are intended to limit the freedom of advertising, including the Association's 'Code of Advertising Practice' and the 'Bureau of Standards' Requirements for Advertising'. For example, this is supposed to stop competitions that are too much like lotteries, to prevent certain products' being advertised to children, to curb nudity, and to stop open comparison or misleading claims. This official voluntary code of the Association bears no relation to reality, claiming among other things that 'testimonials should be the honest opinion of' and that there should be 'no sexual act implied or otherwise'.

The government's interventions were limited. 'Certain agencies, especially the small ones, know damn well you are not supposed to say the best so-and-so, but they will do it. And they know well that the next day there will be a phone call from the

so-and-so saying you cannot run this, but then they have done it.'
In one case it was noted that 'The Director of Public Prosecutions
has a letter advising them to stop the promotion, but they saying
"OK then, sue us." Shows the DPP has no teeth.' In practice, when
the government was backed up by rivalry within the profession
so that a given agency was encouraging it to take measures, then
limitations were often successfully imposed, and campaigns were
either taken off the air, or elements of them were toned down.

I do not want to give the impression that the voluntary code
was without effect. A typical investigation took place as to an
implied claim by a Spanish wine to be a champagne, on the
grounds that it was produced by the same method. It had not
called itself 'champagne', but said that it was 'the best way to fill
a champagne glass'. The objection had been upheld and the
advert withdrawn. The Calvin Klein line, 'You know what comes
between me and my Calvin Kleins – nothing', was also
withdrawn as indecent. For similar reasons Guinness had to
claim to 'keep your vigour up' rather than 'keep your pecker up'.
Various products were also prevented from naming their competitors directly. The adjudications are often rather byzantine,
as when 'it was held that this kind of expression was not an
absolute claim so much as an expression of satisfaction in almost
the hyperbole sense.'

Sometimes the 'truth' about such actions, as representing
advertising competition rather than simply moral concerns,
would come to the fore in aggressive letters from agencies. Since
the Association's chairperson was always a member of a particular agency, chairpersons could be accused of 'a criminal
conspiracy' and 'having rival interests' in pushing for conformity
with its rules. During the period of fieldwork McCann Erickson
withdrew from the association after a particularly acerbic conflict, and remained outside for over a year. The Association may
also be used for companies to attack each other directly, so that
Carib's claim to be 'the beer of Trinidad' and Stag's to be 'the
people's beer' are each denounced by their rivals. Government
may also take direct action, as when a minister complained in
parliament: 'One example of the saturation of advertising
campaigns pays tribute to a mother of 12 children who is able to
cope because of a certain beverage, the same beverage to which
is attributed by implication the father's ability to sire a dozen
offspring.'

This tension between permitted and forbidden advertising was also employed by the profession itself. A good example of this that occurred during fieldwork was an advert by S. M. Jaleel for Seven-Up. The advert consisted of a reprinted page from the national newspaper within the same newspaper, consisting of all the usual news, but then printed over this with the international cartoon 'youth' figure associated with Seven-Up holding a can of the drink. Critics correctly picked up on the idea that this was a deliberate subversion of the 'seriousness' of the news by an image of youth that had more exciting things to think about. This is what made this (I assume) a successful worldwide campaign strategy in relation to the youth market. Although there were complaints, the advert had transgressed in a sufficiently novel direction for no one to have much idea as to what might be done to prevent it.

The Media of Advertising: Television

The most important medium for advertising in Trinidad is television. It represents around 40 per cent of advertising expenditure, compared with 30 per cent for press and 20 per cent for radio. During the fieldwork it was represented by a single company, TTT (Trinidad and Tobago Television), owned by government. Begun in 1961 by Rediffusion and Thompsons (with 10 per cent equity held by CBS) it was nationalized in 1969. Different surveys suggested that between 85 per cent and 93 per cent of homes in Trinidad have television, of which 75 per cent have colour. One survey suggested 89 per cent of the population had watched within the last twenty-four hours. Given that less than 2 per cent had satellite dishes, the dominance of TTT was evident. The normative model was for four advertising breaks per hour, which might be five minutes between programmes and three minutes within programmes.

The costs of adverts had been checked by recession, and had remained constant since 1982. The rates ranged from TT$1,250 for 30 seconds or TT$2,145 for a minute at evening peak time, to TT$302.5 for 30 seconds between sign on and 12.00 noon. Alternatively, a company might sponsor a programme. The costs of television programmes to TTT varied considerably. Imported soap opera might cost TT$1,700 an hour or TT$2,500 for a feature programme. Local programmes, by contrast, would cost TT$4,000 for the news, but TT$8–12,000 for a local competition such as Scouting for Talent. The contract for the main local weekly arts programme had just gone down from TT$6,000 to TT$4,500 per programme. The proportion of local programmes, at around 25 per cent, seemed to have changed little since the beginning of Trinidadian television in the 1960s. Surveys by others have suggested that the proportion of foreign content was growing to 89 per cent of programming, although I feel this exaggerated foreign content prior to deregulation. As with many of these figures, I do not want to imply a spurious objectivity or precision. Differences in such percentages depend partly on how these terms are defined.

Once again the advertising agencies seem to have gradually infiltrated the mechanisms of the institution in order to gain influence over its output. Many of the formal controls over what was to be shown could be flouted. For example, the prohibition on alcohol and cigarette advertising early in the day could be overcome through full sponsorship of programmes. Advertisers were persuading clients to sponsor whole series, thereby re-placing the television authorities as the agents that sold off the advertising within the series to various clients.

The concern expressed by members of the public as to the degree to which advertisers could determine what was actually shown seemed borne out by my research, though denied by the television authorities. A television producer who had made a programme on a political theme noted that he would only be able to have the programme shown if he could pre-sell the programme himself to some companies who would guarantee the associated advertising. He noted that at present 'offensive' churches with evangelical messages could get on air because they could afford the costs, while other churches and religions could not.

Certainly agencies and their clients talked as though they could call the shots in terms of television programming. For example, in a telephone conversation one executive notes 'Yeah, it was a brilliant game, fabulous ... so if [person from TTT] would only tape it off his dish like he did on Sunday my thought it is to put Stag on with us. I don't know if Stag have any money or what. I feel we could delay the broadcast till the weekend and get a better audience. I don't know how much it would cost to bring live, because that's a serious decision. A three-hour game, well, I can imagine. I don't want to own the whole thing, I just want to be in association with it. . . . Well TTT will say no, no, no, but I imagine tomorrow at about half past five they would say they bringing it.' Another conversation complained that they are not informed what film will be shown in the movie slot. 'I wonder why, TTT don't sell the stuff themselves. . . . the reason is that they don't know what the movie is. Its just whatever they thief the night before!'

There were various ways of sponsoring local television shows. One noted that they gave TT$7,000 worth of prizes and received back $5,000 worth of free advertising, while another company gave a car worth TT$150,000 for the first prize. That year a bank had sponsored the whole series for TT$300,000. Another local series was quite blatant about showing only the products of the associated advertisers within the scenes shot during the series. Some of this was acknowledged by officials at TTT. They suggested that 'pre-selling a programme before deciding to put it on is getting more common, like sports events. Where there are rights involved and production charges, I like to get some commitment from our clients before I do anything. Clients can specify their preferences. In 99 per cent of cases they get what they want.'

Still more problematic was the tendency to use television for direct advertising masquerading as news. Companies discussed the main television business news programmes as though they were simply advertising slots to present new products and developments. Denied by the industry, but attested to by various workers in the media, were cases of enormous pressure placed on television by advertisers after something had been said within a programme detrimental to that company's products. An example of this issue came up during fieldwork when West Indian Tobacco Limited withdrew sponsorship worth TT$18,000 from 'Gayelle', a programme about local culture. Parts of the relevant letters were published in the *Guardian* 27/4/88. It is noticeable that the conflict was all handled through the advertising agency. The agency complained of Gayelle's relation to anti-smoking commercials as part of World Smoke-Out day. They claimed: 'It is incomprehensible that material and views in direct opposition to our client's [Witco's] business is aired on the very programme it has made a commitment to.' The programme makers replied that 'Your letter [Witco's] implies that when your client buys advertising identification in the programme, he expects to be afforded editorial influence . . . We offered advertising, not endorsement.' The Advertising Association sometimes became embroiled in these debates, and could see the problems involved in its own strategy of image construction. A case arose when an agency tried to refuse paying for a advert because the associated programme had included derogatory remarks about it [the agency]. The Association's letter noted: 'In fact by threatening this action you are endorsing the point the programme was raising about the power which advertisers wield.'

The Media of Advertising: Other Media

According to a media survey 95 per cent of households have a radio, 21 per cent have two or more radios, and 88 per cent of cars have radios; 79 per cent of the population had listened within the last 24 hours, while 17 per cent have radio on the whole day. While television was dominated by two programmes, *The Young and the Restless* and the News, with huge ratings at around 70 per cent, radio's highest rating was only 29 per cent for the news at 6.00 p.m. The radio is perceived as a more approachable medium, and there are a considerable number of interactive genres such as phone-ins and advice sections, as well as request shows. Indeed, the sixth most popular programme was the death announcements. Radio was divided into four stations owned by two companies (with two stations each).

Radio is still more saturated with adverts than television, with often a third or more of the time on air going to advertising. The highest rate I recorded was a staggering 54 minutes of advertising interspersed with only 15 minutes of music on Radio 100 during a morning just before Christmas! One reason this is possible is the proportion of radio adverts that are themselves sung. I was probably not the only listener often to prefer the music within the adverts to that which separated them. As one advertising executive noted: 'Radio ads more outrageous since cheap, can afford to do it. Also quick. More up to date with what's going on . . .'. Despite this topicality, I did not get the impression that the agencies spent much time devising their radio material, which was certainly seen as secondary to television.

Just as with television, larger companies might decide to sponsor programmes rather than simply provide spots in general. One conversation in a major company demonstrated the degree of sophistication that could be involved. This took place in the light of a detailed media survey by a marketing company, leading to a general review of its radio sponsorship policy. The first step had been to calculate the precise cost of 'delivering' listeners, based on the estimated audience for particular shows and the costs of sponsoring those shows. Each programme was also considered in terms of which other shows were broadcast at that time slot, and what this would represent in terms of competitors advertising. For example a programme might be sponsored through 5 spots in a day or 1,000 per year, with a cost of TT$35 per spot or TT$35,000 per year. This was followed by a lengthy discussion about advertising to the Indian consumer. Since there are relatively few radio programmes based largely on Indian materials and thus known to obtain Indian audiences, these had been charging higher rates. The company not only considered its relative advertising input into these programmes but also alternative strategies, for example, creating an entirely new Indian radio programme on FM. There was speculation about the Indian youth audience and the potential for a 'top 10 Indian music programme.' Further discussion revealed that on the basis that 40 per cent of the audience for a more general show would be Indian it would be cheaper to obtain the 'ethnic' audience through working with the larger general show than by targeting specifically Indian programmes.

The importance of sponsorship is evident in the details of programmes listed in the newspapers. Drinks are particularly prominent. The listing of one day's broadcasts for Radio Trinidad included eighteen programmes plus the news. Of these ten are sponsored by drinks, including the 'Coca-Cola Soca Jam', the 'Pepsi Cola Jam' and 'Light Rock with White Rock.' Sportsview and Test Cricket were sponsored by Carib, and 'Bring Yuah Music and Come' was sponsored by Stag.

The situation in the newspaper industry was rather more complex than that of television and radio. As already noted, one problem was that one of the two major daily papers was owned by a local conglomerate (the *Guardian*, established 1917) and the other (the *Express*, established 1967) heavily influenced by its rival. The weekly newspapers were also seen as representing certain interests. For example, a savage attack on the weeklies by a daily paper accused them all of being in the pay of Indian politicians of the opposition party, leading to continual attacks on African politicians. Market research, however, showed no evidence that readership was split on ethnic lines.

Most advertising went to the daily papers and their sister Sunday editions, where the cost of a full-page advert was in one case TT$5,049 for the Sunday paper and TT$6,806 for the daily paper. When sharing of papers was taken into account total estimated readership was around 350,000 for each of the two main dailies, and not much less for the best-selling weekly. Traditionally, the weekly papers were anti-business and concerned with scandals of various kinds. As an example of the genre's 'depths' the *Blast* for 21/10/88 has for its headlines 'Minister Eats His Own Dog', just below a smaller line about 'Man Uses Carrot as a Dildo.' These newspapers survived by having much lower overheads, while attracting few adverts except for products such as condoms.

One particular bi-weekly paper, the *Mirror*, has been particularly forthright in its critique of business, as in a column (15/7/88) that stated 'over the years, advertisers have always tried to "run" newspapers by threatening to withdraw their business if the reporting staff does not toe the line'. Even here things were changing with recession, and since the *Mirror* took on new overheads it had experimented with a 'business section' in order to repair its relationship with potential advertisers. The same newspaper's revelations about government included suggestions of censorship, in that it claimed evidence that, as a result of its attacks, the government was preventing it from obtaining the foreign currency it needed to buy newsprint.

As with the other media, there are various areas where the relationship between advertising and news content becomes murky. The daily papers have various sections that purport to address public concerns, such as a 'Medical Corner' or 'Food Scene – a fortnightly publication for the Agricultural Development Bank.' These sections of the paper tend to be mainly concerned either with advertisements or articles that are as good as advertisements. There are also many business supplements.

For example, the soap company Cussons for its 21st anniversary took out a 4-page supplement. There are also supplements to mark the opening of a shopping centre. These supplements tend to include a large number of adverts for the companies that are associated with the product or project.

Still more problematic is the tendency to report the company line of the conglomerate that owns a particular paper. Such influences are nothing new. Stories tell of Kirpilani, an important business man of an earlier period, checking the front page of *The Bomb* before deciding whether to advertise with it. Indeed, there was reputed to have been a particularly controversial case in the 1970s where an article by a daily paper criticized a country club that appeared to be running a 'whites only' policy. This led to various advertisers threatening to pull out from that paper.

Sponsorship and Promotions

Apart from direct-media advertising the most important means by which companies attempt to influence consumers in favour of their clients is through sponsorships and promotions. These seemed to be extraordinarily ubiquitous, a point that will be discussed further in Chapter 8. Indeed, since the period of fieldwork, agencies have suggested that there has been still more emphasis on such activities, which are cheaper than a full-blown television advertising campaign. In particular, the early 1990s have seen a growth in 'piggybacking', where companies will combine to share the costs, Supligen for example being promoted as a mixer for rum, representing a combination of Nestlé with Fernandez, the main rum producer. These were not without opposition. The *Express,* under the title 'If you drink milk, buy some coffee', complained that people who hated Milo seemed to have to buy a tin in order to get condensed milk, etc. (29/9/88).

These activities divide into several main categories: competitions, promotions, merchandising and sponsorships. Competitions were a constant feature of life, often being advertised in their own right on television and radio and in the press. A typical advert that appeared in the press, but relates to television, was: 'Amco invites you to enter "The Young and the Restless" competition.

The new grand winner will take off to meet the stars in person at a filming of "The Young and the Restless".' To enter, people have to give evidence of their product use and answer questions about the show such as 'Who was in the car accident with Nina on her way to the wedding?' Competitions may also relate to a current event such as 'Nicen up yourself', and win 'free tickets to M. C. Hammer in concert together with 1,000 dollars to spend in any mall of your choice'. This depended upon answers to questions such as 'Who is the controversial film director of "Do the right thing" and "Malcolm X"?' The ability to conjure up a competition out of the most unlikely materials was evident in a competition advertised in the weekend *Heat* for 15 December 1990, which was not long after the attempted coup by Abu Bakr, and was entitled 'Stage a coup: test your knowledge about current affairs and take part in the big overthrow!'

Competitions often form one element in larger strategies, which may be called promotions. These also have been significant for a long period, and are often credited with first establishing particular products. Larger promotions may be carried out by professional companies attached to transnational firms. For example, I attended a meeting to discuss whether the Trinidadian branch of a transnational wanted to get involved in a competition based around the YoYo which was being carried out in other countries in the region. At the meeting they showed pictures of a promotion the same company had carried out for the Trinidad office back in 1957. Various details were considered, such as how much time the main YoYo experts would actually spend in Trinidad, what might be suitable prizes (the idea of footballs for girls was vetoed), whether there could be special events for the disabled or orphans, how the country would be divided up into regions, and where the promotion would itself be promoted. They were also concerned about how efficient the other countries involved would be in ensuring that the necessary materials were present when they were required.

An advantage of both competitions and promotions is that they are seen as influencing the retailers to stock more product in the expectation that there will be an increase in consumer demand associated with the event.

Not all such promotions were at this international level. One local promoter specialized in putting together small-scale campaigns, particularly for South Trinidad, where these are regarded as most successful. For example, to promote a product for girls up to the age of 14, he produced a see-through purse that contained the product, which he reasoned would be attractive in itself for the forthcoming Carnival season. He not only made and printed the promotional items but liaised directly with the companies, and thereby offered to save them costs through by-passing the advertising agencies. Typically, he would make between 4,000 and 20,000 of his promotional items.

The most local end of promotion was an activity known as merchandising. This was also an extremely common process, and engaged in by most of the major companies in Trinidad that dealt with supermarket-sold commodities. The merchandisers were employed essentially to fight for market share at the retail level. Typically, they would be women in uniforms of the relevant colours or logo, who would stand in the major supermarkets on days of expected high sales. First, they would check the shelves to see that they were properly stocked and provided with advertising materials. They may also be engaged in negotiations as to how much shelving is allocated to a particular product. In the store they may provide free tastes of samples. They may wait and watch until a customer reaches for an alternative brand, and then step in to provide a free sample or special offer of their own brand, while also obtaining the customer's opinion and thus providing feedback for the firm. One particular merchandiser reckoned on improving sales of her product (nappies) by at least 50 per cent by her presence. On a Friday a large supermarket might have around six such merchandisers active in the store.

This degree of sponsorship is related to the obsessive concern by companies to have their logo seen at any site where their rivals' logos might otherwise be found. This was particularly the case if the event might be televised. An example of this came up with a discussion about the finals of the schools' football tournament. The company marketing manager considered where his logo might be sited:

> Well, corner flags, the ball boys – dress them up in our shirts; the referee's garments – we could dress them. A lot of pictures appear in the papers with us on the flag and so on. What we need is a big billboard in the stadium, and the tent opposite the stands where the teams come out, in front of that. A tent for the officials or for the teams, that sort of thing. Last year we had this banner. The other

thing we could do is print flags, not corner flags, we talking flags for the spectators, real cheap stuff. Another thing is we have to reprint jerseys for the commentator and organize track suits for them All Star team, because we weren't ready for them last year.

Market Research

The development of market research has certainly not kept up with that of the advertising agency. Whereas advertising agencies have, if anything, established their presence and range of activities well beyond those that are associated with such agencies in many other countries, the marketing research companies have only recently had much success in persuading companies that expenditure was required in this direction. In large measure this relates back to the observations made on the companies themselves, where given the small size of the country, executives often feel they 'know' their market without having to engage in expensive research. Or alternatively, as another suggested, 'anything my wife picks up and says is good, must be'. As one of the executives giving me an oral history of the industry noted 'Research is a bad word and it shows. In my experience with the Trinidadian business man he tends to react by saying "Forget it." Indeed, most marketing workers feel it is the home-grown Trinidadian rather than the foreign official who is most opposed to marketing, particularly when, as is often the case, they have come up through the ranks of salesman.'

This situation did not change until the mid-1970s when, thanks to the oil boom, companies felt able to indulge in expenditures even in areas they were not entirely convinced would pay dividends. These were the best years for such research. One executive recalled paying US$80,000 for a Jamaica, Puerto Rico and Trinidad project, but assumed this could not happen today. Things did not simply go into reverse, however. The recession saw some retention, owing to insecurity and the sense that anything that might help retain markets should be attempted. The exceptions to this history are one or two of the transnationals that have imported their traditions of market research over a much longer period and mainly supported the one marketing research company that had been around since the mid-1960s.

Marketing research may be derived from three sources: the marketing section of the company itself, the advertising agency, and professional market research companies. There are several of the last category offering their services, but there are probably only two that enjoy a significant reputation amongst businesses, plus a third that mainly works for governmental agencies. Research that is done within companies or advertising agencies is most likely to be based around focus groups, which are held to be 'representative' of certain kinds of consumer. For example, one such study consisted of seven focus groups, each from a particular region and characterized by class, ethnicity and gender, for example 'Pleasantville – working-class Indian males.' In general the advertising agency will do the pre-testing of products and the client company will be responsible for any post-testing, which might include dealer surveys, feedback from merchandisers, or recall tests in a supermarket. The marketing companies may work through either agency or client. One advertising agency claimed to make use of four different market research companies.

Full-time marketing companies are used for more extensive research, but also for mundane tasks such as standard recall tests. For example, a company paid TT$3,750 to examine the effect of a particular promotion. For this around 500 interviews were conducted in four malls, to find out (a) how many people knew of the promotion; (b) how many knew which company was associated with it; and (c) which prizes they would like to have won. Typical other surveys included questions about where people would like to travel to, what goods they perceived as having gone up in price, and blind tests on preferred fragrances. A typical company pays interviewers TT$60 per day to work from 9 to 5 and to obtain an interview every ten minutes.

There are two main uses of more extensive market research. One is regular 'omnibus' surveys, where major companies wish to keep track of general trends in consumption through surveys carried out every two to four months. The advantage of such surveys is that they may indicate general trends, mapping brand preference against age, income, ethnicity, gender and region. One might thereby spot a sudden interest in a product amongst youth, or a change in the degree of dominance of the leading brand in a region. The other source of intensive research is for the launch of new products, where the market research forms part of the development of a new campaign. Such research may cost in the order of TT$25,000 for an important new commodity.

Market research may be used by companies to justify changes in campaigns from international to local themes, and thus the employment of local advertising agencies. In general there is not much market segmentation. Mostly the divisions used are obvious enough, and follow from the information available in the national population census, which is usually used as a baseline to determine the parameters for samples. Occasionally, more complex indices might be used, such as 'amount of money spent on food'.

Detailed marketing research is normally done on the kind of product where the creatives are fully involved because of the importance of the campaign. In meetings, between the advertisers and the clients, such research would be mentioned from time to time in order to justify or repudiate a proposed campaign theme. At some point an executive might note 'but when we were doing the thing in Maloney, we had 15 guys aged 15–30 and they said . . .'. More generally, a campaign's overall strategy might be justified by saying 'We are going to launch a [product]. Research shows it's an African thing.' In general, all those working outside the marketing profession itself agree that research is largely used to legitimate strategies whose source comes from elsewhere, and is rarely used to initiate directions or confront decisions based on hunches or some other foundation. In this the evidence from Trinidad parallels that for the use of marketing research in advertising more generally as being little more than a 'comfort mechanism for decision makers' (Schudson 1993: 54).

There are exceptions, and one of the most successful campaigns of the time was based on close co-operation between the company's marketing manager, the director of a marketing company and a senior executive in an advertising agency. These three managed to show much more concern with 'ordinary life', and themselves attended many events in order to keep a sense of the market. The marketing research was tightly integrated into a multi-faceted strategy concerned to keep their 'collective ear to the ground'. In this case marketing material could be interpreted within a larger qualitative context of knowledge. This meant it was both more respected and used; but this was rare. Not surprisingly, those within the marketing profession affirm its necessity. The marketing manager for one transnational recalled the launch of a drink that failed miserably 'It should have been predicted, since tetrapack is associated with children's things, not alcohol, it was more expensive than beer and in the tasting sample only 50 per cent liked it. Dumped 800 cases after 8 months. The whole exercise costs them TT$400,000. The manager insisted you have to test waters like that, but it makes for a very expensive form of marketing research.'

Structural Tensions in Advertising – A Case Study

The general discussion so far cannot convey a sense of the atmosphere within which key decisions are made. A case study provides this much more effectively, and thereby complements the previous analysis. Since the semiotic aspect of advertising is the subject of the next chapter, I have chosen a case that seems to minimize the question of symbolic linkage, and emphasizes rather the institutional context. In practice these two cannot be easily separated, and what will emerge is that the semiotics, and even the degree to which the commodity is subject to overt symbolizing, is itself closely bound up with the internal tensions and imperatives of the agencies in their relationship with their clients. The other reason for starting with this rather de-contextualized product is that in most campaigns it would be impossible to retain even a hope of the anonymity of the companies concerned while giving details of the conversations that took place. I have also changed some of these details by amalgamating evidence from other campaigns, in order to help retain anonymity.

As noted above, although in a small country the directors are the key people in determining which advertising agency obtains which contract, they may not be personally involved in any but the most important or sensitive campaigns. In this particular case, I was not aware of any involvement of the director of the agency. All the action that I was able to observe took place between two groups: the account manager and a team of creatives on behalf of the advertisers; while for the company it was the overall marketing manager together with a more junior product manager responsible for this particular product line. There are two companies that dominate this product, and I obtained some information on both their strategies; but I will conflate this into a single company, to be called 'Cal'.

For the purposes of this case study I will use the following terms:

Advertising Agency = Adab
Drink Producing Company = Cal
Rival Company = Dag
Account Manager at Adab = AM
Marketing Director at Cal = MD
Product Manager at Cal = PM.

The first meeting took place when Adab, represented by a team of Creatives and the AM, came to the offices of Cal to hear a briefing from Cal's PM in the presence of the MD. The MD was one of the most senior officials of the company, a post which in earlier times would have been held by an expatriate. The PM was a junior official, who clearly felt under some pressure to prove himself in the presence of the MD. The agency and company had worked together previously on various products and were well known to each other. The same company also used other advertising agencies for other products, so that the agency was well aware that the company could shift products to other advertising agencies at any time were they not satisfied, while a particularly good campaign might bring them more business. In this particular drinks division, the two had recently collaborated on what was generally regarded as a highly successful campaign for another product.

The meeting was based on the decision to re-launch a drink, both in itself and as part of a range. There was to be a 20-second television advert for the drink and a 30-second advert for the range. The total advertising budget was TT$ 75,000. The MD started by providing a general discussion of the commercial climate for this launch. He noted that, thanks to the recession, things were terrible, the country's GDP had contracted by 26.6 per cent in five years, and another 6.1 per cent in real terms between 1986 and 1988. This was the first year they had recorded a dollar for dollar decline. In 1986 they had made no money on a turnover of 10 million dollars. In 1987 prices had increased to some degree, and they made a little over a million dollars from a turnover of 8.5 million. Cal was maintaining an 8 per cent price differential over Dag and was also offering retailers 25 per cent, while Dag only offered 18 per cent; but Cal was still selling only half Dag's quantity. That year they had not increased prices, but just absorbed costs. The PM did not feel many options were left: 'If I could drop my price by even 15 per cent, which would make it significant to the consumer, I have to double the amount of volume to make up, and there is no way you can sell double the volume.'

The PM then proceeded to give a very upbeat description of the kind of advert he had in mind. Most of the description was provided using strong images of a war with the opposition, and dramatic gestures of aggression, for example, 'I would like to see what would happen if I dropped my price to . . ., because I am quite prepared to wipe them off the market prematurely. If I drop, they cannot match, in a month, they are losing money.' At another point he states 'I just want to be on top. I want to be the market leader, . . . so I want to be seen as what I am, the leader.' The presentation was intended to be exciting, although at one point he noted 'the sky's the limit, I mean the number of approaches I have sat down and thought about. I said I'll just not write anything down, because the client is not supposed to tell the agency what to do.' He concluded that 'we want the packaging to look so appealing and the advertising to be so stupendous that people just go like zombies and buy this product'.

This bravado was also evident in the details of the brief, which talked of using the country's top calypso artists, with visions of exciting scenes and glamorous images that would devastate the opposition. For example 'If you had a woman and had brown tan, and skin close up, in a hammock, the sort of wrap they have . . . it could melt into a dream product, intermingles into fantasy; not sex thing, I don't want to abuse womanhood; but if you drop a woman there, dark tan, can see the pores of her skin, and you are looking at TV and, say, going for a beer . . . "Later . . . let me see what they are trying to tell me." I want a scene that sucks you in. Romance in a real way, that people can touch.' The MD, by contrast, provided a more sober brief, mainly concerned that the brand name would be prominent and the drink's attributes clear.

After this briefing the creative section of Adab had some time to come up with a suggested 'storyboard' that would outline the intended adverts. This they presented to the female AM in the presence of a senior executive who had not been present at the meeting with the client. The three younger female creatives presented as a group. They argued that the most important attribute of the drinks was the new way the packaging was to be opened by pulling off a tab. They suggested as the key line 'Only Cal could pull it off.' They suggested 3 or 4 different scenes when people are doing something but it all goes wrong, and because they bring out the drink, they pull it off and save the day. The example given was a school play, where the manager trips up, the donkey comes out in two different halves. The line would have been 'How could we ever pull this off? Nothing's going right. Pull out Cal's new . . . pull off the tab and enjoy a taste delight.'

At this point the AM interrupted and loudly proclaimed 'This commercial is too people-orientated; we have taken a decision that we will stay away from people, the whole thing is people. What we wanted to do was to cover the attributes of the products, use the studio for strong branding, its new packaging, new product, former flatness, by getting across the thick appetite appeal of the new product. In my opinion you are on the wrong track totally.' There followed half an hour of argument, with the creatives being berated by the AM, supported by comments by the executive, who claimed that the creatives hadn't read the brief properly, etc. The creatives gave each other moral support by muttering comments to each other. For example, at one point a creative noted in a whisper 'I wish we had known that this is what they wanted before, from the very start, because we wouldn't have wasted all this time at all.' She then stated aloud 'I really thought that, OK, it is a new product and image, right, and is supposed to be original and creative.'

I want to dwell on this meeting rather than the first, since three points emerged clearly from it. Firstly, the realities of the context were stated far more baldly. Secondly, the distance between what is being said and what was supposed to be heard became evident; and thirdly, the structural relations between account managers and creatives were brought out with particular clarity. With regard to the first, the AM noted:

Unfortunately, we have one negative, which is that the product has flopped twice on two launches prior to this one. Not because of advertising, since wasn't any. The product failed because of the quality of the product and the perception. Especially before they had competition they were able to get away with a certain amount, since there wasn't any choice, but there is now even greater comparison. Don't forget Dag has been very well received as a good tasting, whatever that good tasting might be, the thickness, bubbliness, the strength.

The grounds for paying for an advert at this point were precisely the possibility that the previous failures might have been partly because of lack of advertising.

Most important, however, was the difference between this product and its rivals. After a while the AM became still more honest: 'You have a perception of a flat, horrible-tasting product to deal with; OK, you have that perception, it exists, they are being beaten out of the market to the point that they had to withdraw two, and if this continues they will have to discontinue.' Such statements were based on the company's own research, which showed a clear preference for the rival's drink, on the grounds that it was sweeter. The further problem was that Cal simply could not produce a product as bubbly and thick as that of Dag, because the kind of machinery they used would not allow it.

However, things did not all go Dag's way. Their bubbly product cost more to produce, particularly because of the main ingredient. The suspicion was that they were often changing the actual constituents. It was suggested 'maybe the content goes up and down with the price of [an ingredient].' There was evidence that consumers were starting to notice this inconsistency and that the product was sometimes found to have gone bad. They speculated that this was also due to production problems: 'In addition they have tried to reformulate, which may be part of the problem, since when you reformulate you don't know how exactly to handle the machinery. They have reformulated to try and make the product a bit more profitable.' What this demonstrated was that the known 'sub-text' to their brief was the necessity to address the key difference between Cal and Dag, which was that the new product had tried to improve its bubbliness, though marketing research showed that it still did not match their main rival.

The second point to emerge comes from the discrepancy between what had so far been said and what was supposed to be heard. It was quite clear that the original meeting was understood by the 'experienced' advertising executive as having very little to do with the actual intentions behind the campaign. The exciting bravado of the PM at Cal was seen to be a necessary public performance in the presence of his MD, to demonstrate that he was an up-and-coming team member with masses of fresh ideas and drive. Despite the fact that they had all sat around in the first briefing and discussed the detailed proposals for hours with complete seriousness, it was evident back at the agency that no one was expected to take any of that discussion as having any further significance. The only difference was the degree to which this was understood to be the case. The creatives at Adab clearly still felt that there was an argument here for something fresh and exciting. At one point one of them laments, saying 'I really thought we had to come up with something, the way they were talking at the brief. All the time is they wanted something original and different.' This was dismissed as mere *naïveté* by the more senior staff. As far as they were concerned, it should have been 'obvious' that the advert was a launch ad that was primarily concerned to present the new image of the packages and the attributes of the drink itself, in particular with reference to this 'problem' of taste and bubbliness. They should have known enough to ignore the entire content of the PM's presentation.

It was, however, not only the meeting with the client that was in many respect not at all what it had first seemed. This further meeting within Adab had many ritualistic elements, in the sense that arguments were evoked that seemed to belong to a standard rhetoric that was more to do with the establishment of the structural relations between sections within the company than about the actual advert. As Moeran points out (1993: 88) many of the rituals of advertising, such as presentations to clients, 'are part and parcel of the processes that serve to define and maintain the advertising community as a whole'. At one point the AM said 'We came here for a frank discussion. I give you my opinion. Immediately you start to read to me, and I am waiting for my product to appear in the ad. Down the road and I ent hearing the product yet, and that worries me, and I think this is a genuine concern.' She is clear that the focus should be on the product and its package, noting that 'They don't want any consumption shots in the range add.' The creative replies 'That's very, very limiting', to which the AM noted 'It is the confines under which you are working; that is the difference between fine art and graphic art, right, it would be nice not to have confines, but that is the real role.' The creative then queried 'Where is the entertainment value in that? . . . you have just limited the introduction 30 secs to 10 secs of pouring each product and hoping that the package mesmerizes everybody. OK, maybe there is too much activity, but I believe for an introductory ad you need something that people will look at more than once.' The AM then concluded 'When I say show product for 30 secs you don't have to be literal; I am talking to people who do creative, who do copy and thing.'

This exchange is, I suspect, one that could be repeated not only many times within this and other Trinidadian advertising agencies, but in advertising agencies round the world. It is based upon the best-known structural fault within advertising agencies, which is part of the organizational 'habitus' inculcated in the training of those taking part. The creatives are supposed to be budding artists, wishing to demonstrate their artistic abilities through this medium. It is generally assumed that, if they could make a living through art, they would have done so, and that they resent the limitations imposed by commerce. The AM, by contrast, is expected to identify with the commercial concerns of the client and to be primarily identified with the drive towards a profitable product. Thus, in the final comment made before the meeting broke up, she demands 'Just treat my product strongly, my branding and my product attributes.'

The degree to which this is in a sense an evocation of a ritual encounter was especially evident in another section of the argument. At one point the AM stated 'That is what people feel might be acceptable to a European taste or whatever it is, but it is not acceptable to a Trinidadian.' This was, in that context, a totally irrelevant comment that bore no relation to the actual issue, just as the comment made about fine art and graphic art above was irrelevant, since no one could see the botched school play scene as 'fine art.' Rather, both relate to a vocabulary of argument in which creatives by definition are expected to have their ideals sanctified in a European tradition of fine art that is far too distant from the immediate concerns of local commerce. The fact that the criticism did not actually apply in this case was no more an issue than the fact that Cal's PM's description of what he would like to see was not supposed to be acted upon.

These are perhaps extreme examples, but they indicate how much the conversational content within commercial institutions such as these major companies and advertising agencies has often as much to do with the reaffirmation of organizational roles through studied performance as it has to do with the actual creation of the image itself. In both meetings it was the status of the junior members, either trying to impress or being put down by the senior figures, that was the key to comprehending the exchange. The AM was using the opportunity to show how 'typically' creatives cannot be trusted and must be carefully controlled, while in their muttered asides the creatives confirmed amongst themselves their prejudices about account managers who have no concept of how advertising could actually work.

Sometimes such exchanges seemed to bear little on the actual result in terms of the advertising made, but this particular encounter did seem to establish a trajectory of constraint that helps account for the final advert produced by the campaign. It may even be that the effect of this classic internal contradiction within the agency bears directly on why the final advert produced was possibly less appropriate and successful than might otherwise have been the case. The advertising agency saw itself as being 'mature' enough to read between the lines of the brief and prepare an advert that was true to the unspoken 'realities' of the commercial context. They assumed that this meant, despite everything said to them in the brief, a highly cautious, conservative approach was called for, given the precarious situation of the brand. The marketing manager at Cal had certainly expressed the cautious side of their demands: 'I don't want to risk it in terms of "Everybody, this is something new." I don't want that. I want something that will work. They can do that on Stag or Carib, but not on my drinks, boy.' He is here suggesting that one could afford to try to be experimental on prime brands such as beer, but this drink was not the appropriate place for true innovation. It was such statements that Adab's AM chose to focus upon as the 'true' brief. As was suggested in a later conversation with me, 'When you hear that what they want is something slick with a calypso you know you have to keep translating as you go along.'

Adab therefore read one message and ignored another in deciding what Cal 'really' wanted. But they may well have 'over-compensated', resulting in a much blander de-contextualized advert than even Cal's marketing manager had originally envisaged. Indeed, this was to create a problem for Cal. As their marketing manager noted later on in the campaign 'I said sharpen the product a bit more, but now we have taken away everything else and only have product alone. While there is nothing wrong with that, what it has done is that it has totally created a launch ad, which means the life of the ad is much shorter. Don't know if I could go a year. It just says this is the brand, that is the delicious taste and that is it.' As such Cal felt in some ways they had been let down by not being pushed into being more adventurous by Adab. As one of their executives commented towards the end of this round of meetings 'It seems like in this second approach it was like "If that's what you want to see, OK, you got it."'

Conservatism in the context of creating an advert takes the form of complete concentration on the product itself and its brand name and form, as opposed to relating the product to a given context. But it took more than the meetings so far described for this to happen. There was at least one more stage of further de-contextualization to go through. The next meeting was a presentation by Adab to Cal which, of course, made no mention of the previous conflict. Instead, it provided the result of a compromise that retained some inclusion of person and context in the proposed advert.

The proposal was to place the drink within a 'lazy Sunday morning'. This might be viewed as a consumption context, suggesting to the viewer an appropriate time for drinking this flavour. But the creatives clearly saw this as rather less specific in its impact. Rather, it was a way of objectifying the concept of 'flavour' itself. At one point the conversation went: 'Sunday morning is not a time, but a mood, a character. You know, just as you hear certain types of music on Sunday morning, classical music'. 'And religious music', chimes in another voice, and they all laugh. The point is made by the joke. Religious music would have really meant Sunday morning, as opposed to the mood symbolized by that time, which is what the creatives wanted to evoke. The discussion used the concrete case to deal with more general semiotic issues. When one opined 'You can't create a mood without a situation' the reply was 'But sometimes you don't need to describe the situation: for example, if you were to open on a Sunday morning, it could be a Sunday morning because its not a workaday, the person not rushing nowhere, relaxing; so I am drinking . . . on a lazy Sunday morning.'

Later on in this meeting an executive noted that, with the recession, actual Sunday mornings rarely fitted the image being discussed. The unemployed were not working on weekdays, and even those in work might be hustling to find some further ways of making money on Sundays. The reply was that 'That doesn't go on in reality, but this product could help you feel that way.' This was to suggest that the strategy might have been particularly attractive, as the drink would help at least to evoke a temporary sense of something desired but largely lost. Cal's PM could see a further problem as he noted: 'I would not say *lazy* Sunday. I find that a negative; something like "laid back" or "inactive", but not "lazy".'

This illustrates how advertising operates within the schema of what Schudson (1993: 209–33) called capitalist realism. This is a realism that is not based on verisimilitude to the outside world, as in showing a typical person drinking in a typical fashion. Rather, this is a realism constituted by the long-term role of advertising in constructing a genre within which commodities are supposed to be part of a kind of hyper-real idealized world of consumption.

The discussion that took place in the meeting was covering ground that has been increasingly the focal point of academic discussions about the nature of the semiotic relationship. This is not surprising, since many of these ideas were first formulated in the critique of advertising, and later became a major part of the training of advertising personnel. For example, at one point an executive referred to an article he had seen in a magazine of the advertising industry looking to future trends. 'I found that where he said ads were going, I remember their script, because he said the ads that were moving your brand was a feeling, it wasn't a product; but I didn't agree with it. I don't want to risk this, it is something new. I don't want to totally eradicate what you had before.' The creatives, however, were keen to relate the strategy to such trends, since they might thereby salvage some status-enhancing discourse from the realities of their constraints. They may have been refused the more overt creative advert, but they could argue that this degree of de-contextualization was in line with a more subtle form of suggestive mood/flavour construction that was now in favour. What had started as a constraint (i.e. the emphasis upon the product) was being re-termed as something 'sexy.'

From the perspective of the client the move to de-contextual-ization was fine if argued to be a strategy to concentrate on branding and product image. But the client became nervous if told that this was actually some kind of new-wave attempt to create what academics have termed 'a postmodern decoupling of the sign from the signified'. Once again the desire felt by the creatives to feel good about what they were doing could end by turning others against them. But this was only part of the issues involved in considering explicitly an advert as a semiotic form. The problem is that the company cannot control this order of evocation between sign and signified. There is the equal possibility that that the viewer will see the product as itself captured by the context of this mood creation, so that desire for the product is reduced to the specificity of the particular time evoked (and by implication consumers would restrict their drinking to those occasions). As one executive put it 'Every time you put in a setting you are going to fix consumption time or pattern or occasion. If it was a soccer match you could say "fixes it with sport". You said you didn't want setting, wanted it in the middle of nowhere.' The fear now was that 'Sunday morning' would not be read as a mood, but would limit consumption to actual Sunday mornings. Within the general climate of caution this lack of confidence in their ability to control the semiotic direction of their own images was enough to sink the suggestion. When the adverts were finally produced, all consumption contexts were eliminated, and the result was solely one of product and pouring. By this stage it was clear that branding was the sole focus, not some elusive sense of mood or character.

The concept behind this campaign had passed from telling a story to specifying a consumption context to total de-contextualization. This in turn produced another problem, put succinctly at one meeting as 'pouring too boring.' But this was in turn rejected by the AM of Adab in talking to the creatives. The point she made was that, given the right creative input and appropriate technological capacity, this action of pouring could be made to look exciting and, more importantly, enticing. A decision was therefore made early on to go abroad for the production. Trinidadian advertising companies often have agreements with agencies abroad to assist them with the more sophisticated graphical devices for which facilities do not exist in Trinidad. An agency such as McCann Erickson, of course, has no such problems. Other agencies have agreements in Florida or more often in nearby Caracas to use facilities there to create those parts of their adverts that require special skills.

The clients themselves were sceptical as to how far this could be taken; as one put it after hearing a briefing 'I have just seen a whole avalanche of pouring shots. All I see is a band of blue coming across the screen, something coming from nowhere and going nowhere, it doesn't impress me, just a band of blue.' As is often the case the 'pour' is already constituted by the memory of past campaigns. So that people will say 'Pour should not be a regular [Brand A] pour, but must be something interesting, so want to know how they execute that, something more like a [Brand B] pour.' These conversations refer to adverts shown in the last few years for other drinks that used pouring shots. This is true for most aspects of advert production. Anything from the models employed to the way a text appears on the screen can be discussed in terms of recent examples of adverts shown on Trinidadian television. Not surprisingly, behind some 3 seconds of visual image meant to evoke a sense of viscosity may be an expensive mixture of mock-ups made from entirely different materials. As one executive noted, liquids that will solidify once they are poured are often helpful, with these days often some added computer-generated graphics.

The advert that was finally produced seems at first relatively bland and innocuous. It makes some reference to the ingredients the drink is made from, but the emphasis is on the pouring, the bubbliness and the new package. There is, however, a considerable irony here. By following structural tensions between the account manager and the creatives that led to ever-increasing conservatism, the end result is probably about as risky as any advert for this particular product at this particular time could have been. The entire advert is focused around the concept of bubbliness and thickness, which were exactly the features that all the marketing research had shown this product to be weaker in than its main rival. It certainly 'addressed' what was the true main issue, but, as all the participants must have known, it therefore contained a disastrous potential for simply drawing the attention of consumers to why they should buy the rival's product.

Indeed, what might be seen as the dishonesty of the campaign is highlighted further, in that the spoken section referred to the product as 'true to you', juxtaposed with what was shown to be a particular bubbliness and thickness of texture. This, of course, was exactly what would not be true as soon as the consumer purchased the drink. The advert made, by creating visuals based on quite different materials, to produce an evocation of something that, even if the drink was nigh perfect, could not have been created merely through the sensation of drinking. In this case, the hidden suggestion is a promise to be bubblier and thicker than the rival that is manifestly untrue. When watching the campaign over several months I could not help the feeling that this slogan about 'true to you' arose almost subliminally, despite the many hours of discussion over each detail, as a symptom of the worries that both the company and the agency felt about the commercial prospects for this drink, given the intense competition.

This may be generalized from the single case study and stand as a conclusion to my observations of advertising production. The primary factor in determining the actual advert produced is commonly neither profitability *per se,* nor a consideration of the consumer. It is a reactive fear of the competition. In many cases this may act to hinder rather than promote consumer desire and actual profits.

6

The Content and Consumption of Advertisements

The intention of this chapter is to undertake the kind of textual analysis of advertising that has been developed in cultural and media studies, but in addition to place my interpretation within the wider context of ethnographic enquiry, including the reading of these materials by some of people who were also main informants within the ethnography as a whole. The text that was analysed comprises of 100 television advertisements, mainly based on whatever came in sequence while recording, but with some bias towards drinks, given my general emphasis upon that sector. The selected 'sample' consists of 16 adverts for alcoholic drinks, 18 for other drinks, 9 for medicine or vitamins, 12 for food products, 5 for utilities, 15 for household products such as detergents, 11 for building or furnishing materials including electronics, 4 for baby products, 3 for banks or insurance firms, 2 for cars, and 2 each for shops and clothes, plus single adverts for products and services ranging from education courses to security firms.

Television advertising in Trinidad includes groups with just still cards and voice-overs, usually lasting between 7 and 10 seconds. My sample were taken from longer adverts. Roughly half would be 30 seconds, and the other half 15–20 seconds. They all include movement, either with persons or animation or graphics. A few adverts are longer, and a quite exceptional advert is that of Huggins furniture, which lasted for a full five minutes. This is longer than some of the gaps between advertising breaks! It is possible that one or two adverts that I have taken to be local were in fact made by agencies abroad, for example, with American black models, but in most cases there are clues that help one to discern whether there is a local element in the production. Imported adverts are particularly common for certain products, such as perfumes and hair products. By contrast, shops, utilities and insurance are largely local, as are most beverage adverts other than some Colas. Detergents and household objects may come from either source. I also have an equally unsystematic collection of radio adverts collected by tape recording and press adverts obtained from cuttings. In addition I have the information obtained by sitting around within the advertising agencies when campaigns were being constructed and on some occasions asking advertising executives to comment on the adverts that I had recorded from television.

Of the many perspectives from which the content of the advertising could be analysed, mine is derived from one of the sub-themes of this volume, which is to document the nature and extent of localization in Trinidadian commerce. This will first be addressed explicitly, including the industry's own conceptualization of the local. I will then take four examples of aspects of advertising content involved in localization: the portrayal of Trinidad, of ethnicity, and of gender and sexuality, and the use of language and music. Much of this is based on relatively overt statements and contents. But, in parallel with the last chapter, I want then to move from this treatment of adverts as representations of society to a more analytical treatment of the role of the commodity itself as image in advertising. This analysis of content is then followed by an analysis of the way adverts are viewed by Trinidadians.

The Analysis of Content

The Issue of Localization

In Chapter 3 it was noted that advertising lies at the centre of one of the most paradoxical findings with respect to local and global business. It is advertising, often regarded as a major source of global homogenization, that turns out to be a fierce proponent of localization. This is because of a contradiction by which the local firm or even the local office of a transnational only becomes of a significant size if it is asked to create its own advertising rather than to use 'canned' adverts. This in turn can only be justified by arguing for the specificity of the local. Localization of theme need not imply localization of personnel or vice versa. For example, the last few years have seen a massive promotion of Australian beer and wine in Britain based on explicit images of Australia, but analysis of these campaigns shows that no help was sought or accepted from the British marketing firms: 'one thing that stands out is that the marketing campaign for beer was conceived in, and directed from, Australia. The same is true of wine' (Merrett and Whitwell 1994: 185). In Trinidad, however, it is only local agencies that would bother to render something Trinidadian.

The issue of localization in advert content cannot easily be separated from that of the history of localization of the advertising industry discussed in the last chapter. It is highly unlikely that there would be the same pressure towards local production if the personnel involved were not entirely Trinidadian. In turn, the decline in expatriate personnel was a result of political pressure. An advertising executive made the point:

> In the sixties there were various foreign directors. None of them worked. But by '70 all the managing directors were local, due to black power and Eric Williams. Prior to 1970 there was no pressure to try and make a Trinidadian commercial. You would have used the best available model in terms of looks and appearance. After 1970, when I got into advertising, you had to get that happy mix, you know, the Indian, the Chinese, the Dougla, the mix. Before 1970 would be clear-skinned, could be local Creole or local White, even Chinese, but had to be very fair to give that status. Since wealth and capital and anything the lower classes might be aspiring to was epitomized by the fair-skinned.

What this quotation does not reveal is that localization of personnel was mainly a move towards giving power to local whites, even while (as it suggests) the same move in terms of representations was to shift away from local white models. As a result of such pressure one estimate suggested that 70 per cent of advertising is local, 20 per cent is adapted, and only 10 per cent is canned. I think this exaggerates the proportions for television advertising, but is probably a fair estimate if the other media are taken into account, since they are almost entirely local products.

The ethnicity of models is one of the most common examples given to stand for the process of localization, but there are several others. The need was to show that there was something different about Trinidad. The starting-point would be a remark such as 'They don't really understand the local scenario. They took ads done in England and Jamaica and just plonked them on television.' Contexts of consumption are therefore a favourite point of legitimation. For example, it would be noted that in international adverts for spirits such as whisky, the drink is poured straight into a glass of ice and consumed. In Trinidad, however, spirits are almost never drunk on their own, but with a wide variety of mixers, making the advert inappropriate for local use. Another example was in a confectionary product 'They got it wrong since foreign company. So they targeted . . . to children which is how it is used in Europe. So advertising is kid-centred, while in Trinidad it is women who are the true consumer and proper target.' The observation with respect to the product may then be extended to the inappropriate nature of the clothing and life-style that accompany it; as one put it: 'There are certain types of commercial where you have to relate it to the populace, say for a beer commercial or a sweet drink. You are relating it to the environment, to how people consume, and basically it is the beach, the lime, the dance and this, and those things are specifically Trinidadian in the way people get into the car and go to Mayaro beach and Maraccas.' Obviously there is a degree of product differentiation here. It would have been a great deal harder to justify a foreign rum, for example, than a foreign toothpaste.

Not surprisingly, executives will dwell on cases where they feel localization has produced dividends.

> A lot of our advertising was imported, tailored to the North American market or the Continental market, but then we began to look at ourselves and our own customs and target our people differently. We went to them with their own message. Quite clearly the success of this type of campaign there with our supermarket chain, where we went to the grassroots and we got them. I am not saying that this is the only reason why our fortunes have changed at this time, but what is interesting is that we have been able to keep it that way. When we researched the market, this segment, the retail outlet types, in the end we realize that there is this vastness of our customers that don't come to our sophisticated outlets, they are serviced by the country shop and the small family-owned super-market, but our ads over the years were developed towards the higher-class consumer. It is only when we decided to mix this that we see these gains in sales and market share.

Here elements such as the use of dialect represent both localiz-ation and a shift from élite to mass within Trinidad.

Outside these specific cases of differences in context and targeting, there is a much more vague and general impression created about how Trinidad is 'different'. Business men and women will remark with clear pride how complex and hard to read the local market is, and how it is 'totally cockeyed'. The claim is made that there is more brand loyalty elsewhere, but in Trinidad there are sudden switches: 'before all whisky sold was Old Parr, then a sudden shift to Dewars'. Typically such shifts are put down to the idea of 'town say so'. The idea is that a feeling emerges around the time of Carnival when new ideas come in and people, particularly in Port of Spain, are looking for a change. This is when the sudden shift in dominant brands will occur.

These various attempts to justify localization do not go entirely unchallenged and are not without associated problems. The first difficulty is that a local advert may not have the same production values (quality) as a foreign-made advert. In a conversation during a meeting with an advertising agency and their client, the latter remarked 'Your storyboard said a golden glow coming from the top of the machine. I look at the ad and I see vaseline nursery jelly has been put on the edges of the lens, and that was what the glow was supposed to be. I don't want that to happen to [his product]; let's not cheapen it with cheap visual effects.' But when the client described the effect he wanted to show, the agency responded 'That whisk cost £500,000–700,000; it was done in an aquarium with oversize clothes and an underwater camera. So to achieve whisk you are talking out of the question. Now you see a lot of things which come out of London which look very good, but they cost £800,000. American companies often have commercials done in the UK for that very reason.' To which the client suggested 'The alternative is to buy existing footage and use that, rather than trying to reinvent the wheel at considerable cost.' Local products were often unable to fit the image of how they should ideally be, as one agency found when the locally available potatoes would not produce the quality of chips needed for the close-up treatment of advertising copy.

Another disadvantage of localization was in the small size of the market. This meant that both advertisers and clients might be less interested in targeting, since a smaller share of an already small market might seem unattractive. It was suggested that this produced a rather bland, broad-based product approach. A creative complained: 'Another thing about advertising over here is that they tell me "Well, we are too small to have a particular kind of market." Is that we are always aiming towards everybody, so that what happens is that you are afraid to say something that somebody might not understand or somebody might misinterpret.' A larger unit such as the Caribbean region might justify targeting. This, it was argued, might produce more adventurous and perhaps more successful adverts.

The second negative issue is scepticism as to how far companies are indeed localizing their images. As noted with the supermarket strategy just described, this may come down to questions of class emulation. One executive remarked that 'Localized agencies were not in the vanguard of localized imagery, since clients just as likely to want from them an upmarket image, while foreign agencies might provide just as good local work. Foreign still generally connotes upmarket in its images. The danger is that local may appear as the poor man's brand in relation to multinational products, which will continue.' Others imply that although the advert is made locally the ideas for it always come from abroad. More damning are accusations that I suspect are acute in focusing on the central cause of localization. 'A fellow called . . . who was greatest for being local, saw a way to make a fast buck with every commercial. Costs are more in this country since they dub it, put a local voice-over, which to me is ridiculous. When they make a local ad it is just nepotism. Their friends and relatives who want to get in on it.'

Advertisers also noted that Trinidadians were more likely to judge material harshly if they saw it as local. This in a sense makes the paradox of localization the more complex, because although localization is legitimated as enhancing profitability it does not follow that this is the case. One of the larger transnationals was 'puzzled' that his own recall research showed that it was the canned adverts that seemed to have the best response, and sought various ways to dismiss the obvious implications. Companies may therefore simultaneously argue for local production but shy away from some aspects of local imaging. When advertising concentrate on 'the pour' or 'the whisk' they have actually demolished their own legitimacy for creating local adverts, since 'a pour is a pour' wherever it is poured. But they hope that the cause of localization is now sufficiently established for this to escape notice, as in this case, where they still managed to make the advert locally.

The same issue applies to the products as to the adverts. There is considerable uncertainty as to whether to claim that a product is local. The recession and the renewed interest in agriculture have seen a rapid increase in the use of local ingredients, to the extent that products such as coffee and cocoa were actually Trinidadian in origin. The relevant companies, however, were not at all sure whether to use this fact in advertising, or to avoid allowing it to be generally known that these were local products. They were afraid that these would then be seen as intrinsically inferior to foreign goods. This was despite international adjudication that suggested that Trinidadian-grown cocoa, for example, was of quite unusual excellence.

Overall, then, advertising was moving from foreign to local identity and vice versa at the same time, mainly because there was no consensus as to which was the better strategy. My own hunch would be to side with the executive who suggested that 'in advertising either straight American style or very dialect works best, not the stuff in between.' What is striking is how far many advertisers had succeeded in obtaining funds for local production of adverts only to produce adverts that had in effect very little that was local about them. Since, however, one of the themes of this book is to investigate how localization is created in business I will ignore for now the kind of advert discussed in the case study of a new drink in the last chapter and examine some examples of actual localizing strategies.

Images of Trinidad

Given the issues surrounding the project of localization, its most obvious manifestation is in portrayals of Trinidad itself. There is little doubt that advertising gives considerable encouragement to the nationalistic project of asserting the special nature of the people of Trinidad and their difference from others. The desire by advertisers is to associate this nationalism with particular products. This is in a sense a commodification of a prior tendency to objectify one's sense of locality in material culture. Just as expatriate Trinidadians might focus upon the consumption of certain home-made foods and drinks such as eating *toolum* or drinking Sorrel to stand for what they miss from the land of their birth, so now commodities attempt to embody a similar sense of attachment that they know will then stand them in good stead in terms of retaining long-term demand.

By far the most evident example of this strategy during fieldwork was the battle between Carib and Stag beers. Carib has a far greater time-depth, and remains a fully local brewery although taken over by the local conglomerate of Ansa McAl. There was a slight tension between its association with Trinidad specifically and the fact that it is also marketed in several other Caribbean islands, such as Grenada, as the beer of those particular islands. Its status as market leader had been relatively secure almost since its inception. Stag, which was backed by Heineken, had, however, by dint of some impressive marketing, succeeded in associating itself with the problems of recession. This was achieved through a combination of initiating a price war and a focus on its role as 'the recession fighter' in its adverts.

Many commentators believe that if Stag had kept its nerve in the price war it might have ousted Carib, but in the event the two agreed a price differential of 4 cents in Stag's favour, which settled down to a market share of around 40 per cent. Stag's marketing had emphasized the poorer African of the East–West corridor, and its attempt in 1988 to re-focus on the Indian market will be discussed below. The present issue is the way both beers attempted to objectify themselves in relation to a concept of Trinidad itself.

An example of a television advert for Carib in that year shows the explicit nature of this project. The voice-over goes: 'There is nothing like your Carib, its a classic. Ah Trinidad and Tobago, emerald islands in the sun, your beauty abounds, you are our pride, our joy. There is nothing like a Carib, its a classic. You were the land of the proud and the fearless Carib people. Yes, you are indeed Carib country. There is nothing like you anywhere, just as there is nothing like your beer.' The visuals consist of a kind of tourist brochure. These include well-known river valleys and beaches, trees in flower, cows in the fields and the scarlet ibis, the national bird, during their spectacular mass flight back to roost in the evening in the Caroni swamp. On the basis of this intense nationalism another advert concentrates more on the product itself, with visuals only of the beer, but tries to emphasize its long association with the land in the voice-over, which states 'Your Carib, brewed to perfection for over 35 years. In this land of ours, you know and I know that Carib is truly beer at its best. There is nothing like your Carib. Its a classic.'

Against this Stag was continuing its own immensely successful campaign, in which localization was more specifically targeted to the shared human problem of survival in recession. Within this there was a similar bid for characterizing the peoples and culture of the nation. One advert sung by the calypsonian David Rudder includes the lines 'You might be on the breadline from tomorrow. Pressure come and go, but you are the kind of man . . . and for people like you there is a friend in need who's always at hand. There's a jungle out there; but you are part of the winning crowd, and when you coming, you are coming from the heart, so we know we will survive. Me and you and Stag the people's beer. The recession fighter. Stag the people's beer.' The visuals for this advert were unusual in being based on urban life in Port of Spain. Scenes include selling shoes on the pavement, using a public phone box, greeting friends and familiar urban areas such as the market.

In other adverts Stag links this urban life with other elements of Trinidad. In another advert sung by Rudder the emphasis is on the productive sphere. The lines go 'You are the people working the land, building the nation each and every man, the ocean, your strength and pride, a friend for tomorrow will be a friend for all time, and for a job well done, a celebration, there's the only one. The recession fighter. Stag the people's beer.' The visuals start with a tractor driver in the cane fields, and then include construction site workers, workers repairing a telephone line and a fisherman with his catch (the same who sells the fish in the market in the urban advert). The emphasis is entirely male, and runs through various ethnic typifications. This pluralism was also evident in the third advert within the sample, which showed scenes of various cultural activities. The song includes the lines 'people wining on the stage, soca blasting in a rage. Everybody going wild, everybody making style. Carnival is here, but bacchanal running wild. Trini people coming out to show what its all about. Drink a Stag to that. Stag the people's beer.' At the end of this advert the four scenes of local cultural activity were shown as quarters of the screen while the Stag label appears in the centre. The effect is as of a flag, with Stag as the national symbol uniting the disparate parts.

Beer is not alone in this strategy, however: rum is another

product with a strong sense of nationalism, as in 'Vat 19 the spirit of Trinidad and Tobago', or 'in Trinidad and Tobago, appreciate the distinct difference of Royal Oak Deluxe Rum'. Most adverts made in Trinidad make no mention of their locality, but in a sense they are merely taking for granted that which the beer and rum adverts made explicit. What is much more common is to locate adverts in familiar locations. By far the most common seemed to be the beach, and the idea of either sitting by the beach or swimming seemed itself to stand for the quintessence of a leisured Caribbean 'paradise'.

Often location is only the backdrop for an activity that equally stands for what was is seen as the quintessence of Trinidadian life. Thus a scene at Piarco airport is evocative because of the enthusiasm of the welcome given to some returnee, be they a lover or family member. Given the transnational nature of most Trinidadian families, this activity of seeing off or greeting people makes the airport one of the most important and well-known public sites on the island. Newspaper adverts have much more difficulty in portraying local scenes. Instead they tend to emphasize local events. Many press adverts refer to 'Mother's Day', Christmas shopping, an 'Eid' sale 'Divali', 'Carnival', 'Independence', and so forth. Often they pick up on obvious connections. Thus shoe adverts are prominent in talking about the 'jump up' associated with Carnival, as are vitamin supplements. The electricity company goes as far as having the Carnival masquerade figure Midnight Robber announcing to those who haven't paid their bills: 'I am the prince of darkness come to out your light.' The shop Liberty announces 'Independence begins with Liberty', following with 'To celebrate Independence Day Liberty offers you freedom from high prices.'

Sometimes the connections are even more tenuous. To take the festival of Divali as an example. 'Follow the light this Divali' is appropriate for an advert for light fittings. Otherwise puns are used as in Liberty's 'The Price is Light.' Often there is a featured prayer, as in the Bank of Commerces 'May the light of Mother Lakshmi continue to shine upon us all with greater brilliance', rivalled by the National Commercial Bank, starting with 'From the very beginning there was light' and ending with 'Om Maha Lakshmi Mata.' Many adverts at this season would feature the Om sign, or a oil lamp or figure of Lakshmi in order to make the association.

The newspapers were also more at the forefront than television in dealing with another aspect of localization – that of the regions. A series that was clearly addressing this issue came out in the press when Stag featured articles on each of its area managers in relation to the region covered. A photograph appeared in a recognized spot in the area with their name. In the text one talked about his support for the local steelband, another about of the self-reliance of people in her area. Similarly a newspaper series for Royal Bank featured the individual branches together with the local cultural features of places such as St James and Chaguanas. Nevertheless, these are exceptional.

Ethnicity

Ethnicity is probably the most sensitive of all aspects of localization that the agencies have to deal with. It is a topic that is much discussed by advertisers, and, as has already been noted, it is sometimes used synonymously with localization. Clients are also deeply concerned, as an advertising executive noted: 'All our clients would want to see photographs [of models] before they would even consider. They want to see a whole range; sometimes we shoot 30 or 40 different possibilities before they make up their minds.' These models are usually selected from data files held by the agencies, which increasingly liaise with the modelling schools, which have expanded in recent years.

The dominant policy of advertisers was summarized as follows:

You will find ethnic representation produced by the agencies in terms of a locally conceived campaign of brown-skinned people as it were, which is supposed to represent in essence the Indian and the African community, who are the majority of the population, and the reason these people are used, they translate across those two boundaries. More recently there has been a bolder approach to the market in terms of ethnic segmentation, and in product positioning there is in some cases a direct Africanization or Indianization. For example liquor, cigarettes to some degree. For products that are very profitable and you can afford that degree of segmentation.

The emphasis, then, is on the brown-skinned. These may either be Dougla, the local term for the child of an African and Indian, or 'red', which implies a more general mixing, often slightly fairer than a Dougla. Their importance may be seen as simple financial expediency: 'because of the limitations of budget, and many situations where not too many people were involved, you particularly avoided identification with only one ethnic group, unless that was specifically the intention. Now one tended to find someone who looked as much Negro as Indian, in other words a cross between the two.'

The overt discussions of advertisers help with regard to the analysis of the sample of television adverts. While it might seem questionable to indulge in the local practice of deciding what 'ethnicity' a person has by virtue of their visual appearance alone, with respect to television advertising we are dealing not with real people but that kind of capitalist 'realism' (Schudson 1993) in which ethnicity is one of several categories into which models are deliberately divided. Thus in advertising we do not have the same range of physiognomy that might be met with in a street. An Indian model is chosen to be conspicuously and unambiguously Indian, while mixed models are chosen precisely because they do not lean towards any particular appearance. The irony is that a host of young Indian women are trying to enter into modelling by styling themselves as sexy or erotic. This may get them booked for 'girlie' photos in the weekly newspapers; but advertising requires Indians who conform to a highly conservative concept of 'Indian'.

In contemporary advertising there is a tendency to see either blackness or whiteness as problematic, depending upon the context. In one case the agency noted a problem with light-skinned presenters: 'We have first to come up with the right TV like . . ., but problem of colour factor there. Why not just get TTT to light her dark, like put her in shadow. I don't think she would be that much of a negative appearance. But if there is someone who is of a good TV personality and is of the neutral colour situation then we go for them first.' Similarly, another agency noted 'This is the East–West corridor, it is predominantly Negro. Therefore this has got to be Negro, we don't even want Dougla we want Negro.' By contrast a company marketing a higher-class rum suggested 'You can use Negro or whatever, but make sure he fair-skinned, make the woman Dougla or Indian, but make sure she fair-skinned.'

In contemporary advertising the African has replaced the White as neutral, while the Indian has become the 'ethnic.' Historically there had been very little focus on Indians *per se,* although an early series of adverts for each local branch of the Kirpilani group had used Chaguanas as an Indian centre, with portrayals of potters at the wheel and bullock carts. The Indian was often still seen as hard to target: 'What I have come to understand is the Indian is a very hard person, very clannish. You would quickest get the Indian vex' for doing pan [steelband] than get the African vex' for doing Indian orchestra. I have done advert mainly in Hindi, mainly in Indian programmes. Taking the existing jingle and sung it in Hindi.' Executives were trying to find out the proper strategy to deal with this situation: 'Who you portray makes a difference, I was reading about what it takes to win with Hispanics [in the USA]. Not just if on television, have to get into the cultural family community. So we encourage area managers to get involved in the community, give a trophy, organize a concert, get involved in a heart case, kidney case, that's how we do it.'

The construction of these 'hyper-real' models of ethnicity is even more evident for Whites than for Indians in the actual commercials. Almost all Whites that appear in the sample were females, with long blonde hair: for example the disc jockey in a Dixi Cola advert, or the female who teaches ballet in a Nutriment Gold advert. This reflects something also found in the American and English adverts shown in Trinidad, for perfumes, for example, where by far the most common White females are again those with long blonde hair. Hair is one of the key elements in demonstrating ethnicity in advertising. Where it is clear that ethnicity is an intended attribute, Africans will be both dark-skinned and have thick curly hair, while Indian women will have long straight or slightly wavy hair. In one discussion about a company calendar the client suggests 'I want nice-looking Indian girls', but the creative reminds him that 'We have to think Caribbean', to which the client replied 'Alright not totally Indian, straight hair then.'

The same differences go for clothing. Most models are shown wearing modern stylish clothing. Even though clothes are not the item being sold, a selection of the right contemporary clothing is part of the general sense of the up-to-dateness of the product. But if ethnicity is to be indicated, then this may be brought out in the ethnicity of clothing. For example, an Indian woman is presented in a sari, an African woman in a Nestlé flavoured milk advert as though doing a traditional dance with coloured cloth, her head swathed in scarves and large earrings.

In advertising, then, as has been remarked about ethnicity in real life, although the ideology emphasizes the role of physiognomy, it is usually contextual information that leads people to read physiognomy as related to a specific category (a point well made by Khan 1993). Apart from these accoutrements, the key context is the other people who appear in the advert. As already noted, the most common advert strategy is to attempt to avoid ethnicity altogether. A friend of mine was often asked if she would be interested in appearing in advertising, because she was not only mixed (of African and Indian parentage), but looked what might ironically be termed conspicuously 'typical' of this mixed Dougla status.

In advertising this relationship between ethnicities is largely by juxtaposition, rather than interaction. It is rare to find ethnicity actually commented upon in the voice-overs. The only exception in my sample is a Sudsil advert. At the end of the advert the African housewife looks at her clean clothes and says 'What clean whites!' At this the white 'German' (see below) puppet looks up at her and says 'And what beautiful coloureds!' The housewife gives a slightly embarrassed laugh, bends down, and kisses the puppet.

Commonly an advert will not try to use ethnicity as its theme, but will simply throw in various models to give a general impression that it has covered the field. For example, in a Nestrum advert a dark, curly-haired African baby is followed by a lighter, straight-haired, clearly Indian toddler. If there is more time then a Chinese or White may be added in, as well as some mixed. In such cases, even if one would not otherwise see the models as conspicuously ethnicized, their juxtaposition in a series makes this their evident grounds for inclusion. Sometimes this becomes awkward. For example, an advert for Aquafresh toothpaste includes a family that looks generally African until the last scene, when another woman is added to the family, although this produced a family of two adult women, a man, and the child. In all probability the woman is added as the 'token Indian'; but the result is to confuse what had previously been a simple nuclear family scene.

Pluralism may also be addressed by using a series of adverts. One advert for Broadway cigarettes has only Indians, who are used to illustrate the idea of generational transmission of crafts, while another advert for the same product concentrates on Africans. A third has both groups represented, with the main action showing an Indian in a band cadging a cigarette from an African also in the band. As noted in the conversations around the Adab advert, there are many strategies other than merely 'reflecting' what are seen as social norms. If Stag seems to be targeting Indians it is because the drink is already well established amongst Africans. Cannings's red drink may have traditional Indian associations, but the adverts are orientated towards a generic youth partying atmosphere where ethnicity is absent.

The problem for many advertisers is that ethnicity is rarely the entire issue in targeting. It may be cross-cut with other variables such as age. As one executive in marketing noted 'The Indian younger generation is trying to oppose their fathers. They therefore smoke Du Maurier in order to oppose themselves to Broadway, smoked by their fathers. So the latter has a problem of how to get them back.' Similarly, there is a problem in that if ethnicity is seen as itself a conservative old-fashioned concern by cosmopolitan youth, the agencies become confused when they are trying to target an Indian youth market (a confusion I was witness to on several occasions).

The representation of ethnicity in press adverts is remarkably different from that of the television advertising so far discussed. Indeed, the difference provides strong backing for the sense that these have to be taken as independent genres, within each of which ethnicity is constructed structurally as a set of relationships between categories that are as much a product of the internal differences as of reference to some prior sense of 'ethnicity' as existing in society. In this case my evidence comes from a sample of all the adverts in newspapers that appeared during a week in May 1988. From these the 80 within which persons were portrayed were selected. The 'ethnicity' of press adverts is as problematic to discern as that of television, but there are many contextual cues when a particular ethnicity is intended. For example, I would not wish to see the graphical outlines of figures as White simply because the interior of the figure is not filled in. Rather, there is evidence from hairstyle and face that often indicates the artists' intentions. Although given these difficulties I have tried to err on the side of assuming mixed ethnicity, there is a marked difference from television, in that this category come to only 20, or a quarter of the total. Even more divergent from television is the relative scarcity of adverts that follow the strategy of having several persons of markedly different ethnicities in order to demonstrate overall coverage. Only 9 of the adverts indicate this strategy. There are 4 where the person is clearly Indian (the name is often given to assist this), and 13 that I took to be clearly African (often the hair is shown in a manner that would not be possible for other groups). The biggest difference from television is the preponderance of Whites. At 34 cases, they are easily the most common group represented.

To have such a high proportion of White figures in a country where the number of Whites in the population was falling below 1 per cent clearly posed a problem. While of the 46 other adverts only 5 are drawings, the rest being photographs or based on photographs, in the White category there are only five photographic images, and the rest are all drawings. In terms of associated commodities there is again a marked difference: 14 of the 34 adverts featuring Whites were for clothing fashions, which accounts for all but 2 of this category. By contrast, there is only one White advert for alcoholic drinks (wine), and 7 associated with other ethnicities.

There may be several reasons for this discrepancy with television. Firstly, there is conservatism mixed with established tradition. Prior to the 1960s most advertising featured White models, and some of the contemporary press advertising for fashion seems remarkably similar to the kind of drawing styles that may be found in newspaper archives for that period. By contrast, television has largely expanded its advertising in the post-1970 atmosphere, which was more overtly opposed to this hegemony of Whites as the model to be emulated. Secondly, the continuation of a graphic tradition in the press allows Whites to be portrayed while in a sense appearing as neutral. This is only a ruse, since it would be quite simple to create drawings that are clearly African or Indian, as is the case in many other countries. In television, where drawn figures are relatively rare, it would be comparatively hard to have such a concentration on White models. I also suspect that the graphic side of the advertising agencies is generally a more conservative element than the audio-visual sections. By seeing this as largely a tradition of genre I am not, of course, suggesting a less powerful ideology of White dominance. Quite the contrary, it demonstrated how far the naturalization of White aesthetic models from the colonial period still perseveres in areas where there has been no explicit challenge through bringing to consciousness the issues involved.

Voice and Music

The use of voices seems to be one of the most predictable and structured elements in this sample of Trinidadian adverts. The predominant voice overall is the male 'mid-Atlantic' voice. The term mid-Atlantic is commonly used by Trinidadians when talking about the media. As in many countries, the intonation used by the vast majority of the people is not recognized as the 'standard' accent, but is represented as a marked accent constituting 'dialect.' The standard accent is one which is heard amongst the élite population in normal conversation, but most particularly in the media. Partly as an explicit policy, partly through evolution of practice, there has developed a voice that speaks with a strong emphasis on clear intonation and is related to both formal media 'BBC' English and North American media voices. An advertising executive explained the term 'which means it is not a complete American accent nor is it a complete English accent. It is a sort of mid-way between, that is acceptable in the market place.' The term acknowledges, then, that it represents not so much Trinidad as a mythical place half-way between the two main influences.

As any advertising agency will readily acknowledge, a key place in Trinidadian adverts is played by music and musical jingles. The emphasis on music is the second most common definition of localization after ethnicity. A company director noted 'In my experience, if you have a good jingle you have a good investment; you know a good jingle has tremendous appeal.' A marketing survey on the recall for an advert showed that while 40 per cent of the sample had learnt both music and the words, only 30 per cent recognized the character and 21 per cent recalled the action. The essence of the jingle is the music. Not even the advertisers who make them up regard the associated words, such as 'good Cannings good', as anything other than banal; but the point is made if the product or company name is associated with a musical phrase that is constantly sung, hummed, or, as the calypsonian Shadow famously sang of a bass riff, seems to have taken permanent occupancy inside one's head. The soap Refresh was a conspicuously successful example of a product more or less entirely sold on memorable music. The musical aspect of the jingle is complemented when the wording itself is memorable. Typically advertisers will try and come up with a pun, so that one hears 'Zero in on a Cole Cold', or 'Toyota – driving quality home.' Most important is the actual singing of the complete advert text, which took place in 27 of the 100 adverts.

Music seems to have its own history in commercials. At one time: 'calypso very rare. Calypso too dangerous, ads, they grew up when steelband was taboo. Calypso tent was all dirt, and they didn't want their product associated with that at all. The respectability for that only came in the 1980s.' Other evidence suggests the 1970s was the high point for calypso. Advertisers waxed lyrical about the contribution of the calypsonian. 'Sparrow in my experience is one of the greatest copy writers that I have ever seen . . . He has a knack, if you give him a brief he brings a tape which is totally finished . . . remember one particular calypso jingle for a Guinness that almost any line in that jingle could have been a theme for a campaign; it was utterly fantastic.' Or 'We did the best thing with Sparrow. That jingle was *the* jingle. It just hit this town like a bomb. If you were out the room when it came on you would run into the room to hear it.' Sparrow's main long-term rival Lord Kitchener also continues to be involved as in a successful jingle for Angostura rum. Calypso still features in ads as sung by David Rudder and others; but they seem to have passed their peak in use. Phrases out of calypso are, however, often used, especially in press and radio advertising.[8] Indeed, unless one knows that phrases such as 'wet meh down' or 'ease the tension' are referring to calypsos, many of the texts of press adverts would make little sense. It is likely

8. The use of phrases from calypso music and the general influence of calypso as it emerges from the ethnography of everyday life is currently being studied by Justin Finden-Croft, a postgraduate student at the Department of Anthropology University College, London.

that both radio and press exploit the relative speed of their production to retain this link with current phrases that calypsos have left in daily discourse, as against television adverts, which, if they tried to be as in touch, would be in danger of being dated by the time they came out.

Singing varies in intonation, as does text. Most songs have an equivalent to a mid-Atlantic accent, though with probably a move somewhat closer to the North American voice that becomes generic to pop music. This would not be true of songs recorded as calypso. The equivalent in the sample to the *comédienne* with heavy dialect is a highly successful advert for the insecticide DET made by the calypsonian Brigo. Brigo here uses his 'grass-roots' quality to sing with a normal dialect accent, and this is completely in keeping with the name of the product, since DET is itself simply the dialect spelling for 'death', and the calypso consists of Brigo trying to deliver this death to all insects within his home.

Gender and Sexuality

Unlike the cases of ethnicity, music and nation-building, the topic of gender is not so evidently an aspect of localization. The fact that gender stereotypes found in Trinidad may be common elsewhere does not, however, detract from the sense amongst local producers that this is a particular issue that has to be addressed within the local social context. This is still more true of the issue of sexuality. For example, in Trinidad, there are forms of authority that are granted to females when in other societies the male might take this role. Though males' voices dominate as sources of knowledge, in visual terms the female stands for knowledge. For example, in an advert for Sunshine Bran Flakes the housewife on sitting down for breakfast says 'You know what's good about this?', to which her husband replies 'Yes, it tastes good.' She comes back with 'More than that, it's got wheat bran and oat bran, so you get all the fibre you need.' He responds with 'But it still tastes good.' After she has gone on to explain the importance of eliminating cholesterol for avoiding heart attacks he finally makes (to the embarrassment of his son) the joke 'So the way to a man's heart is through his stomach.' Quite commonly in the scene shown (as opposed to in the voice-over) it is the female who stands for either the utilitarian or the symbolic advantages of the product, while the male simply takes the role of satisfied consumer. In Maggi soup adverts, again the men simply know that things taste good; it is the woman who has to explain what the key ingredients are or the nutritional benefits. Quite often the men are made to look stupid or acknowledge the woman's greater wisdom, as in a Comtex advert where the woman explains that her bathroom cabinet, with only Comtex, is better than his cabinet, which is full of all those medicines needed to treat each of the ten cold symptoms individually that her Comtex treats together. The extreme example of female dominance is shown in the Ronco gas advert, where the large female *comédienne* shouts at her thin henpecked husband who has brought the wrong gas canister. This scene enacts a well-established genre of family domestic dominance, with many local dialect words for the dominated male. It is also not unknown for men to give advice on screen. A man wearing work overalls explains how he needs to get in touch with customers when servicing their cars in an advert for the telephone company, while in another case the advantages of an insurance scheme are explained on screen by an elderly male.

Female dominance in giving advice and knowledge about products may be set against their subservience in assumed occupation. Again these figures depend on how one specifies gender involvement, but on my assessment all but one of nine scenes of blue-collar work situations are based on males. There is one male and one female office scene (with the male being handed a drink by a female secretary). Other portrayals include one of female housework and five scenes of female cooking, as well as four female and one male scene of playing with children and one female washing clothes.

There are eleven adverts showing couples. Single-sex situations outside of mother–daughter interactions are relatively rare. Males tend to appear together; as work colleagues, either at work or taking a drink together, but there are no examples of conversation between them. The only clear female couple of the same age are in a domestic setting for a telephone company advert, which shows them chatting together when one hears her name on the radio.

There are nine families portrayed in the adverts. There are sometimes additional relatives; two families are shown with both grandparents, and one each with additional older female and male. The housewife tends to take responsibility for the family, as where 'I give my family complete mouth protection with aquafresh.' The number of families shown is relatively few, considering that there are ten situations with mothers and children but without men present.

The only times we see men and children on their own are a portrayal of two elderly fisherman repairing nets, one with a young boy on his knee, and an Indian older man appreciating his son's ability at jewellery-making. Compared to this there is an overwhelming preponderance of females showing direct concern for their children, from babies to young adults. They may be teaching them to dance, advising them on courses they could take, watching over them while doing housework, or trying to get through on the phone. It is noticeable that in full family situations that include active fatherly participation it is mostly with a son: for example discussing the different breakfast cereals, or playing football. Mothers, by contrast, are shown far more commonly interacting with daughters than with sons. With grown-up children it is invariably daughters; but even with young children, daughters are more often shown. The mother's concern is particularly evident in an advert for an educational course in which she says 'Well, child, don't waste your time: go straight to Zenith educational courses and register and I will pay for it.' She may be sentimental as well as practical, as when the daughter asks 'Will you wash my nightie in Softlan too?' Where it is both children or just a son the mother is usually explaining the advantages of the product. In a case where a grown son advises his mother in a advert for the water authority, she is resentful of his thinking that he would have anything to tell her about practical matters.

Sexuality is one of the key devices used to sell products. Females may be used simply to give a glamour element without referring to sexual activity as such: for example, the manicured female hand that caresses the upholstery of the new Toyota car. Or there may be an attractive model, as in Cole Cold. There were six adverts where women appeared in either leotards or swimsuits. Male bodies are also quite commonly used for glamour purposes. A more general use of romance, as with a couple making eyes at each other, is quite common, with 17 adverts showing some element of sex or romance as the setting.

To conclude this section, one extended example and three supportive examples have been given of adverts being set in contexts that reflect the importance of localization. The point that comes over clearly in all four cases is that localization is rarely in practice simply a question of putting the product in a setting that is typical of Trinidadian life. The simplest form of localization seems to lie in the representation of Trinidad itself, as in the beer adverts, which try to objectify their brands as that which forges the plural culture and diversity of landscape into a national unity. Equally straightforward are the transformations of brands such as Stone's Ginger Wine and vitamin supplements into commodities sold as sexual enhancers, which is either absent or a minor part of their sales pitch in other countries (see Wainwright 1990 for the more usual promotion of Stone's).

Where there is more of a compromise with international expectations this may produce the very reverse of this project of localization, in that what at first appears to be the 'local scene' is actually a transference of international norms. A case in point is food advertising. In advertising consumption shots are almost always based upon a group of people, most often the family sitting together for meals. This reflects international norms in advertising, but is entirely at variance with the practice of most Trinidadians. Apart from certain élite groups, most Trinidadian families do not eat together except on more 'ceremonial' occasions such as Sunday lunch or Christmas. The usual practice is for the woman of the household to make the food, which is then kept warm, and eaten by all other members of the household as individuals, often when they return from work.

These cases employ a fairly simplistic criterion for 'localization', based on whether the scenario depicted is more similar to local or to international social expectations. In most cases, however, the issues are rather more complex. Often advertising genres play a powerful role in creating a model of locality that relates in different ways to what might otherwise be seen as normative practice. Often this consists of creating some generic form that stands for Trinidad, rather than reflecting its diversity. Thus the mid-Atlantic accent or the 'red' model are certainly localizing, in that they make sense within the context of Trinidad and not elsewhere; but they work through constructing their own normality of representation, which would certainly not be the voice or look of the bulk of the population.

Trinidadians don't spend all their time singing jingles; women rarely lecture their husbands on the advantages of particular products. Nevertheless, the Trinidad that is constructed as genre is intended to be easily comprehended, either in terms of what Trinidadians do encounter, or, as is often the case with genre, because the particular 'norms' of advertising itself quickly become a self-reverential system that have established their own expectations. It seems, then, that localization is better understood in the manner noted by Wilk (1990) as the emergence of a dialogue about how Trinidad might represent itself to itself within particular genres, rather than a reflection of some external norm. How this might come to be can best be understood by a wider examination of the cultural context of advertising production and consumption.

A Context of Fear and Contradiction

Both the analysis of advertising agencies in general and the campaign for a new drink in particular suggested that adverts are constructed primarily in a context of fear about rival products. The major legitimation for spending on advertising was the sense that in business, if one did not constantly move to protect and develop one's brands, then others would move in and take away market share. This climate of fear about what the consumer might hold against a product does not just stem from the action of rivals. It is in some sense intrinsic to the business of advertising, because the various qualities that the product is expected to objectify are often themselves held in contradiction. Thus promoting a product because it is cheap may be perceived of as promoting a poor-quality product, while promoting a healthy product, may be seen as promoting a boring product, and so forth. What I want to suggest is that contradiction and fear are the most important contextual attributes that help to explain the content of most of the adverts that were analysed in the sample. This emerges in the television adverts through the duality and multiplicity of the messages portrayed, which can be accounted for by their relationship to the internal contradictions within the wider society that are commented upon in the adverts.

The concern of the advertiser to cover the various possible sources of demand is unusually conspicuous in an advert for the car Nissan March. The advert is structured 'for those who seek economy . . .', 'for those who seek comfort . . .', 'for those who seek space . . .'. In each case the concern may be that audiences will feel that a cheap car will necessarily be a small car, etc. The same problem is coped with through visual effects. Small cars seem blessed with a Mary Poppins effect by which huge objects such as windsurfing equipment are taken out of what might otherwise seem minuscule car boots.

Duality and multiplicity are often also evident in the use of different sections of the same advert. A comic advert will be interrupted by a section half-way through in which an off-screen voice provides the serious information about the benefits of this product. An advert for White Magic Rum, aiming at a high-class image that would not deign to be concerned with anything as vulgar as thrift, is complemented through a very common device, subtitles that move across the base of the screen, in this case referring to a sale of the product in the True-Value supermarket at that time. Similarly, an advert for Klim milk powder that emphasizes how children are growing up all around the world on Klim contains a central section about a current competition related to the Klim mystery shopper. In all these cases fear of a commitment to a given strategy has led to the direct juxtaposition of opposing attributes. Often it is only knowledge of the wider context that makes sense of the prime emphasis in the advert. The slogan 'switch to Dixi' has a particular resonance in view of the relatively low market share held by the drink at that time.

The focus is very often on exactly what the product might otherwise seem to lack. An artificial-looking fast food such as Maggi soups will therefore concentrate upon the natural ingredients and a female figure who embodies the values of home cooking. She in turn is reassured that she 'and her pot' will gain all the credit for the meal she produces. A soft drink based on artificial flavourings will refer to the 'real fruit flavour.' When one watches the massive excitement of a family telling the world that they have just discovered that there is 'A new Aquafresh', it is hard not to read into the this the fear of the agency that by now everyone is bored stiff with a constant development of new versions of toothpastes. It is by the same logic that here (as in other countries that permit it) cigarettes seem constantly to sponsor sports events to whose success they might otherwise appear to be inimical.

The Means to this End

I do not want to suggest that all advertising messages are motivated by fear and contradiction, but only that this may be the dominant context. This leads to the question of how such a concern effects the delivery of the advertising message to the public. The primary method of much advertising is metaphorical juxtaposition through visual images. Some adverts are crudely constructed to make this evident. One advert for a Toyota starts talking about the sleek and sophisticated with reference to a glamorous model and, only after this is established, attempts to demonstrate the same attributes in the car. This is followed by various to-ing and fro-ing to establish the classiness of her jewellery and the car's accessories, etc. Another Toyota advert announces a new car through the motif of the discovery of a pearl. The first adverts simply depicted a closed shell, with no clue as to its contents. These were on display for some weeks before the television campaign showed the shell opening, to reveal the car at the centre where a pearl might be expected. Graphics are obviously the most flexible means of juxtaposition, as when a combination of ice cubes and the red lips of the model transform to 'become' the logo for Cole Cold.

Nearly as common is a kind of fetishism that has objects or aspects of persons acting as though they were full agents. In animation, biscuits can be anthropomorphized, or sparkling stars can be seen as the active force of a detergent, literally pushing out dirt between fibres. The applause at the end of an advert for Vaseline Care is given, not to the conductor of the orchestra, nor even to his hands, which are shown conducting, but to the product revolving on a pedestal with lights shining on it. The message is that the hands that do the clapping are well aware of what is good for them, even if the brain still needs to be educated. Babies can also be set dancing, or talking as though they were adults discussing the merits of a new diaper/nappy.

Central to this object fetishism is often the package that the consumer is actually buying. The advertising agencies are well aware that, although they may be discussing a product, the shopper has first to respond positively to a cardboard pack or a can, which is what they actually take from the shelves and pay for. This container may be reproduced in giant size as a kind of pseudo-shrine. Hundreds of children dance around a giant tin of

Klim milk powder at the top of a hill. A family dance in front of a giant cereal pack. Packs move across and fill screens. The pack itself may complement other vehicles, for messages about the product such as 'rich in protein' are often written on the pack, and very evident when a close-up of the pack is shown. The pack will often be integrated visually into the advert to help the consumer to be reminded by one of the other. In a Nestlé milk drink advert the pouring of the drink in the advert transforms into the picture of the same action on the pack. Maggi soups often show the action through a cut-out shape which is the same as that used on the pack. The penetration of the pack is most evident in Royal Gelatine, since the theme of the advert is the mother who finds that she can't escape the pack since her children keep putting it wherever she is likely to look (for example in place of her alarm clock, or filling her bathroom cabinet).

A common theme in these adverts is the attempt to make the product in the shape it is purchased stand for both the processes that create it and the consumption that follows it, through a kind of magical transformation. Williamson suggests this is a form of 'naturalizing' the technologies that have replaced natural processes (1978: 103–21), though I suspect such criticism involves to a degree the analyst's 'naturalizing' the previous low-tech production method as though it were 'real nature'. For example, the Nestlé drink adverts have a giant peanut, which when broken open has the finished peanut punch pour out from it; and a similar approach is taken to eggnog pouring out of a cracked egg. The pack of Richmond cocoa appears by emerging from a sea of drying cocoa beans. On the consumption side, Lion *phoulourie* mix appears beside a plate of the perfect *phoulourie* it creates, as do baked products beside flour. Detergents, in turn, appear beside the marvellously white clothes they might produce.

The product itself may have to reveal qualities that normally might not be evident from its visual appearance within the pack. Liquids are a case in point. Milk drinks are trying to appear thick and rich, so that they are shown whirling around clinging to the edges of cups or slightly frothing. Fizzy drinks burst like fountains from White Rock cans, or fizzing over the top of Cannings bottles (although any consumer who thereby lost half the drink might be none too happy about this!). With beers it is usually the sense of cold, given by the droplets on the outside of the bottle that stand for it, that is the essential attribute to be communicated. In one Stag advert the bottle taken off a table miraculously has the word 'Stag' left in droplets on the table itself.

Not surprisingly, the commodity attempts to interpolate itself as the solution to a given problem, providing the purchase is made. Thus the 'Hoover solution' presupposes that viewers have a problem, in that they cannot afford a fully automatic machine and thus would welcome a Hoover that costs less but can do more than an automatic washing machine. More subtly when Richmond cocoa proclaims that it is the family favourite it appears as the potential resolution of that most common of problems for the shopper, which is how to please all the various constituent members of the household. This kind of pre-emption of solutions may sometimes have to take a less direct route. The advert for Dantsteel, which sells building materials, emphasizes that 'Now is the time to build.' Of the various justifications for this statement one of the most prominent is that 'Labour is available.' What this refers to is that, with recession, unemployed masons are quite cheap. But it would hardly be diplomatic to be so clearly exploiting the misfortune of others. Instead, this claim is illustrated by the main graphic figure who is thinking of doing the job, flexing his arm muscles. His labour thereby stands for what everyone knows is the reality of the low cost of building labour in recession.

As Carrier has noted with respect to catalogues (1995: 126–44), the advert tries to pre-empt the context of consumption, helping people to imagine themselves in the consumption context. The advert will often use terminologies of inclusion such as 'your partner in saving' or 'you and me and Shandy Carib.' The reasoning behind these various techniques is made very clear by Williamson (1978: 48) 'You do not choose in the shop, but in response to the advertisement, by "recognising" yourself as the kind of person who will use a specific brand. You must have already chosen when you buy, otherwise the advertisement has failed in its purpose. That is why it is so crucial for the ad to enter you, and exist inside rather than outside your self-image: in fact to create it.' This is particularly true for the kind of supermarket products that dominate television advertising. Larger one-off purchases tend to be subject to active shopping, where one goes to several shops to compare. These small items are regular repeat purchases, where most of the decision-making is done prior to the visit to the shop, where they are mainly just collected. Where shopping is less an active choosing, the crucial phase is the advert working on the choice of brand (Wilkins 1994: 20).

The techniques described in this section clearly derive from the imperatives of advertising discussed above. For example, the desire by advertising agencies to address several concerns at once is obviously assisted by highly creative and dynamic forms of pun, metaphor, visual juxtaposition and fetishism. I hope my evidence helps show that this reflects more than just peer rivalry over 'cleverness' or the workings out of a structural logic in the means of communication. Rather this must be analysed as much in terms of how it acts as a resolution of the anxiety of the advertisers as of how it stimulates complex forms of inference in readers.

Intertextuality

Another major strategy for creating effective messages is intertextuality, especially in relation to other television genres. The importance of intertextuality would follow from what I have already suggested is the degree of autonomy in the genre itself. Television personalities are often used as voices of authority. The presenter of the advert for Huggins furniture is the presenter of the weather forecast on the main evening news. The advert starts with 'Good evening. I am Robin Maharaj. Tonight we are going to talk about a storm of a different kind. Huggins' storm of savings, its thundering bargains.' Later on he talks of a 'tropical depression of prices. Down payments are as low as possible. The storm has really damaged prices in every department. In the bedroom section winds have blown down prices to an all-time low.' Jai Parasram, a former news director for TTT, attacked the advert (pers. comm.) for Cheekies diapers/nappies, which is presented by June Gonzalves, a news reader. He argued that 'you cannot have your anchor person presenting the news in one breath and telling you about the state of the world; and in the next, telling you this brand of diapers is the best. There's a conflict there.' He suggested that during his time of office this was forbidden.

An advert for the water authority is based around the typical quarrelling between the mother and son characters from the main locally produced soap opera *No Boundaries*. Here the pastiche of the programme as an example of intertextuality is itself compounded when the mother says accusingly during the advert 'like you making a commercial for WASA (the water authority) or something.' Another advert, not in this sample, was a pastiche of the soap opera *Santa Barbara* using the ongoing story of 'Sam and Barbara' in relation to the product. As well as these television genres there is considerable use made of the classic film genres. The cowboy and Indian of Canada Dry are an obvious example. Three adverts are based around science fiction images. One has Frico milk powder being encountered by astronauts in space, another has Daytron televisions whirling as weightless objects in space.

Sometimes the choice of a well-known phrase or genre would seem unlikely, at least in this context. Thus a cornsnacks advert that portrays black primitives being seduced by the goods distributed by a confident white explorer might have been thought to give offence. The slogan 'The Final Solution' for Doom spray in the elimination of cockroaches is probably sufficiently abstracted when used in Trinidad from its origins in ethnic genocide to work as intertextuality, on the basis that the phrase is a familiar one objectifying a sense of efficiency in killing while not evoking the precise origins of the phrase in the Nazi holocaust.

Intertextuality also works from other media to the television. The newspapers may discuss a person featured, for example 'Jason Alleyne is not just the guy in the Cole Cold ad, he is also a rap artiste' (*Sunday Punch* 27/12/92). Many of the newspaper adverts refer to current television advertising, featuring either a shot from the advert or a comment or slogan. For example, the Hi-Lo adverts included a 'colour Tanti Merle' competition and a 'Tanti Merle say . . .' series. It was through billboards that the images of the pearl shell were used to build up anticipation prior to the television 'Toyota in a pearl shell' advert. Often the newspapers can expand upon the overall theme, with the characters pointing out a particular sale or event in a way that can otherwise only be done through television wordovers. For example, once Dr Sud the German Puppet was established through television he can then appear in a series of press adverts, each one providing 'A Grime Prevention Tip' from Dr Sud, such as how to remove a grease stain from a blouse.

Transience and Transcendence

Both the discussion of localization and the techniques of image and message construction have tended to imply that we are dealing with a relatively abstracted and artificial medium that is being related to a 'reality' made up of unmediated everyday life. Most ethnographic writings imply that the people of a particular place and time are themselves engaged in relating the events in which they participate and observe to generalized expectations and cultural projects, with often powerful moral and normative implications. Genre is a concept as applicable to them as it is to the media (Goffman 1979).

Furthermore, my own ethnography of Trinidad in common with advertising is not attempting simply to describe that which was observed as a series of encounters, but rather to abstract and clarify the underlying models that Trinidadians themselves may be using both to make sense of and to determine their stance to any particular event. It would be quite surprising, therefore, if the advertising industry did not itself evoke and employ these larger cultural projects. I have argued (Miller 1994) that the specificity of Trinidad was best understood within a framework of comparative modernities in which a particular contradiction played a highly significant role in articulating the flux of everyday life to longer-term normative expectations. This was not based around the more overt symbols such as ethnicity and language, but around a foundational dualism that I termed transience and transcendence (compare Wilson 1973 on reputation and respectability). I now want to reintroduce these concepts through the manner by which they are constructed in advertising.

Attributes most fully associated with transience are individual freedom and choice within a context of fun and comedy. These are expressed most often through the idiom of the body as a site of pleasure and sexuality. By contrast, the commodity that is associated with transcendence is more likely to proclaim itself as the objectification of inter-generational continuity, a property of the land and of serious concerns such as thrift, utility and social or moral virtue (for details see Miller 1994).

The ideal context for a sense of transience is at a party or by the beach. In several cases the advert places children or youth in the kind of party situation that would normally be only achievable for adults. This is marked in an Ovaltine advert, in that the boys wear the hard hats of construction workers, and the context for what is half-party, half-musical is a kind of bright, coloured factory for the product. The soft drinks tend to use more realistic beach-based parties, with adults dancing and drinking with the exhilaration and excitement of the Trinidadian 'fête'. The emphasis on the self-cultivation of the body as site of pleasure tends to lead to a sexual innuendo when it is adults who are portrayed. Women working out in leotards are also women with assumed sexual drive, as is true also of the male engaged in body-building or having the muscles to show that general sense of being well-built. The sexy voice, or the blonde White, are also accessories that invite fantasy and sexual innuendo.

There are many adverts that stress that the consumer is free to choose. This is most common when a product of low market share is challenging the consumer to switch from the dominant brand, as in 'Move to the sparkling world of White Rock' or 'You have to know how to move, and when to move, and when to move is right now. Move to the one that suits you best, Canteen the mellow one.' The visuals for this last advert are concerned with a man 'making a move' on a woman he fancies at a party. These are all low market share products; but a market leader such as Carib can also focus on the message of moving on when it is threatened by an up-and-coming challenger. In this case, however, the slogan is 'and move with the leader.' This sense of choice is important in the overall project of transience, which attempts to minimize the sense of the individual as controlled by institutional forces.

Themes concerned with transience tend to be to the fore during Carnival, where indeed it is Carnival itself that often provides the visual materials than back up the message. Themes related to transcendence are most fully to the fore during the Christmas season. The concern to keep in touch by phone is that much more poignant when the older woman starts to cry, having found that she cannot wish her relative a Merry Christmas because the latter's phone has been cut off. Similarly, the Electric Company's threat of a black spot is that much more effective when it is clear that the Christmas lights on the tree are only going to light up if the electric bill has been paid on time, in which case one can indeed hope for a 'bright' and Merry Christmas.

By contrast, there are many products that emphasize the seriousness of the project of transcendence, and make the commodity deny its transient nature and its commoditized abstraction, to become instead a kind of pseudo-heirloom, standing for traditions of family, nation and continuity. Not surprisingly, institutions such as insurance companies and banks, in particular, stand for long-term values. The theme is that one is putting oneself into safe hands well tested by time. One bank associates itself with classical music (as played on steelband), orchestrating its various different kinds of accounts the way a good conductor orchestrates a symphonic form.

An insurance company sells the idea of life assurance that is received when one has a critical illness, rather than after death, through the slogan 'life is love' and by showing a daughter in the arms of her father. A similar concern is central to Fernleaf milk, which shows a daughter taking pride in the achievement of her father, who is wearing a medal. The theme is explicit in the final phrase of an advert for Royal Gelatine focused on mother–child relations, which is 'somehow something may be remembered'. There are also a very large number of adverts in the newspapers around the time of Mother's Day and Father's Day that focus upon this theme.

The wider environment of love within the family is featured in a Softlan advert, in which the wife tells her husband that he recalls the blouse she is wearing since she wore it when they first met, and it is only because of Softlan that it still looks new. This is then transferred to the daughter, who is told of her nightie that 'I did with my very own hands.' The message is reinforced by the verbal phrase 'tender loving care', as a pink fluorescent heart appears behind the product. The elderly are also prominent in such adverts, as with the elderly female who sits in a rocking chair next to the telephone and tells us 'I look forward to seeing my grandchildren every weekend, and during the week I feel so good knowing that I could always get in touch.'

A cigarette advert focuses upon this theme in relation to a rural Indian family, which in many respects fits the stereotypical context for a concern with transcendence. The text runs 'Time itself, the very essence of appealing to generation after generation. The traditional skill of fine jewellery has to evolve from one generation to another. With each passage must come new inspiration and refinement, breathing new light into the art.' The same sense of time may be associated with the product itself, as in 'When we first started making Three Plumes matches in 1887 we made a commitment to quality and perfection. That's why over a hundred years later Three Plumes are a stroke ahead of the rest.'

Bacchanal

Transience and Transcendence may be major cultural projects in Trinidad, but, as suggested in Miller 1994, these are not static forms but constantly in conflict, with each trying to subvert the other. This conflict is objectified in the concept of bacchanal, which I argued has become the single most common word used by Trinidadians to describe the particular character of Trinidadian society. This makes it a suitable closure to the general theme of localization in advertising. The specificity of the term reflects its local meaning as the moment in which transcendence gives way to the cultural project of transience. Rather than seeing localization as a simple process of accommodation of the external to the internal, a consideration of this term also reveals the more complex dynamics of articulation involved.

Just before the end of my fieldwork a new set of adverts by Carib appeared on television. That it should be Carib that provides this quintessential case of the specificity of Trinidad should not be surprising given that this is probably the beer that (despite the attempts by Stag) remained the most closely identified with Trinidad and Tobago for many consumers.

The advert in question was based around the personality of a singer who was the son of a well-known calypsonian. Indeed, when the advert first came out a weekly paper reported this as front-page news. The point was that the calypsonian was also a Rastafarian, and therefore against the use of alcohol. For his son to be fronting an advert for the country's most popular beer was seen as likely to have produced a certain degree of tension in the family. This became a near-perfect example of potential bacchanal, i.e. transcendence collapsing into transience, since it becomes a moment in which not only sobriety but inter-generational continuity is subverted by short-term desire. Bacchanal is most clearly designated when it emerges as a conflict within the heart of the family project of continuity.

If we turn to the content of the adverts themselves the theme fits this context precisely. The main advert starts with everyone at work. A van filled with Carib is trying to cross a bridge in a remote part of Trinidad. The scenery and the population, which is mainly African, suggest the North-East region around Toco. The bridge is blocked, and at first the point seems to be to get everyone involved in helping overcome this problem by working together, for example to carry things by hand over the bridge. This would allow them to continue on to their destination, where the visuals suggest they are trying to put on some kind of show for this singer sponsored by Carib. This overt 'good' message is, however, subverted if one examines the action that actually takes place. Because in effect what the singer and his followers do is to seduce various hard-working labourers from their labours in order to enjoy a beer and join a procession of happy, dancing drinkers. Thus an elderly woman is relieved of the clothes she is carrying on her head, and a male labourer of his wheelbarrow. More and more workers end up having nothing more to do with their labours, and instead become more concerned with having a spontaneous party, lubricated by abundant supplies of beer.

Another advert in the series makes the same point with respect to that shrine to transcendence, the serious business of shopping at Christmas. The scene here is a group of shoppers trying to choose their poinsettia plant, which with its red leaves is seen as the local 'Christmas' flower. At first the singer seems to be helping them with their choice, but once again, as soon as the beer starts to be handed around the shoppers leave off their onerous Christmas tasks and join in a spontaneous party atmosphere, dancing to the (genuinely) infectious rhythm of the advert's song. In this campaign, then, we see a key product attempting to turn a corner in its fortunes by attaching itself to what I have argued elsewhere is the concept that most succinctly defines the specificity of Trinidadian cultural formations.

The Consumption of Advertising

The Nature of the Evidence

The consumption of advertising is something that would best emerge from a general ethnography devoted to its influence on everyday life. There are examples of such work within this volume, for example in the chapter on drinks, as well as in Miller 1994 (see also Gillespie 1995: 191–204). In this section, however, the evidence is derived from a somewhat more artificial but nevertheless informative attempt to obtain the opinions of Trinidadians about advertisements through asking them to watch a video of typical television adverts and to comment upon them. This was conducted with twelve informants, all women. All of the four areas of fieldwork were included, that is people living as squatters in Ford, more 'rural' Indians from St Paul's, an African woman from the government housing scheme in Newtown, and women from the middle-class residential area. They ranged from viewers almost entirely without education to a part-time lecturer. Most interviews were conducted singly, but I also showed the video to groups of two and three women who could discuss their interpretations with each other. The video was not the same as the hundred adverts analysed above, which would have been too long to show at a sitting, although there is considerable overlap between the two.

I would not wish to suggest that what people say about an advert is the same as what the advert means to them. Responses are as much a product of normative genres of acceptable speech and legitimation as are the adverts themselves. Furthermore, the circumstance of these discussions itself constructed particular attitudes to the material that might not be typical. Certainly there are discrepancies between what people say when asked about adverts and what can be discerned as the influence of these adverts upon them through observation of their actions. For example, most people deny the influence of adverts, even when it is otherwise clear that the influence is there.

I do not then regard such evidence as immediate access to some true subjectivity to be posed against the previous section consisting of my interpretations of these texts. I do not assume, therefore, that I am always mistaken in my interpretation where I am contradicted by 'real' Trinidadians. In all cases one is dealing with the articulation between genres: of television, of speaking, and of academic tradition. Nevertheless, there were times when I was astonished by the results of this particular investigation, and aware that none of my previous work had prepared me for what people in fact told me. The two topics of ethnicity and sexuality were the most surprising, especially since I had already worked for some time on both topics.

To view adverts systematically is of course artificial. Ordinary advert viewing is often not much focused upon and remains in the periphery of consciousness, absorbed while people are largely engaged in other activities. Furthermore, this was a far greater concentration of unremitting advertising than would ever otherwise be seen by viewers. People might normally never really care about or even consider the fact that the adverts use terms that are completely unfamiliar to them. The manner in which this artificial exercise in part creates its own results is evident in the following quotation: 'Seeing these ads, just brings to my attention how much Negroes. They don't show East Indian people, then. Don't know why, since that's not something I noticed before.' Watching adverts, particularly in company, also tends to bring out humour and riposte, as when a viewer says of an Eno advert 'Oh, that's an advert for greedy people', or suggests 'Yes, car is like a woman, old car stays at home just like a woman.'

What emerges quickly is also the degree of consistency with which particular individuals respond to the adverts. Some viewers take an almost entirely utilitarian stance to whatever advert is shown. Their comments are largely of the form 'It is a good commercial. It says exactly what it does. It shows you effectively' (for a roofing compound). Or 'She has a headache because the baby is crying and it is irritating her. She has a lot of housework to do, which could really drive you up the wall. Yes that's a good advert, it is really related to everything' (an advert for Phensic headache tablets). Another viewer tends to see almost all adverts in ethnic terms, being absorbed by the ethnic identity of who takes part and a sense of the under-representation of her own [Indian] community or looking for any possible signs of bias against Indians. Still another viewer takes a fiercely critical view of everything she sees, belabouring the ads, partly for false claims, but much more for low production values or poor choice.

For example, referring to 'The Blue Danube' waltz used as background in one advert she stated 'The music sounded like funeral music for the dead.' One of the most impoverished viewers constantly asserted the advantages of home-made equivalents to these commodities. But in contrast others emphasized their advantages, for example 'I like *accra* [a salted fish dish] mix, since before you used to have pick out the bones. Here you get it as a mix.'

Most viewers claimed that, as one put it, 'I hardly ever buy anything because of ads.' Such claims were sometimes contradicted within the same sitting. For example, watching a claim that a deodorant is more cost-effective than its rivals, a viewer noted 'I wonder if you would really use four of those before you would use one of these. I want to buy it to try it.' Equally, when it came to approval of adverts the utilitarian was often expressed. For example, one of the most approved of adverts included a scheme for obtaining a year's supply of schoolbooks, just after the government had withdrawn the subsidy on these items. Nevertheless, much of this may reflect a context within which people were trying to find a highly acceptable reason for asserting legitimacy. It was when conversations became more relaxed and jokey that the other, more indulgent, criteria tended to come to the fore, such as the music.

Advertising as Genre

In much of the literature on advertising it is assumed that, while producers are primarily concerned with genre, consumers are more likely to see adverts in relation to the world around them and their own experience. The evidence here was, however, that most adverts are first considered by viewers with respect to the genre of advertising itself. Indeed, there is considerable empathy with the advertising industry. This is also the main source of criticism of adverts, especially when adverts are seen as Trinidadian. There are two main aspects of this interpretation: the first stems from knowledge of the advert's manufacture, and the second from a sense of the relative autonomy of the genre. The background to this first point may be an observation often made by anthropologists, which is that with a shift in context what appears to be an identical object of comparative enquiry may not be.

In some respects advertising in Trinidad is equivalent to genres other than advertising abroad. In larger metropolitan countries, the vast majority of viewers rarely relate adverts to knowledge about their production or the advertising industry. There is also a relatively clear boundary between known celebrities who are placed in adverts as celebrities and the actors and actresses that play what are intended to be anonymous and fictive roles.

In Trinidad there is a much smaller pool of persons involved, and this has clear repercussions. Viewers can often recognize, not just a few, but sometimes the majority of the off-screen voices, and state which television or radio announcers they represent. Similarly, the people playing parts are much more often recognized, even when they are not playing themselves but a supposedly fictive character. They often appear in the press, and there is general knowledge about them as individuals.

Trinidad has no local film industry of any size, and even the number of programmes made for television are limited. By contrast, the advertising industry is a major and flourishing business, with large numbers of local productions employing a high proportion of known celebrities, models, voices and so forth. Adverts are therefore themselves quite often discussed in the newspapers. A case in point is the bacchanal surrounding the use of the Rasta's son in a beer advert, discussed above. In addition, some adverts were in effect reviewed much as a film might be in another country. Their quality and content were commented upon, the level of acting, direction and production. There was speculation about how successful the campaign might be and how it reflected on the agency that produced it. This 'film' review treatment tends only to occur for major new advertising series; but it does indicate that to understand the nature of advertising in Trinidad the correct comparative equivalents may not be simply advertising.

This knowledge of the individuals concerned has many different consequences. Sometimes it is quite personal, as when a viewer stated 'I hate that commercial, she was Miss Trinidad and Tobago once. I did a modelling show with her once and she is very unfriendly and very cold and aloof person.' In such circumstances people tend to assume they will recognize someone even when they don't, as was clear in viewers' claimed but mistaken knowledge about the British athlete Daley Thompson, who appeared in a Lucozade commercial. Known celebrities may incur very different responses. Following an advert with the comedian Sprangalang one viewer commented 'I don't like him. I don't like how he speaks. I just can't stand it. I don't look at him at all.' But another noted that he is 'like myself, who don't really speak proper English. It makes us feel good because it have people who would go an' do it on TV. Well, there is nothing wrong with the way we talk. If they could put him there it means there are people who would like to hear us talk in that way.'

This quotation leads to the second aspect of identification with genre, which is an explicit concern with what is appropriate to an advert as a television genre. The topic of gender was much better understood in relation to genre than as a reflection of some more general sense of gender issues. Where it was felt that a beautiful woman was appropriate to the product the feeling was that the advert had failed if she was not sufficiently attractive, irrespective of whether the viewer could identify with her. As was stated of a perfume advert 'I think she is ugly; they could use a nicer-looking person.' However, the gratuitous inclusion of sexy females where it was irrelevant was condemned, as in a soft drink advert where a viewer complained 'She just come and show she [her] bust.' Where an ordinary-looking woman can appear as a role character she is not viewed as appropriate to talk directly about the product to the viewer. This was especially evident in an advert for a disinfectant, which was almost universally condemned. 'I don't like that commercial. I find that she should use some herself. She doesn't look clean, and she is supposed to be promoting a detergent.' Another commented 'She is just ordinary, she should try to be something better.' Such comments demonstrated the degree of conservatism, not of the industry, but of the consumers of adverts. There has clearly developed a strong sense of how an advert should work, and innovations may be condemned as inappropriate even if they improve the information given about the product. This concern with the norms of the genre is clearly linked to its 'film'-like potential. Viewers feel that a Trinidad-made advert is always also a potential advert for Trinidad, and that high production values are required of something which (like a local film industry) is viewed in nationalistic terms as a creative product to be proud or ashamed of.

The Known and the Unknown

As in so many areas of commerce, the workers in the advertising industry quickly forget that the knowledge they have come to take for granted and is necessary to interpret advertisements may not be available to the average viewer. Viewers often struggled with imported images and substances that they had never met. Of course, it may not matter very much that no one knows what the 'malt' is that is the basis for a 'Malta' drink (something like a cocoa bean was one suggestion), or what a blackcurrant is (something like a grape, was another suggestion). This becomes more of a problem if it leads to a misidentification, as in an advert for Canada Dry: 'They use a very skinny girl because of the word dry in the advert. Its not a good thing to be dry or skinny.' Another viewer suggested dry meant it wasn't watery, though some did see it as equivalent to 'dry' in wines.

Instead of a foreign word or product causing a problem, it may be the social norms that are portrayed. An advert for 'night nurse' cold treatment made in England was condemned by one viewer, since 'they are treating the man like a child.' However, the same advert showed that importation can also give an unintended bonus: 'When you think of England, you think of the weather, the cold. If it works there it should work anywhere.' Imported adverts still retained a certain amount of prestige, given the emulation of the foreign that was inculcated under colonialism, as in the expression 'our babies are not active like that', though in general it seemed that this deferential attitude to the foreign had declined considerably from earlier periods.

Confusion that arises from imported adverts was more than matched by locally made adverts. Advert producers are often trying to compress a whole story line, or chain of associations, within 30 seconds, which may prove too much to digest. An advert for Dixi Cola is based upon a radio phone-in programme sponsored by the drink. Some viewers understood this, but most did not. Interpretations ranged from (a) she is making a phone call from a foreign land since she is foreign; to (b) she seems to be a singer and is being phoned by her daughter; to (c) this woman is on the phone and the men are bothering her. A similar problem arose with an advert that included the conductor of a steel band orchestra in white gloves waving a baton, who was assumed to be, amongst other things, a magician or somebody about to play cricket.

The localization which results from picking a well-known television personality can also have negative repercussions. There was almost universal bewilderment at the picking of the weather forecaster to present the Huggins advert, since, as one viewer put it, 'Nobody would listen to him because he is always wrong. If he says its going to rain tomorrow, bet your bottom dollar its going to be blazing sunshine . . . so I don't think he is a particularly good choice for this commercial.'

In general, the degree of 'correct interpretation', in the sense of interpretation according to the intentions of the advertisers, was closely related to class and educational background. Not surprisingly, those with a similar educational level to the advertisers were most able to follow the intention behind the advert. They were also more likely to engage in the kind of analysis that an academic would produce. For example, one viewer decoded the Stag advert that placed the commercial motif in the centre of various cultural activities in precisely the same way I had seen it, that is creating a sense of nationalist unity through transcending the plurality it had first created. Such viewers are likely to have been through the same kind of university degree system in social studies or business studies as both the advertisers and myself, applying the academic 'habitus' that Bourdieu so ably shows is thereby inculcated.

By contrast, viewers who had not spent as much time within institutions of education were more likely to reinterpret the advert as something quite different. These differences are highlighted when the product can be appropriated by rural and 'traditional' beliefs. The best example came from an advert for Tisane de Bourbon, a 'blood purifier.' One viewer described her attempt to use the product for her infertility: 'Some people say it's a drink that it will clean your womb. My grandparents, mother, father and other women, everybody is telling me use Tissan, but the doctor tell me something totally different. I drink four bottles as a course to clean my womb.' She was surprised by the advert's being based upon football, since 'I never knew men used it.' Another viewer noted one 'should not take it after a lack of sex, since it could kill you, but it is OK for early pregnancy'.

Sexuality and Ethnicity

The relation of 'class' to knowledge is hardly a surprising finding, and would probably not worry the advertising industry too much, since their prime concern is with wealthier viewers, who tend also to have the relevant educational background. By contrast, the evidence for the interpretation of sexuality and ethnicity does not conform to either my or their expectations. With regard to sexuality, it was not that there was either more or less emphasis upon this factor than expected. As most Trinidadians would probably anticipate, it was very commonly commented upon. Rather, what was surprising was the choice of adverts that were assumed to rely upon this strategy of sale.

In some cases the explanation for difference was not hard to find. For example, by far the most offensive advert on the video, and the only one to cause considerable disgust, was an imported advert for 'Close-Up' toothpaste that would have been seen as utterly innocuous in, for example, western Europe. The difference is simply that while Trinidadians have certain erotic movements and gestures that might offend others but are taken for granted locally, the public kissing that is common in many of the countries where these adverts are made is quite unacceptable to most Trinidadians. One viewer noted 'A child watching that, I don't know what they would really think . . . In Trinidad we say that is disrespectful. You leave that for home.' Another suggested 'There has never been an advert like that, with kissing in. It's rather shocking, I don't like it . . . it's embarrassing. In Trinidad people wouldn't kiss like that, would feel embarrassed if see other people kissing in public.'

Of the adverts that were clearly intended to be sold through an emphasis upon sex, that for Stone's Ginger Wine was viewed more or less as the advertisers would have predicted, with a certain amount of joking, but in general an acceptance that this is a well-established process of commoditization. As one viewer put it 'Anything that would give you upliftment before or after sex, people would be at least willing to try.' The most surprising result was the complete and consistent rejection of Supligen as related to the theme of sex, which is discussed as a case study in the concluding chapter. Other adverts where there seemed no particular link to this topic, were, however, interpreted by some viewers as appealing to such concerns. For example, one viewer said of an advert for Carnation hot chocolate drink 'That ad, they try to sell it with sex, because they didn't tell you in words, but the way the people act it, that he would reward her when she comes home. So you get the impression that she would get something special.' The idea of a sexual strengthener was also ascribed by viewers to a malted drink, eggnog, stout and Tisane de Bourbon blood purifier.

The viewers' reading of ethnicity was discussed in Miller 1994, since it proved a turning-point in my interpretation of the general topic of ethnicity in Trinidad. The ascription of highly specific ethnic categories to persons is extremely common, and is often the primary way in which people are designated. I had come to assume that there was considerable consistency in this 'folk science', which classifies by physiognomy. Indeed the practice is common even with new-born babies, when there is a desire to challenge claimed paternity. I was therefore much surprised at the considerable diversity with which the characters who appear on adverts are given their ethnic labels.

For example, the advert for Stone's Ginger Wine is almost entirely based on a close-up view of a muscular man discussing the attributes of the drink. I was informed by viewers that this individual was Negro (twice), Indian (twice), Dougla (twice) and Mixed Negro-Spanish. Despite this diversity, classifications are usually given in an authoritative tone, as though this was not something that could be disputed or refuted. Khan (1993) demonstrates how the use of the term 'Spanish' is influenced by contextual knowledge; but it seems that still more basic categories, such as Negro and Indian, are subject to considerably divergent responses, even with good contextual information.

As noted earlier on, advertisements would hardly give an accurate picture of the actual spread of images available. This is because of the considerable emphasis on the use of mixed ethnicity as an alternative to a pluralism based on the juxtaposition of several persons representative of different ethnicities. From the perspective of the producers this was a quite understandable strategy, but it does not follow that it was well received by viewers. On the contrary, it was one of the most commonly criticized features of contemporary advertising. One person (not in this group) commented 'What is this thing about mixed persons? Almost every commercial based around them, but why do that? Don't they realize this can offend people . . . it ends up exerting a certain pressure.' The word not used in this quotation, but very commonly employed by other Indians talking about advertisements, is 'Douglarization'. This was part of the general belief amongst Indians that the government was largely unsympathetic to them. A belief generally sustained by the evidence of the policies of the PNM government, which had been in power for most of the time since independence (Hintzen 1989). One part of this accusation was the idea that the government had a specific policy of encouraging mixed marriage or sex in order to dilute the purity of the Indian population. This was argued by some to be the reason behind the construction of Newtown, a largely African settlement in the middle of Chaguanas, a town dominated by Indians.

Many Indian viewers assumed that big business interests, including the advertising agencies, were in cahoots with the government, and that they were deliberately trying to encourage people to view positively mixed ethnicity, and in particular the Dougla. The fact that so many adverts portray romantic situations or couples only reinforced this idea that there was a concerted anti-Indian plot in the casting of advertisements. The predominance of the 'red' or Dougla did not, however, fare any better when viewed by the African consumer. On this side there was considerable prejudice against this group, especially as advertisers tended to emphasize the lighter-skinned examples of the mixed group. These actors and actresses were reminiscent of an important category of 'high-brown' light-skinned Trinidadians, who usually had some element of white ancestry as part of their inheritance. During the colonial period this group almost came to form an independent class that mediated between the colonial whites and the mass population. In general this class was seen as highly emulatory of the whites, and in some sense betraying the remainder of the population in their repudiation of their own origins. Although the older calypsos show that they also appeared as sexually desirable (Rohlehr 1988), by the 1980s this group no longer presented as a clear demarcation in Trinidad ethnic consciousness; but there was still a sense that they tended to be positively discriminated for in job interviews. Hence there remained a strong prejudice against them as likely to be arrogant and self-important.

All of this was very evident to my research assistant, who was well aware that those who only judged her on her appearance almost always tended look down on her as a 'red', a term which most commonly included a pejorative element. So that what made her attractive to advertisers by no means made her popular more generally. It seems, then, that advertising agencies, in their desire to find a solution to what they perceived as the problem of ethnic representation, had devised a strategy that pleased very few and caused considerable offence to the majority of viewers.

The advertisers are certainly correct, however, in thinking that ethnicity poses a problem for them. Prejudices in favour of one's own group were very evident in viewers' comments, as was perceived bias in the adverts: for example, a Stag advert was viewed as 'showing you that you have to be a particular group, Negro or African, in order to enjoy the beer.' In particular, this was essentialized in the 'taste' and criteria of beauty that were applied to the advertisements. For example an Indian viewer found it peculiar that a dark-skinned African should be chosen for a skin care product: 'I don't think they have the best of skin to display this product. I don't know who would have the ideal skin, but definitely not African. It doesn't look appealing.' Indians were much more rarely shown, but here also Africans looked askance, as when an advert for diapers (nappies) imported from America with an acceptable white baby was replaced by a locally made advert using a clearly Indian baby. The same prejudice applied to products such as Maggi, which were assumed to be suitable for Creole cooking but not for Indian cooking. This use of ethnicity should not be exaggerated. There were viewers who seemed to show little interest in this factor, and were able to find models attractive irrespective of their ethnicity.

Bacchanal

To say that advertising attracts scepticism is probably a highly generalizable statement around the world, for obvious enough reasons. But in Trinidad scepticism takes a very specific form, bound up in the particular moral and ideological stances that generate the concept of bacchanal as the key defining feature of Trinidad. Looking for bacchanal is something like a national hobby. Many adverts prompt this kind of viewing, since they are attempting to represent a particular kind of respectability, which in practice is relatively rare but has become the dominant genre in the world of advertising realism (Schudson 1993). Traditionally, it is precisely this attempt to create respectability by those who can only do so by hiding various aspects of their origins and relations that is the primary target of the search for bacchanal.

The quintessential uncovering of bacchanal is through looking for sexual indiscretions that have been covered up. Here is the imperative to uncover the 'true' father of the child, of the fact that a claim cannot be sustained. There are many ways in which advertising can be taken apart in the interests of eliciting bacchanal; but the most common was when viewers reacted to the fictive family created for the advertisement. The problem from the point of the advertisers was once again one of ethnicity. On the one hand they wanted to portray a family that was plausible as a family; but on the other hand they had a dictum that when several people are being shown there should be some sensitivity to the pluralist nature of the Island. This caused endless mirth amongst viewers, as one put it 'You laugh about it, especially when you are in a group, in some ad you know that child couldn't be for that father.' Typical examples of such remarks were 'In fact that can't be her family because some of the children. Look, the husband is African, she seems to be African. The children seem to be Dougla . . . definitely think that it is from an outside man. It can't be his. A lot of people would think that is funny.' Or 'The mother is Chinese Negro, the little girl looks like a Dougla, the father is a Negro, so it couldn't be a family.' The implication of disputing paternity is of course that the true father has been revealed by the birth, which is a favourite source of bacchanal in everyday life.

Conclusion

Advertising should not be analysed as an artificial construction opposed to something called 'society', which is understood as natural. Advertisers, anthropologists and ordinary viewers are all engaged in the creation of generalized models and normative expectations. In all three cases these may or may not be either abstracted or reflexive. Indeed, many instances have been given in the last two chapters of advertisers' lack of reflection upon their own creations. If anything, it is the anthropologist who is most concerned with the project of abstraction, because of a commitment to comparative study. The critique of advertising that dominated social science accounts in the 1970s and early 1980s projected considerable abilities on to advertisers in terms of their ability to manipulate both messages and audience. Observation of the industrial context for the production of advertising in Trinidad would certainly leave one sceptical of such claims.

On the whole I have concentrated on what might be seen as the negative drives to advertising, the fear of competitors and the fears about known weaknesses in the products, because advertising was found to be a rather more reactive and defensive industry than used to be portrayed. It tends to be studies that are more in touch with the industry itself that have affirmed this rather more ambivalent and uncertain foundation to contemporary advertising, where perhaps the most important contextual feature is that they often have very little idea themselves of whether an advert sells goods, or whether anybody is much influenced by the images they create. It is this that leads the academic in turn to be rather more circumspect about assuming the effects and consequences of advertising (cf. e.g. Leiss *et al.* 1990; Schudson 1993). A parallel case could be made for the consumption of advertising, since, as Schudson notes, the issues involved in what he calls 'the consumer's information environment' (1993: 90–128) has many parallels with 'what advertising agencies know' (1993: 44–89).

The advertising literature seems to follow a general trajectory, reflecting a more general trend in the analysis of language. The first critiques of manifest content (often called 'content analysis') were replaced by the desire to investigate the underlying structures, equivalent to syntax and grammar. This gave way to a concern with the technologies of meaning that seemed more equivalent to semantic analysis. Finally, works such as Tanaka (1994) have espoused the rise of pragmatics and more particularly of theories of inference. This trajectory is reasonable enough if we consider that this cycle started in a dissatisfaction with content analysis as too simplistic a link between manifest representation and the world outside advertising. Returning to the articulation through theories of relevance means coming back to this linkage with a much more sophisticated theory of the contextual cues that guide the inferences that might be made by viewers of advertising.

I do not claim to have echoed the degree of sophistication that may be found in many of those books devoted specifically to the topic of advertising. My analysis is also highly synchronic, and cannot offer the same kinds of insights that are emerging through long-term work on change in advertising (e.g. Leiss *et al.* 1990). But the last two chapters represents an approach that seems to be demanded but not fulfilled by the recent literature on the topic (e.g. Tanaka 1994). This increasing concern with context and inference seems to place far greater weight upon the wider environment within which an advert is constructed and read. As long as this remains within debates about language, however, there is a problem, in that the linguistic analysis seems to assume complete familiarity with the contexts from which meaning is generated, which is unlikely to be derived from any study that remains within the context of linguistics alone.

The aim of an ethnographic approach is therefore at least to start to give more consideration to these problems of our limited knowledge of context. In the last chapter I attempted to show how a particular advert came into existence through the rejection of various alternative scenarios. This was based on an ethnography of that particular campaign, which it was argued gave clarity to a more general argument about the importance of fear in advert construction. Similarly, my interpretation of the new Carib campaign in terms of the concept of bacchanal as the pivotal point of localization depends upon the weight of ethnographic material that led me to the conclusion that bacchanal had a quite different meaning from that which this term usually connotes. In this case it objectifies the particular contradictions of Trinidadian cultural projects of the late 1980s. Without the ethnography of Trinidadian values and contradictions developed in Miller 1994 this larger implication of the Carib advert would certainly have escaped me. What the present volume adds is ethnographic material that now includes the situation of advertising as one moment in a history of products that includes also their production, distribution and consumption. It is to the next stage in this sequence, that of retailing and shopping, that I shall now turn.

7

Retail and Shopping

Introduction: The Shop as Urban Symbol

The problems of generalizing ethnographic materials are notorious. Sometimes the case study is given as though it were typical of many similar situations. In other ethnographies it seems as though the case is a heightened exemplification of some aspect of social life that is being investigated, atypical but instructive. A study of shopping in Chaguanas is of this second variety. Shops and shopping have a special relationship to the town of Chaguanas that will provide pointers to the wider cultural context within which an analysis of shops ought to be conducted, but in itself represents something of an extreme case.

The people of Chaguanas are very much aware that shops and shopping are in some respects a symbol of the town itself, both for them and for the rest of Trinidad. Chaguanas, a location that on most maps and in most accounts is still not designated as a town, has three shopping malls, being second in this respect only to the capital, Port of Spain. The symbolic relationship between the town and its shops is mediated by ethnicity, since Indians are themselves often associated with shopkeeping. Historically, the predominance of Indians in shopkeeping is a relatively recent phenomena, and there were many early rivals to ethnic specificity. In the nineteenth century, outside Port of Spain, both the Portuguese and the Chinese were seen as 'natural' shopkeepers. The earliest accounts from oral history suggest that the Portuguese ran the most important commercial enterprise in Chaguanas, while the Chinese dominated the local groceries and rum shops. Both were in a sense dwarfed by the commercial clout of Woodford Lodge sugar plantation and mill, which is where most of the people of the town were employed.

Nevertheless, there were early examples of shops opened by

Indians who had served their indentureship and established sufficient capital. The nineteenth century census information suggests the rise of small outlets for bakers and jewellers in particular. By the early decades of the twentieth century these came to dominate the high street of Chaguanas. Already, what had been a sleepy village, an adjunct to Woodford Lodge and a train station, was growing into a commercial centre for its immediate hinterland of villages. The Chinese and Portuguese continued to have influence, but increasingly it was Indians who were being used as outlets by merchants distributing stock imported through Port of Spain. In addition to shops the town's market served as a symbol, since it has for long been a market of some renown – indeed, probably the most extensive open market in the country outside Port of Spain.

The importance of shops is evident in the earliest extensive portrait we have of the town, that given for the late 1930s, reflecting the childhood of V. S. Naipaul and fictionalized as Arawak in his novel *A House for Mr. Biswas*. Biswas, having failed to become an apprentice priest, turns to sign painting, especially for the Christmas season:

> Occasionally there were inexplicable rashes of new signs, and a district was thronged for a fortnight or so with sign-writers, for no shopkeeper wished to employ a man who had been used by his rival. Every sign then was required to be more elaborate than the last, and for stretches the Main Road was dazzling with signs that were hard to read. (p. 77)

Biswas then marries into the shop at Hanuman House, then and now (under its true name 'The Lion House') the most impressive older property in the town.

The stereotypical relationship between the Indian and shop-keeping is not in fact a reflection of true economic power. Until recently, Indians had virtually no presence in the main retailing concerns of Trinidad, which were controlled largely by White and Syrian interests. The one exception was Kirpilani, a relatively recent immigrant from India who was briefly highly successful before going bankrupt. In this respect retailing repeats the picture already noted with respect to manufacturing; but if anything the 'layers' of ethnic involvement are still clearer with retailing. Indians do, however, clearly, indeed conspicuously, dominate at the level of middle-range and small retailing and as owner-occupiers who serve the consumer, especially outside Port of Spain. As a result, the image of the shopkeeper held by the consumer is resolutely Indian. Within Chaguanas this is particularly the case, and until recently non-Indians had considerable difficulty getting employment even to serve in shops in the town. Indians are themselves subject to this stereotype about their 'natural' propensity towards retailing (Ramsaran 1993).

For Chaguanas this relationship is compounded by the image of the town as itself self-made. It is known to all its inhabitants that the government has constantly favoured Couva to the southwest as the central place within the region, and favoured the latter first by having more government posts stationed there and more recently through links with industrial development at Point Lisas. Nevertheless, it is Chaguanas that, thanks to the placement of the main North–South highway through the town (and according to its shopkeepers, their industriousness) has clearly won this rivalry for dominance of the central region of Trinidad. As a Ford resident noted, with the exaggeration of pride: 'Chaguanas is a city. Right now you have almost every store in town has a branch in Chaguanas. Chaguanas is a total city. Now you don't need to go into town to get anything. Now the only time you go to town is for the drive, anything you think about in Chaguanas, you could get it.'

This also makes Chaguanas the established alternative 'ethnic' capital of Trinidad. Although there has always been a substantial minority of at least a third of non-Indians in the main part of the town, the dominant population is Indian, and this is the only urban location in Trinidad where this would be true. Indians are a clear minority in Port of Spain, San Fernando and Arima, the other three urban areas. Chaguanas thereby stands out as the proper site for any activity, such as Divali Nagar, that is seen as reflecting Trinidadian Indians as a national community. In the 1990s Hulsi Bhagan, a vociferous local member of parliament for the constituency, has cemented this identification through providing the most explicit focus upon ethnicity in politics of any current politician.

In contemporary Chaguanas this triad of ethnicity, urbanity and shopkeeping is fully established in three symbolic forms. Firstly, there is the continued success of the market, which dominates the centre of Chaguanas and constantly threatens to expand beyond the area allotted to it, so that market stalls have to be prevented from occupying much of the roadway around. Market activity still often threatens the flow of traffic through Chaguanas's already congested one-way system. This remains a market of national reputation. The second symbol is the bustling high street, with constant anecdotes about how this is commercially the most viable high street in Trinidad, and how they have a higher turnover than shops in Port of Spain, especially after the looting that followed the attempted coup of 1990. The third is the malls. They are certainly much less impressive malls than the single mall at Gulf City in San Fernando or some of the larger malls around Port of Spain, but the fact that there are three malls, close together, all within sight of the highway, has become symbolic of Chaguanas as a successful commercial venture. There is also widespread acknowledgment that this fact accounts for the presence of the malls in the first place. Each mall is directly associated with an individual Indian family, and was seen as their family monument. One – 'Ramsaran' Mall – is directly named after its founder, another – Mid-Centre Mall – is just as commonly called after what has probably been the single most successful family firm in the area, and the third – Centre City Mall – is less commonly personalized, though its significance as a memorial to a particular businessman is still clear to all.

The malls are the abiding legacy of the oil boom, when there was the money and self-confidence to engage in this kind of monumental construction, though even before their construction there had been an earlier local shopping development, termed a 'plaza', which was a conglomeration of shops again associated with a successful local family. The advent of recession is also visually marked by the malls. Ramsaran is built in two blocks, and the foundation structure of the third, never completed, phase stands forlorn at one end. Few people are aware of the grandiose scale of the original plans for Centre City, of which the built section represents only a fraction of what had been intended.

The combination of these three, the market, the high street, and the malls, makes Chaguanas the symbol for the area of that which is 'bright', that is, modern and cosmopolitan. This is, of course, only true for a certain population. In many respects, Chaguanas shops are symbolically important less for the people of the town than to those of villages in the surrounding areas.

The people who live in The Meadows and other middle-class suburbs of the town, the children of the shopkeepers, see themselves as too sophisticated, and prefer to shop in Port of Spain. For them the word 'town' is shorthand for the capital, and that is the only place that is really 'bright.' But for the people of the largely Indian-dominated surrounding villages, as well as the less affluent element of Chaguanas itself, Port of Spain remains either intimidating or over-associated with non-Indian Trinidad, and it is to Chaguanas that they come to lime[9] and that they take pride in. The most important form of this liming around Chaguanas has become shopping.

The function of shopping as a symbol of Chaguanas certainly affects the degree of vertical integration between retailing, manufacturing and distribution, but only in certain respects. It means that shops are still largely related to local ownership and control, and the proportion of outlets of national chains was up to the 1990s low when compared with that in other centres. This statement must be qualified by type of economic activity. It is obviously not true of banks, for example, which are all national chains, or of insurance companies. National chains are also conspicuous in electrical goods and in fast-food outlets. Nevertheless, at least three-quarters of retailing is locally owned. This is true even of the malls. In Centre City mall, for example, all but two outlets were locally owned in 1989.

Local ownership had been virtually complete with respect to the two dominant retail forms in the town. These are clearly divided, in that the area to the west of the highway, the traditional high street, is dominated by 16 clothing and fabric shops and 6 shoe shops (out of 76 outlets on the street). By contrast, the Montrose area to the east of the highway has 23 outlets concerned with the car, but no predominantly fabric or clothing stores. In at least one retail field, that of car upholstery, Montrose has unrivalled dominance over the whole of Trinidad. On the other hand the fabric shops have for long been in rivalry with the mainly Syrian-controlled fabric shops of Port of Spain. In 1990, when the first Syrian-owned fabric shop opened in Chaguanas, it was as though the integument of the town had been violated. There was also the simultaneous opening of a pizzeria (also part

---

9. See below for a more extended definition of liming, which is a form of 'hanging around' in groups.

of a Syrian chain) in the very centre of Chaguanas, and the event was treated with extreme ambivalence by the Chaguanas people, who admired the slick styling and cosmopolitan feel of these new outlets, but also seemed almost bemused that the relationship of locality could be so swiftly compromised. These events were followed by a call to form a Chaguanas Chamber of Commerce in order to prevent the spread of Syrian and French Creole business, which were seen as being aided by the banks (*Express* 13/12/90). The weekly newspaper *The Bomb* put this in more graphic terms. Under the title 'Cold War over Central Stores'(14/12/90) it reported 'The businessmen of Chaguanas, the ones "wid we navel string born and bury in Chaguanas" are visibly upset with people whom they deem as "outsiders" cutting in on them and trying to control their "turf".'

The Shopkeeper's Perspective

Establishing Shops

My main source on the views and histories of the Chaguanas shopkeepers is interviews conducted with twenty-five retail and service outlets, all within central Chaguanas and its extension into Montrose. The study centred on small to medium enterprises. This meant that although the discussions were held in all cases with the shopkeepers, these same individuals were also involved in direct selling to the public. Only one case represented a branch of a Port of Spain firm. Out of the twenty-five interviewed there were two Africans and one Portuguese, and the rest were Indian. In almost every case the owners lived locally in the Chaguanas area, though in many cases they were born elsewhere in the region of central Trinidad, and moved into Chaguanas with the oil boom.

This retail sector is dominated by East Indians in a manner that far outweighs their demographic dominance. Indeed, one shop claimed that: 'In the whole of Chaguanas we were the first shop to introduce Negroes or any variation, or what we call true, true Negroes, which is real Africans, and it was a bit alarming for some people, but . . . started to work for us around 1980, and

Negro people would say this is the only shop who are hiring Negroes, and that made a great influence on people buying. The Indians never said anything about it, and I can't detect any loss; but I can detect in that regard a gain in sales, and it was not done for business.' The implication being that this attracted more African customers. This is almost certainly an exaggerated account, and in 1988 there were many African sales staff and a number of shops run or owned by Africans; but it gives a sense of the assumed dominance.

In most, but not all cases, the key influence in establishing retail outlets was family background, since there would have been other members of the same family who were already involved in either retailing or wholesaling. For example, in a family where there were parents and siblings with fabric shops, a daughter decided to open a shop that specialized in bridal wear, transforming what had been a specialist section within the other shops into a shop on its own. In another case, a carpet shop was started by a member of a family already involved in hardware. In other cases, the new generation was opening up in retail on the basis of wholesale or manufacture by the older generation, as with a daughter whose newsagent's shop is mainly supplied by her parent's wholesale enterprise, or a nephew whose furniture in part comes from his uncle's wholesale business. Retailing could extend previous work, as in a furniture shop that had started by manufacturing furniture in the yard behind the shop, or a woman who had manufactured clothes to supply to a mall in San Fernando, but who was now establishing her own retail outlet. Where families were important in the shop's origins they may continue to play a vital part, often as main suppliers. In one case a wife runs a gift shop on the basis of a much larger export–import and distribution service for giftware run by her husband.

There were also one or two persons who were establishing themselves in business for the first time. An example was a music shop whose owner's parents worked in the cane-fields. Some shopkeepers were women previously in paid employment, but now trying to start their own enterprise, such as the ex-airline hostess who decided to open up a specialist second-hand baby goods store as a result of her experience in helping in a garage sale. She had been 'flabbergasted at the people coming, negotiating, bargaining, buying junk like pantyhose and cutlery that had been used. And the calibre of people, well-to-do people that you wouldn't think would be using second-hand things.' Even here there was family involvement, as it was the husband who, though in waged sector employment, used his spare time to clean and fix the equipment prior to resale. In general it was rare for a shop-owner to have had any specific training. One had been on an accountancy course, while the owner of a pet shop who had lived in New York for many years had a degree in business studies.

In many Indian families, here as observed elsewhere (e.g. Shaw 1988), there is a sense of the household as a whole controlling the economic choices made by the individual. This is most often seen in the form of family members working within the shop. Some of the smaller retail outlets were devised as occupations for women whose husbands were in waged labour. In this case the husband or other relatives; would assist after office hours, in order to give the women time to buy in stock or undertake domestic responsibilities. The concept of the immediate family could also be of considerable importance in the structure, ownership and scale of the enterprise. It is sometimes assumed that the only genuine business partners are relatives; as one person suggested: 'I don't have anyone I can ask to come in it with me, so I prefer to keep it at a size I can handle by myself.' In another case one of the owners noted that, in their family, if they could only have had more siblings, they could then have had more shops. The family and the business thus become to some extent synonymous. In a typical instance a sibling had been a teacher; but when business expanded with the oil boom and another shop was seen as viable, then the teacher gave up his profession in order to manage a shop for his brother.

There is some suggestion of a 'developmental cycle' operating, where the children at first grow up helping in the parent's business, but, as tension develops within the family, respond by setting up their own establishments in a connected or in effect a sub-franchised system. About half the outlets seem to be involved in larger family structures. This relationship to the family is, however, looser than that described for cases in India (e.g. Fox 1969). Firstly, the labour laws in Trinidad attempt to restrict the use of family labour (although they are not much enforced). More important is the government auditing of accounts, which means that Trinidadian shops do dissaggregate their commercial interests from their household interests, and don't merely regard the stock as serving both groups equally, as is commonly the case in India (Fox 1969).

Trinidadians of all ethnicities tend to characterize themselves as highly entrepreneurial and as often ready to try various money-making strategies of quite different character, simultaneously if necessary. In other areas of the economy they might drive taxis, carry a government public service job and grow crops at different times of the day. Given the strength of this stereotype it was a surprisingly absent characteristic of retail, which seemed to be treated as a full-time occupation. Some shopkeepers had trans-formed their enterprise radically as such, as with the owner of a 'pub' who had transformed it into a paint shop after a conver-sation with a customer over a drink about the need for an outlet for a particular paint company in the area. This was exceptional, however; and although there is a fast turnover of small retail enterprises, this seems to reflect those initially trying to establish themselves. Otherwise, retail does not seem as flexible or as fast-changing as might have been expected from the self-characterization of the dynamics of Trinidadian involvement in business. Most of the present enterprises date from the oil boom; but a number had been in the family for several decades. In these two respects, stability and intensity, detailed investigation differs markedly from the 'impression' that would be given from casual conversation about the nature of retailing, which constantly asserts the opposites.

The main cost involved in establishing a business is the rent and the stock. In Centre City Mall monthly rents had just decreased to TT$3.5 per square foot (upstairs) and TT$4.5 per square foot (downstairs). This was for properties of around 500–600 square feet. The best positions in the high street might be twice as expensive, while at the outskirts of Montrose typical rents were at that time being reduced from over TT$1,000 to around TT$800 as a result of the recession. In addition, a shop might have taken out a loan to get established during the oil boom, and would be suffering the consequences of this during a recession. The shopkeeper of a small outlet for cassette tapes and videos noted that after he took out a bank loan in 1984 'to pay the first instalment I hustle money in a week, that was TT$3,800, and now they break the loan down to TT$2,600 and is taking a month and a half to hustle that less money.' The mark-ups on goods during the oil boom had rocketed, but during recession they were gradually coming down as profits were squeezed. One clothes shop still achieved a 100 per cent mark-up. Most outlets recalled a similar or larger mark-up during the oil boom, but had now come down to around 25 per cent for most goods and 40 per cent or 50 per cent for a few chosen items.

The shops had a variety of strategies with respect to suppliers. The period of fieldwork was marked by an extreme emphasis on one particular factor that would not normally have been of such concern, that is the lack of access to foreign exchange referred to in earlier chapters. This is of particular importance, since one of the key decisions made by shopkeepers is whether to obtain supplies directly from sources abroad or through Port of Spain-based merchants and importers. In some cases goods are made or completed locally. One furniture store produced a large quantity of its own goods; an undertaker required imported raw materials, but made the caskets and coffins on site; a fashion store produced all its own clothes from bulk-purchased rolls of cloth.

Most shops, however, dealt mainly with the direct sale of imported commodities. In some cases this required a co-ordinated policy. For example, a dress-shop, linked through family connections to others, organized to allow selected members of the family to travel abroad for collective purchasing. In the last year this had meant two trips to the United States and to Canada, and specialist trips to England for buttons and Switzerland for silks and embroideries. They specifically differentiated themselves from other fabric shops in Chaguanas, which took supplies from Port of Spain. Connections are often made through the West Indian community in New York or Toronto; but shops will equally find suppliers anywhere from Japan to Czechoslovakia if they can obtain good-value materials. While some have specific policies with regard to their source of supply, and others are more eclectic. A gift shop takes some ceramics from a local factory, and others through a wholesaler who concentrates on Caricom imports and exports, while still other goods come through merchants dealing with Far Eastern suppliers.

There is no necessary relation between decisions made in relation to suppliers and decisions about how to present these same goods to consumers. First, consumers are seen as having very little interest in the source of goods. A curtain shop noted

'They don't care one thing about whether or not it come from Canada, England, American or Japan.' Second, even where a shop might advertise 'Belgian fabrics' they may equally well have been obtained directly from Belgium or through a Port of Spain intermediary. The perception of what makes a significant selling point for the public is therefore quite detached from the decision how best to obtain stock. In research on the history of furniture sales in Britain, Attfield (1992) has found that shops that stressed traditional craftsmanship in their advertising might be taking their stock from mass production, while retailers who actually took their stock from hand-manufactured sources might prefer to stress its modern and functional qualities. Similarly in Trinidad, although retail is a link between manufacture and sales, in practice it tends to a Janus-faced policy that treats the commercial logic of supply as quite independent from the symbolic self-representation of goods to the public. This is not always the case. While the particular source abroad may not matter, Trinidadians may regard home products as inferior to imported goods as a general category (see the questionnaire material in the last chapter). A review in the *Sunday Express* (16/1/91) provided the following quotation: '"I regret having brought local clothes to sell here, because people only seemed to want the foreign stuff – not because the local thing weren't good quality but because they wanted something exclusive and local manufacturers were selling the same thing to everyone. Never again", concluded Ali (owner of a fashion store in a Chaguanas mall).'

These establishments employed between one and ten members of staff. The descriptions given of employment by the shop-owners often differed considerably from accounts collected during the household survey interviews where the householders happened to have worked as shop assistants. The shopkeepers tended to have a matter-of-fact attitude. Some noted the credit or discounts that might be made available to staff; most implied a long-term relationship, with job security. From the perspective of shop assistants two factors, in particular, were noted. The first is the low wages, and the tendency to hire them for a period of six months and then dismiss them. This was confirmed by a manager who had come into Chaguanas in order to restructure the finances of a bankrupt company. He noted:

The assistants are local, since they are so cheap; you wouldn't get anyone from Port of Spain for that – if they make TT$150 a week, that's good . . . The way they treat staff here is abominable: hire a kid, keep her working 12 hours a day; after she's been with them for 6 months they get rid of them, since if they don't, they got to give the holiday leave, sick leave, etc. After that period they find something wrong with them and send them away and find someone else.

The second complaint was of sexual abuse, and the pressure on young women to sleep with employers in order to obtain or retain a job. Such accusations are hard to verify or confirm; but the household survey happened to include one woman who was working for one of the outlets interviewed, where the owner acknowledged that she was pregnant by him. One shop-owner implied that this was the result of female employees 'thrusting their charms' upon owners in order to be able to bargain for days off, easy working conditions, etc. The balance of evidence, however, was for pressure from owners, or in larger businesses from senior staff, upon unwilling employees. Within Trinidadian popular culture – for example, calypsoes by female calypsonian-ists, or scandals reported in the weekly newspapers – the degree of sexual exploitation and abuse at work is a constantly reiterated theme.

Selling Goods

There was considerable variation in the parts of Trinidad shop-keepers saw their customers as coming from. Although there was a group of outlets that mainly served a local market, in many cases they perceive their customers as deriving not from Chag-uanas itself but from the villages and suburbs around the town such as Enterprise, Felicity and Longdenville. In one case an African hairdresser who had moved from an outlying area noted that before this move her clientele were specifically not local people. She attributed this to a jealousy that meant they would not wish her to advance herself, since they feared 'you might have bread on the table' (compare Ryan and Barclay 1992: 60–1). The small 'parlour' does serve an immediate neighbourhood; but this is much less often the case for the more formal shop.

Some saw their market as the general area of South and Central Trinidad. Other more specialist centres, such as the second-hand baby goods or the motor accessories, not only saw themselves as servicing the whole of Trinidad, but might see the capital and the East–West corridor as more important sources of custom than the local area. In such cases there was the temptation to think about opening up a store in the capital. For example, the owner of the Bridal Shop had recently had a stall in the national 'expo' event, and as a result of the good reception received there, was encouraged to think of expanding into the capital. She recognised that many Trinidadians would simply not come down to shop in an area they regard as 'country'.

In many cases the customers break down into several discrete fractions related to the specific situation of the outlet. For a gift shop, for example, there are regular customers from a factory nearby who buy gifts for social occasions. There is the custom from the nearby wealthy suburb, who would prefer to buy gifts at more prestigious locations, but will drop in for cards or paper or when they have a last-minute demand. There is also a noticeable passing trade from those who have just come off the highway at this junction. They would buy cosmetics, stockings, and other items to smarten themselves up before going on to the social function that occasioned their trip to this area.

One shop-owner who was not local and had his main branch in Port of Spain was able thereby to discern a notable character-istic that differentiated shopping in Chaguanas from shopping in the capital. This was the importance of shop loyalty and personal relations in Chaguanas shops. Indeed, he was one of the few who mentioned a specific strategy in the hiring of shop assistants. This was to aim for someone local who would talk and be friendly with customers, in order to build up such customer loyalty. This difference may not be entirely due to the desires of the cust-omers, since, as he noted for Port of Spain, 'the shopkeepers are so busy looking for dishonest people that they don't build up a customer relationship'. Most shops mentioned a core of loyal shoppers, although in no case was this seen as the sole source of custom. Where the customers are unknown some attempt will be made to evaluate their potential as customers, and, as so often in Trinidad, it is the make of the car in which they arrived that will be viewed as the key clue to their identity and spending power.

The binding of a customer to a shop may be secured in a

number of ways. The advice of the shop assistant is often sought by customers, who then develop a relation of trust or friendship with a particular assistant. This may be mainly practical advice as to what colours suit, or which materials are appropriate to an intended context. A pet-shop owner expects to continue to service his customers with advice: 'A man might complain that his parrot is ill. You have to tell him to use sunflower seeds, and whenever you give him fruits to make sure you wash out the container and clean the cage' (for an extended example see the case of Obeah below). In some cases the commodity is part of a much larger network of discussion. This is certainly true of clothing. Style is an important part of general discourse, and customers may chat for a considerable time about fashion changes and stylistic developments.

Shop-owners may have networks with other shops in the area, so that a customer at a furnishing shop will be sent to one shop for a repair and another for materials. This is based on reciprocity and friendship, as I found no case of formal commission being paid. An individual who was in the habit of asking for commission after claiming (falsely as it happened) to have 'introduced' some relatively wealthy outsiders to certain local shops was considered rapacious. Shopkeepers do, however, have their own gossip network. One group of shops in Montrose found their custom so concentrated in the evenings and at weekends that they would spend the early afternoon playing scrabble, breaking off only if a customer should enter one of the shops concerned.

Customer relations are also affected by forms of payment. Virtually all retail is done on a cash basis. The use of cheques is limited, and is always based on an accompanying bank card. Most shopkeepers remain suspicious of them: 'you have to know who to take a cheque from, they have to look sincere'. One shop resolved this problem by only taking cheques from people who worked in banks. Credit is an important element in establishing a core of customers, although it has little of the importance it once seems to have held in retailing, where six months' credit was a norm for regular customers. A gift-shop owner gave credit only to the twenty customers she knew best; another shop noted only four credit customers, while a fabric shop only gave credit to staff. Credit is often regarded as rather old-fashioned (at least by shopkeepers), though it is coming back with the recession. Ambience may determine whether people feel free to ask for discount, as an upmarket clothes store reported that people did not ask, while an ordinary furnishing store estimated 75 per cent of customers asked for credit. Most customers who place a larger order or an order for several items will demand and receive some discount in most shops. In part, this is a modern version of what is seen as the distinctly Trinidadian tradition of the *Lagnieppe,* a little 'extra' consideration that secures a deal.

The retailer is in a sensitive position between the pressures from distributors on the one hand and the demands of customers on the other. Their survival depends on becoming an effective conduit between these two. Different kinds of business vary in their relative leanings towards the customer and the supplier. The key place that determines the balance between these lies in the strategy for the selection of stock. At the time of fieldwork the dominant concern was recession, and the shopkeepers could all see the growing concern for thrift as radically affecting the materials they could stock and the factors that should be emphasized in selling. 'Plenty people not asking me for a big pack of that or a tin of that. They would ask for a pound of sugar or half pound of that or 25 cents of that. That's how business now: cigarettes – ask for one, and he want a light.' Indeed the shopkeeper then presented a calculation of the effect of this demand for a 'light' on his overall profitability, based on the cost of matches. There remained, however another end to the market, where keeping up status was paramount: 'Some of them want real silk. They don't want the artificial silk because they can't see themselves being asked "You are wearing an imitation silk?" It's not their style, it's not their life.'

The shopkeepers often assess their own skills in stocking, as in part a pre-empting of influences that are likely to relate to the consumer. This may consist in watching the most relevant television serials, or attending key events in town:

> If a prominent person gets married or it have a big show, some big entertainer comes to town and sales will go up. So when Run DMC came it is stud goods and that sort of thing. If Gloria Estefan like big earring, so people will imitate. For *Young and Restless* – big rhinestone, anything big and shiny, big rings from Mrs Chancellor [a character within this soap]. That is the biggest influence right now, so I take an interest. There is a lot of parties and weddings in that show. Even the buyers have to keep up with *Young and Restless*. I

watch it and have to keep up, because when a woman say 'I want
something like came on *Young and Restless.*'

This interest in potential outside influences is then tempered by
judgements as to how they are likely to affect the home market.
For example, the owner of the Bridal Shop quickly saw that the
wedding dress used by Princess Diana in Britain was far too
simple to be of interest to her customers, and therefore decided
not to let it influence her choice of stock.

Stocking is also the mundane task of checking on sales if one
has several outlets, and getting feedback from shop assistants as
to customers' comments about the stock. This can be especially
important in a fashion domain such as fabrics, where considerable discussion often takes places about the goods themselves.
In other areas retailers may be more influenced by the various
pressures coming to bear from merchandisers and their relationship to particular suppliers. They will hope to promote and thus
disperse stock that they have obtained cheap from a supplier or
to become involved in a promotional campaign based on special
offers and discounts. The one strategy that circumvents this
whole problem is that of working to order, where there is no risk
of over-stocking; and some shops do have this as at least an element in their sales.

All retailers note the importance of fashion, or simply 'newness', as a factor with at least a section of their consumers.
Typical comments were: 'In Trinidad people love their cars, and
once something new comes on the market the people put it in
their car'; or 'They don't want to see the same things we had last
year, they want to see something new. So during the year most
people enquire about these things: "When are you going to get a
new shipment?", and that has a strong bearing on where they are
going to shop and what they are going to buy and what they
plan.'

Shops may act to supply themselves with what are seen as key
sources of information with regard to fashions and innovations.
The bridal shop expects customers to browse through the latest
magazines imported from North America and to instruct their
seamstress to copy or adapt one of the dresses illustrated. The
shop assistants may then advise on the type and quantity of
materials and appliqués that will be required. They might also
remind customers of the doggerel about 'something borrowed,

something blue' in order to sell them some blue item, such as garters. Some shopkeepers seem to feel that their role as advisers is diminishing as there is more direct comparison made between the shoppers to determine how fashions will develop. The pet-shop owner commented 'What is happening with the small dog, I am not sure. A lot of the Indian women long ago were involve only with the home. Now you find a lot more of them are driving cars, going to the shopping malls, seeing different styles and how other women behave differently, so they are beginning . . . so this is why you see the small dogs – it is more like a fashion.' The larger implication being that his advice on the 'appropriate' kind of pet is becoming less important than the observation of peers.

Apart from fashion, a temporal element is important in stocking for particular seasons. A clothes shop expects to display a range of 'dressy' dresses for the office parties associated with Christmas, and a range of swimsuits for the long weekend at Easter, when people traditionally go to the beach. A shop selling lights would be particularly concerned with the advent of the festival of Divali, which is the festival of lights. The following quotation, which is only around a quarter of the original discussion of seasonality, illustrates the importance of this factor to the wholesaler and retailer:

> January, after Christmas finish, people tend to replenish stock. Around the second week in January they will then think about Carnival. Lots of jeans, shirts, blouse, hats, caps, shoes, socks. I won't deal with liquor. You will be shocked to learn what people do with clothing after Carnival time. They will cut it up and make all sorts of designs, just for Carnival time, and then they might throw it away. After the Carnival we might deal with slippers. In March month it's a bit slow: more replenishing, and we sort of prepare for the Easter clothing, again dresses for children, gifts for weddings. Especially in the Chaguanas area its predominantly Indians, so you have lots of East Indian weddings, mainly from January to mid-June. The favourite wedding gift is glassware. I notice ceramics is taking a very important place. . . . We also got to remember that Mother's Day is around the corner in May month. Some people buy wares for Mother's Day gift, others clothing, some buy handkerchief, etc. . . . Ceramics is very important for Easter. They buy more clothing because of the long weekend holiday. By then school will close, and when school re-open the children will probably need a shirt. In June month you have Father's Day, when people buy a lot of jerseys . . .

July, when school close, you have lots of children home. We don't do much business around that time, because parents are looking after the children . . .

A temporal consideration also comes into judging the likely quality of the customer in terms of when in the day they shop. Those in work will tend to be constrained by that fact. As a café owner noted 'if working then would come at lunch, or buy before they go to work, but the limers will buy anytime: once they find they have some change in their pocket and they find their belly going *gu gu gu*'. There is also the historical legacy of the way people used to spend money, which was closely tied to the regular wage packet. From the time of the plantations, employers had tried to arrange matters so that the time between the receipt of wages and the giving up these same wages back to the plantation store was as short as possible. The tradition was to spend when the money came in, especially as much of the money went to service the debt accumulated during the period since the last wages were received. Shopkeepers still found a tendency to spend out money as it was received. By this period, however, the historical link with regular wage packets and debt was becoming linked to the question raised in the next section about the moralities of spending and saving money.

Shopkeepers are obviously concerned with the social relations of their customers, since in many cases shopping is based on a purchase by one member of a household for others. The Bridal Shop, for example, usually serves a group of three, the prospective bride, her mother, and their seamstress who will make up the dress. One of the key considerations is the relationship between men and women, in particular in terms of who makes decisions and who spends the money. A clothes store found that men were coming in to buy clothes for their wives: 'I had quite a lot of men coming in to buy outfits for their wives, for their kids to give them on Mother's Day.' She has also decided to institute a small selection of men's clothes for the wife to buy as gifts to her husband. An exception was the motor accessory outlet, where women were mainly noted as being much more particular about the way items such as stripes were affixed to the car.

Another shopkeeper commented that 'if man alone would come and look, then go for the wife. Wife alone would buy – that is the main one. If they stay for a bit the wife could convince the husband a little bit more. I guess the wife has the greater say with buying furniture.' A typical arrangement seemed to be that 'women will come alone, but when ready to buy will bring in husbands for a final nod of approval'. With regard to paint 'a man may just come in, wants a gallon, sees, likes it and that's it. Women take much longer to choose. Most walk in, take a colour chart to take home and keep matching the walls, and then come back and choose.' Several shops devoted to domestic items gave 5 per cent as the number of male customers in general, although there are domains in which males dominate as shoppers, of which the car industry is of considerable importance to Chaguanas. This does not diminish the consensus about women being the 'natural' shoppers, and the sense in which men distance themselves from this activity, so that for example car-related purchases do not tend to be referred to as shopping.

The Shopper's Perspective

There are three ways in which shopping may be related back to the shopper: as part of a more general concept of provisioning; as a form of spending money; and as an event in and of itself. Shopping as a topic is starting to attract the attention of anthropologists and sociologists (e.g. Carrier 1995; George and Murcott 1992; Humphrey 1995), though research on the topic's social aspects is still rare in this region (see Hay 1990; Simms and Narine 1994). An exception to both of these statements is the extensive work on retail geography associated with Potter (e.g. 1982) for the Caribbean (but see Wrigley and Lowe 1996 for more general work).

Provisioning

From the first perspective shopping in Trinidad is not the only, and in some cases not even the dominant, form of household provisioning. The first alternative source of goods is direct access to agricultural produce. This is particularly important for the Indian population that shops in Chaguanas, many of whom grow crops or have relatives who grow crops. An exchange relationship often develops between the individuals in Chaguanas who work in the public service, for example as teachers or bureaucrats, and their relatives who live in villages. The more sophisticated urban dwellers may visit the relatives at the weekend or be visited by them. Prior arrangement is not usually made or expected. Quite often the villagers use their urban relatives for advice over filling in forms or dealing with some governmental or commercial bureaucratic problem, such as choosing schools or paying taxes. In return, the urban dwellers may receive a quantity of whatever fruit or vegetables are growing at that time of year. A businessman suggested that the supermarket Hi-Lo had a hard time establishing itself in Central Trinidad precisely because of the extent to which people were provided for by their kin.

Another supply of goods is those that come around the residential area without people having to go shopping. There can be quite a variety of hawkers plying their trade. Fresh fish is often sold at street corners or from vans. People come door-to-door selling items such as perfumes or household cleaners. Some of these are regular sellers, who operate in residential areas as though they were weekly markets. Others are primary producers, such as fishermen, who are trying to cut out the middle man. In some cases it is more *ad hoc*. A householder in the Meadows noted sympathetically of an individual calling from the street that the man was claiming that he had only one more dress to sell. In reality, it was suggested that this was a cover for the degree of poverty the family had fallen into, and the single dress was really his wife's.

Another source of provisioning is items sent by relatives living abroad, who in most cases include a member of the nuclear family. This is often one of the main sources of goods. The extent to which this is taken for granted is illustrated by a conversation with a person whose job was to invent and carry out promotional programmes for companies. He carried out a project based on selling kitchen towels through supermarkets in the South of Trinidad. He claimed this had revealed that 'a lot of Trinidadians buy their kitchen towels from away, so they had no idea of the price of retail towels in Trinidad.' There are probably quite a range of products of which this would be true. The 'away' referred to here is mainly the United States and Canada and the sending of goods by relatives, as well as the buying of goods when on holiday abroad. In addition to this, there is the suitcase trade with Venezuela (see below).

Attitudes to Spending

The following quotation from a saleswomen in the Chaguanas market indicates some of the key dilemmas in assessing attitudes to spending and shopping:

> Sometimes when men shop they do it stupidly, because like sometimes when they go in the market they see this thing here they would not walk. You tell them 6 dollars per pound, they would say 'Give me that.' Many men like that. While women would get even better products at a cheaper price, because they walking and checking out prices. Yes, when men have money they spend it all out and they don't control it, and many men will tell you that if they have a woman, they control their money . . . Sometimes they don't have no woman at all, so they wondering what to do with the money. So they gone with the boys to drink now, and they find the money just going down, and when they catch themselves they have nothing . . . Some women can't save at all. Women like shopping: you have to be aware of the woman who sees everything in the store and wants it . . . these are women that men have to be careful with, or they will make them spend spend all the time. Women love to spend their money on clothes. Some eats a lot, because I have a friend, she hardly buy clothes, she like she men to carry she out and she like to eat a lot. Whole day she could be eating all the time. Some people worry about spending on the house. They like ornament and so on; and some people just bank their money.

This quotation is unusual in as much as it does not homogenize gender into two single types. There are spendthrift women and thrifty women. On the other hand, while forms of spending are dissaggregated, there are underlying generalizations about gender with respect to shopping as an activity. On the whole, shopping is a female pursuit, which makes women expert at it and the proper gender to carry it out, but also leads them into an over-commitment to spending, and potentially an insatiable desire for goods. In a sense, this latter is viewed less as a social pathology than a natural potential concomitant of their propensity to shop. In each case one can only refer to 'some people', since there are some, as the quote ends by saying, who 'just bank their money.'

The different tendencies to spend and save were examined in Miller 1993. In particular, a distinction was noted between the qualities of what may be called spending 'in', associated with Christmas, and spending 'out', associated with Carnival. The Christmas spirit sees spending as permissible as long as it is done carefully and is understood as an investment in the household, either in the form of goods that are stored in the home interior, or for some larger social event such as a wedding. It is a form of spending in which any extravagance is made compatible with a larger ethos of thrift. The Carnival spirit is concerned to abjure saving and storing, which constrain the possibility of spontaneous and free expression of the self in society, and is devoted to the purchase of goods that will be consumed by the event and then discarded.

Miller 1994 argued that these are powerful differences, which can then be projected on to social distinctions. In the above quotation the emphasis is upon their application to gender, but storekeepers also gave evidence as to the application of the same distinctions to differences in ethnicity: 'The African will spend all that they have, the Indian will say "For Christmas I want to buy a TV set." He will start to save that money from February, even if it is only the downpayment he will make in December, he will then do it. But the African, he will wait until he get all his money and go right away and buy it.' As with gender, the stereotype is also often contradicted. There were other shopkeepers who stated that there were no discernible ethnic differences.

Such a context leads to considerable self-consciousness about the way one spends. For many men, and some women, there is a bravado in the 'spending out' of money as quickly as possible, as an act that demonstrates one's commitment to a network of peers with an ethos of generalized reciprocity and maximum sociability, as opposed to the individual retention of resources. Such money is spent mainly on alcohol, frequent changes of stylish clothing, and liming. Shopkeepers tend to assume that such people are relatively easy to exploit, since part of the bravado is competitive spending on conspicuously expensive things, where price is an important element. The shopkeepers claim that the shopper won't buy unless a high price is charged, and that they raise prices to match the expectations. The constantly reiterated example of such forms of spending is whisky in the oil boom, and the desire to find increasingly expensive labels in order to demonstrate one's generosity. Such behaviour is in direct contrast with the thrifty accumulation of cheap but abundant possessions, based on considerable comparative shopping in order to locate the cheapest example of the product.

These attitudes to spending have a considerable impact on the more general attitude to shopping and the degree to which this is seen as pleasure or burden. Many women clearly regard shopping as a pleasurable and relaxing experience. It has the capacity to 'ease the tension' (the title of a popular calypso of that year). 'For me shopping is a very relaxing thing to do when I am bored; some time ago I told my husband – "Oh gosh ! you know what I could do with right now is just get a thousand dollars and just go out and shop."' The important point is that this relates neither to the act of shopping as an event nor the question of provisioning. It is the idea of spending out money that has an independent resonance associated with shopping.

Campbell has argued that for Britain there is a clear distinction for women between the pleasure some women obtain from shopping for clothes, which they experience as a form of self-determination, as against their food shopping, which as a necessity was less likely to be viewed so positively (Campbell, forthcoming). In Trinidad the contrast is rather between saving and spending out. Such spending out has strong metaphorical links with the realm of sexual experience, which in turn provides a dominant idiom for many other areas of behaviour. Spending out has therefore its own sensuality, as exhilarating, exhausting and relaxing. The context of its alternative to thrift and storage as mediated through the opposition between transience and transcendence cannot be understood outside the larger cosmological order within which shoppers operate. It is this which links it irrevocably with basic ideas as to the 'nature' of men, women, Indians, Africans, youth, Trinidadians and so forth (for details of this argument see Miller 1994).

Not surprisingly, therefore, there is actually considerable ambivalence about desire as experienced in relation to a visit to the shops. This emerges, in particular, through contrary attitudes to window shopping. Window shopping is understood as a search for things that one potentially might purchase, but has either no means or no intention of buying at that moment. Several informants made comments similar to this one: 'I don't like window shopping. If see something I like I must buy it straight away. It really digs me when I see something I like but I can't buy it, so I rather not see.' This was a widely recognized attitude even when not shared: 'some people would see it like that, they cannot afford it and just looking at it would develop something inside of them, but not with me.' Not surprisingly, this problem was deepening with recession: 'Before, I would have spent money to ease the tension, but right now it hard. The money that you have now you keep.' There is a palpable sense in which an activity such as window shopping can be transformed into an expression of frustration analogous with sexual frustration, and the recession into a kind of concomitant period of forced celibacy. This is, however, resonant for only certain sections of the population. Those who tend towards what I have called transcendence do not share this experience of window shopping, and many in the questionnaire described it as their greatest pleasure and the main hope for getting 'out of the house.'

Talking about Shops

Shopping may also be considered as an activity in itself, apart from the factors of provisioning and spending. Four aspects of shopping are considered here: the way people talk about shops; shopping as spectacle; shopping as skill; and shopping as a social activity. When a shop is constructed it attempts to create an ambience that will influence its reputation. But few people come to a shop 'cold', and are solely influenced by the visual effect. A shop that is attempting some sort of spectacle or any new larger shop is quickly the subject of conversation. It is part of town talk, people give opinions on it. One has heard these before one goes. A visit to this shop becomes an event. People then want to 'check it out' for themselves, to know it and so be included in conversations about it, to have an opinion on it, to say whether it will succeed or not.

A helpful example of this kind of town talk as a genre comes from the fictional *Lal Shop* by Paul Keens-Douglas, which seeks to pastiche humorously the talk at a typical rum shop, where everyone wants to express opinions about everything. Each piece ends with the phrase 'Is town say so!' It is quite common for the topic to be some new commercial venture. One piece, called 'She doh want to smell like de central market', is a response to a newspaper items stating that they want to develop products from local fruits like 'mango mouthwash, banana deodorant, guava perfume'. Another piece called 'She say a pizza is a social bake' mocks the pretensions of those who go for the latest thing, since the word 'social' means 'anti-social' and pretentious. The implication being that there is nothing wrong with the traditional bake, but that some 'big-shot' people have added a topping and created a pretentious new item that everybody feels obliged to turn to. Typical complaints are about changes in commerce. The piece 'Kus now it go have squatters in bottles' complains that customers are now being asked to allow for 'settlement' of bottle contents: 'dat mean dat when dey full up de bottle de coffee go settle down low'. In a similar way the first response is often to mock the pretensions of a new retail outlet, and ask what was wrong with the old choices; but this does not seem to delay the actual interest in the new, at least for the moment.

The opening of a larger shop will often feature in the newspapers as a four-page spread, with mixtures of adverts and articles by the main suppliers 'congratulating' the new enterprise and providing a display of its goods. Given the recession, the newspapers generally talk in terms of the 'bravery' and 'courage' of the entrepreneurs who are attempting to 'buck the trend'. Not surprisingly, the extreme example of this comes with the launch of a new mall. The *Sunday Guardian* for 11/7/88 produced an eight-page 'Town Centre Mall Supplement' under the title 'Show of Faith'. As is commonly the case, there is commercial association, since the company that owned the *Guardian* was largely run by the same family that was opening the mall. The article notes that 'against overwhelming odds, Ramon Carlos and Richard made a decision to display their faith, and confidence in the land of their birth – Trinidad and Tobago – by getting into a multi-million dollar venture in the middle of a cutting recession.' The mall was on the main shopping road in Port of Spain, but included the second branch of the Bridal Shop in Chaguanas mentioned in the previous section. Entries in the daily papers often read as though there has been very little change from their original form as commercial promotions issued by the company's marketing agents. By contrast, any revelation about the 'undeclared' purposes of the new business is more likely to surface in the weekly newspapers as gossip.

Subsequently the reputation of the shop becomes established, through a variety of factors. The owner may be known; the ethnicity of the shop may be cause for comment, and also its decor, its value for money, the attitude of the shop assistants. Sceptical criticism often remains the norm. A shop may be seen as a dodge to show losses in order to avoid taxes. When the shop closes shoppers will exchange an 'I told you so' with reference to their claims that the shop was a 'scam' [dodgy enterprise], even if the shop is closing after a decade of profitable trading and they have been frequent customers. A grand sale is seen as evidence of forthcoming bankruptcy. Such cynicism is almost always directed at locally owned and managed enterprises, and less often directed against multinational operations, except under a rather vague and general notion of American capitalism.

Shopping as Spectacle

The centrality of shopping as an end rather than just a means is perhaps more evident in Trinidad than in many other places, since it is admitted to readily. While most people go to the shops to get things to dress up in, there is in Trinidad no shame attached to the idea of getting dressed up to go to the shops. It is by shopping that one is being seen. For younger Indian women, who are restricted in their other social contacts, shopping is quite clearly the main arena in which they can see and be seen, and as a result it is quite common to hear of a group of young women spending all morning getting themselves ready to go shopping. Paul Keens-Douglas pokes fun at this ironical foundation for the act of shopping, as both end and means, with reference to another kind of outlet – the gyms that had become a key fashion event in Trinidad. Once again, officially one goes to the gym to get in shape; but as he relates in *Lal Shop*:

> Is at dat point Dorothy drop in de shop, she dress-up in one fancy jogging outfit wit' a sweat band roun' she head, an' ah towel over she shoulder. She tell Lal, 'Lal boy, is only water ah drinkin' today, ah have to make three rounds roun' de savannah. Ah have to lose weight before ah go an' lose weight up in de exercise club. Is only nice man dey have up dey an' yu girl cannot go up dey lookin' out ah shape, so ah have to get in shape before ah go an' get in shape!'

In the same way, many people feel they have to look well dressed before they can go to quality dress shops.

Once a person arrives in the shop, it is the decorative framework represented by the shop itself that is important. At this point the desires of some shoppers articulate closely with distinctions in the way in which shop-owners choose to present their shops, and how they try to draw the eye of the potential consumer to particular aspects of the shop. An undertaker might not be expected to provide a glamorous ambience. The gaze is not directed at the shop itself. Nevertheless, the caskets on display are dominated by the 'up-market' varieties, which are in a sense highly glamorous, with their elaborate silk and satin upholstery and ornate silver handles and trimmings. Again a shop called 'glamour and glitter' tends not to concentrate on ambience created by shop fittings, but rather on the dense arrays of costume jewellery and accessories, which become an Aladdin's cave of spectacular forms. Shop décor tends to be much more prominent in shops where the customers are in a sense themselves on display and expecting to be seen. This includes the bright and ostentatious displays of the more fashionable fast-food outlets, and also some music shops or fashion shops, as well as the malls themselves, which become a kind of 'super-shop', providing the décor and thereby the ambience for the diversity of retail and service outlets they enclose.

While the shopkeepers may thereby draw attention to their décor as display, it does not follow that the gaze is thereby drawn further to the goods within the shop. This is often because the sight is drawn to the shopper who inhabits this glorious environment. The effect is to draw, to the shop, shoppers who wish to be seen in such 'bright' surroundings, and will hopefully purchase goods while there, as they do in fast-food outlets in order to be there. The spectacle consists of the shoppers viewing each other within the décor of the shop or mall. In a sense the shopper is trying on a set of décors while out shopping, in an analogous sense to trying on a different set of clothes. As with clothing, it is not certain that they feel this is the 'right' place for them; rather, in trying out an ambience they are trying to determine the nuances that specify what kind of person is appropriate to the place and whether they see themselves as either already or potentially that kind of person. This concern may blend into other forms of fantasy. The bridal shop almost always has its complement of schoolgirls, who simply want to use the sight of all the wedding paraphernalia around them as a prop to their fantasies of their own futures as brides.

This emphasis on the external appearance of the person dressed up by their clothes or surrounding shop fitments and atmosphere has to be understood within the context of what I have elsewhere described as a particular ontology, which renders words like 'superficial' quite meaningless. It is an ontology in which the sense of being rests on external appearance and the reaction of others to that display, rather than on some imagined 'deep' core inside oneself (see Miller 1994: 219–31). Trinidad is, after all, one of the countries that has developed the festival and ritual of display through Carnival into what is globally regarded as an art.

The idea of 'dressing' as metaphor is not my invention: the semantic field of this term is much broader in Trinidadian than in other forms of English. Trinidadians talk of 'dressing the house' and 'dressing the car', as well as dressing themselves. Without the burden of the critique of superficiality they allow themselves much more freedom to construct surfaces that are granted significance. A clue to this practice may lie in the alacrity with which the car was appropriated by Trinidadians, to move from being a relatively rare form of private possession prior to the oil boom to becoming the central prop for the experience of being distinctly Trinidadian, as demonstrated in the Spot the Trini competition of 1988 (Miller 1993). The car in Chaguanas is not merely conspicuously dressed (car upholstery is after all the dominant industry in the town), but also the form in which individuals dress. As already noted, the identity of individuals is more likely to be read from their cars than any other attribute, even clothes. If we move from the idea of people being dressed in their clothes to the more transient feature of being dressed in their cars, there is then a little less distance to travel to the idea of their being temporarily dressed in shops that they do not own, but parade within. In this context the 'transience' of what is in effect trying on a new shop is no bar to its significance for the identity of the shopper.

Trinidad differs from some other shopping contexts, however, in that the determinant of ambience may be as much aural as visual. Music, and sound more generally, is of extreme impor-tance to the sense of ambience, and Trinidadians may feel more 'attuned' to the subtle distinctions suggested by music as sound-scape (Tacchi 1997). Both the visual and the aural have their constraints. The music may represent no more than which radio station is tuned to, though the loudness may be as important a factor as the form of music in expressing the kind of customer to be attracted. Sound can also be developed in other ways. A Rastafarian who practises as an MC (master of ceremonies) with rap and dub is also often hired by high street stores that specialize in cheap mass-market goods. He sees his job as providing the kind of atmosphere Trinidadians like:

> People want to hear slang, they want to hear something to entertain them that is what Trinidadians like. They like fame, they like scenes ... they like words, plenty words. He will bring them in to buy clothes and other goods. The shopkeeper might tell him 'Boy, look, I have some seamoss selling $2.50.' ... I will say – 'Seamoss, boy, take it for your back, your bottom and your waist – don't miss the taste – following the race.' You have to influence them.

Sound is central to the process by which 'ambience' is constructed as a relation between shopkeeper and shopper. The individual shoppers transform their behaviour in accordance with their perception of what is appropriate to each context, taking cues if they choose to do so from elements of décor and music in the shop. A certain way of walking and talking may emerge, as one tends to 'pose' using clothes held against one as props in an up-market clothes shop, while one's voice and posture signal how relaxed and 'cool' one is feeling within a bar. Often the nuances come from the slight ways in which the body moves in relation to and thereby acknowledges the music coming from the surroundings. Although I have not heard anyone express the relationship in this way, it is clear that many Trinidadians dress themselves above all in music.

With respect to both the aural and the visual aspects of display the effect is more often to draw attention to the shopper than to the product, a situation which in many cases therefore militates against elaborate displays. Another factor is the position of Chaguanas as a place regarded as particularly cheap and of good value. Local shopkeepers keen to retain this reputation tend to avoid the more spectacular forms of window display. They prefer a kind of 'pile them high and sell them cheap' aesthetic. The shopper is faced with an impression of the quantity of goods almost spilling out through the plate glass frontage on to the pavements or mall ways, with a clear message that the primary concern is not to waste money and thereby put up prices by a concern for the aesthetic of presentation. There are of course many exceptions and alternative strategies, but this one dominates the town. By contrast, in districts in the capital where style rather than thrift is of greater consequence the local shopping malls do indeed have a concern for eye-catching display modes that resonate with a desire for aesthetic pretension.

Traditional theorizing of this aspect of shopping seem quite unable to appreciate such possibilities. Perhaps the most influential source of such theory today remains Benjamin (1973), and rather less brilliant attempts to render partial aspects of Benjamin's vision of mass commodities on display. As Buck-Morss (1989) makes clear, Benjamin conceived of his historical analysis of the Arcades as a deliberate strategy of revelation. Starting from the premiss that there is nothing quite as dead as the discarded fashions of yesterday, he hoped that this debris would reveal the unreality of such façades, thereby helping to puncture the mythic enchantment of the commodity world of his own day. It is this feature of mere spectacle, the 'Just Looking' element, that tends to pervade most recent work (e.g. Chaney 1991; Goss 1993; Shields 1992). Benjamin himself had a more contradictory stance, also recognizing the images of social revolution and democratization contained in shopping, but often submerging this under the rather claustrophobic form of Marxism associated with colleagues such as Adorno. Thus the radical potential could only be allowed as embryonic, to be realized when society woke up from its trance condition, a catatonic state induced by an overdose of commodity spectacle.

This same refusal to acknowledge the 'reality' of commodity worlds, through the retention of this spatial model of the superficial façade against some inner 'real' core, remains the 'conclusion' of even the most vanguard theorizing of today. Most writers continue to inhabit a metaphysic where there is a hidden reality, both a pre-modern authentic subjectivity of the person and a global capitalist motivation or hidden logic. Both of these are mystified in an enchanted brilliance of refracting lights and colours of commodity imagery. In most recent literature, therefore, shops act merely to symbolize some generic sense of capitalism. By simultaneously representing both the surface and the core of capitalism they are held to mystify its presence to the shopper. In effect, the perspectives of neither retailer nor shopper are considered in this simplistic semiology.

The Trinidadian context can only be understood by a refusal to project ideological constraints derived from different historical legacies. It is not just that there is less fear of superficiality as a vice, but there is less problem with commodification and with the seriousness of identity construction. Overall there is much more playfulness about the relations between subject and object, especially within the sphere of transience. The 'lightness of being' is much more bearable and liveable, as one is transcribed in transient and multiple imagined identities. The point is to keep objects on the surface and changeable; the horror is a relationship, as in *obeah* (witchcraft), where objects stick to one like leeches. In *obeah* the object becomes a kind of heavy attachment, draining one of the capacity for self-expression and rendering one subject to the will of another. The key spectacle in shopping is in most cases not the shop in and of itself, but the shop as a form of dressing or, more accurately, an accoutrement to the display of possible selves.

This means that individuals can easily see themselves in many roles, both as consumers and producers, and the distance between these two is less. The person who can simultaneously be a bureaucrat, a farmer, and the middleman in distributing some imported goods can also be experimental in the nuances of shopping as performance. There is studied nonchalance as 'cool'; there is conspicuous buying of rum, coke, or anything that signifies that one is going to have a 'good time'. There is less of the class consciousness that alienates whole categories of commodities as more appropriate to some other group. There is an absence of that dissatisfaction Campbell (1987) describes between the imagined possession and the actual possession, because there is much less 'riding' on the individual purchase. Shopping often becomes an extension of the verbal banter at which so many Trinidadians are highly skilled. The pretensions invested in association with objects, whether purchased or not, are constantly subject to the appraisal of those around you. In particular, women out shopping find themselves subject to the verbal taunts of the limers who hang around the malls and other shops, and are quick to subject any sign of pretentiousness to a barrage of 'fatigue.'[10] As long as the relationship to clothes and other forms is not over serious, then little is lost by being 'put down' by those around you, and shopping remains fun. None of which makes the Trinidadian stylist 'postmodern', since these values derive from particular local historical trajectories and concerns.

Shopping as Skill

The other major lacuna in the recent literature within critical social science on shopping is the consideration of what might be called non-spectacular shopping. In this case shopping, whatever its role as an experience, is also a means, the end being to acquire particular commodities; and the source of the desire lies in events prior to the shopping activity, usually in having run out of an object one is habituated to the possession and use of. This kind of shopping dominates overall in Trinidad, as probably in most countries today.

Such mundane shopping may appear a rather utilitarian and mechanical provisioning; but as with hunting, farming or wage labour, it is not without its rituals, skills and moralities. To strip it down to its clearest form we have to imagine shopping for goods that are barely affected by fashion, and where the brand choice is limited and stable. Typical items would be household cleaners and basic foodstuffs. In many ways, it is precisely such goods as these that highlight the wider context of skill and choice. Such shopping is dominated by housewives, who in carrying out the mundane tasks of cleaning and cooking and keeping house often find themselves discussing, and reflecting upon, not just the differences between the available brands, but also the skills of obtaining them.

One of the items I most often heard discussed in day-to-day conversation was a liquid disinfectant, available in a variety of bright colours and strong smells, probably dominant in the Trinidadian market, but with a number of competitors that were used by people the conversationalists were aware of. Colour was not explicitly discussed, but smell and efficacy certainly were.

---

10. Fatigue or *picon* is a kind of verbal assault that is designed to 'put down' the person addressed.

Each worker in the domestic domain was concerned to take decisions with respect to the purchase of such cleaners that reflected a careful balance between a large number of factors. One of these was to minimize the value spent on this commodity, in order to maximize that available for others. Conversations that discussed the comparative price of the same goods at different outlets helped secure this aim. Another factor was concern as to whether a consensus was emerging as to the preferred smell out of the range available, and whether it was better to conform to or stand out from any such consensus. Alternative, more expensive brands could also be justified on the grounds that they lasted longer or were more effective. Overall such comments reflect the gamut of social relations. In some contexts, a daughter-in-law may exact revenge on a dominating mother-in-law through her superior knowledge of changes in the market and by constantly implying that her rival's products and choices are out-of-date or inappropriate. In other contexts, two housewives freely exchange experiences of consumption in order that both should be protected against critical comments from what is regarded as the ignorant but malevolent world of men.

Shopping as skill is hardly ever valued positively; rather, its existence as a skill emerges most often in instances of failure, as when the house runs out of something. This may be merely a symptom of a deeper *malaise* whereby the house is out of money to purchase goods; but where this is not the case it is viewed as a failure of planning and organization of time. Here shopping is also set against other provisioning strategies, such as borrowing from one's neighbour. A second failure is when it comes to light that one has paid more for an item than someone else. This may be excusable in part, if the shop is prestigious and it is recognized that one has paid for the status accruing from shopping there; but to have picked one of the lower-end supermarkets, but the wrong one, is clearly a failure. Other failures may be to have retained loyalty to a brand when others have moved on to what is regarded as a preferable product, or to have tried a new brand that the *cognoscenti* know to be an inferior type.

Another aspect of shopping as skill is its routinization as part of household activities. Many households have clear strategies as to the frequency of shopping. As one housewife commented 'I used to do a big monthly shop in the boom; now I shop weekly, plus the market on Saturday.' This move from the monthly to the weekly shop was commonly remarked upon as an effect of recession, or in some cases the failure to be able to maintain a working refrigerator. Shopping planning may be a part of shopping thrift, as with those who shop when they think the best bargains are to be had, either at a certain time of the week or during sales: 'like mothers day is coming, you will see lots of ads, buy this, buy that; you get discounts in stores, so people buy'.

It cannot be assumed that the self-perception of savings reflects real savings. Sales are by tradition associated with particular events, but there may be very little discounting of goods, and lower prices are usually to be found by going to the less prestigious shops at any time of the year rather than to the kind of store that will advertise its sale in the national press. Similarly, shoppers often justify loyalty to a particular store on the grounds that they will gain discounts by being known. The shopkeeper may follow such a strategy; but there is also the well-established custom of enticing loyalty through providing genuine discounts at first, but, once the customers are hooked, charging them premium prices thereafter. Unless this is spotted by an outsider, however, it need not detract from the ability of the shopper to claim foresight and skill for her labour as a shopper.

Some Shopping Forms

The discussion so far has been based on the somewhat contrived distinction between the shopkeeper's and the shopper's perspectives, and remains at a rather generalized level. The actual relationship often centres on the particular forms of shopping that have evolved. It is therefore easier to highlight and illustrate these points with respect to particular shopping 'genres'. Although there exists the superordinate concept of shopping, which may be discussed and perceived as a whole, in practice people frame their shopping behaviour according to these 'genres'. Six of these have been selected here, to emphasize six aspects of shopping. These are: Shopping as a holiday; the parlour and gossip; the *obeah* shop and advice; the market and thrift; the supermarket and class; and the mall and liming.

Shopping as a Holiday

Although shopping is often considered in relation to leisure activities, Trinidad is probably rare in the degree to which the concept of a holiday and of shopping have become synonymous. The background to this elision consists of two recent phenomena. The first is the experience of shopping in Margarita; and the second the experience of going abroad in the oil boom.

The island of Margarita, 300 km to the West of Trinidad, is only 850 sq km, with a population of 250,000. For Trinidadians it represents something of an extreme attraction. It is part of the state of Venezuela, whose prices for most commodities are considerably lower than those in Trinidad, and within that country it has been designated a free port, which even in recession has been granted quotas of preferential dollar exchange rate. As a result the cheap goods available around the town of Porlamar act as a magnet for Trinidadian consumers. There are two main ways in which Trinidadians use this resource. The first is a personal trip to the island (or alternatively to Caracas). The explicit aim of this is for shopping, and it is the money saved that justifies the trip; but most Trinidadians will also visit the 'sights' on such trips, and view this as a holiday. Margarita justifies its free port status precisely by the tourist trade associated with it, which has allowed it to construct some 2,000 tourist establishments.

As an example of this kind of 'holiday' two sisters from The Meadows went to Caracas. The trip cost them each around US$400, including meals. They reached their hotel at nine in the morning and had that and one more day to conduct their shopping and sightseeing. They returned with 20 items of clothing, 13 pairs of shoes, 2 handbags, 9 pairs of stockings, 5 bottles of toiletries, various creams, cosmetics, and underwear, and presents for their immediate family.

The other main use of Venezuela is in what has become known as the 'suitcase trade'. For example, a housewife from St Pauls collects orders from her relatives, friends and neighbours. She travels to Margarita twice a year, estimating her costs at US$500–600. She then spends around US$2,000 on items for herself and those who have ordered goods from her. Orders tend to be dominated by children's clothes. In her case 'most of them who bought from me is mostly relative, so I just make about US$500–

600. So it would pay for the ticket.' Others organize their trips on behalf of a group of secretaries working in an office and the like. The individual shoppers may escape without paying any duties; the suitcase traders pay some duty, but not so much as to prevent a profit being made on the trade.

In the oil boom this kind of shopping was greatly enhanced by the possibility of shopping in the United States and Canada. Most such trips were based on visits to relatives; but middle-class Trinidadians flew to Miami and New York for what were in effect shopping trips, and some still managed to do so in 1988, tending to concentrate on more sophisticated goods that were less readily available locally, such as computer software or alarm systems. Once again the trips were punctuated by general sightseeing.

There is, however, little need to differentiate shopping as a utilitarian exercise from sightseeing as a leisure activity. For most people the malls and shops are themselves amongst the most interesting sights, and many people find formal tourist 'sights' boring and less attractive. If anything, the shopping becomes the pleasurable leisure activity and the 'sightseeing' a formal requirement that 'justifies' the trip. In recession times few Trinidadians feel they can afford a formal holiday, with the exception of a few days in Tobago. As a result, the concept of holiday has become in effect an amalgamation of visiting relatives abroad, time off from work, and shopping. It is likely that this sense of shopping as the primary holiday activity may well have implications for the sense of shopping more generally as an activity within daily life, and the ease with which people can associate shopping with the notions of pleasure and leisure.

The Parlour and Gossip

The rise of supermarkets and malls has not led to the demise of that most traditional form of Trinidadian shop – the parlour. There is no residential area where these cannot be found. The parlour is not only important as one of the main institutions of shopping, but also because consideration of the parlour highlights certain more general questions about the social relations of shopping that remain important in many other shopping contexts.

There can be no strict definition of something so resonant of the informalities of popular culture as the parlour, but in the main it is a shop that is constructed out of a household's own home, which sells basic goods and where the customer is over a counter. In the larger context of shopping, I was surprised to find that the parlour is not an equivalent of the traditional 'corner shop' of countries such as Britain. When people talked of a strong personal attachment or loyalty to a particular shop they usually meant a supermarket. Only those parlours that are also places for 'liming' (see below) attract this kind of relationship. Most were viewed pragmatically, rather than with affection. While in other countries the corner shop may remain the preferred location for general shopping (if price discrepancies did not in practice make this a rarity), the parlour is more a place to be resorted to for a few primary goods such as bread, newspapers and sweet drinks, or to 'top-up' goods forgotten or run out of in between larger shopping expeditions.

The case of a newly opened parlour in Newtown is instructive, since it indicates the kinds of goods for which such demands will arise. This parlour had been open for three months. It was constructed by opening out the back of the yard on to the street. The capital was raised by the owner when she worked in the local bread factory, and then by selling cooked meals in Port of Spain streets. She decided to open a parlour, as being more compatible with her domestic responsibilities and child care. She spent TT$8,000 on construction and a further TT$8,000 on stock. She started with 'a little juice, cake, paper, and then the meanwhile people started coming an' asking for certain things; and, as they ask for things, according to what they ask for, I buy it'. By three months she had tinned juices; spices; crystals for drinks; essence; royal icing; seasoning; mayonnaise; pigeon peas; red beans; split peas; oil; breakfast cereals; tea; coffee; liver salts; sauces; vinegar; packet soup: sweet drinks; washing powder; disinfectant; toilet paper; soaps; toothbrushes; toothpaste; oxford blue [soap]; bread cakes; frozen goods; rice; sugar; biscuits; frozen goods, such as sausages and chicken parts; drawing books; small sandals; hair clips; sanitary napkins; various sweets; pencil sharpeners; cosmetics; starch; and bar soap.

Parlours are supplied with bread and sweet drink by vans that come to them; but for most other goods they have to go and purchase from wholesalers for themselves. Some smaller enterprises will have little more than sweet drinks and bread, and would establish themselves with only TT$4,000 in total. Others, such as one in The Meadows, have become virtual shops, though still selling over the counter. Parlours spring up with some frequency, since they require relatively little capital; and some areas seem to have developed at least one parlour on every street. In one case a church had helped an older woman who had been a devout congregant over many years to establish herself in a property made up as half residence and half parlour. There are also parlours on the main street; but these are more likely to be rented in the more usual fashion of shops, with the owners living elsewhere. Parlours tend to have two distinct types of customer. Those on main roads or feeder roads deal mainly with car-based customers who stop for their papers, a drink or bread as they pass. Parlours inside residential areas such as Newtown and Ford deal mainly with the residents 'mostly children – parents send their children, and the men would come and buy their cigarettes and sweetdrink'.

A problem for the parlour is the number of goods that are on the government's scheduled list of fixed prices, which include common commodities such as tea and sugar. On such goods very little profit is to be had, but there is a risk of a heavy fine (TT$5,000) if such goods are sold at above official prices, and many parlours obey the law by having a listing of such goods with their prices on the doors of the parlour. Some parlours extend their trade and profits by selling some home-made foods. These may be pickles and sweets, or, as intended by the owner of the Newtown parlour, full cooked meals. Profits from parlours are usually low. Several interviewed claimed that they were not making any real profits at the present time, but felt the enterprise was just about worthwhile, since they also consumed the goods they traded. Exceptionally, the parlour in the main feeder road into the Meadows probably makes much more profit than most medium-sized shops, as is evident in the quality of the house it backs on to.

Apart from its place in the sale of basic commodities, a parlour has to effect a strategy with respect to the kind of sociality it encourages. In effect, a parlour can easily become a liming spot or centre for gossip if it chooses to do so, as people would hang around chatting to the person selling and consuming sweet drinks. The extremes in strategy with respect to this potential may be illustrated by a contrast between the Newtown parlour discussed above and another parlour on the main road. Two factors probably determine the response in Newtown. First, the owner is a woman; and second, she is dealing with her own neighbours and friends. She noted:

> I don't encourage chattering in the shop. People would do it, but I always busy, because you see these things cause a lot of confusion, and I don't like that. If they come to gossip, is about the neighbours they talkin about. They might talk about the neighbour do something, the neighbour might have a dog across there and the dog may be worrying them . . . and they get vex' or so . . . and then again they might talk about their husbands. But I don't want it, you could lose customers, because if you come to this parlour all the while and you seeing a big gossip and a crowd always here gossiping, eventually it must have a confusion. And they would say it come from the parlour. So people might find that I say something and some customers would vex if I hear something about them, and I didn't tell them anything: 'I am not coming back here to buy.' Gossip cause confusion and fight.

This standoffishness in part explains why shoppers tended to mention supermarkets rather than parlours as places evoking personal loyalty and identity. By contrast, the parlour on the main road is run by a man who is also a local politician. He has encouraged the development of the parlour as a liming spot by having a television that faces out towards the customer and also providing chairs, tables and a game of chequers for those who like to play. This is not a liming spot for the youth, but rather attracts those with an interest in community matters, since the owner has established himself as a highly popular local personality on account of his persistent battling for the rights of poorer people in the area. As such, it tends to be a meeting ground for those who have come with stories of hardship and debt and those who have influential positions in, for example, a mosque or the government party. The owner can survive his refusals of the constant requests for credit that otherwise would destroy his business, because it is evident that he and his family have nil capital and live at the same level of daily hardship as those who make these requests. Running a parlour is also quite compatible with his other communal activities. When, for example, he wants to organize a local sports competition he can make his requests or send messages through the people who stop to buy bread and papers. The particular wit and wisdom dispensed by the owner is an attraction beyond the utilitarian aspects of the supply of goods. In this case there is also the further attraction that, as a politician and previously a journalist, the owner is a good source of news and gossip as to what is going on in the town at large, and this may prove an irresistible bait to many.

It is not only parlours, however, where people come to chat and gossip. A large number of the shopkeepers interviewed noted the tendency of their customers to engage in such activities when given the chance, though much depends upon the character of the shopkeeper. Some convey an instant air of being too busy. Some would discuss the goods themselves, such as clothing fashions, but are clearly not interested in 'people business'; while others seem to invite the confidences and requests for advice that customers bring to them. As one shopkeeper noted 'They won't just buy, will chat for a while. Some will discuss private and family business, but not everyone will want to tell you their business: men would not do that, only women. If you do find men talking it means they are up to some scheme. Some women afraid they will get licks [beaten] so they won't talk.' There were no reports of any problems with drunks or violence, although one of the local supermarkets had been the scene of several attempts of armed robbery. By contrast, all retail outlets are commonly subject to requests for donations towards local community events, for example a residential area sports day or some charitable function.

Selling *Obeah* and Advice

A special instance of this relationship between shopkeeper and customer is the advice that shopkeepers may be expected to dispense as part of the service they provide to the customer. Perhaps the clearest illustration of the close relationship that may develop between a commodity and the advice necessary for its use comes from the sale of products associated with the system of symbolic magic and ritual known as *obeah*. This is the Trinidadian version of a magical system, common to many African American groups, with roots in Yoruba religion. Over the past several decades *obeah* has become increasingly syncretic and commercialized. Like other systems principally used for

problem-solving, it has become modelled on professional pharmaceutical practices. Often a ritual expert (as doctor) assigns an
individual (as secretary) to write out a list of items required (as
prescription) for the performance of a ritual, and they are then
obtained from the shop (as pharmacy). In the Montrose area of
Chaguanas there are a number of shops that are recognized as
supplying goods for *Obeah*.

The first point that emerges is that a shop cannot necessarily
control the way its goods are seen or its overall purpose. One
shop has as its explicit purpose the supply of goods for Hindu
religious ceremonies. There is nothing to suggest that the owners
would have anything to do with *obeah* by choice; but, given the
general syncretic elements in Trinidadian religion and the rise of
particular cults, such as Kalimai, that have strong *obeah*-like
elements within a predominantly Hindu structure, it is not
surprising that customers feel that some of these goods possess
properties that make them suitable for *obeah*. Thus there is nothing the shopkeeper can do to prevent this shop being widely
known in the area as a useful source of *obeah* supplies. There
is rather more ambiguity with regard to the main pharmacy.
Once again, there is certainly nothing explicit about the sale of
obeah-related products. But there is a section that relates to
general goods, such as incense and oils of various kinds, that
while having other uses does have the effect of incorporating
most of the products that would be of interest to *obeah* users
within the same general section of the shop. In this case there
may be some complicity in the consumption of these goods,
though the intention is almost certainly commercial. In both cases
these shops do provide advice in the use of their goods as long as
they are for the purposes intended by the shopkeepers. They
would not be asked about the uses of goods for *obeah*.

There would also be little point in asking advice from the
small outlet that took a completely cynical attitude to its sales:

> It is completely stupidness, because people would come and ask for
> 'luck oil'. What is luck oil? It have nothing such as luck oil. If they
> ask for it, you could give them some, any, kind of oil. You know
> somebody ask for commanding powder. You give them some My
> Fair Lady powder. Most of them come for money, for man, that is the
> two main problems they does come for. Some want come-to-me oil,

commanding powder, they want love oil and this kind of stupidness. When they ask for these things, I give them. Well, we have a whole lot of oils at the back; and so to know: nah, we just put names on them.

The situation is quite different with the other two outlets for *obeah* material, which were much larger suppliers of such goods. In both cases the sale of *obeah*-related goods is quite explicit. In only one case, however, is the outlet exclusively for such goods. This started as a small outlet working behind from a grille, but by the end of the fieldwork period had moved into a proper purpose-built shop with associated advertising of its goods. The second outlet was in most respects an ordinary newsagent supplying stationery to schools, with government bonds and a range of popular magazines, but underneath the main showcase was a section full of imported *obeah*-related materials, and behind this was a section of magazines devoted exclusively to this and related topics.

The two shops differed markedly in their source of supplies and their representation of these supplies to the customer. Neither in a sense related primarily to what might be called formal *obeah*, with its specific rituals and experts, though the materials sold at both outlets might be used for such purposes. The newsagent clearly works to a slightly more up-market version of this trade. The owner in effect differentiates the quality of her service by noting that 'You can make your own, but somehow people prefer imported thing with labels. If you sell anything in a bottle they will figure you are mixing it and that it is not pure.' In her case the bulk of supplies was purchased from New York, which is regarded as something of a centre for such materials and their associated powers. Goods include oils, candles, seals and parchment. She also sells booklets with titles such as 'White Witchcraft', 'The Modern Witches Spell Book', 'Famous Voodoo Rituals and Spells', 'The 7th Book of Moses', 'How to Protect Against Evil.' She is a Muslim, but finds more objections from fundamentalist Christians, who complain that such materials should be thrown away or burnt. She sees occultism and *obeah* as essentially the same thing, with *obeah* as simply a Trinidadian version. There is also a fashion element in such a market, such as a recently passed fad for voodoo-related material.

As part of her work she expects to impart a considerable amount of advice to her customers. The owner has been working with such material for many years, since her parents are wholesalers for such goods. When a customer comes in with a particular problem she may provide a number of stories of similar cases and the actions taken in those cases. As in general conversation about *obeah*, these are often begun with the observation that the doctors had given up hope in relieving this particular symptom or preventing that severe illness. When *obeah* is then resorted to it proves much more efficacious thus demonstrating that the original cause was not physiological. She works in informal tandem with ritual experts who prescribe specific rituals, much as the pharmacist complements the doctor. There are many such 'experts', who signify their expertise in various ways, for example, by calling their home a Baptist church with associated flags, by hosting a Shango feast, or by working within a Kalimai temple. In all such cases they will suggest the remedial ritual and list the items that must be purchased for the ritual to be carried out. The newsagent also deals with a large number of 'do-it-yourself' rituals, based on individuals' trying to follow the advice in the kinds of booklets she sells. The single most common problem brought to her is from women who feel their men are straying and wish to find methods to retain their attentions, and she provides many analogous stories and successful outcomes.

In the case of the shop exclusively selling magical goods, the emphasis was on a related complex of oils with transformative properties. These were sold mainly to less well-off Baptists, but also to many people with no particular religious affiliation who hoped that the oil would help them in some matter. A range of oils would be available in small bottles, with names such as 'conqueror' and 'money oil'. In this case the original source is in no case substances made for this purpose; indeed, the principal supplier was the firm Johnson & Johnson, the manufacturer of baby products. The shopkeeper explained that she obtained a number of different oils, such as baby oil or oil of thyme, and had the power to discern their magical potential and in turn transform the substance so that this power would be released. She claims it is a property intrinsic to her: 'The spiritual field is not something you could just learn or purchase, you have to be born with that instinct, it's a gift.' In effect, though, consumer expectations were of importance, as with the idea that 'money oil' must be green: 'Sometimes you sell something else and they say, no, the green one is the money oil, so you know the market is there – green is for money.' So oil of thyme becomes 'uncrossing oil' and another oil an unjinxing power. A similar transformation is effected with Lavender water, rose water and calendula water. Many shops in the region put down 'money oil' in the hope of increasing sales. Many young men anoint themselves with items such as 'conqueror' in the hope of seducing women.

She also gives out a certain amount of advice, for example to elderly people who hope to retain control over their children's actions, though mainly to young people. 'I like to listen to their problems. When some people talk to you they feel like a burden lift from them, and I does be glad to give these things to people that helps them.' Such shops are typical of a wide range of services, from electrical repairs to beauticians, where there is no simple distinction between the commodity purchased and the accompanying time and advice, which is not formally paid for but an anticipated part of the general service.

The Market

As already noted, the market has for a considerable period been the symbolic marker of the distinctiveness of Chaguanas itself as a centre. It is probably the main source of the town's enduring reputation for being a cheap place to purchase goods. It remains one of the main reasons why people from surrounding villages want to come into Chaguanas. The market has a core of relatively fixed facilities divided into specific domains of goods. These include a core area of fruit- and vegetable-selling. On one side of this are the areas for fish and meat, an area for spices, and general dry foodstuffs. At the other side is an area of textiles, household items and cheap plastic gifts. There is a tendency for the market to spill over from the designated area, especially on busy days, and the additional stalls may sell a variety of goods such as are proffered at the roadside, though with fruit and vegetables clearly the dominant items.

The market has competition, less from Port of Spain than from the fruit and vegetable stalls that are to be found at the verges of the main roads that lead from the capital to Chaguanas and San

Fernando. It clearly dominates, however, the sales of these goods in the central area. According to Griffin (1981) Chaguanas market was at that time the third largest in Trinidad after Port of Spain and San Fernando. It is unusual in obtaining more than half its supplies from local sources rather than wholesalers (p. 97), and is one of only three that also act as wholesale markets. In his questionnaire Griffin found that 81.9 per cent said the market was their sole source of fresh produce.

The market's character is familiar from markets in other countries. The sales patter, the style of the seasoned market sales-people, who mix a slightly aggressive sales pitch with humour and satire seems familiar. The market seems to provide surprisingly low profits, and there are many market sellers living in Ford who clearly work extremely long and unsociable hours for comparatively little reward. One suggested that he puts out around TT$700 every day on market produce and expects a profit of around TT$150 on that. These residents in Ford were my main informants as to the workings of the market. While working the atmosphere between traders may be 'dog eat dog', but the stereotype is of a quick temper and easy forgiveness, and traders will act sociably out of work, for example, organizing collective expeditions to the beach, and *susu* (rotating credit schemes). Prices start high, but by mid-afternoon may drop to the price they paid for the goods. Market sellers freely accuse each other of various sharp practices, such as altering the scales with a little magnet or other device to give low weight. But in a sense this is almost an expected corollary to the cheap prices on offer.

Visits to the market had become a routine activity for most people in the area. A questionnaire administered within the market showed that the vast majority of shoppers had last visited the market within the last week, mostly exactly a week before. Only two gave a time period longer than a month. This finding is confirmed by the household survey (see Table 7.1), which also suggests a weekly or bi-weekly trip as standard.

Many consumers have developed strong views as to how to deal with the market. Most common is the assertion that one goes at particular times, such as early in the morning, to obtain the best-quality goods rather than to get bargains. Others used to drive slowly along the traffic-filled main road while their partner purchased goods from the market and then was picked up by them at the other end. To shop at the market has its particular

Table 7.1: Time Since Last Visit to the Chaguanas Market by Monthly Income (in TT$)

Time since last visit	Below 1,000	1,000– 2,500	2,500– 5,000	5,000– 8,000	Above 8,000
One day	6	5	2	3	1
A week or less	11	31	19	11	6
Two weeks or less	2	5	7	5	1
More than two weeks	3	5	3	1	0
Don't go	0	1	6	2	2

connotation of a continued commitment to traditional values of thrift, of in a sense still being prepared to fight for one's value. The principal shoppers at the market were Indian housewives, who had often been brought up in a regime of self-made foods and the virtues of thrift. These values had been severely curtailed by the oil boom. During recent years conspicuous consumption came to rival thrift as a means to status elevation, but with the recession people simply did not know in what direction 'proper' behaviour was moving.

Despite this it is increasingly common to meet people who will not go to market, especially amongst the young. The market is seen as dirty and smelly, and the jostling and crowding is seen as dangerous to the respectability and class of the buyer. The response to this is varied. Many middle-class Trinidadians still affirm their thrift and sagacity precisely by their determination to market early and frequently. Other are ambivalent, as was evident in a conversation in which a middle-class Trinidadian was being gently 'ribbed' for her refusal to shop there. First, the claim was made that one couldn't park; then, when a parking spot was pointed out, other reasons were given that were clearly intended to escape having to admit that one didn't go simply because it was seen as too dirty and crowded. Others, however, say with pride they have not gone for four years. These are still a minority, as is evident from the questionnaire. But their concerns are also shared amongst more regular shoppers: 'The reason why I don't dress for shopping in Chaguanas is because you end up going to the market, . . . So I say it make no sense. Like if you going to town you might dress in a different way. You might wear a watch or a pair of something, you might put on a little makeup, but if I going to Chaguanas I don't really dress that way.'

Supermarkets and Class

Most shops in the Chaguanas area are relatively neutral in terms of any social symbolism that accrues to the shopper. That is to say, people who consider themselves 'grass-roots' and people who are considered by others 'big-shots' can patronize a store equally, provided they have the funds to do so. With respect to the market the more important division is probably that between younger and older shoppers, since the greatest antipathy to the idea of shopping in the market was found amongst school-children (who did not appear in the questionnaire), many of whom clearly loathed the experience. The supermarkets are, however, much more important in the emergence of a sense of class, though this may at this stage be more a structure of taste and difference rather than the clear differentiation of behaviour amongst discrete groups of people.

Within Chaguanas there are several categories of supermarket. Most conspicuous are the supermarkets attached to the malls. At the beginning of the fieldwork two of the malls had large food supermarkets; but a third was open by the end of the year. In addition there are half a dozen supermarkets on a smaller scale that are known as particularly cheap sources of goods. Finally there are some larger groceries that serve more specific areas of the town. Supermarket shopping is part of routine provisioning for all income levels, as is shown in Table 7.2, which indicates a slight tendency for lower income levels to shop at intervals, of around a week and higher income levels to shop at monthly intervals, presumably because of better refrigerated storage.

Two supermarkets stood out as symbolic of the general differences amongst the group. At one end is Hi-Lo, which is attached to Mid-Centre Mall. Hi-Lo are easily the best-known chain of supermarkets in Trinidad. They are found close to most of the major centres. They are well known to be part of the Neal and Massy group, and are clearly the highest-status range. They produce the glossiest publicity, including recipe books and well-known advertising campaigns, and a promise of money back in cases of dissatisfaction. They are expensively outfitted and air-conditioned, and usually provide the quickest service at the check-out counters, often with help in packing and carrying groceries. Hi-Lo as part of Mid-Centre is associated with the best car-parking facilities available in the town and the most evident security.

Table 7.2: Time Since Last Visit to a Supermarket and Frequency of
Shopping at Supermarkets by Monthly Income (in TT$)

Time since last visit	Below 1,000	1,000– 2,500	2,500– 5,000	5,000– 8,000	Above 8,000
Hi-Lo	3	3	3	3	7
Other Mall	4	10	2	8	4
Ramphalies	3	9	4	3	3
Other cheap	2	12	7	3	1
Frequency of Shopping					
One week or less	2	8	9	3	1
Two weeks or less	5	6	5	0	2
One month or less	0	14	14	9	6
More than one month	0	0	1	0	0

If any of the stores still intimidates people from the country-
side or the elderly unfamiliar with mass marketing then it is
Hi-Lo. There is little evidence, however, to suggest that this is a
deliberate strategy of up-market targeting. The main advertising
campaign of the period of fieldwork featured Tanti Merle, probably the best-known fictive character of the country, invented by
dialect poet (but also previously advertising professional) Paul
Keens-Douglas. Tanti Merle's humour comes in part from the
degree to which as an ordinary black housewife she could never
be intimidated by anything or anybody. She is featured 'wining'
her way down to the check-out aisles, in a manner which would
best translate as a 'swagger'.

The supermarket that represents the opposite end of the
spectrum is Ramphalies. This shop has become an important
symbol for Chaguanas as a whole, since it seems to epitomize the
claim that this region is indeed worth a special trip in order to
find the cheapest prices. In practice Ramphalies is one of a series
of low-cost supermarkets. The store has worked to pare away
costs over the years. There is no freezer section; the meat section
it once possessed has gone. During the fieldwork period it
principally brought in larger quantities of a relatively restricted
range of goods and piled them crudely within a confined space.
It also worked on a minimal mark-up that was bitterly resented
by some other retailers in the area. The owners employed kin and
close friends to serve. The net effect was that this type of
supermarket provided the lowest prices any retail outlet could

hope to manage while remaining a profitable enterprise. The shop became immensely popular, and was constantly over-crowded, with long waits at the check-out desks. The parking problems were notorious, and very different from the controlled and patrolled car parks associated with the malls.

A comparison was made of prices in six of the Chaguanas supermarkets during the same day. This was based on 11 common products such as fruit juice, diapers/nappies and detergents. The Ramphalies total came to $131, and was matched by the two other examples of supermarkets renowned for their low costs, which came in at $131 and $132. The total of super-market serving a suburb, and thereby acting more like a parlour, was $135. Of the two mall supermarkets open at that time, the Ramsaran Mall supermarket cost $136, while Hi-Lo came to $146. I doubt these figures would come as a surprise to most of those who shop in the Chaguanas area. The only explicit reason ever given for disliking Hi-Lo as a place to shop was that it was too expensive. Similarly, the reason given for not wanting to shop at Ramphalies was typically that 'We don't go there because my husband doesn't like crowds. We would rather pay more money and feel comfortable, so we go to Hi-Lo or Ramsaran Plaza.'

To shop at either Hi-Lo or Ramphalies was, in a sense, a different order from other supermarket shopping. In their different ways both were a conspicuous 'experience' and provided images of what life at a particular class level should be like. Hi-Lo, with its calm uncrowded spaciousness, its lighting and range of choice, its corporate imaging and promotion, conformed to most people's image of the metropolitan experience of consumer culture. In Ramphalies, by contrast, one had the supermarket equivalent of the market, the necessity and enjoyment of direct social contact, the sweaty crowded ambience, the banter as a checker calls one out to a different counter or the negotiations needed to unpark one's car from the scrum of cars around it. There was a deliberate unpretentiousness. In these ways the two supermarkets probably provided the clearest instance of a polarity that would conform to Bourdieu's representation of modern French taste in his book *Distinction* (1984).

There is, however, an important difference between the distinctions of class made evident by Bourdieu for France and those distinctions that emerge from the differences between these two supermarkets. For France, Bourdieu is able to talk of a habitus that lies 'deep' in the processes of socialization and differential class upbringing. Most of the differences in taste are systematic, but not deliberate; the opposite class's taste remains extraordinary and inexplicable to those who do not share it. Each feels uncomfortable, if not nauseous, within the ambience intended for the other. These things would hardly apply in Chaguanas. Table 7.2 shows a preference for Hi-Lo amongst the highest income group; but all income groups use both Hi-Lo and Ramphalies.

Most of the intimidation and foreignness of Hi-Lo to ordinary agriculturalists and workers was dissipated by the oil boom, and for the young at least is no more. Most of those who might have thought of themselves as destined never again to enter into places such as Ramphalies are taking stock of such assumptions with the deepening recession. These huge economic fluctuations have not aided any stable class formation. Yet this statement is only true if class is based on 'habitus' (Bourdieu 1984), a subjective interiorization of the objective world that becomes doxic in nature.

What has emerged through the Chaguanas supermarkets is a clear representation of class around the objective differences in available worlds, which is however interiorized rather as a choice of identities, either or both of which may be appropriated by the shopper. Our understanding of class in Trinidad has then to be returned to the understanding of spectacle. Class becomes less an enduring aspect of personhood than an alternative 'dressing' for the self. Very few shoppers remain aloof within Ramphalies; they also sweat and enter into the pushing and the *bonhomie*. At Hi-Lo their voices are lower, their movements are calmer. Not even Tanti Merle would really 'wine' in Hi-Lo. In effect, these become two of the most important sites in which the inhabitants of Chaguanas can try on 'class', if the term class remains the proper word for such a transient condition of identity.

Not surprisingly, these are the two shops that come up most frequently in people's conversations about shopping for groceries. Ramphalies managed to incur particular notoriety owing to a number of armed attacks made on the store, which included the killing, in defence of the store, of an attacker. Precisely because of the clarity with which they represent much more than simply an act of provisioning, people want to discuss the relative merits of both possibilities, and thereby form their views as to who they might themselves become. Views can be expressed with some anxiety and ambivalence or with some bravado. The parameters of class are by no means isolated from other factors, which in this case included ethnic stereotypes, the dynamics of oil boom and recession, and the changing role of thrift as a personal virtue. This combination made many people very unsure as to what pose to strike, what represented respectable action, and what decision granted one self-respect.

To borrow Peacock's title (Peacock 1968), supermarket shopping has become a 'Rite of Modernization' within which people form their views as to the nature of class as difference. The supermarket does seem to be changing the criteria for such evaluation. The previous discussion of the parlour represents issues that are relatively localized to the region and based around terms such as 'bacchanal' that are not easily translated into some generic notion of class as used elsewhere. The issues of the market in part overlapped with this, since the atmosphere is very much connected with the sense of verbal wit and assertion and public name-calling that is associated with bacchanal. With the advent of the supermarket, however, the people of Chaguanas seem to be moving towards dilemmas that are much closer to conventional notions of class in metropolitan countries.

Malls and Liming

In 1988 it was impossible to think of Chaguanas without its malls, and hard to appreciate that they had only existed for a few years. This was because they had almost immediately become the heart of Chaguanas. This was because of their dominance not so much over shopping sales as over the conceptualization and use of public space. With regard to sales the malls do not in fact dominate. The main high street has not merely withstood the impact of the malls, but rather if anything seems to have been enhanced by their presence. The relationship between the two is evident in the higher rental costs of high street positions and in their higher volumes of sales. But in a sense what the malls have done is to render the high street unambiguously a place for the more mundane and utilitarian activity of purchasing commodities. With regard to shopping as an social activity or event, it is the malls that have become supreme.

The Chaguanas malls emulated developments elsewhere in Trinidad (which in turn followed the establishment of malls for tourists in Barbados). Several larger prestigious malls had been established in Port of Spain and one in San Fernando, although the earliest true mall and one of the most successful was established at Valpark near the junction of two highways close to a wealthy residential area some distance from any urban centre. Valpark was still managing to trade at a TT$1.7 million profit before tax in 1988 (though this was a fall from TT$3.7 million in 1983).

As already noted, the Chaguanas malls have in two cases had their original plans curtailed owing to the recession. Centre City represents one out of the original four 'corner' blocks planned, which would have had a seven-storey office block in the middle. It was almost sabotaged by the revelation of the financial scams of its original sponsor. All the malls are heavily dependent upon local Chaguanas capital.

The use of the mall was researched partly through a questionnaire administered at Centre City (which has only a single entrance/exit) on 12 occasions during the course of a week. The results revealed that out of the shoppers asked 76 came from Chaguanas, 83 from the suburbs, i.e. contiguous areas including the four sites of field study, and 133 came from villages in the Central district. There were 7 shoppers from the South, 8 from Port of Spain, 7 from other parts of the East–West corridor, 1 from Tobago and 1 from Martinique. The busiest time of the week was midday Saturday, when approximately 800 people an hour entered the mall. This drops to around 400 at less busy periods. On weekdays the maximum reached is closer to 600: a typical figure would be 350, though this can drop to under 100 an hour at the quietest periods. The survey also revealed the following categories of shopper: 89 single females, 43 single males, 35 couples, 12 pairs of boyfriend and girlfriend, 3 groups of brothers, 13 groups of sisters, 12 groups of parent(s) with a daughter, 78 friends, 9 nuclear families, and 12 other family combinations. While 132 came to shop on their own, the 174 social groups comprised 420 persons. Even those who come initially on their own tend to meet people they know when shopping, and they may then join up to shop or eat together. This means that shopping in the mall must be considered as predominately a social activity.

This social aspect of shopping was also clarified by enquiring as to the primary reason people had come to the mall. The results for this were: 51 'liming'; 47 general shopping; 45 window shopping; 26 phone calls; 20 shoes; 17 gifts; 16 clothes; 10 meals; 7 to visit friends; 6 postcards; 6 toys; 6 on business; 5 flowers; 5 looking for girls; 4 ice cream; 4 jewellery; 3 nappies/diapers; 3 wedding materials; 3 snacks; 2 stationery; 2 video; and 1 each for visiting a toilet, looking for a mirror to comb their hair, photos, cribs, books, sweets, having their hair done, and a zip.

Dividing these answers into three main classes results in 94 respondents who came to shop for a particular item, and 92 who came shopping in general, of whom half had no expectation of buying anything. This leaves 110 whose primary purpose was social or having a meal/snack. In general, the majority of visits to the mall could be said to be predominantly of a social/leisure variety rather than with an emphasis on more mundane provisioning. The suggestion that people come as a leisure activity is also supported by evidence for the frequency of visits. In the questionnaire 74 had last been to the mall the day before, 160 had been within the last week, a further 55 within the last month, and 26 within the last year, while 5 said it was their first visit. This suggests that a large number of people are visiting the mall daily or every few days. There is a marked discrepancy here with the evidence from householders as to how often they visit the mall. Table 7.3 shows that most householders had visited the mall within either the last week or the last month. This suggests that many of those questioned at the mall are youths or others who did not count as the 'main shopper within the household', and therefore did not participate in the survey of households reported in Table 7.3, which also suggests a slight tendency for frequency of visits to the mall to increase with income.

The Trinidadian expression appropriate to visiting the mall as a leisure activity is to describe it as a 'lime'. The term 'lime' has had to change its meaning for this juxtaposition to make sense. Before the oil boom it referred merely to the activity of standing around on street corners and waiting for some action, and was associated with lower-class blacks (Lieber 1981). With the oil boom the term widened its semantic field to become almost any time two or more people set out to have a good time, and for the Indians of central Trinidad this was typically a car-based activity. Ericksen (1990) provides a recent account of this 'art of doing nothing', which has come to include going to the beach, or up

Table 7.3: Last Mall Visited and Period Since Last Visit by Monthly
Income (In TT$)

Last Mall Visited	Below 1,000	1,000– 2,500	2,500– 5,000	5,000– 8,000	Above 8,000
Mid-Centre	0	10	9	7	3
Centre City	3	8	9	4	1
Ramsaran	1	8	10	5	0
Time since last visit					
One day	3	4	5	2	4
One week or less	5	21	16	11	3
One month or less	4	13	9	7	3
More or never	10	5	7	1	1

river to cook a duck as a kind of picnic, trying to pick up some
women and take them into town, or even going to a bar for a
drink in company.

Although quite a few people talk of 'liming' in a mall, few
people will actually refer to shopping itself as a 'lime'. This is
because shopping as a term suggests a purposeful event that is
contrary to the spirit of the 'lime'. Furthermore, 'liming' is first
and foremost associated with men, though women increasingly
see themselves as 'liming', while shopping is largely associated
with women, although men also do it. Despite this, when I
suggested the idea of shopping as a 'lime' this was instantly recognized and affirmed. In a sense what has transpired is a meeting
between an expansion of the term 'lime' and the expansion of the
activity of shopping. This would imply that to go shopping is not
a directed activity towards household provisioning, but a generalized leisure activity that involves hanging around, spontaneity in
deciding what to do next, and accumulating companions as one
goes along, which are all key attributes of the classic 'lime'.

Within this idea of shopping as a 'lime', the three malls seem
to be increasingly occupying specialist niches. Centre City is the
clearest example of a 'liming' mall, but is so especially for the
schoolchildren and youth. The degree of 'liming' by children is
related to the shift system operating in some local schools. In
order to maximize the use of school facilities children are taught
in two groups, one from early morning to midday and the other
from midday to later afternoon. This means that most children
have half-a-day in which to occupy themselves. As one schoolgirl
who finished her studies at 12.00 noted:

Our parents don't want us to find work, but I would really like to get a job. Yes, I am really bored most times. I will go by my friend and from there to Chaguanas to lime in the plaza and the malls. Sometimes it is just me and my aunts who go to lime, we just go and walk around the shops; and sometimes we does buy anything they selling, and we find it nice. My aunt and they bought clothes and shoes, also jewellery. We does buy ice cream.

This activity is not unchallenged, and the most prestigious secondary school in the area regularly sends monitors in to check if any pupils may be found 'liming' in the mall, in which case they are disciplined. Other schools will permit 'liming' as long as the school uniform is not being worn; but no disciplinary procedure can make much of a dent in the imperative to congregate in the place where one is most likely to hear about what is going on within the town. The children respond by bringing a change of clothes to school or changing in a friend's house close to the mall. The particular attraction of this as opposed to the other malls is: the central position (for example it lies quite close to what was then the favourite public eating area for those who could afford it – Kentucky Fried Chicken); but above all the presence of a bank of public telephones, which is the basis of youth's ability to make assignations.

Ramsaran is equally important to the youths, but for slightly different reasons. It is the site for the main fêtes. At weekends, the empty upstairs section of one phase of the mall is host to the key 'selectors', who mix tracks of rap, dub and other music and keep several hundred youths dancing through the night. As a youth in one of the nearby villages commented:

Years ago they used to use the community centre; but that abandon, don't use it much. Most of the parties take place in Chaguanas in the Malls. Malls made the place brighter, but the money not there to make the place as bright as it should be. When it bright it better, so you wouldn't have to go to Port of Spain. Port of Spain too hot, Chaguanas is more relaxing. Port of Spain is a hustle.

Most of the parties that would attract such a youth are held in Ramsaran, which also had two associated bars, both very popular. Up to the second half of 1988 this mall also held the most popular pizzeria in town. This attracted the same youth, who overlapped with a larger swathe of Indian youths who would not have been permitted or would not have desired to fête, but who came either in groups of peers or with families. Families also used the larger public space of the mall through the establishment of Indian musical events, and in the late 1980s and early 1990s this has crystallized around the development of 'chutney', a syncretic form, based on Indian film and classic music but with elements that emulate black dancing, including its lasciviousness. 'Chutney', while frowned upon by the establishment developed enormous popularity within the Indian community, and the mall would be packed to capacity in its weekly shows, held on Sunday.

The same pizzeria moved that year to Mid-Centre Mall, and with it a considerable amount of custom. Later still this was in turn replaced as the place to be seen eating by a joint pizzeria and hamburger site established on the high street as a branch of a Port of Spain enterprise. This represented another triumph of the high street over the malls. Although Table 7.3 does not show a very marked relation to income, the ethnography suggested a more middle-class orientation for this, mall assisted by its inclusion of Hi-Lo. It is also the most expensively constructed and adorned of the three malls, and in a sense the only true mall with a larger open and rounded centre, as against the other two malls, which have more the appearance of covered-over shopping streets on two floors.

Mid-Centre also attracted its population who came to 'lime', but in this case they might be more respectable Indian families with higher incomes. They were less likely to hang around as such, and more likely to purchase goods as an integral part of their expedition to the mall. While Centre-City had a popular cheap restaurant and snack bar, and Ramsaran appealed through the presence of two bars for drinking, Mid-Centre was more likely to be used to give one's children an ice-cream as a 'treat' element within the family expedition.

Perhaps not as important as the development of the malls themselves, but an innovation with its own considerable impact, are the car parks associated with the malls. In this case it is Mid-Centre car park that is easily the most important, and Centre-City to a lesser extent. The car park of Mid-Centre Mall has within a few years become the most important venue for public occasions in the town. This status was most clearly established by the holding of Divali Nagar over several years. This is an annual festival devoted to the celebration of East Indian culture in Trinidad, and includes many stalls with a combination of commercial and cultural interests. For example, banks and racing bikes are juxtaposed with information on religious movements within Hinduism, the sale of Indian foods, and exhibitions about the settlements of Indians in the area. The festival is held for several days, during which time the car park is entirely devoted to the fair. The car park is also used during evenings or Sundays for competitions (such as for Indian music), political meetings and other public events. Occasionally similar events will be held in the car park or annexe to Centre City, such as a sponsored fashion show for Indian clothes. Not all such events are exclusively the concern of the Indian community. Mid-Centre car park may also be used for a day's 'wind-ball' cricket competition and similar events, but Indian themes dominate.

The Chaguanas malls do not have the resources of some of the other malls in Trinidad. These capitalize on the sense of shopping as an event. As well as the many forms of festival exploitation, such as the 'week of events' which will surround Christmas and similar occasions, such malls may put on a particular attraction, such as a 'learning is fun' educational exhibition with associated activities, or an oriental evening with Indian dance, song and fashion. Such corporate activity is intended to encourage a move from the association of malls with 'liming' to one with the atmosphere of a family outing.

The importance of viewing the malls and their car parks in relation to 'liming' and public leisure events relates to the centrality of outdoor life more generally in Trinidad. The dynamics of 'liming', in particular, are crucial to the development of contemporary Trinidadian society. The malls have helped to resolve key conflicts that were emergent in the increasing importance of the 'lime'. The 'lime' had been simultaneously one of the most attractive and one of the most threatening forms of activity for many Trinidadians. In its earlier form 'liming' had been associated with a male youth culture that seemed devoted to avoiding the taint of purposeful activity, especially work, and was viewed by others, especially women, as a potential source of harassment. At the same time most Trinidadians are attracted by the elements of spontaneity of action, freedom and easy sociality associated with the 'lime'.

The use of the car for 'liming' during the oil boom extended the possibilities for those who otherwise would not have wished to lose their respectability, and who were in any case afraid of the youth culture associated with 'liming'. With the malls, however, we see a new phase, in which walking and hanging around become much more acceptable, partly because of the relatively protected environment which is their context and partly because of the ambiguity with respect to the idea of purposeful activity. In practice, 'liming' in malls is a highly heterogeneous activity, which includes more traditional youth hanging around, but is more commonly a kind of attenuated version of this performed by schoolchildren. At the same time it has come to include the window-shopping of family groups and the sitting and gossiping of work colleagues. Even though they don't use the term, many groups are clearly feeling that their leisure has the *frisson* of freedom and modern life associated with 'liming', while in practice including a strong continuity with alternative uses of public space such as the traditions of dressing up and going out to see and be seen by peers. In this way the advent of the mall is used to resolve what had been an emerging contradiction in the manner in which Trinidadians seek to use their leisure time.

Conclusion

For shopping in general and the malls in particular, while these institutions may arise out of the developing economic structure, it would be quite wrong to limit our consideration of them to those economic factors that are responsible for their creation. Once established they become public space, and public statements about décor, taste and class. The malls have radically transformed the whole sense of place and space in Chaguanas, a town that was always dominated by its shops both physically and symbolically. There is much cultural specificity here, and the appropriation of the malls is quite different from that in other societies, relating as it does to specific local traditions such as 'liming' and fêting.

The ethnography itself therefore makes a relativistic point against any assumption that 'shopping is shopping is shopping'. Even within Trinidad there is a diversity among the institutions homogenized by the term 'shop'. As I have tried to show in the latter half of this chapter, these are better divided into a series of 'genres', each of which lends itself to distinct forms of social relations and symbolic systems, such as the parlour, super-market, market, mall, etc. There are also no grounds for seeing the effect of these as creating an overall homogenization that makes Trinidadians more like any other people, or less internally diverse. In many respects, shops have been used to extend and 'complete' cultural desires that already existed, of which the most important is objectified in the notion of the 'lime'. This means that 'hanging about' around shops in Trinidad has distinct characteristics and connotations, which are by no means to be equated with what is coming to be called 'malingering' else-where (cf. e.g. Hopkins 1990).

None of this precludes the possibility of comparative analysis of shopping in cross-cultural perspective. Such an approach would help situate, for example, the shifts in gender, the evaluation of shopping skills and the understanding of the relationship between shopping and spectacle described here. Shopping is neither simply a form of globalization nor simply one of localization. The particular forms of shopping here have clearly been influenced by the local historical trajectory in the use of markets and public space. There are many innovations, represented by the introduction of new forms such as malls and supermarkets. In some cases these are appropriated by these older trajectories; but there are also newer forms of specific use that owe little or nothing to the past.

Contemporary shopping has become integrated as a sphere of possibility throughout the gamut of Trinidadian social relation-ships and cosmological imagination; it is used in gender exchange, in 'dressing' the self, in objectifying the sense of 'bright', in the competitive skills of housewifery, in mobilizing youth against their parents, in establishing taste as class, as well as in many other modes of interaction. To borrow Bruno Bettel-heim's phrase, shopping in Chaguanas turns on the development of skills in 'the uses of enchantment'. Shopping is evidently as important to the development of new skills of identity formation as of provisioning. There is no reason why the anthropologist should collude with certain cultural biases largely objectified in gender stereotypes that denigrate shopping as mere super-ficiality, and refuse to acknowledge these skills as fundamental to modern life.

8

Consumption and Capitalism

The first chapter of this volume set out the main issues that the book was intended to address. Since most of the intervening chapters have been descriptive accounts of particular sections within the Trinidadian economy, it remains the task of this concluding chapter to draw together several threads of discussion and determine the contribution of the ethnography to these larger issues. There is, however, a danger that the structure of the book in and of itself might reinforce a misleading image of the relationship between business and consumption, which was the issue with which the whole project began. Placing the consideration of the consumer at the end of each chapter, and indeed at the end of the book, may reinforce a model of the economy that implies that goods come to exist as a result of imperatives in production and that the role of the consumer is reactive – either to accept or to reject. This would make the study of the consumer a manifestation of some kind of 'reception theory' that was developed to understand the response to media forms. While the more sophisticated versions of reception theory allow for considerable 'work' to be done by consumers, they remain the end-point of a process that starts with creative production.

Any detailed reading of this volume alongside Miller 1994 should, however, quickly dispel any such directionality in interpreting the articulation between consumption and production. Indeed, in business and economics the most explicit model is often based on quite the opposite premiss, which is that consumer desires are some kind of natural force arising out of a given attribute of the consumer called a 'need', to which business benignly responds by providing the best means by which such needs may be satisfied.

This chapter will attempt to balance the remainder of the volume, by reversing this direction of presentation. The chapter is divided into four sections. The first of these explores those areas in which there is an explicit or official objectification of the consumer *per se*. These are mainly bodies that are responsible for consumer protection, and also the consumer co-operative movement. The second section concludes the arguments within the book that explicitly address the general issue regarding the articulation of consumption and production. It employs two case studies that give instances of collusion and of autonomy between these domains. The argument then moves towards a conclusion for those sections of the volume devoted to the ethnography of business. Starting with the impact of the capitalist ideology, it then considers the more general arguments about the nature of organic capitalism and the rootedness of business in Trinidad. It then returns the discussion to the question of the articulation between organic and pure capitalism.

By the fourth section, a road has been driven back from consideration of the consumer to the issues of macro-economic change with which the volume began. In this final section the articulation between consumption and business is moved upwards towards the more general issue of the relationship between consumption and capitalism. Here what might otherwise appear as the two loose ends of the volume are tied together – on the one hand the discussion in Chapter 2 of pure capitalism, and on the other hand the micro-ethnography of consumption. Through confronting the relationship between these two, a larger contradiction is revealed, which becomes the final conclusion of this book and a pointer towards a further theory of capitalism in the age of the consumer society.

The Official Consumer

Consumption is mainly a practice of everyday life. There are relatively few points at which the consumer is objectified as such. These may, however, be slightly more common in Trinidad than in some other countries, since the idea of consumerism is relatively well established, with particular bodies directly responsible for representing the interests of the consumer. In the nineteenth century, the explicit construction of the consumer as an identity probably arose most strongly in countries, such as France, with a strong consumer co-operative movement (Furlough 1991; Williams 1982). By contrast, in this century more countries have seen their consumer movements develop through state involvement in their promulgation, as in Sweden, or through consumer protest movements, as in the United States.

In contemporary Trinidad the main areas in which the consumer is clearly constructed as such are: first, the various government and non-governmental agencies for consumer protection; second (though much dependent upon the first), the media representation of consumers; and third, the consumer co-operatives and wider economic institutions that are intended to benefit or represent consumers.

State Consumer Protection Agencies

During fieldwork in 1988 a conference was held in Port of Spain under the auspices of the regional office of the International Organization of Consumers Unions for Latin America and the Caribbean. Consumer groups from all over the region assembled along with invited guests, such as the head of the British Consumer Association. Discussions were held on a large number of consumer concerns and also on women's issues more generally. To give just one example, many Caribbean countries had found that they were being used to dump electrical goods that at first seemed good value, but were largely end-of-the-line stock with no back-up or spare parts available. Guests were invited to take part in a specially sponsored competition to write the best calypso about consumer interests. This was in part because one of the officials in the relevant government consumer office is a well-known calypsonian, 'Lady Wonder'. Indeed the winning calypso was not, as might have been expected, a bland appeal to be concerned about one's rights, but a rather hard-hitting attack on the Trinidadian consumer who claims to have such concerns, but then avidly spends the 'Yankee dollar' on shopping trips abroad for foreign-made goods.

That Trinidad should host such a conference reflected on the sense that this was a relatively progressive country in terms of its active pursuit of consumers' right and interests. The word 'relatively' is important here, since the consumerist movement is largely a fledgling one in most countries. Nevertheless, I found considerable evidence to support this claim. The period of the oil boom, with its abundance of facilities and a considerable public service sector, had allowed Trinidad to consolidate its concerns. Legislation was in place with respect to a wide range of measures to protect consumers against poor-quality or unsafe goods. In my investigation of the drinks industry I found a number of cases of active intervention to test products or challenge claims. This was mainly carried out by the Food and Drugs Commission, which analysed around 6,500 samples a year, including most major products on the market. For example, in 1986 their *Annual Report* lists 128 samples of carbonated beverages analysed. Their concern was with issues such as the type of sweetener being used in diet drinks, or the enforcement of laws preventing the use of portrayals of fruits on labels that gave the impression that an artificial drink contained real fruit juice. They also destroyed goods found to be out of date or otherwise unfit for human consumption.

In addition to the Food and Drugs division, there was a Bureau of Standards that establishes such things as sizing and the labelling of materials used in various products. For example, they followed through the considerable public concern at the low standards of women's shoes, where the glue would come unstuck and parts fall off soon after they were purchased. Their laboratory could also test products such as detergents, though given the recession they were being asked to use their expensive equipment to conduct work on behalf of business as well as to keep a check on business products.

Equally active was the Consumer Affairs Division of the Ministry of Industry, Enterprise and Consumer Affairs. With eight members of staff, its research division carried out various reports on, for example, seat belts in cars and taxis, the air travel industry, or the false implications of adverts. They also ran a complaints division, which typically dealt with 200 to 500 specific complaints a year. These tended to come from local Port of Spain clerical workers and production line workers. Relatively few complaints were received from housewives or rural residents. Cars, including spare parts, fridges and footwear were the most common subjects of complaint. Finally, the Price Commission, whose activities with respect to placing price control on sweet drinks were discussed in Chapter 4, was also seen as an agency representing consumer interests, although, as in the case mentioned, it would be more accurate to see it as an instrument of political strategy.

At least one important body, the Consumer Guidance Council, was originally established by government, but was supposed to represent the public directly. In addition, there were groups that arose without the aid of any governmental prompting. Some of these were small-scale and short-term. More substantial was an active association for housewives of Trinidad and Tobago, which claimed 900 members. There was also a long-term lobby group called 'The Informative Breastfeeding Service'. These groups were hoping to promote their interests through the recently established Minister for Women's Affairs.

While scientific testing of products was assumed to be largely a governmental responsibility, the Consumer Affairs Division and the non-governmental groups recognized that to be effective they depended upon interest generated through the public in the form of requests and complaints. Only these would represent the kind of pressure that would ensure that they remained a political priority. To this end there was considerable encouragement for any media contribution on consumer matters. These varied considerably, depending upon whether a media outlet felt that there was an audience. Thus the Consumer Affairs Division was able to show videos on morning television, but could not afford to pay the fees that would be charged for peak-time transmission. A programme called 'Live Issues' was also allowing public debate on television over concerns such as legislation concerned with severance pay, although these discussions by relevant experts tended to be more 'live' than 'lively'.

There were sporadic radio programmes, depending upon whether there was an issue available that could fill up particular time slots. Various newspapers also had columns from time to time, or special articles. For example the *Express* (7/6/88) had a double-page spread termed a 'debate' on how consumers could fight back against poor-quality goods and services, including inter-views with members of the public as to whether they would return faulty goods. Items ranged from 'tips to consumers' provided by the Consumer Affairs Division to individual cru-sading columnists, such as 'Action Line by Angela Martin' (*Express* 1988). Such columns claimed to expose the villains behind any scams that were reported to them by the public. For example, a company that tried to attract consumers by claiming a very low price for one commodity but mysteriously seemed to have sold out of that particular product before the day's trading began, might be the subject of a media exposé.

The weekly papers also reported scandals and exposures against particular products and companies, but such was their reputation that, while on the one hand they would hit against bodies that the more establishment dailies might not feel free to attack, on the other hand there was always the suspicion that their attacks were partial, echoing personal scores and rivalries. There were, however, several examples of debates relevant to soft drinks in which there is no particular reason to assume partiality. For example, there was a discussion through the letters section as to harmful effects of NutraSweet (*Blast* 12/8/88). The *Blast*, (11/3/88) under the title 'Soft Drink Scandal', claimed 'thousands of people across the country have injured themselves and broken fingernails struggling with the bottle caps at one time or another . . . Some has [*sic*] unfortunately cut their lips attempting to get the caps off with their teeth also. And on go the horrors.' The article ends with 'Over to you, Bureau of Standards.' The government institutions realized that it was often more effective for individuals to go directly for news coverage. This is made rather clear in an article in the *Express* (21/6/88) titled 'Beware those soft-drink covers', which notes 'Harper and Mollineau have already gone to the Bureau of Standards and the Consumer Guidance Council, who advised them to go to the media.'

In addition, the Consumer Affairs Division attempted to develop an educational role. This was partly through leaflets and information made available in public places and informing shoppers about their rights, how to make complaints, and the proper definition of terms such as a 'sale', or 'the hazards of flammable liquids', etc. They also held events such as a lecture for 'World Consumer Rights Day' and provided materials for schools. For the region more generally there is a well-produced textbook called *Consumer Affairs in the Caribbean* (Seepersad and Bernard 1984) that forms part of the standard curriculum. When I asked pupils in secondary schools, most could remember having had a specific lesson on consumer issues, though the detail of recalled content was usually minimal.

To summarize, there were sufficient numbers of people specifically employed by the government to generate a general concern for the standards of goods available in the market-place. At the time of the oil boom these had been relatively effective controls, and I could find many examples where their authority had been implemented. They were not therefore just bureaucratic sinecures. Many of the responsible officers had a strong nationalistic concern that their country was increasingly subject to dumping and to other excesses of international capitalism, and had a genuine interest in the preservation of the standards that they had been able to set during the oil boom.

Unfortunately, it is most unlikely that these standards can be retained. The recession was eroding these interests on a whole series of fronts. The influence of structural adjustment was generally opposed to state intervention in commerce, and promoted the cutting of the public sector. There was less will to combat powerful companies when the general economic situation was so precarious. Indeed, the fact that the Bureau of Standards' laboratory facilities were being looked to as a source for raising money through their use for commercial purposes pointed the likely future direction. This would mean a reduction of consumerism in favour of the power of commerce. This is particularly to be regretted inasmuch as such protection as these agencies can offer is likely to be more acutely required as recession leads to the importation and production of goods of lower quality and ingredients that are chosen in order to cut costs.

I do not want to give the impression that consumerism was ever particularly powerful, except in comparison with other countries, where it is generally a weak movement. The evidence suggested that the main use of its facilities was based around the Port of Spain community that was employed in the public service, and had developed into a middle class during the oil boom. In other words, it was a bureaucracy that largely served its own social milieu, rather than Trinidad as a whole. But my evidence suggests that this was not the result of a deliberate strategy, but rather the distance and relative lack of trust in governmental bodies that was still prevalent in lower-class communities outside the capital. Furthermore, arrayed in opposition are considerable commercial forces. An example of these was provided by a friend who sold medicines for a pharmaceutical company and reported the large percentage of doctors whose first question was invariably about the availability of cheap out-of-date medicines.

The Consumer Co-operative Movement

Apart from consumer protection agencies, the main other domain that explicitly addresses the identity of consumers *per se* is the Consumer Co-operative movement. Once again this is the result of largely state-based initiatives designed to enhance social welfare; but such bodies also look back to a much wider tradition of popular institutions, such as saving schemes, that developed as part of the informal economy of the household. By far the most important and most prevalent today are the *sou-sou* (Miller 1994: 35), which are entirely informal and based on trust. Probably the majority of Trinidadians have been associated with them at some time or other. Historically important were various forms of friendly society and masonic lodges. Today rather more important in terms of actual saving schemes are credit unions, which have grown up mainly since the Second World War, and some of which are considerable in size (up to 35,000 members in one case). Finally, there are various forms of producer co-operative societies, especially in agriculture and fisheries.

Consumer co-operatives, in contrast to all of these, deal with goods rather than with money and services. They are basically alternative retail organizations. As a movement they are closely tied to government promotion. They mainly developed following the establishment of a relevant government department in 1949, slowly at first, and then received a boost as a result of government's being pushed further along this road after the Black Power movement of 1970. Although this could be thought to constitute popular pressure, various commentators suggested that the movement was too dependent upon government sponsorship to survive. Another factor was the enmity of business, which saw them as a threat and would attempt to prevent access to cheap imported goods. It was difficult to locate firm evidence, but it does not seem that there had ever been more than 25 groups involved; some, like those in Tobago, had lasted for quite some time; but by the time of the fieldwork the only major consumer co-operative was at El Dorado on the East–West corridor. This had started in 1949 with 3 employees, and had made good profits up to 1965. In 1969 it had closed after suspected mismanagement; but it had re-opened in 1973, and by the time of the fieldwork was well enough established to advertise on television in competition with the main supermarket chains.

Since the advent of structural adjustment there have also grown up rather shadowy organizations designed to provide cheap access to imported goods. They may be rooted in the expatriate populations in Europe and the Americas. I have not been able to obtain detailed information, and these are very recent developments. I suspect they are partially based on 'pyramid selling' principles, with each investor being paid back through the recruitment of further investors. They seem to work largely through middle-class consumers who can still afford imported goods. A friend who is a lay preacher in an evangelical church remarked that the efforts made to recruit his household to this scheme was reminiscent of the most zealous missionary activity.

Consumer Culture

The degree to which the consumer is explicitly objectified as an agent is little indication of the actual importance of consumption either to the economy or to the social lives of consumers. Most of the previous chapters have attempted to relate consumption to production with respect to particular sectors. Advert creation is set against advert viewing, retail against shopping, sweet drink branding against sweet drink consuming. The emphasis has, however, generally been on the imperatives behind production and distribution, rather than those of consumers.

The relative lack of attention to consumption as an imperative is a reflection of the complementarity between this volume and its predecessor (Miller 1994). The broader nature of consumption is better considered within an ethnography of society rather than an ethnography of business, because it is mainly related to the objectification of values. The ability to make purchases as an economic function gives little guidance as to the extraordinarily complex, contradictory and nuanced background to actual consumption, which is the selection of particular strategies of prioritization and taste.

In Miller 1994 it was argued that in many respects the projects of value that are being constructed through commodities are more a continuation of projects that previously were objectified through social categories such as kinship, household and ethnicity. For that reason one has first to comprehend the earlier history of the region that gave rise to the particular concerns with transience and freedom on the one hand and with the long term and the establishment of roots on the other. Once these fundamental projects could be elucidated it was possible to see how these determined such minutiae of everyday consumption as the decoration of living rooms, car interiors and the use of style in clothing. By contrast, I cannot in this volume provide much insight into consumer imperatives, since I believe the production and marketing institutions that have been described here would not in themselves throw much light on this question. What is central to this volume, however, is the question as to whether consumption is best viewed as a derivative merely of business or more generally of capitalism.

The Articulation of Business and Consumption

As noted in Chapter 1, a primary incentive for undertaking this fieldwork was to combat justified accusations that the new studies of consumption had merely created an autonomous arena to match the study of production. What was required was a more mature consideration of the two in relation to each other. Already one very impressive attempt has been made to construct such a relationship, though I feel that Fine and Leopold (1993) are too strongly wedded to what might be seen as the obvious direction of causality, whereby the nature of the market for a particular domain of goods is seen to be constructed in terms of the relations of production for that same domain. By contrast, I am open to the possibility that there is indeed considerable autonomy between these various parts of the economic system, and that the appearance of this is not just an artefact of researchers only focusing upon one or other element within the economy.

The relationship should not be viewed simply in terms of particular campaigns for particular products. As was evident in the detailed case study of drinks, the cultural categories that are the environment within which the consumer operates have developed over many decades. During all this there has been a constant and dynamic interaction between the development of new branded drinks by the industry and the various social concerns with issues such as ethnicity or artificiality that have become expressed in consumers' use of drinks as an objectification of values. In practice we have seen that this may give rise to a wide variety of situations. Sometimes there is a surprising gulf between these arenas, with advertising campaigns or the development of new products that seem entirely autonomous from any sense of the consumer, or new fashions and tastes developing that seem to bear no relation to any campaigns by producers. In other cases there is close collusion between the two, so that to ask which is responsible for the innovation becomes a pedantic 'chicken and egg'-style enquiry.

To supplement the argument given so far two examples are now provided that may help summarize this argument with respect to the relationship between consumption and production. The first example, which examines the place of competition, illustrates the problem of trying to isolate either business or some notion of 'society' separate from business as the prime agency in the development of a general trait. In the other example, taken from the drinks industry, we can see how far a gulf may open up between the two domains of production and consumption, even where each is predicated on the other.

Trinidad: The Competitive Society

Although the topic of competition and sponsorship was discussed and illustrated in Chapter 5, this may not have indicated just how ubiquitous these commercially sponsored competitions have become as a feature of Trinidadian life. They attract considerable public participation. For example a Colgate-Palmolive competition called 'Realise your Dream' was reputed to have obtained 35,000 responses. Some of the radio-based competitions involved in, for example, finding slogans or providing examples of verbal display such as mock wedding speeches, and similar commercially sponsored events may attract a response of up to 25,000 (see Miller 1993 for the analysis of one example). Such competitions may in turn become events. A newspaper reported how 'an estimated 10,000 people armed with boxes of paper planes gathered at the mall to participate in this exciting competition, which was televised on TTT . . . The winner managed to shoot 100 out of 250 of his paper planes into the window and trunk [boot] of a Toyota Corolla, which they now own.'

During the survey I inquired about the competitions people had entered for. Out of 160 households, 47 confirmed that they had recently filled in the form for a commercial competition. Most of these, especially within the poorer community of Ford, were not actually sent in. This suggests that the figures for those who enter competitions understate the number of those who have actually responded to them. In many cases several members of a household are involved in a single entry. Putting these figures together implies that some 10–15 per cent of the population aged over 15 may be involved in a typical major company promotion; and there are several taking place at any given time.

The commercially sponsored competitions are complemented by media competitions. Competitions are a regular feature of phone-in programmes on the radio. These usually take the form of answering questions about some aspect of Trinidadian history or culture, such as the runner-up in the southern division finals of a steel-band competition in the 1960s, the calypso they played, and the name of the director. One such programme, organized by a chain of pizza restaurants, was one of the most popular radio programmes according to marketing surveys done that year. Since the lines to the radio were continually jammed the usual policy was to phone in and then ask for the question to be repeated when one got through, rather than wait until one knew the answer. Once again, many people in the survey noted that they had phoned in, and one had even won a pizza! Such competitions are not new to Trinidad: Naipaul (1967) describes similar events in his novel *The Mimic Men*, and during conversations with marketing personnel, records were discussed showing the massive participation in a competition in the 1930s that the company was considering repeating. At another level there are continual raffles to raise money for charity, a major national lottery in which the great majority of those asked said they take part, and a popular, if illegal, numbers game known as *whewhe*.

In effect, commerce tries to make all forms of cultural competition an aspect of commercial competition. Two obvious examples are Carnival and sports. For Carnival commerce provide the prizes and the motifs used in display. Angostura reports in the 1988 volume of its journal *The Distiller* that during the Carnival they had sponsored the parade of bands, given first prize for the Young King, and sponsored three 'steel bands' or 'pan around the neck' and 4 mass camps. For this they had designed and executed 54 banners. When, during fieldwork, the Chaguanas steel band 'Tropical Angel Harps' quite unexpectedly did well in the early stages of the classical steelband competition, there was almost a panic, since they were entirely without sponsorship up to that time, which seemed quite inappropriate to the business community. A writer with considerable knowledge of the steelband movement has suggested that it is hard to exaggerate the level of sponsorship that accrues to the contemporary steelband from commerce.[11] Even a children's band may be festooned with sponsored items. The same would be true of sports. The soft drink company S. M. Jaleel not only reported ploughing TT$100,000 into one tournament, but also noted support for athletics, secondary school cricket league, football, hockey, volleyball and basketball, either through teams such as Cole Cold Hornets or competitions such as Cole Cold National Football League (*Express* 14/5/88).

At this level branding becomes not merely the competition between rival products in the supermarket, but a kind of superordinate level to almost every sort of competition that is otherwise taking place. All music sports and social gatherings become re-categorized as Cannings drinks, as Broadway cigarettes or as rival oil companies. For one day picked at random (21 May 1988) the two daily newspapers provided 23 example of sponsorship. These ranged from reports on the Trintoc cricket trophy and the Malta Heineken sponsorship of the St Peter and St Paul's grand fête and bazaar, through to the Mario Pizza's sponsored school radio broadcasts. About the only thing in the newspapers not sponsored seemed to be the horoscope.

This presence of competition is equally evident when we move from more explicitly commercial realms to a more general consideration of Trinidadian society. Indeed, the notion of 'culture' in Trinidad is virtually synonymous with that of competition. All the major cultural festivals take the form of competitions. These include two major steelband competitions and the various calypso competitions, of which the most important is the Calypso King announced on *dimanche gras* at the beginning of Carnival; but there are half a dozen other major competitions also involved. There are competitions on a national

---

11. Personal communication, Kim Johnson.

scale for the Christmas music of *parang*, for a variety of East Indian dance and song categories, and for 'best village', which emphasizes Creole culture. Many members of a village are required to prepare the entry to the best village competition in terms of dancers, costume makers, choreographers and so forth. Most people have friends who take part in any given competition, and there is fierce local interest. At a slightly lesser level there are a wide number of beauty competitions and fashion shows with a strong competitive element, local song and talent competitions, a vast number of sporting competitions, including national leagues for local events such as 'small-goal football', 'windball cricket' and the 'all-fours' gambling game. These are events where every village may expect to put up a team. A high proportion of local input into television broadcasting takes the form of annual competitions, with the screening of all the heats. These include events for children 'twelve and under', in 1988 a new competition for youths called 'party time', and Mastanha Bahar and Scouting for Talent, which deal with Indian and African cultural forms respectively. The drawing of the national lottery is made into a much-extended weekly televised ritual. The major competitions are organized at a state level, for example for Carnival; but there are a host of minor ones, since local restaurants, bars, charity committees, schools village councils and other such bodies organize their own.

At this point the evidence of ubiquitous competition in commerce and cultural events may be matched by the evidence for the centrality of competition in everyday life that arose from the observational material that forms the basis for *Modernity: An Ethnographic Approach* (Miller 1994). The following section was based on a study not of commerce, but of gender relations and the transient mode discussed in detail in that book (1994: 222–6).

Intensive competition is particularly a trait of the transient mode. The quintessential display of such competition is probably within groups of females sharing the same office. In the survey questions were asked as to the clothing of those surveyed. One of the figures to emerge was that many females engaged in extensive purchase of shoes relative to other aspects of their dress, and relative to their incomes. It should be noted that shoes are classified in such a way that only dress shoes are counted in this number. Items that come under the category of 'sandals', or 'flats', etc. are not counted as true 'shoes' and do not figure in

these numbers. Indeed, what appears to have happened is that
the semantic category 'shoe' has contracted precisely to those
forms of footwear that are implicated in such competition, since
flats and casual sandals are for informal home wear outside such
a competitive arena. Also, in many cases it appeared women only
counted shoes that were wearable at the time. In fact women's
shoe imports are not well made and do wear out; but these figures are for presently wearable shoes.

The figures for 'when did you last buy a pair of shoes' also
indicated a considerable intensity of purchase, given that this
was a period of recession when money was scarce. In very many
of these cases the same informants had given details of the
degree to which their groceries had been pared down to the basic
necessities. In all cases shoe purchase would have been far more
vigorously pursued in the oil-boom period, and the continued
involvement for many is testament to its continued prioritization.
Other evidence comes from discussions about trips for shopping
at Caracas and Margarita. One of the main motivations behind
these trips was the relatively cheap cost of shoes abroad, and the
result was that people would return with large numbers. This
extravagant purchase of shoes tends mainly to be made by
women who are working, but is not necessarily confined to them.
Dress shoes are also used for weddings, parties and so forth.
Women who fête regularly would endeavour to afford shoes
through other means. Many women excused the number of shoes
in relation to stylistic matching, arguing that all new dresses
required a new pair of shoes to match, although observation
suggested that acceptable matching was not necessarily
so tightly orchestrated, and there is considerable use of neutral
colours such as black, white and silver, especially for dressy occasions.

A more revealing insight into the logic of this activity comes
from comments about who observes what one is wearing. There
seemed to be a consensual view as to what women wear to
impress men. Essentially these are items drawing attention to the
breasts and buttocks, short or slit skirts, tight tops and so forth.
As one commentator noted, however, about the last place that a
man looked at would be the feet, and very few men would show
much interest in the shoes worn by their partners. However,
there was some consensus that shoes would be one of the first
observations made by other women in assessing the dress

display of women, and that judgements would be made for appropriateness and then style. It seemed reasonable to conclude that the enormous emphasis placed on the wearing of shoes is testimony to the stress on competitive display amongst women, rather than a product of dressing for men.

Both observations of office life and comments on what happens in offices seem to confirm this. In general, women strongly assert the degree of competition. This is not to say that there is no co-operation. Women involve themselves in *sou-sou* (rotating credit schemes) and also organize suitcase trade, where one member goes abroad to make purchases on order from the others. In Ford women often seemed better able to form co-operative groups geared towards local politics than the males, who tended to be more formally responsible for this activity. Alongside this, however, is often also intensive distrust, competitive display and sensitivity to factions and so forth, of which ethnicity is often an additional element. Very few women regard the office as an appropriate locale for informality in dress: if anything, work dressing shows as much intensity and anxiety as dressing for a fête.

Many similar examples could be given for both genders, including competition in house renovation, intense competition over cars and car interiors, in sports, and especially in the verbal exchange of insults that is known as *picon* or 'giving fatigue'. The intensity of competition was evident in such mundane examples as the local sports days that most communities are keen to organize. One such sports day in Newtown pitted the three phases by which the community had been built against each other. In terms of establishing good relations in the community, the event was a disaster. From the beginning there were continual accusations of favouring by judges, and questions as to the interpretations of rules, for example, whether a balloon burst at a given stage counts in a total or not. All decisions were interpreted as reflecting the interests of particular phases. The affair deteriorated to threats of violence and intimidation. I hardly encountered a community-based competition that did not include quite serious accusations of favouritism.

Overall, then, competition seems to have a particular salience within Trinidadian society. It is characteristic throughout, but accentuated amongst women and in association with transience, where it is conjoined with the excitement experienced in gambling. But how should we account for its centrality to Trinidadian life? If I had just included the first half of this case study – that is, the evidence for commercial involvement – then one would undoubtedly have concluded that this was evidence for the degree to which competition, which is inherent in capitalist institutions, has infiltrated into everyday life, so that the culture of consumption has become subservient and a mere reflection of the dominant forms that arise through business. There are many example of social analysis that continue to assume such effects of capitalism (cf. e.g. Harvey 1989: 343–5; Jameson 1991).

If, by contrast, I had discussed the latter part of this case study, that on competition between women or in sports days, and not the former part, then an equally obvious conclusion would result. There has been considerable work done on intense competition, for example, on the verbal insulting that existed prior to commercialization and that exists in the least commercialized parts of the Caribbean today. One of the points made in Miller 1994 is that Trinidadian competition rarely constructs stable hierarchies, but is renewed with each event, i.e. each new party or day at the office. Most of the analysis by anthropologists such as Abrahams and Wilson suggests that this is a sign of radical egalitarianism arising out of the particular histories of slavery and oppression. It is a common observation that competition reduces its players to an equality of chance, and that each competition may be in effect a reduction of all to the same starting-point. Competition, it might be concluded, represents a radical opposition to hierarchy.

That this affects even the commercially sponsored competitions can be seen in the disparity between government and popular perspectives on such competitions. On the whole, the State preferred competitions that involved the encouragement of talents of various kinds, local culture, and semi-institutionalized forms. Government legislation actually forbids commercial competitions that are only dependent upon chance, and the only exception to this is the government's own lottery. For participants otherwise associated with the transient mode, by contrast, there is a marked predilection for competitions in which chance plays a major part, in which results are immediate, and in which each competition starts as essentially a new event, not tied to any tradition or institutionalization. By far the most popular new

competition during the year was the government's own introduction of a national lottery based on scratching out a section
of a card, providing instant results. The introduction of this
competition created traffic and pedestrian congestion and general disruption. As anthropologists have observed for gambling
elsewhere, the type of competition that relies on luck rather
than ability may serve an egalitarian rather than a hierarchizing
ideology.

One could therefore construct equally plausible arguments to
suggest either that the ubiquity of competition is simply an
expression of capitalism or that it is an expression of radical
egalitarianism. It seems much more sensible to note how competition may arise from the logics of both business on the one
hand and moral cosmology on the other, and how the two
reinforce each other. As in so much of consumer culture, what
emerges is elements of collusion between these two relatively
autonomous sets of interests. Competition might have been
restricted to intra-business relations; but in such a conducive
environment as it finds here it flourishes and spreads across
many other domains. The result is that even American academics, who come from a country that others regard as extreme
in its predilection for competitiveness, have told me that they
regard Trinidad as extreme by comparison with the US in its passion for competition.

Supligen

The example of competition illustrates the close collusion over a
long period of time between the development of what might be
called a 'culture of business' and more general social norms, so
close that we cannot easily locate agency as cause in either the
one or the other domain. In Chapter 3, where the case study of
sweet drinks was presented, and also in Chapter 4, in the study
of advertising, various examples were given where agency could
be clearly located as the interests of producers or advertising
concerns. It is harder to argue that social imperatives cause
commodities, since initially products are created by commerce.
There is, however, still the possibility that the acceptance of a
product bears no relation to the meaning attributed to it during
its production and advertising. Just such a case arose amongst

one of the products that was being closely followed during field-work.

For a considerable time I could not understand one of the most unexpected results of asking viewers to comment upon adverts. When I had watched the advert for Supligen it had seemed to me the clearest example of a product that was being sold on the theme of sex. The drink is a soya milk product, made by Nestlé and sold in a tetrapack.[12] The television advert consisted of a female in a leotard working out as though in a gym, followed by a male with rippling muscles and a pneumatic drill between his legs. The female is shown throwing a carton of Supligen to the male and giving a clear wink to the viewer as they leave together through a door made from a Supligen pack. The slogan to the advert is 'the nourishment behind performance', and the off-screen voice notes 'it will help you perform longer'. The pack itself is based on the profile of what might be taken to be a comet, but is clearly intended to be also taken as a penis in action. All of this would seem to make the advertiser's intentions pretty clear.

In order to confirm my interpretation, I discussed the advert with the 'creative' who had produced the material for her agency. She confirmed everything I had thought, and described the campaign as being based entirely upon sex. The theme was also further clarified inasmuch as the merchandising associated with the sale of the product at supermarkets was based on offering free packets of peanuts or chick-peas. Both of these are trad-itionally foods that are supposed to help men sustain their sexual drive. An example is the oft-quoted street-corner peanut-seller's cry of 'Bullets for your gun.'

As was clear in Chapter 5, the viewers of advertisements were not at all reticent about ascribing sexual innuendo to advertisers trying to sell products. Indeed, my surprise had been at the extent to which adverts, such as that for Carnation hot chocolate, that to me did not to have such connotations, were read by viewers as being sold on sex. I could not therefore assume some prurience or reticence when viewers of the advert for Supligen simply refused to see it as associated with the topic of sex in any way. None of them saw the packet as related to the theme. All of

---

12. It had previously existed as a canned product. By 1995 the product had largely returned to being marketed in cans, suggesting that this innovation had not proved suf-ficiently successful over the long term.

them saw the message as based on the drink's giving nourishment and help in strenuous work or leisure activities, but not sex.
Typical responses were 'It's a sort of health drink, shows people
working hard' or 'They just put someone there to show he is
doing a good job after he drinks it. He is very energetic, he is
doing something very hard. I don't see any other thing in it. The
package – I think it's as light bulb.' In one case it was only after
considerable prompting (of the kind ethnographers are supposed
to avoid!) that a viewer stated 'I was wondering if I is really right,
but I could be wrong, I don't want to say, I don't want to start the
idea, because I doubt they would be as blatant to put something
like that.'

No such hesitation was shown with other advertisements,
such as those for Stone's ginger wine. My experience was not,
however, an aberration, since this consumption of advertising
turned out to be a fair reflection of the consumption of the
product. The manufacturers found that, while the product sold
reasonably well, marketing research showed that the product
was mainly being used, first by children for their lunch boxes,
where it was regarded as more sustaining than the usual milk
drinks, or as a meal substitute by those in a hurry. Both of these
are traditional categories.

Two questions arise. First – what led the manufacturers to
choose this particular theme? Second – what led the consumers
to reject it so emphatically? The producers may have followed
this theme since they felt they were being boxed in by the
complex internal competition amongst milk drinks. There was
intense competition at this time between Nestlé and Cannings
over the range of chocolate milk, eggnog and peanut punch,
which are the standard milk drinks. Supligen was situated
between these and 'build-up' drinks such as Nutrement. There
was a further incentive for the advertising agency. The relevant
'creative' was looking for an opportunity to express her creativity
without heeding the constraints of the field of milk drinks as
already constituted. She therefore chose sex as one of the several
possible alternative strategies that were well established in the
industry, being used for many other products, but not at that time
having an established niche within the field of milk drinks.

The second problem is to account for the rejection of this given
meaning and the imposition of another by the consumer. In this
case I assume that the consumers are faced with a new product,

and they are given a potential image from the advertisers that should act like a shoehorn. That is, it would ease the product into their lives through simple incorporation into a given category of products and their commoditization. These attributes can, however, be appropriated in other ways, and the advertisers have certainly left open the route to other connotations, such as those given by the idea of soya, and through the ambiguity of terms such as 'performance'. The consumer has in turn found particular niches in which this particular commodity appears to be an improvement upon previously available alternatives. Parents are concerned that their children have a drink at school that will sustain them. Parents are often battling against their own children, who would prefer sweet drinks. Chocolate milk is seen as more a woman's drink than a child's drink, and the only real competitor in this niche would be Milo, which is sold as good for sports. A product that has qualities that are supposed to sustain one in strenuous exercise has an obvious affinity with the needs of highly energetic schoolchildren. What Supligen added with its soya content is the idea that it was also rich in protein, which is often viewed as part of a general category along with vitamins as helping to sustain mental activity in addition to physical strength. I assume that some parents came to this conclusion for themselves, but other parents took it up through copying the innovators, until it became a reasonably widespread practice.

Inasmuch as this was becoming the consumer niche for the product, the sexual connotations of the campaign were rendered inappropriate. About the last thing parents want to do for their school-aged children is enhance their sexuality or sexual drive. This then establishes a contradiction, making the advertising campaign inappropriate. I believe that as a result viewers simply could not see the advert's sexual aspects. The result is rather like those popular visual illusions where you can either see two candles in black or the figure in between in white. Consumers had constructed a consensual appropriation of the commodity that led it in one direction rather than another. Obviously, this will not apply to all consumers. There are no doubt many Trinidadians who drink Supligen to enhance their sexual drive. Judging from the variety of opinions given to the reading of most adverts, there will also be a number of other routes to the appropriation or rejection of the drink that have developed.

Nevertheless, the evidence is for a generalizable cultural norm that has developed through the collectivity of consumers as an appropriating body. If I am correct in my interpretation (and I fully acknowledge that there are other possible explanations), then it reflects upon the formation of cultural normativity. Bourdieu by applying a variant of Durkheimian analysis to the area of taste established that moral orders are applied to the world of commodity purchase. My case study shows this principle in rapid motion, occurring as it were in front of my eyes.

As an epilogue to this campaign, the next stage taken by the producers was to attempt an entirely new strategy with regard to the adult consumption of Supligen, which was to market it mainly as a mixer for rum. In this case the strategy merely followed upon developments in Jamaica, where Supligen had become rapidly established as a rum-mixer. There was no evidence that this had become a common practice in Trinidad, and this in effect meant that the local developments were being ignored.

In the course of this volume, quite different examples have been presented of highly successful campaigns to place a particular commodity in a niche that objectifies some immanent cultural value and thereby sells surprisingly well. An example was the launch of Canada Dry, where clever advertising drew the consumer away from the given category of ginger ale into a new conception of the tough soft drink. There are many other cases where some functional advantage or competitive price have been equally important in promoting sales without any such mediation through image construction. Nevertheless, as people working in business know to their cost, huge amounts of time and money are constantly being poured into the arena of commodity image construction, mostly with little or no effect on the market. Although it might seem wasteful to spend so much for so little, this activity dominates most commercial companies because they know that some of this work may bear fruit, and that they are struggling against rival companies who will devote at least as much of their resources to doing the same thing.

We cannot, then, read off the significance of industrial image construction from the amount of effort put into it. We can only gain some insight into its significance by being present in the consumers' world as these images are relayed to them, and as the new products emerge in the market-place. Commerce is enormously important to consumers: they provide the goods, and often the side-effects of their existence can have a massive impact. It is hard, for example, to imagine Trinidadian culture without business sponsorship. Nevertheless, I would remain firm to a point made throughout the two volumes I have written about Trinidad, which is that if one is seeking to understand consumption most of what one needs to know is to be found within the values and imperatives of Trinidadian culture rather than in the study of Trinidadian business. Taken together, the two cases described here may suggest that in many respects the literature on business has been too concerned with its overt purpose, that is the sale of goods, while often from an ethnographic perspective it is the way it fits as an institution within society that is most important in terms of its overall social impact. This is the 'culture of business' implied by the term 'organic capitalism'. In parallel with politics, religion and other such forces, business operates in society as employer, sponsor, and ideology, just as much as producer. To reach the next stage of any conclusion about the nature of business we need to move from an examination of the articulation between commerce and consumers and to address the larger issues posed by the notion of an organic capitalism.

Organic Capitalism

One of the aims of this volume, introduced in Chapter 1, was to explore business as a specific practice encountered through ethnography rather than in terms of general models. This aim is fulfilled through the descriptive materials that make up the bulk of the book. In many instances this also became subsumed within a second aim, which was to consider to what extent these materials could be considered specifically Trinidadian. It is hard to substantiate such claims without a comparative study. For example, in Chapter 3 I noted the degree of local control over business. An economist might prefer to find a quantifiable comparison, such as the relative degree of locally held equity. My qualitative approach cannot provide such firm evidence. Instead, it uses ethnography to broaden the idea of local control to a larger sense of authority in practice, which is very different from the formal authority given in equity holdings. It might be possible still to engage in comparative analysis, but only when other ethnographies have been carried out elsewhere covering similar terrain.

For purposes of this conclusion a balance must be assigned between the evidence for localization of business practice and conformity to wider international models of capitalist practice. There is plenty of evidence to support either contention. Generalized economic theory as capitalist ideology flourishes in contemporary Trinidad. An example is an article in the conservative daily newspaper *The Guardian* (11/7/88) by Dr Morgan O. Job, a Trinidadian of African descent. He launches an attack on the president of the Public Service Association, who had argued for income to be shifted from consumerism to investment, and for a modified Keynesian-style multiplier effect in which employment would produce demand that would generate a boom. Directly noting the experience of Margaret Thatcher and similar politicians, Job attacks what he calls socialist theorizing. The article contains an extraordinary repudiation of Eric Williams's (1942) condemnation of colonialism in *Capitalism and Slavery*. Job suggests instead that 'We have never understood Massa as the manager of a vast profitable enterprise.' Massa is then argued to have navigated oceans, innovated, made endowments, and produced a surplus, and is in general lauded as the model for the future. It might have been thought that praising the slave-owner as the model capitalist would hardly be the best way to promote the image of capitalism in Trinidad; but the existence of such articles shows the degree to which within Trinidad the discussion of economics is established within the parameters of capitalism understood as successfully applied market theory.

Approval of such an ideology might also be expected within business practice itself, where many practitioners have been to business schools and similar institutions. As such it can lead businessmen to act in ways that are against their own interests, but help them conform to an ideal of capitalist practice. As an example I would take an interview held in 1993 with the director of an advertising agency about the impact of deregulation in the media.

For several decades the advertising industry had worked with TTT, the single, government-owned television channel. For some time, however, there had been a feeling that this was inappropriate for a modern capitalist economy, and that the media should be opened up to competition. The director noted the constant support and indeed powerful advocacy by the advertising industry for this move: 'Oh yeah, I think the whole country wanted it, we couldn't very well continue the way we were going could we?' This commitment in principle overcame the clear evidence that this change would be highly damaging to the advertising industry. With a single channel, rates charged for advertising were relatively high, and because advertising was concentrated and produced a large audience for a given advert it made sense to make high-quality and relatively expensive adverts. The agencies benefited considerably from this situation, since they were employed to make the quality adverts, and took large cuts from placing materials with relative ease.

As soon as two new channels came on the air the situation changed dramatically. A price war developed, so that the rates paid for adverts plummeted, and, particularly with recessionary conditions, there was also a squeeze on the amount it became worth spending on an advert. Adverts might be better targeted, but this was a small market, and it was more important that one now had far less ability to predict the consequences of any given advert, since the potential audience was much more fluid. This also meant it often became easier to adopt foreign-made 'cheap' adverts rather than to invest in locally-made campaigns. All of this was clearly predictable to people in the industry. The contradiction between a belief in the principle of the free market and experience of its effects gave rise to several contradictions within the description by this director of what was going on: 'It hasn't done a thing for the agencies as such, not really. That doesn't mean to say this wasn't necessary, firstly, and secondly, it doesn't mean that down the road it's not going to mean something . . . I know there are some agencies that are struggling, including our own. I don't think there is any agency that is fat.'

In the same interview he also remarked on a new sweet drink: 'Is a product that came in as a result of trade liberalization. It couldn't get in before. They spent a lot of money on advertising. The local importer is spending the money. He is using imported advertising material . . . all you get is the media commission, you don't get production.'

Such details may be expanded, but these constant contra-dictions are testimony to the ability of capitalism as ideology to transcend organic capitalism as a practice. Even if they are largely wiped out by the free market, such businessmen are unlikely to be any less convinced of its merits. After all, governments in many countries appear to have become more ideologically committed to pure markets the more disastrously they damaged the local economy. Clearly, then, there is abundant evidence for a homogenization of practice and, in particular, of ideology around international norms. At the same time, this book has provided considerable evidence for the opposing trend towards localization.

Within the general category of localization, there are cases of what I would call *a priori* diversity, where commerce may be seen to have been altered in order to fit pre-given local structures. There are other cases of what I have called *a posteriori* diversity, where it is the institutions themselves that have diversified into quite new forms that owe nothing to some historical legacy. Most commonly localization fits neither of these two pure models, but reflects a constant dynamic between commerce and context.

Examples of *a priori* diversity are found throughout this volume. For example, where particular advertising campaigns have been accounted for in terms of bacchanal or the interplay of transience and transcendence we see business adapting its general images to long-standing tensions within local values. In Chapter 7 a supplier to retail outlets remarked on the considerable impact of the yearly cycle and its various festivals upon almost all commodities. The topic of ethnicity and presumptions about the supposedly intrinsic nature of 'Negro', 'Indian' or 'Chinee' again pervade all the levels and stages of economic activity.

On the other hand, when distribution bottlenecks in the soft drink industry are explored, or the relationship between supermarkets and class, these may also be quite particular and different from what happens in the drink industry or retail in many other countries. But I do not pretend that I can link these with some deep 'roots' in Trinidadian values. It is similarly the case with many business activities and decisions that are affected by the small size of the business community and the ways 'Who you know' becomes more important than 'What is most profitable.' Rather than anthropologists' having always to depend on history as cause it would be better to regard much of this new heterogeneity as created when institutions that we generalize by labels such as 'capitalism' diversify through all the contingent considerations of commerce in practice.

In any case, most localization should not be viewed as a case of change in commerce as it adapts to a context that is stable. Considerable evidence has been presented on the importance of commerce in helping to construct a concept of Trinidad itself, in some cases because this was in the commercial interest of the local offices of advertising companies. It is the combination together of all three types of localization, *a priori*, *a posteriori*, and dynamic interaction, that justifies the concept of organic capitalism. We should not conclude, however, that the propensity of business is merely to give way to local considerations. On the contrary, there are many forces that drive it upwards towards pure capitalism of the kind espoused by Job or the head of the advertising company discussed above.

To understand organic capitalism we have to acknowledge the constant struggles by which people in societies have attempted to tame capitalism in order to ameliorate some of its negative consequences for them. Historical causes include the growth in labour organizations in the first half of this century, and the impact of democratic government dependent upon a mass electorate in the second half of this century. There have also been fortuitous causes, such as the oil boom.

Today Trinidad is as far from the oppressive conditions of extreme inequality of many South American countries as it is from Scandinavian equality. The most important foundation to inequality in Trinidad has been ethnicity; but even here there has been considerable movement since the portrait painted by Braithwaite for the 1950s (see Henry 1988). The clear dominance over transnational companies by white élites has been gradually diluted, so that most middle management is now occupied by African and Indian elements of the population. The PNM government may never have lived up to its rhetoric of caring for the poor and oppressed, and many of its more benign measures may have been partially diverted into abused and corrupted schemes, but the achievements of democratic government in Trinidad are many. At least a nascent welfare state was in place. Working in one of the poorest areas in Trinidad I was able to see that while there still existed the most abject poverty, some at least of the proceeds of the oil boom had filtered down, and the basic infrastructure of clean water, electricity, and basic resources was gradually becoming established. Educational levels for the mass population have for some time been amongst the highest in the region.

Organic capitalism exists within this context. Capitalist corporations both foreign and local can take little credit for any improvements. These are the same companies that extracted profit with little concern for the impact on workers in all those decades that saw far more unremitting conditions. Both as employers and in terms of dumping unhealthy goods on markets with little protection, transnationals have an unenviable reputation for exploitation in the region (cf. e.g. Kowalski 1982; Ledogar 1975; see also Mattelart 1983 for the global perspective). The recent ethnography of a factory by Yelvington (1995) provides a contemporary portrait of a typical Trinidadian capitalist firm, and it does not suggest that capitalists any more than leopards are given to changing their spots. Nevertheless, politics can push business into localization and accountability, and moreover over the long term capitalism finds that an affluent workforce comes to constitute the market it requires for profitability. It certainly helps that in a small country business élites may be more directly answerable to a population they live amongst. The media, especially the weekly newspapers, enjoy being as intrusive as possible. The situation is, of course, only relatively benign: relative to the harshness and cruelty that preceded it as the norm of commerce, and I fear relative to what pure capitalism may yet engender in Trinidad.

Pure Capitalism

In the discussion of organic capitalism I have stressed the positive side of the changes of the last few decades, not to be complacent about the advancements of liberal democracy, but to ensure a recognition of the fragile advances that are now in danger of being lost, not only in Trinidad but in many similar countries around the world. With hindsight the 1980s appear to have been one of the most regressive periods of this century. This was also the view of most Trinidadians with whom I discussed political and economic development. The opportunity for dissent arose, just after the period of fieldwork, with the attempted coup by Abu Bakr. The population in Ford saw this as a punishment for a government that was reneging on progressive development, even through they did not generally support any revolutionary transformation.

From the perspective of an outside observer, however, the Abu Bakr episode does not seem a response to any indigenous movement towards conservative politics within Trinidad. Rather it was the first tremor set off by the earthquake represented by the impending structural adjustment discussed in Chapter 2. There is nothing in the intervening chapters that should lessen a critical assessment of the likely impact of the IMF, or the World Bank, economists and bankers. This also implies a regression in terms of an increasing influence by non-Trinidadian 'experts' and a subservience of local politicians to the dictates of outside forces that may well warrant the term 'neo-colonialism'.

If organic capitalism focuses upon the way commerce becomes rooted in local context, pure capitalism constantly struggles to lop off these local roots, which allow even transnational companies a rhizome-like quality. Instead, it seeks to draw them back towards criteria of international capitalist competition. It does so less by addressing the capitalist corporation than by turning the State itself into a kind of super-competitor that goes beyond the firm in its eagerness to suppress welfare costs and de-contextualize itself from local concerns that might humanize it.

With respect to the companies described here, structural adjustment asserts an ideology that corporations can only compete in a global market if they transform themselves into the image of the lean, mechanical, pure companies that extract maximum profit for minimum cost. This will be backed up with pressure on the government to dismantle any nascent welfare services that might otherwise have lessened the blow dealt by any new, tough regime of exploitative business.

As George and Sabelli (1994) point out, most of these changes fly in the face of any empirical evidence as to what makes companies actually profitable. In the same way, recent conservative regimes favoured by these economists have cut taxes on the grounds that capitalists need incentives to invest, notwithstanding the lack of any evidence to support this contention. Politics has little to do with this. The PNM came back to power because of its greater commitment to social welfare, being seen as a lower-class party. In power it made hardly an iota of difference as compared with the equally competent but less accessible NAR that proceeded it. This is because of the extent to which Trinidad and Tobago are now in the hands of the receivers, and it is hard to imagine when the international bankers and economists will loosen their disastrous grip. Even regions the size of Europe find their protective legislation undermined by arguments that free markets will make their workers comparatively uncompetitive.

There is a considerable literature of critique of the effects of structural adjustment in the Caribbean, and on the consideration of alternatives. Most of the relevant books look to local solutions, which means withdrawal from rather than integration into the global economy. McAfee emphasizes the role of Non-Governmental Organizations in developing self-reliance and what she calls the holistic alternative (1991: 159–248). Korner *et al.* focus on self-sufficiency and prioritization of basic needs (1986: 162–86). In general, then, such prescriptions assume a more isolated economic regime, rather than one that is more open to world markets. The emphasis is on local peoples consuming local products, rather than First World standard goods. In such a scenario the concepts of local and global seem entirely appropriate. The beneficiaries of global processes seem always to be First World consumers, who gain more goods at lower cost through extreme competition between producer countries, while Trinidadians would be unambiguously the victims of such a process, as a case study within the developing world. The alternatives suggested in these books will be contested in the next section.

Conclusion: The Trinidadian Consumer and Shiny Peanuts

In moving from an ethnographic description and analysis towards a generalizing theory I would wish to take as my model Karl Marx, with the proviso that anyone attempting to emulate Marx has to bear in mind some key historical lessons. Of these, the most important is that a dialectical approach cannot be ahistorical. What Marx said was most powerful for the time that he said it. What was ignored by many later Marxists, but should have been evident, given that it was entirely explicit in Marx's own writing, was that theory should be changing at least as fast as history. The need is for generalizations about the political economy that relate to the contemporary world, in full knowledge that these theories will inevitably be made redundant by further developments.

Some of Marx's work retains considerable relevance to the contemporary Trinidadian economy. There remains a fundamental contradiction between labour and capital. This has, however, changed radically. At the time of Marx, conditions in Trinidad, with its legacy of slavery and indentured labour, were at least as bad as those Marx and Engels described for Britain. Much of the historical writing on the early decades of this century in Trinidad is about strikes and other movements for the amelioration of poor conditions for workers. Rheddock's (1994) recent work on women workers is particularly illuminating. The means to bring this up-to-date is available through the ethnography of Yelvington on a contemporary factory. His study suggests that within the factory context there is still a capitalist class, mainly identifiable through its relation to the development of various ethnic élites in this region. There is also a clear proletariat, taken from the descendants of slaves and workers in indentured labour.

What has changed, however, is that the factory and the plantation are no longer the unambiguous foundations for the formation of social relations in Trinidad. The categories that determine social identity have become diluted and mixed, particularly since the oil boom. Most workers in Trinidad no longer belong to an industrial proletariat, but work in government service or distributive sectors. Here their relations to the means of production are not easily recognizable from a portrait painted at the heart of the industrial revolution. Many others occupy the kind of lower and middle management that has been described within this volume. Macdonald (1986) may have exaggerated the importance of the middle class in Trinidad; but, compared to the other countries in the region, Trinidad has certainly possessed a larger and more significant middle class for a longer period.

Obviously to reduce Marx simply to an analysis of class as contradiction is once again to vulgarize a much more profound corpus. Certainly Marx saw capital and labour as intrinsically opposed sets of interests, such that profitability for the capitalist came directly through the exploitation of labour, whose value was extracted in congealed and fetishized commodities, where it could no longer be recognized as the product of labour. This analysis was based, however, on a perspective that transcended merely the observation of the social relations of that time. Before he claimed to understand the economics of contemporary capitalism, Marx was committed to the principles of dialectical analysis as founded in Hegelian philosophy (Marx 1975). He understood that even something as grounded and apparently autonomous as economics could be merely the manifestation, at a particular historical period, of a more fundamental set of contradictions based in the very nature of culture as objectification.

For this reason Marx saw the contradictions of capitalism as based less on the circulation of capital *per se* than in the manner by which through this mechanism the ontological nature of human beings in collectives, that is, what he called the 'species being', is split apart. As with the best anthropological theory, he did not separate objects and persons as mere animate and inanimate material. He understood that material culture was precisely the place where the humanity of persons was located. Our humanity does not reside in our bodies or our brains, but above all as it is reflected back on to ourselves through the historical production of culture as the objectified essence of a potential humanity. This tradition has influenced many anthropologists, and is well exemplified in Bourdieu's (1977) analysis of the manner by which social beings are founded in the trivial and practical taxonomic orders and distinctions of the object world. Hegel foresaw how the development of ever more complex institutions would render ever more difficult this reconciliation between ordinary humanity and the forms taken by culture. Culture becomes, on the one hand, ever more abstract and, on the other, ever more varied in its specificity. The most powerful modern expression of that contradiction is the contemporary consumer economy.

Class analysis remains relevant to the situation of labour in Trinidad, but I believe its relevance is diminishing. Instead, I would re-locate this contradiction in terms of the shiny peanut mentioned in the introduction. To recall, this emerged from an interview in London with the firm that provided the bulk of the peanuts supplied to the Trinidadian economy. Peanuts here are not some local resource grown as groundnuts, but an international commodity that is sold in packets, usually as a salted snack. This is familiar in most countries of the world today. This company had achieved close to monopolistic control of the Trinidadian market, on the basis of a particular attribute. Their peanuts, which were imported from China, were more shiny than the peanuts that their rivals imported from the United States. Trinidadians preferred shiny peanuts.

Peanuts are not merely a luxury product for élites. Even in the most remote rural parlour, products such as peanuts and crisps are to be found appearing amongst the stripped-down corpus of those 'essential' commodities that the most isolated outlets feel they must stock. Trinidad is not, then, a country where a concept of 'basic needs' would have the slightest chance of reforming the people back to some utilitarian set of priorities established by the United Nations or nutritionists. As already noted, even soft drinks, often regarded as one of the most wasteful or even harmful of commodities, would vie in this region with rice and wheat (both largely imported) to be protected as a basic need. This is in the same spirit through which the squatters in Ford chose television sets powered by car batteries over the supply of water and regular electricity as a priority for their expenditure. It is possible for a government, through manipulation of taxation and other controls, to ban or reduce goods that are particularly harmful, such as cigarettes and other drugs; but a regime that attempted to ban television and soft drinks in order to force people to obey the priorities given by international experts in nutrition would be likely to be regarded as an extreme form of neo-imperialist oppression.

Peanuts and soft drinks have thereby become fundamental to the daily lives of the mass population as consumers, who use such commodities and a vast range of other goods in order to construct themselves in terms of historical projects of value and identity creation. Trinidadians as consumers do not identify with the 'solutions' that are proposed by radical opponents to structural adjustment. I found little identification with the values and ethos found in most of the non-governmental agencies that are described by academics looking for a way out of the present impasse. Most Trinidadians see access to high-quality international goods as amongst the most basic of their 'rights'. They believe that, just like First World consumers, they should be able to purchase 'shiny' goods of the highest quality without blemish, at the cheapest possible price. As consumers they do not consider themselves to be Trinidadian in some simple parochial sense, which in turn would lead them to favour import-substitution. Their being Trinidadian is increasingly linked to a sense of their being global, with similar rights and expectations to those of any metropolitan country.

In practice both consumers and business people identify actual consumption most closely with imports. Indeed, in business circles this is clearly concretized in the very specific image of 'the container'. Trinidadian small- and medium-sized businesses tend to think 'containers'. This is because most businesses are involved in importing. Sometimes, when overhearing telephone conversations, it seemed as though there were relatively little concern with the contents of the container: rather as Venetian merchants were portrayed by Shakespeare as conversing about the 'ships' they had invested in, there is a sense that it is the container load that is the conceptual merchandise. The concern is to raise sufficient capital to bring in a container and then ensure its passage. If at all possible the contents of a container are already sold before the goods actually arrive, and so the risk is minimized. Often there is also a concern over how far the container is subject to inspection, since adding goods at the far end of a densely packed container is the favourite method for a business man wishing to smuggle through restricted goods. Transnationals will also measure the relative success of a new product in the number of containers per month that can be sold, rather than through some notion of the overall profitability of the product.

An advert from the local tyre industry sports a coffin in the middle of a tyre with the caption 'Imported (used tyres) Lethal Weapons Available Nationwide.' An Article by 'Craftmaker' in the Express (2/2/88) states:

> Most retailers have no regard for locally made items even of good quality. They always seem to prefer foreign items, and sometimes you are confronted with the remark that your items, items that took you days and even nights to produce on time for them, are like trash, compared to the more expensive items which they sell, on which they can secure exorbitant profits. They prefer foreign items, and it's certainly a shame and a disgrace that so many of our souvenir items

are made in Taiwan and Hong Kong. If this continues, then with the growth of tourism many people in the handicraft industry would lose revenue, since retailers would prefer to get these foreign products of very cheap quality just to secure profits.

The fault cannot be simply laid at the door of the importers of containers or the retailers. Amongst the questions in my survey was one that asked which countries made the best- and worst-quality goods. Taking just those that gained at least three votes, the best-quality goods were ascribed to:

Country	Votes
USA/AMERICA	36
ENGLAND	28
JAPAN	12
CHINA	10
CANADA	9
JAMAICA	5
TAIWAN	5
ITALY	3

The worst-quality goods were ascribed to:

TRINIDAD	27
TAIWAN	21
VENEZUELA	8
CHINA	7
CARIBBEAN	4

It was in the squatters' settlement of Ford that the strongest vote came for Trinidad as the producer of the worst-quality goods. In such circumstances one could hardly blame the retailer for stocking foreign goods in preference to local ones. None of this, however, prevents Trinidadians from taking up a strongly nationalist stance in public with respect to business. At a political level consumers certainly expect business to favour local interests at all times, to preserve local currency, favour local suppliers and so forth. They claim they will vote for governments that serve such local concerns. As long as politics is kept separate from consumption this contradiction is not experienced as a problem, in the same way that most people can (and unfortunately do) vote for lower taxes at the same time that they demand better welfare provision. The responsibilities of government and the individual are not combined into a clear concept of citizens who also have responsibility.

In an article entitled 'Could Shopping Ever Really Matter' (Miller 1997) I argue that it is a particular ideological construction that defines the choice made through political elections as important, and the choices made through the myriad daily decisions taken in shopping as trivial. This ideology retains a considerable element of gendered distinction, inasmuch as the political choice is identified in countries such as Trinidad as a particularly male concern, while the decision-making of shopping is disregarded, at least in part, because it is viewed as distinctly female. In posing the question of what 'matters' we are partly asking which has the greater consequence – the political vote or the myriad votes of the shopper?

It is being brought home to Trinidadians more clearly each year that their political vote is losing its ability radically to affect their future. This is because, whichever party is in power, and whatever its claimed programme, it is faced by a growing impotence in relation to larger economic forces that dictate not only its economic policy but increasingly also its social and welfare policies. This is a general tendency on a global scale; but it is most acute for countries undergoing structural adjustment.

The economists who implement structural adjustment beat down protectionism, destroy price control, insist on the elimination of welfare expenditure, on the grounds of an international search for ever lower prices for international goods. The Trinidadian shopper votes on a daily basis for these policies by choosing the cheapest available source of international standard commodities. The constant refrains about needing lower prices and better availability for branded goods become an aggregate force that pushes governments in all countries to support international bodies that are forever promising greater economic efficiency on a global scale. As in one locally infamous case, a Trinidadian will emigrate on the grounds that the country can no longer supply 'real' cornflakes but only locally made substitutes that cannot be borne by cosmopolitan people with taste.

Trinidadians, along with many other countries of 'the South', have seen emigration as one of the main solutions to this emergent contradiction. Many countries see their local economies becoming ever more harshly suppressed. Their main bastion of agricultural production is likely soon to fall to the development of bio-technologies in the North. At this point the people of the South have nothing to contribute to the productive process, and thus no stake, no role and no wages with which to gain goods. The only solution is for the South to come North, to partake directly in the North. Trinidadians have gone beyond many in appreciating this. They are already one of the most transnational communities in the world at the nuclear level. But they don't emigrate through any particular attachment to the Northern states. As one ethnography of Trinidadians in Los Angeles has shown, they are a case study in non-assimilation (Ho 1991). Their ties are largely with family and friends, constituted much as they always were. They travel frequently around the US and to the Caribbean, taking advantage of Northern affluence to minimize the disruptive effects of having to live in another country. At times when they feel they need to be in Trinidad, such as at Carnival, they will be there. The reason for moving is that it is the only way they can retain a stake in the consumption forms with which they identify as fully as any other inhabitant of New York or Los Angeles.

It would be only too easy to identify with Trinidadians as victims of the world economy, exploited by neo-imperialist forces for the benefit of the First World. It is not that this is untrue, but that, so far from being mere victims, Trinidadians as consumers every day vote for these same policies. The justification given by the economists who serve the Bretton Woods institutions is that ultimately pure markets will provide the highest-quality goods at the lowest prices. When Trinidadians demand that shiny peanuts are made available at a price they feel they can afford they are 'voting' to exclude West African producers, who cannot maintain sheer consistency of product, in favour of what is becoming a global conflict between the cheap labour of countries such as China and the high technology of countries such as the United States as to who can produce the higher quality at the lower price. The future will very probably see the rise of high-technology, high-investment economies that may outcompete even the cheapest labour, leaving the rest of the world ever more destitute.

It may be that at present it is largely First World consumers, rather than those of the developing world, that extract any benefits from a lowering of the cost of production of such commodities. It may be that as high-technology states they will continue to reap the benefits at the expense of others. But we cannot pretend that populations of the developing world would behave any differently if they had the chance. When Trinidad was in the midst of the oil boom Trinidadians took to affluence like ducks to water. As was argued in Miller 1994, they used mass commodities not to repudiate value in some mindless bout of materialism, but finally to fulfil many projects of value that had previously utilized other domains such as kinship for their realization. Commodities were on the whole put to profound rather than thoughtless use. What this suggests is that instead of looking to groups of persons as victims and villains we need to focus on the structural contradictions that lead to a situation where most people at one level vote for the same forces that may oppress them at another level. We have to face a modern political economy where contradiction is more subtle and in some ways more invidious than that analysed by Marx, since it is increasingly located within the same persons.

Time after time one finds 'good' consumer concerns turned into 'bad' structural effects. In the current fieldwork I am conducting in London, the single most important concern when shopping for most consumers is thrift, understood as taking mature responsibility for the welfare of households. Virtually all spending is actually experienced as a form of saving. Thrift is generally regarded positively, as the proper 'skill' of the rational and sensible consumer. Yet thrift is also the justification behind the fight for the cheapest possible goods, which, higher up the economic chain, becomes the argument for the most rapacious cost-cutting by companies.

This desire of the Trinidadian consumer for the shiny peanut, then, has consequences that may prove disastrous for Trinidadians. When company executives were discussing the future of the local economy there were various proposed 'solutions' to the current crisis in terms of potential new sources of income. One of the most commonly quoted was the idea of cut flowers, which one of the major corporations (amar) was already developing with some success. Cut flowers are like shiny peanuts, in that they have no value for the consumer unless they are essentially perfect examples of their kind. Trinidad is by no means the only country in the tropics to be looking to flowers as a replacement for older plantation crops. Kenya, for example,

already exports 23,000 tonnes per annum. This is a highly pol-
luting form of agriculture, where each hectare must be fed with
10 tonnes of fertilizer and pesticides each year, which often
results in contamination of local water supplies. With cheap,
often female, labour and only a small proportion of the profits
going to the growers, this threatens to be only the latest in the
long line of exploitative agro-industry that Mintz (1985a,b) has
shown was the foundation of the modern Caribbean. As long as
this remains the model of world development that arises out of
structural adjustment, then the historical distance travelled from
the sugar plantations upon which the West Indies were first
founded is woefully short. The main difference is that contradiction has moved from being centred in production to being
centred in consumption.

In comparison to the consumer the position of Trinidadian
capitalists, when faced by the pure capitalism of the Bretton
Woods institutions, is still more ambivalent. Businesses that have
grown under protectionism, controlled exchange rates, and similar governmental measures know full well that the bitter and
chill winds that will blow when these covers are taken away may
well destroy them; but they are ideologically wedded to these
developments. The very largest conglomerates, such as Neal and
Massy, try to respond by becoming transnational Caribbean
companies rather than merely Trinidadian. Others almost take
refuge in the growing poverty of an island that simply can't
afford imported goods in the way it once could, and whose
population therefore have to swallow their pride and ingest the
local goods that they claimed to detest. Either way, it is very hard
to imagine that structural adjustment will be the friend of local
capitalism.

Two conclusions appear to follow. First, the problem with
'pure capitalism' is as much that it is bad capitalism as that it is
capitalist. The rise in affluence in the First World generally
emerged as companies evolved complex relationships to local
and global environments that included the gradual development
of higher wages to provide better markets for their products, and
a pragmatic link to state provision of welfare services. We might
one day have had 'market socialism'. In general, it is capitalisms
with the strongest social roots, such as those in Japan or Germany, that have been the success stories of post-war economic
regeneration, at least until they too are subjected to the onslaught

of pure capitalism. Meanwhile, pure capitalism regards this history as merely a catalogue of distortions to a market model. It thereby truncates a historical process that might have produced a modified Keynesian economy committed to full employment and harnessed in the cause of social democratic egalitarianism. Instead, the market acts only to sustain and deepen inequality and oppression.

But the second equally important problem is that the increasing objectification of aspects of individuals as 'consumers' separates us from ourselves in our other social capacities. What Hegel foresaw as the solution to these forms of rupture was the notion of a citizenship that transcended the distances between massive and abstract institutions and our subjectivities – in short, a citizenship that recognized itself in forms such as government and the economy and took responsibility for these (Wood 1990). This would be a citizenship that voted for higher taxes in order to gain welfare benefits, and voted for shopping for 'green' or 'red' goods, in which the morality inherent in acts of consumption is inscribed clearly back on to commodities and thereby infused within acts of consumption. This would be the final defetishism of commodities. The individual becomes a citizen not just every few years in a single political vote, but every day, in the choices being made when goods are being obtained.

At this level Trinidad is only a piece within a much larger jigsaw. There is a need to link these findings with research on consumers in the First World, where power is increasingly located today, as well as to the larger study of the political economy. These other pieces would need to be in place before such an analysis could be turned into a fully-fledged political agenda. Reform of capitalism in Trinidad is highly unlikely unless the pure market is opposed by new forms of stakeholder or corporate citizenship reforms that would need to be implemented first in metropolitan regions. This chapter started with the 'official' consumer, that is domains such co-operatives and consumer protection movements, where individuals are explicitly located as consumers. But to focus upon these alone would be a travesty of the centrality of the consumer today, upon whose actions so much of the contemporary political economy has become dependent. A better definition of the consumer is simply as the primary location of dialectical contradiction in the capitalist world.

Bibliography

Acheson, A., Chant, J. and Prachowny, M. 1972. *Bretton Woods Revisited*. London: Macmillan

Alexander, P. 1992. 'What's in a price?' In R. Dilley (ed.), *Contesting Markets*, pp. 79–96. Edinburgh University Press

Alleyne, D. 1988. 'Petroleum and development (1962–1987)'. In S. Ryan (ed.), *Trinidad and Tobago: The Independence Experience 1962–1987*, pp. 19–26. St Augustine: University of West Indies

Alvesson, M. 1993. *Cultural Perspectives on Organizations*. Cambridge University Press

Attfield, J. 1992. 'The role of design in the relationship between furniture manufacture and its retailing 1939–1965'. Ph.D. Thesis, Brighton University

Auty, R. and Gelb, A. 1986. 'Oil windfalls in a small parliamentary democracy: their impact on Trinidad and Tobago'. *World Development*, 14, 1161–75

Barclay, L-A. 1994. *The Syrian–Lebanese Community in Trinidad and Tobago: A Case Study of a Commercial Ethnic Minority*. St Augustine: Institute of Social and Economic Research. In S. Ryan and T. Stewart (eds), *Entrepreneurship in the Caribbean*, pp. 203–26

Barthes, R. 1973, *Mythologies*. London: Paladin

Bayart, J.-F. (ed.) 1994. *La Réinvention du Capitalisme*. Paris: Karthala

Belasco, B. 1980. *The Entrepreneur as Culture Hero*. New York: J. F. Bergin

Benjamin, W. 1973. *Charles Baudelaire: a lyric Poet in the era of high capitalism*. London: New Left Books

Bentley, G. and Henry, F. 1969. 'Some preliminary observations on the Chinese in Trinidad'. In F. Henry (ed.), *McGill Studies in Caribbean Anthropology Occasional Paper*, 5, 19–33

Besson, J. 1987. 'A paradox in Caribbean attitudes to land'. In J. Besson and J. Momsen (eds), *Land and Development in the Caribbean*, pp. 13–45. London: Macmillan

Bourdieu, P. 1977. *Outline of a Theory of Practice*. Cambridge University Press

Bourdieu, P. 1984. *Distinction*. London: Routledge and Kegan Paul

Bourdieu, P. 1988. *Homo Academicus*. Oxford: Polity Press

Braithwaite, L. 1975 [1953]. *Social Stratification in Trinidad*. Mona: Institute of Social and Economic Research

Braude, F. 1972. *The Mediterranean and the Mediterranean World in the Age of Philip II*. London: Collins

Brereton, B. 1981. *A History of Modern Trinidad 1783–1962*. London: Heinemann

Buck-Morss, S. 1989. *The Dialectics of Seeing: Walter Benjamin and the Arcades Project*. Cambridge, Mass.: MIT Press

Campbell, C. 1987. *The Romantic Ethic and the Spirit of Modern Consumerism*. Oxford: Blackwell

Campbell, C. (forthcoming), 'Shopping, pleasure and the context of desire'. In G. van Beek and C. Govers (eds), *The Local and the Global: Consumption and European Identity*

Carnoy, M. 1993. 'Multinationals in a changing world economy: whither the nation-state?' In M. Carnoy, M. Castells, S. Cohen and F. Cardoso, *The New Global Economy in the Information Age*. University Park, Penn: Pennsylvania State University Press

Carrier, J. 1995. *Gifts and Commodities*. London: Routledge

Carrington, E. 1971. 'Industrialization in Trinidad and Tobago since 1950'. In N. Girvan and O. Jefferson (eds), *Readings in the Political Economy of the Caribbean*, pp. 143–50. Mona: New World Group

Chandler, A. 1990. *Scale and Scope: The Dynamics of Industrial Capitalism*. Cambridge, Mass: Harvard University Press

Chaney, D. 1991. 'Subtopia in Gateshead: the Metrocentre as a cultural form'. *Theory Culture and Society*, 7 (4): 49–68

Clairmonte, F. and Cavanagh, J. 1988. *Merchants of Drink*. Penang: Third World Network

Clarke, C. 1986. *East Indians in a West Indian Town*. London: Allen and Unwin

Clegg, S. and Redding, S. (eds) 1990. *Capitalism in Contrasting Cultures*. Berlin: Walter de Gruyter

Corbridge, S., Thrift, N. and Martin, R. (eds) 1994. *Money, Power and Space*. Oxford: Blackwell

Crouch, C. and Marquand, D. 1993. 'Ethics and markets'. Oxford: Basil Blackwell

Czariawska-Joerges, B. 1992. *Exploring Complex Organizations: an Anthropological Perspective*. Newbury Park: Sage

Dannhaeuser, N. 1985. 'Urban marketing channels under conditions of development'. In S. Plattner (ed.), *Markets and Marketing*, pp. 179–203. Lanham: University Press of America

Dicken, P. 1992. *Global Shift*. London: Paul Chapman

Dilley, R. 1992. 'Contesting markets'. In R. Dilley (ed.), *Contesting Markets*, pp. 1–34. Edinburgh University Press

Douglass, L. 1992. *The Power of Sentiment*. Boulder, Colorado: Westview Press

Dyer, G. 1982. *Advertising as Communication*. London: Methuen

Edstrom, A. and Galbraith, J. 1993. 'Transfer of managers as a coordination and control strategy in multinational organizations'. In G. Hedlund (ed.), *Organisation of Transnational Corporations*, pp. 222–43. London: Routledge

Eriksen, T. 1990. 'Liming in Trinidad: the art of doing nothing'. *Folk* 32: 23–43

Fardon, R. (ed.) 1990. *Localizing Strategies*. Edinburgh: Scottish Academic Press

Featherstone, M., Lash, S. and Robertson, R., 1995. *Global Modernities*. London: Sage

Felstead, A. 1993. *The Corporate Paradox*. London: Routledge

Ferreira, J.-A. 1994. *The Portuguese of Trinidad and Tobago*. St Augustine: Institute for Social and Economic Research

Fieldhouse, D. 1978. *Unilever Overseas*. London: Croom Helm

Fine, B. 1982. *Theories of the Capitalist Economy*. London: Edward Arnold

Fine, B. and Leopold, E. 1993. *The World of Consumption*. London: Routledge

Fox, R. 1969. *From Zamindar to Ballot Box*. Ithaca: Cornell University Press

Franko, L. 1993. 'Organizational structures and multinational strategies of continental European enterprises'. In G. Hedlund (ed.), *The Organisation of Transnational Corporations*, pp. 46–68. London: Routledge

Furlough, E. 1991. *Consumer Cooperation in France*. Cornell Univerity Press

Geertz, C. 1979. 'Suq: the bazaar economy in Sefrou'. In C. Geertz, H. Geertz and L. Rosen, *Meaning and Order in Moroccan Society*. Cambridge University Press

Gelb, A. 1988. *Oil Windfalls. Blessing or Curse?* Oxford University Press

George, A. and Murcott, A. 1992. 'Monthly strategies for discretion. Shopping for sanitary towels and tampons'. *Sociological Review*, 40: 146–62

George, S. and Sabelli, F. 1994. *Faith and Credit*. London: Penguin

Gereffi, G. 1994. 'Capitalism, development and global commodity chains'. In L. Sklair (ed.), *Capitalism and Development*, pp. 211–31. London: Routledge

Gillespie, M. 1995. *Television, Ethnicity and Cultural Change*. London: Routledge

Goffman, E. 1979. *Gender Advertisements*. London: Macmillan

Goodman, D. and Redclift, M. 1991. *Refashioning Nature*. London: Routledge

Goss, J. 1993. 'The "Magic of the Mall"'. *Annals of the Association of American Geographers*, 83(1): 18–47

Granovetter, M. and Swedberg, R. (eds) 1992. *Sociology of Economic Life*. Boulder, Colorado: Westview Press

Griffin, M. 1981. 'The internal food marketing system of Trinidad and Tobago'. Unpublished Ph.D. thesis, University of Aberdeen

Grossberg, L., Nelson, C. and Treichler, P. (eds) 1992. *Cultural Studies*. London: Routledge

Hampden-Turner, C. and Trompenaars, A. 1993. *The Seven Cultures of Capitalism*. New York: Currency Doubleday

Harvey, D. 1989. *The Condition of Postmodernity*. Oxford: Blackwell

Hay, F. 1990. 'Micro-ethnography of a Haitian boutique'. *Social and Economic Studies*, 39: 153–66

Hedlund, G. and Kogut, B. 1993. 'Managing the MNC: the end of the missionary era'. In G. Hedlund (ed.), *Organisation of Transnational Corporations*, pp. 343–58. London: Routledge

Henry, R. 1988. 'The state and income distribution in an independent Trinidad and Tobago'. In S. Ryan (ed.), *Trinidad and Tobago – The Independence Experience 1962–1987*, pp. 471–93. St Augustine: Univerity of West Indies

Hintzen, P. 1989. *The Costs of Regime Survival*. Cambridge University Press

Ho, C. 1991. *Salt-Water Trinis: Afro-Trinidadian Immigrant Networks and Non-Assimilation in Los Angeles*. New York: AMS Press

Hofstede, G. 1980. *Cultures's Consequences*. Beverly Hills: Sage

Hofstede, G. 1994. *Uncommon Sense about Organizations*. London: Sage

Hopkins, J. 1990. 'West Edmonton Mall: landscape of myths and elsewhereness'. *The Canadian Geographer*, 34: 2–17

Humphrey, C. 1995. 'Consumers in Moscow'. In D. Miller (ed.) *Worlds Apart: Modernity through the Prism of the Local*. London: Routledge

Iqbal, J. 1993. 'Adjustment policies in practice: case study of Jamaica, 1977–1991'. In S. Lalta and M. Freckleton (eds), *Caribbean Economic Development*, pp. 47–67. Kingston: Ian Randle

James, J. 1983. *Consumer Choice in the Third World*. London: Macmillan

Jameson, F. 1991. *Postmodernism or the Cultural Logic of Late Capitalism*. London: Verso

Janelli, R. 1993. *Making Capitalism*. Stanford: Stanford University Press

Jhally, S. 1987. *The Codes of Advertising*. London: Frances Pinter

Jones, G. and Morgan, N. 1994. *Adding Value*. London: Routledge

Khan, A. 1993. 'What is "a Spanish"?: ambiguity and "mixed" ethnicity in Trinidad'. In K. Yelvington (ed.), *Trinidad Ethnicity*, pp. 180–207. London: Macmillan

King, A. (ed.) 1991. *Culture, Globalization and the World-System*. London: Macmillan

Klass, M. 1991. *Singing with Sai Baba: The Politics of Revitalization in Trinidad*. Boulder, Colorado: Westview Press

Kogut, B. (ed.) 1993. *Country Competitiveness*. Oxford University Press

Korner, P., Maas, G., Siebold, T. and Tetzlaft, R. 1986. *The IMF and the Debt Crisis*. London: Zed Press

Kowalski, D. 1982. *Transnational Corporations and Caribbean Inequalities*. New York: Praeger

La Guerre, J. (ed.) 1994. *Structural Adjustment: Public Policy and Administration in the Caribbean*. St Augustine: University of West Indies School of Continuing Studies

Lane, R. 1993. *The Market Experience*. Cambridge University Press

Lash, S. and Urry, J. 1987. *The End of Organized Capitalism*. Cambridge: Polity

Latour, B. 1993. *We Have Never Been Modern*. Hemel Hempstead: Harvester Wheatsheaf

Ledogar, R. 1975. *Hungry for Profits*. New York: IDOC

Leiss, W., Kline, S. and Jhally, S. 1990. *Social Communication in Advertising*. Toronto: Methuen

Lévi-Strauss, C. 1969. *The Raw and the Cooked*. New York: Harper and Row

Lieber, M. 1981. *Street Life: Afro-American Culture in Urban Trinidad*. Boston: G.K. Hall

Lien, M. 1995. 'Food products in the making'. Dr Polit. degree, University of Oslo

McAfee, K. 1991. *Storm Signals: Structural Adjustment and Development Alternatives in the Caribbean*. London: Zed

Macdonald, S. 1986. *Trinidad and Tobago*. New York: Praeger

McKendrick, N., Brewer, J. and Plumb, J. 1983. *The Birth of a Consumer Society*. London: Hutchinson

Macmillan, A. 1922. *The Red Book of the West Indies*. London: W. H. Collingridge

Marchand, R. 1985. *Advertising the American Dream*. Berkeley: University of California Press

Marcus, G. 1995. 'Ethnography in/of the World System'. *Annual Review of Anthropology*, 24: 95–117

Marx, K. 1975. *Early Writings*. Harmondsworth: Penguin

Mattelart, A. 1983. *Transnationals and the Third World*. S. Hadley, Mass.: Bergin and Garvey

Mattelart, A. 1991. *Advertising International*. London: Routledge

Merrett, D. and Whitwell, G. 1994. 'The empire strikes back: marketing Australian beer and wine in the United Kingdom'. In G. Jones and N. Morgan (eds), *Adding Value*, pp. 162–88. London: Routledge

Miller, D. 1987. *Material Culture and Mass Consumption*. Oxford: Blackwell

Miller, D. 1993. 'Spot the Trini'. *Ethnos*, 58: 317–34

Miller, D. 1994. *Modernity: An Ethnographic Approach*. Oxford: Berg

Miller, D. (ed.) 1995. *Acknowledging Consumption*. London: Routledge

Miller, D. 1996. 'Could shopping ever really matter?' In C. Campbell and P. Falk (eds), *The Shopping Experience*. London: Sage

Miller, D. (ed.) (in 1997). *Material Cultures*. London: UCL Press

Millett, T. 1993. *The Chinese in Trinidad*. Port of Spain: Imprint Caribbean

Mintz, S. 1985a. *Sweetness and Power*. New York: Viking

Mintz, S. 1985b. 'From plantations to peasantries'. In S. Mintz and S. Price (eds), *Caribbean Contours*, pp. 127–53. Baltimore: Johns Hopkins University Press,

Moeran, B. 1993. 'A tournament of value : strategies of presentation in Japanese advertising'. *Ethnos*, 58: 73–93

Moonilal, R. 1994. 'Structural adjustment, union busting and the future of trade unions'. In J. La Guerre (ed.), *Structural Adjustment: Public Policy and Administration in the Caribbean*, pp. 130–55. St Augustine: University of West Indies School of Continuing Studies

Mosley, P., Harrigan, J. and Toye, J. 1991. *Aid and Power: the World Bank and Policy Based Lending*. London: Routledge

Naipaul, V. S. 1961. *A House for Mr Biswas*. London: André Deutsch

Naipaul, V. S. 1967. *The Mimic Men*. Harmondsworth: Penguin

O'Barr, W. 1989. 'The airbrushing of culture'. *Public Culture*, 2: 1–19

Olwig. K. 1993. *Global Culture, Island Identity: Continuity and Change in the Afro-Caribbean Community of Nevis*. London: Harwood

Ouroussoff, A. 1993. 'Illusions of rationality'. *Man*, 28: 281–98

Pantin, D. 1989. *Into the Valley of Debt*. Trinidad: Gloria V. Ferguson Ltd

Parris, C. 1985. 'Power and privilege in Trinidad and Tobago'. *Social and Economic Studies*, 34: 2

Peacock, J. 1968. *Rites of Modernization*. Chicago: Chicago University Press

Plattner, S. 1985. *Markets and Marketing*. Lanham: University Press of America

Potter, R. 1982. *The Urban Retailing System*. Aldershot: Gower

Prus, R. 1989. *Pursuing Customers: 'An Ethnography of Marketing Activities*. Newbury Park: Sage

Ragoonath, B. 1994. 'Decentralization and structural adjustment: an analysis of the impact of structural adjustment to the decentralization process in Trinidad and Tobago'. In J. La Guerre (ed.), *Structural Adjustment: Public Policy and Administration in the Caribbean*, pp. 171–98. St Augustine: University of West Indies School of Continuing Studies

Ramsaran, R. 1992. *The Challenge of Structural Adjustment in the Commonwealth Caribbean*. New York: Praeger

Ramsaran, D. 1993. *Breaking the Bonds of Indentureship*. St Augustine: Institute of Social and Economic Research

Ramsaran, R. 1994. 'The theory and practice of structural adjustment with special reference to the Commonwealth Caribbean'. In J. La

Guerre (ed.), *Structural Adjustment: Public Policy and Administration in the Caribbean*, pp. 9–37. St Augustine: University of West Indies School of Continuing Studies

Rheddock, R. 1994. *Women, Labour, and Politics in Trinidad and Tobago: A History*. London: Zed Books

Rohlehr, G. 1988. 'Images of men and women in the 1930's calypsoes: the sociology of food acquisition in the context of survivalism'. In P. Mohammed and C. Shepherd (eds), pp. 232–306. *Gender in Caribbean Development*. Mona: University of West Indies

Rosenberg, M. and Hiskey, J. 1993. 'Interdependence between Florida and the Caribbean'. *Caribbean Affairs*, 6: 12–30

Rowlands, M. 1995. 'The material culture of success'. In J. Friedman (ed.), *Consumption and Identity*, pp. 147–66. London: Harwood

Ryan, S. 1972. *Race and Nationalism in Trinidad and Tobago*. University of Toronto Press

Ryan, S. (ed.) 1988. *Trinidad and Tobago: The Independence Experience 1962–1987*. St Augustine: Institute for Social and Economic Research

Ryan, S. 1990. *The Life and Times of Ray Edwin Dieffenthaller*. Port of Spain: Paria Publishing

Ryan, S. (ed.) 1991a. *Social and Occupational Stratification in Contemporary Trinidad and Tobago*. St Augustine: Institute for Social and Economic Research

Ryan, S. 1991b. 'Social stratification in Trinidad and Tobago, Lloyd Braithwaite revisited'. In S. Ryan (ed.), *Social and Occupational Stratification in Contemporary Trinidad and Tobago*, pp. 58–79. St Augustine: Institute for Social and Economic Research

Ryan, S. 1991c. 'Race and occupational stratification in Trinidad and Tobago'. In S. Ryan (ed.), *Social and Occupational Stratification in Contemporary Trinidad and Tobago*, pp. 166–90. St Augustine: Institute for Social and Economic Research

Ryan, S. and Barclay, L. 1992. *Sharks and Sardines – Blacks in Business in Trinidad and Tobago*. St Augustine: Institute of Social and Economic Research

Ryan, S. and La Guerre, J. 1993. *Employment Practices in the Public and Private Sectors in Trinidad and Tobago*. St Augustine: Centre for Ethnic Studies

Ryan, S. and Stewart, T. (eds) 1994. *Entrepreneurship in the Caribbean*. St Augustine: Institute of Social and Economic Research

Sahlins. M. 1988. 'Cosmologies of capitalism: the trans-Pacific sector of the World System'. *Proc. of the British Academy*, LXXIV: 1-51

Samaroo, S. 1994. Public service reform in the era of structural adjustment. In J. La Guerre (ed.), *Structural Adjustment: Public Policy and Administration in the Caribbean*, pp. 156–70. St Augustine: University of West Indies School of Continuing Studies

Schudson, M. 1993. *Advertising: the Uneasy Persuasion*. New York: Basic Books

Seeperdad, K. and Bernard, L. 1984. *Consumer Affairs in the Caribbean*. London: Hodder and Stoughton

Shaw, A. 1988. *A Pakistani Community in Britain*. Oxford: Basil Blackwell

Shields, R. (ed.) 1992. *Lifestyle Shopping*. London: Routledge

Simms, E. and Narine, M. 1994. 'A survey of shopping behaviour of consumers in Trinidad and Tobago: the case of grocery shopping'. *Social and Economic Studies*, 43(2): 107–37

Singh, C. 1989. *Multinationals, the State and the Management of Economic Nationalism: The Case of Trinidad*. New York: Praeger

Sklair, L. 1990. *Sociology of the Global System*. Hemel Hempstead: Harvester

Sklair, L. 1994. 'Capitalism and development in global perspective'. In L. Sklair (ed.), *Capitalism and Development*, pp. 165–85. London: Routledge

Smith, C. and Meiksin, S. 1995. 'System, society and dominance effects in cross-national organisational analysis'. *Work, Employment and Society*, 9: 241–67

Stafford, D. and Purkis, R. 1989. *Macmillan Directory of Multinationals*. London: Macmillan

Sutton, P. 1986. 'The sugar protocol of the Lome convention and the Caribbean'. In P. Sutton (ed.), *Dual Legacies in the Contemporary Caribbean*. London: Frank Cass

Tacchi, J. 1997. 'Radio texture: between self and others'. In D. Miller (ed.), *Material Cultures*. London: UCL Press

Tanaka, K. 1994. *Advertising Language*. London: Routledge

Tewarie, B. 1994. 'Trade liberalisation in Trinidad and Tobago'. *Caribbean Affairs*, 7: 106–18

Thomas, C. 1988. *The Poor and the Powerless*. Latin America Bureau

Tollison, R., Kaplan, D. and Higgins, R. 1986. *Competition and Concentration: the Economics of the Carbonated Soft Drink Industry*. Lexington: Lexington Books

Trotman, D. 1986. *Crime in Trinidad*. Knoxville: University of Tennessee Press

Vertovec, S. 1992. *Hindu Trinidad*. London: Macmillan

Vestergaard, T. and Schroder, K. 1985. *The Language of Advertising*. Oxford: Basil Blackwell

Wainwright, D. 1990. *Stone's Original Green Ginger Wine*. London: Quiller Press

Wallerstein, I. 1974. *The Modern World-System. Vol 1*. New York: Academic Press

Warnier, J.-P. 1995. 'Around a plantation'. In D. Miller (ed.), *Worlds Apart*, pp. 91–109. London: Routledge

Watson, H. (ed.) 1994. *The Caribbean in the Global Political Economy*. Boulder: Lynne Rienner

Weber, M. 1978. *Economy and Society*. Berkeley: University of California Press

Wells, L. 1994. 'Western concepts, Russian perspectives: meanings of advertising in the former Soviet Union'. *Journal of Advertising*, 23: 83–95

Whiteway, E. 1990. *Whiteway's Cyder: A Company History*. Newton Abbot: David and Charles

Wilk, R. 1990. 'Consumer goods as dialogue about development'. *Culture and History*, 7: 79–100

Wilkins, M. 1994. 'When and why brand names in food and drink'. In G. Jones, and N. Morgan (eds), *Adding Value*, pp. 17–40. London: Routledge

Williams, B. 1991. *Stains on my Name, War in my Veins*. Durham: Duke University Press

Williams, E. 1942. *Capitalism and Slavery*. Durham: University of North Carolina Press

Williams, E. 1964. *History of the People of Trinidad and Tobago*. London: André Deutsch

Williams, R. 1980. 'Advertising: the magic system'. In idem, *Problems in Materialism and Culture*, pp. 170–95. London: Verso

Williams, R. 1982. *Dream Worlds*. Berkeley: University of California Press

Williamson, J. 1978. *Decoding Advertisements*. London: Marion Boyars

Wilson, P. 1973. *Crab Antics: The Social Anthropology of English Speaking Negro Societies of the Caribbean*. New Haven: Yale University Press

Wood, A. 1990. *Hegel's Ethical Thought*. Cambridge University Press

Wood, D. 1968. *Trinidad in Transition*. Oxford University Press

Wright, S. (ed.) 1994. *The Anthropology of Organizations*. London: Routledge

Wrigley, N. and Lowe, M. 1996. *Retailing, Consumption and Capital*. Harlow: Longman

Yawching, D. 1991. *Who's Who in Trinidad and Tobago*. Port of Spain: Imprint Press

Yelvington, K. 1991. 'Trinidad and Tobago 1988–89'. In J. Malloy and E. A. Gamarra (eds), *Latin American and Caribbean Contemporary Record*, Vol. 8, pp. 211–31. New York: Holmes and Meier

Yelvington, K. 1993. 'Introduction: Trinidad ethnicity'. In K. Yelvington (ed.), *Trinidad Ethnicity*, pp. 1–32. London: Macmillan

Yelvington, K. 1995. *Producing Power*. Philadelphia: Temple University Press

Index